THEGOOD
web site
GUIDE2006

THEGOOD
web site
GUIDE2006

graham edmonds

HarperCollins*Publishers*

An Imprint of HarperCollinsPublishers
77–85 Fulham Palace Road,
Hammersmith, London W6 8JB
www.harpercollins.co.uk

Published by HarperEntertainment 2005
1

ISBN 0 00 719385 8
Set in News Gothic

Printed and bound in Great Britain
by Clays Ltd, St Ives plc

Designed by Staziker Jones, Cardiff
www.stazikerjones.co.uk

Contents

Introduction

Welcome to the sixth edition of *The Good Web Site Guide*.
We've now sold over 300,000 copies to date. This edition is
fully updated, all the sites have been checked and rechecked,
and I've added over 500 more this year. The book now contains
well over 5,000 sites in all.

I review the very best sites in each category, and then look for
those sites that offer something unique or have features that
make them stand out and recommend those too. I also list
alternatives, especially in the popular genres such as music,
shopping or finance. Essentially I concentrate on what's really
useful, and would like to encourage people to see the Internet
as a tool like any other and not be intimidated by it.

So what else has changed in a year since the last edition? Generally,
standards are pretty high now, and site design is less whacky with
the emphasis on the practical rather than the attractive. The number
of blogs we're including has increased dramatically; we've found that
they can be a really good source of information.

Despite the bright red cover, there's a distinct 'green' tinge to the
book this year as we've included a section listing all the sites
covering environmental issues and help. We've also completely
revamped our Music section, which now includes more details on
downloading plus an expanded section on the iPod. Sharing seems
to be a big trend this year and you can do that in many ways,
but one site that stands out is **www.flickr.com**, which is great for
sharing photos with friends, family and colleagues.

Quality is still a big issue. The costs and time involved in
maintaining a good site are sometimes prohibitive so that many
sites don't seem to be updated as frequently as they should be,
while others just die through lack of interest and funding. Still
hundreds of sites go live every day showing that creativity and
entrepreneurialism are alive and kicking on the Net. Lack of time
and resources often result in site names (URLs) being turned
over to directories, search engines or even adult entertainment
sites. Please do let me know if you find any major changes
to the sites recommended in this book. I can assure you that
all the reviews are accurate at the time of writing this book.
Send comments to: **goodwebsiteguide@hotmail.com**

Keeping Safe

Some people are worried about using their credit card to shop on the Net. In theory it's safer than giving credit card details over the phone, because on most sites the information is encrypted. Before giving out card details, check that you are on a secure line, a small padlock icon will appear on your toolbar, and the http:// prefix will change to https:// Providing you shop from UK sites, you are fully covered by the same fair-trade laws that cover every form of shopping in the UK, but buying from abroad could have some risks attached. If in doubt, shop from reputable firms and known brand names.

There's still a great deal of concern about cookies. A cookie is the popular name of a file which holds some information about your machine and, only if you give it out, about you. They have a sinister reputation but they enable web site owners to monitor traffic and find out who is visiting their sites. In theory, this means they can tailor their content to their customers or provide a better service. If you're worried about cookies, you can easily delete them or set your computer not to receive them. Be aware, however, that many sites do need cookies to function, especially shopping sites. Check out **www.cookiecentral.com** for more information.

Spyware is becoming a real issue. With many sites using it for sinister purposes such as obtaining credit card details, you should always ensure your system is clean of it especially if you have an 'always on' broadband connection. Check out our security section on page 397 if you need more information.

Using the Book

Ratings

Standards are now so high that nearly all the sites included in the book follow the key rules on web design; however, some deserve extra recognition.

 Information merit – this is awarded when the site content goes beyond what would normally be considered reasonable and provides a level of information that is exceptional.

 Service merit – given to those sites that offer something unique or something that otherwise you'd have to pay for, it's not a reflection of how good the staff are or how quickly they deliver.

 Design merit – given to those sites that ignore the web site sausage factory approach to design and produce something definitive or use the technology in an original way.

 Fun merit – for those sites that are unexpectedly good fun to use and see.

 GWSG Top Site Award – reserved for those exceptional sites that offer a combination of quality design, service and content.

In this guide I'm not pretending to be a judge and jury, these ratings are just my opinion, that of a customer and consumer.

Origin – a site's country of origin is not always obvious. This can be important, especially if you are buying from abroad. There may be restrictions or taxes that aren't obvious at the time of purchase. Also, information that is shown as general may apply to one part of the world and not another. For instance, gardening advice on a US site may not be appropriate in the UK.

It's also important to know the origin if you're shopping, as import duties and taxes may apply if you're buying something from abroad. Often these are not mentioned and you could end up with a hefty bill which negates the advantage of going there in the first place.

If you have any suggestions as to how I can improve *The Good Web Site Guide* or have a site you think should be included in the 2005 edition, then please e-mail me at **goodwebsiteguide@hotmail.com**

The Good Web Site Guide's Top 10s of the Internet

New to this edition, we've added some Top 10 lists to our favourite sites in a number of popular categories.

Acknowledgments

I'd just like to end in thanking a few important people:

Firstly, a big thank you to all those people who have written in with suggestions and sites for me to check out, over 100 sites have been included in the book as a result of people e-mailing me.

To the excellent team at HarperCollins.

All my many friends and colleagues for their support and suggestions.

Anyone who bought the first books and the booksellers who supported them.

Especially to Deborah Gray for her great patience and excellent advice and ever increasing contributions to the book.

And to Michaela for all else that matters.

Aircraft and Aviation

A

www.aeroseek.com   US

AVIATION LINKS
An excellent portal offering over 10,000 aviation-related links
in 24 categories – a good place to start for any enthusiast, see
also **www.risingup.com** and **http://luchtvaart.pagina.nl** both of
which are pretty comprehensive.

www.pilotweb.co.uk   UK

PILOT WEB
An excellent overview of the aviation scene with lots of features,
help and information. The site is well laid out and easy to
navigate with lots of interaction, although you need to subscribe
to get the best out of it.

www.flyer.co.uk   UK

AVIATION IN THE UK
A good and well-established portal site from *Flyer* magazine
devoted to all things aviation in the UK, it offers information on
the weather, news, a shop plus chat and forums too. It's
excellent for links and there's a slightly pricey ISP facility too.

www.flightinternational.com   UK

AVIATION NEWS
An online version of the best-selling magazine with articles,
information and news all laid out in a slick but uninspiring site.
Basically it's a taster of what's in the mag and you have to
subscribe to get the best out of it; however, there's good
information on events, a bookshop and a jobs section.

Other sites from specialist magazines:
www.airpictorial.com – another site plugging the magazine,
its got some news stories, some good historical content and
you can buy aircraft schematic plans too.
www.airsceneuk.co.uk – an e-zine provided by a group of dedicated
enthusiasts, this site has lots of information, nostalgia, links to
related sites and personal flying accounts. It's also got an air show
listing with reports, previews and some good photography.
www.airspacemag.com – the magazine of the Smithsonian Air
and Space Museum has a few really interesting articles, but not
much else.

A

www.aeroflight.co.uk
UK

AVIATION ENTHUSIASTS
This site attempts to offer an 'information stop' for all aviation enthusiasts. It's clearly laid out and has details on international air forces, a section on the media (including specialist books and bookshops), a discussion forum, as well as details of air shows and museums.

www.landings.com
US

THE BUSIEST AVIATION HUB IN CYBERSPACE
A huge amount of information on offer from this site including the latest news, history, a route planner, stories and masses of links; use the directory to navigate this massive site.

www.airliners.net
UK

AIRLINERS
With nearly 700,000 photos, this is a huge site, it has a good search facility and should appeal to photographers as well as plane spotters. It also offers a shop, news, chat, links and a huge amount of information.

See also:

www.airchive.com – a labour of love with masses of material posted by someone who is clearly an airline aficionado possibly without equal...

www.airlinerworld.com – better than the usual magazine spin off site; you can buy merchandise and chat to other enthusiasts, there's a small gallery too.

www.zap16.com
US

PLANES, PICS AND FACTS
Excellent site that offers fact sheets and pictures on both military and civil aircraft. There's also news, links and air show information. Beware annoying pop-up ads.

www.raf.mod.uk
UK

ROYAL AIR FORCE
This site features lots of information on the RAF – you can locate a display or fly past, find career advice, check out a squadron or get technical information. The history section is particularly good with data covering aircraft from the very first planes to the latest illustrated by a gallery of pictures; however, the time-line section still only reaches 1989.

See also:
www.rafmuseum.org.uk for the sites dedicated to the museums at Hendon and Cosford.

www.wpafb.af.mil/museum   US

US AIR FORCE MUSEUM
A superbly detailed site with masses of data on the aircraft and their history from the first planes to space flight. The archive section is particularly good with features on particular types of aircraft and weapons, with information about how they were developed.

http://theaerodrome.com   UK

FIRST WORLD WAR
Devoted to the aircraft and aces of the First World War, this site offers lots of background information, personal experiences and details about the pilots who fought above the trenches. For an alternative site on Second World War aircraft try **www.compsoc.man.ac.uk/~wingman** while at **www.fighter-collection.com** you can find out about the remaining airworthy 'war birds' in Europe.

www.vintageaircraft.org   US

VINTAGE AIRCRAFT ASSOCIATION
Events, information, photos plus details of the Association and what it does are all here on this utilitarian site. There is a shop selling a wide range of merchandise but special arrangements have to be made for those outside the US.

See also:
www.battle-of-britain.com – an overview of the battle, the aircraft and those who fought in it.
www.battleofbritain.net – home of the Battle of Britain Historical Society.
www.fighter-planes.com – an overview of all fighter planes from 1930 to date with specifications and some photos.
www.spitfiresociety.demon.co.uk – all you need to know about Spitfires.
www.thunder-and-lightnings.co.uk – a site devoted to British post war military aircraft, with lots of detail, although it hasn't been updated for a while.

A

www.janesonline.com   US
JANES
Janes is the authority on defence forces world-wide and for a
price you can buy books and CD-ROMs which contain all the
information you'll ever need about the world's military might as
well as Jane's Terrorism and Insurgency Centre. You have to
register to get anything out of it, but there are a number of free
newsletter options; anything else, you have to pay for. It's a
little stingy really, but I suppose they are protecting their assets.

www.airdisaster.com   US
NO.1 AVIATION SAFETY RESOURCE
A rather macabre site that reviews each major air crash, and
looks into the reasons behind what happened. It's not for the
squeamish, but the cockpit voice recordings and eyewitness
accounts make fascinating, if disturbing, reading. There are
some really annoying pop-up adverts on this site, which spoils
the visit. See also **www.aaib.gov.uk** for the Air Accident
Investigation Branch, which has a monthly bulletin with details
of crashes and current investigations.

www.aviationconsumer.com   US
EQUIPMENT RATED
A consumer site dedicated to the aviation world with reviews
and tests done on everything from planes to sunglasses. To get
the best out of it you need to subscribe. Unfortunately, the dull
layout makes it tedious to use in some respects.

www.gliderpilot.net   UK
GLIDER PILOT NETWORK
Weather, news, links and information on all forms of gliding,
plus chat and classified ads. You need to register to get the best
out of the site.

www.iac.org   US
AEROBATICS
The site of the International Aerobatic Club and the place to go
for information on the sport. See also **www.aerobatics.org.uk**
for the British Aerobatic Association.

A

Other aviation sites worth checking out:

http://avia.russian.ee – a not that up-to-date overview of the world's helicopters.

http://exp-aircraft.com – all you need to find out about experimental aircraft and where to buy one.

http://hotairballooning.com – an American site devoted to hot air ballooning.

www.aerostationery.co.uk – maps for aviators.

www.babo.org.uk – the British Association of Balloon Operators.

www.globalaircraft.org – a vast site with information primarily on US aircraft with lots of information and interactivity.

www.helicoptermuseum.co.uk – which isn't great but has good links.

www.pprune.com – gossip, news and trivia from the Professional Pilot's rumour network.

www.rotor.com – helicopter industry news plus information and links.

www.ulflyingmag.com – oddly designed, but informative site on ultra light flying.

Most Useful

The Good Web Site Guide's Top 10s of the Internet

1. **www.google.co.uk** – the world's most used search engine.
2. **www.kelkoo.co.uk** – for finding the best price for everything.
3. **www.yell.co.uk** – the yellow pages.
4. **www.met-office.gov.uk** – we all need to know about the weather.
5. **www.expedia.co.uk** – for all your travel needs.
6. **www.newsnow.co.uk** – create your own news channel.
7. **www.which.net** – when you want to know which is the best.
8. **www.ukonline.gov.uk** – government information.
9. **www.nhsdirect.nhs.uk** – help from the NHS.
10. **www.pti.org.uk** – transport information, route finding and more.

A

Antiques and Collectibles

The Internet is a great place to learn about antiques, it's also full of specialist sites run by enthusiastic collectors. If you want to take the risk of buying over the Net, then the best prices are found on the big auction sites such as eBay, see page 41.

www.invaluable.com
UK

ART MARKET INTELLIGENCE
The aim of this site is to provide 'impartial electronic information on antiques, fine art and premium collectables to dealers, private buyers, museums and other institutions'. It proves to be a great resource providing contact details and links to hundreds of dealers, catalogues and auction houses world-wide. Use the 'ideal' section to search dealers' stock. The links section is particularly good. Since our last edition they've introduced live auctions which enable you to participate in international sales.

www.atg-online.com
UK

ANTIQUES TRADE GAZETTE
A comprehensive and wide-ranging site covering all aspects of antique buying from auctions to dealers and classified advertising. You need to register to get the best out of it though.

www.antiquesbulletin.co.uk
UK

INTERACTIVE WORLD OF ANTIQUES
A well-laid-out site with good information and links to more specialist sites and dealers. It aims to be comprehensive and does a great job, there are details on auctions, advice on buying and selling, and a bookshop. You can also buy and sell from the site. To access the articles archive, you need to purchase a site licence.

www.antiquesworld.co.uk
UK

AN ALADDIN'S CAVE FOR THE ENTHUSIAST
Catch up on the latest news, obtain details on major and local fairs and events, book a course or indulge your interests by linking to a specialist online retailer or club. You can't buy from this site but the links and information are very good.

A

www.antiquestall.com UK

ONLINE ANTIQUES STALL
A no-nonsense site devoted to selling antiques at fixed prices
rather than by auction. There's a good search facility and each
item has a picture and details of shipping.

www.dmgantiquefairs.com UK

FOR THE LARGEST ANTIQUES FAIRS
DMG run the largest fairs in the UK. Their attractive site gives
details of each fair, including dates, location and local tourist
information.

www.portobelloroad.co.uk UK

THE PORTOBELLO ROAD
The traders from London's well-known antiques market have got
together a great site which not only gives information about
Portobello Road itself, but also offers excellent links and a directory.

www.lapada.co.uk UK

ASSOCIATION OF ART AND ANTIQUE DEALERS
Get information on their fairs, advice on buying and selling antiques,
learn how to care for your antiques as well as useful links.

www.bada.org UK

BRITISH ANTIQUE DEALER'S ASSOCIATION
Attractive and informative listing site for antique dealers in the
UK, grouped in 16 categories, it's easy to find a specialist in a
particular area of interest. There's also information on their
events and lots of advice on buying antiques.

www.bafra.org.uk UK

THE BRITISH ANTIQUE FURNITURE RESTORER'S ASSOCIATION
If you have an antique that is in need of restoration, then this is
a useful place to visit as it helps you find the right restorer.
Apart from the usual links page, there's also information and
articles on caring for antiques and how to find a course if you
want to become a restorer.

www.antique-furniture.co.uk UK

EUROPE'S LARGEST SELECTION
An attractive site from a specialist dealer offering a wide range
of furniture to choose from, good photography and the promise
of a high level of service to match.

A

Finding more dealers:
www.antiques-atlas.com – an interactive regional listing of dealers and fairs.
www.antiques-uk.co.uk – a slightly confusing database of dealers and information with an international section.
www.antiqueweb.co.uk – a messily designed portal and dealer listing site.

www.finds.org.uk   UK
THE PORTABLE ANTIQUITIES SCHEME
An interesting site devoted to volunteered archaeological and antiquity finds made by individuals who offer to register them so that they can be researched properly.

Collectibles

www.collectiques.co.uk   UK
COLLECTIBLES
Despite its fairly naff name, Collectiques is a good resource if you're searching for information or that elusive piece for your collection. It covers an impressive array of areas of interest from toys to models, kits and architectural antiques, it's easy to use and it's great for background info and links.

www.collectorcafe.com   UK
ONLINE COLLECTING COMMUNITY
A portal site which is great for classified ads links, articles and chat covering most of the major areas of collecting.

www.worldcollectorsnet.com   US
BY COLLECTORS FOR COLLECTORS
Great for discussion groups, collector's message boards and general chat about collecting. There's also a good online magazine plus plenty of advice and links.

See also:
www.collectingchannel.com – another good US site.
www.collectingnetwork.com – links to collectors around the world.
www.collectors.com – great for Americana.

Some specialist sites worth a visit:
www.antiqueprintshop.co.uk – a good selection of antique prints.

www.oldbear.co.uk – antique teddy bears...ah.
www.sandracronan.com – antique jewellery from Burlington Arcade; upmarket, interesting design, but doesn't give prices!
www.tademagallery.com – to kill-for-art deco and nouveau jewellery, most prices on application.
www.tvtoys.com – links and information for memorabilia from old US TV shows.
www.wwii-collectibles.com – mainly stamps, covers, posters and coins.

Ceramics

www.studiopottery.com

UK

THE POTTERY STUDIO
Divided into three sections (pots, potters and potteries), this site gives information on the history of studio pottery. It's a huge site with over 5,100 pages and it's continually being updated. Everything is cross-referenced with good explanations and photographs.

www.claricecliff.com

UK

THE FIRST LADY OF CERAMIC DESIGN
A must for fans of Clarice Cliff pottery. There is information on auctions, biographical details, patterns, shapes, also a newsletter and forum for related chat. The site offers reproductions and related merchandise for sale.

www.chinasearch.co.uk

UK

REPLACING LOST CHINA
A company specialising in finding china to match services and lost pieces, they also buy unwanted tableware. The site is easy to use and they have items in over 2,500 different designs in stock so they should be able to help.

Antiques on TV

www.bbc.co.uk/antiques

UK

BBC
A typically excellent site from the BBC with links to the major shows and a very useful price guide covering some 5,000 antiques, plus expert guidance and tips.

See also:
www.david-dickinson.net – all you need to know about the man...
www.pbs.org/wgbh/pages/roadshow/ – home of the US version
of the Antiques Roadshow

Apple Mac Users

*The following sites specialise in Apple Mac technology and programs.
See also the general sections on Computers, Software and Games
that may also have relevant information.*

www.apple.com/uk   US/UK

HOME OF THE ORIGINAL
Get the latest information and advances in Apple computers at
this beautifully designed site. You can buy from the Applestore,
they do offer finance deals and help for businesses, so software
is surprisingly good value.

Hardware

www.cancomuk.com   UK

APPLE MAC HARDWARE AND SOFTWARE
A messy site offering a wide selection of hardware, peripherals
and software all developed for Apple computers. There are plenty
of deals and free delivery on all orders over £200 before VAT.

www.macwarehouse.co.uk   UK

GREAT PRICES ON MACS
Part of the Microwarehouse group, they specialise in mail-order
supply with a reputation for excellent service. Good prices and
a wide range make this a good first port of call if you need a
new PC or an upgrade.

See also:
www.macassist.co.uk – buy the Mac that's right for you.
www.macreviewzone.com – more reviews and buying help.
www.mrsystems.co.uk – a London-based specialist store.

Software

www.versiontracker.com   US

SOFTWARE FOR MACS

A software specialist that's a great place for downloading the latest programs, it has a huge selection and many are free. You have to subscribe to get the best out of it, but it's well worth the effort.

See also:

www.macupdate.com – good for the latest hot software and updates.

www.theapplecollection.com – a huge site with lots of information and downloads but principally a collection of all things sporting the apple logo.

Information and help

www.macintouch.com   US

THE ORIGINAL MAC NEWS AND INFORMATION SITE

If you have a Mac then this is the site for you. It has lots of information, bug fixes and software to download, but it is a little overwhelming and it takes a while to get your bearings. Once you've done that, for the Mac user, this site is invaluable.

See also the following:

http://thinksecret.com – the latest information and predictions about what's going on at Apple.

www.applelust.com – a site devoted to forums discussing all things Apple.

www.everymac.com – another good guide to the world of Macintosh.

www.google.com/mac.html – Google's useful Mac-only search engine.

www.macaddict.com – very comprehensive, one for the experts.

www.macfixit.com – fix your problems.

www.macinstein.com – which has a good directory.

www.maclaunch.com – the latest news.

www.macnn.com – the Mac News network, lots of ratings.

www.macobserver.com – more news, tips and forums.

www.macrumors.com – a great place to find the latest information and ideas about what could be on the way from Apple, good for tips too.

A

Music for Macs

Here's a selection of sites that offer the Mac owner a place to go to download the latest digital music files. Please be aware that downloading some types of files may be illegal.

www.macintouch.com   US

HOME OF THE IPOD

A huge amount of material to choose from including the latest tunes, classics and audio books, great design.

Other places to look:

www.dailytunes.com – linking to i-tunes, here you can get recommendations and tips on what to download and buy.

www.limewire.com – a file-sharing program that is suitable for Mac users, more stable than some.

www.macband.com – a well-categorised site covering free music donated by bands.

www.macidol.com – news, discussions, free downloads and even an album.

www.macjams.com – an Apple Garage band community site.

www.macmusic.org – keep up to date with the latest music news, software and hardware. There are over 3,500 music-related links and also forums and advice.

www.mp3-mac.com – lots of downloads and links.

Games for Macs

Here are some great sites to help you if you feel restricted by having an Apple Mac.

www.macgamer.com   US

MAC GAMER MAG

A very good online magazine with all the usual features we've come to expect: news, reviews, links and even a few giveaways. It's all neatly packaged on an attractive website.

www.macgamefiles.com   US

MAC GAME FILE LIBRARY

To quote them 'Macgamefiles.com is the one-stop source

for Macintosh game files. The web site features lively libraries of Macintosh demos, shareware, updaters, tools, add-ons, and more'. And they're right; it's a very useful site with some really good games and software.

www.insidemacgames.com   US

IMG MAGAZINE
A magazine devoted to Mac games where you can find the latest demos, updates for the games, loads of shareware games, news and reviews.

Architecture

www.greatbuildings.com   US

ARCHITECTURE ONLINE
This US oriented site shows over 800 buildings and features hundreds of leading architects, with 3-D models, photographic images and architectural drawings, commentaries, bibliographies and web links. It's all well packaged, easy to use and you can search by architect, building or location.

www.emporis.com   US

SKYSCRAPERTASTIC!
An excellent technical and entertaining resource covering high rise and many historical buildings, it has good search facilities and is always being added to. It's run by a company who specialise in the field so the data is pretty authoritative.

www.architecture.com   UK

THE ROYAL INSTITUTE FOR BRITISH ARCHITECTS
A massive site from the RIBA with some 250,000 pages on all aspects of architecture including history, jobs, events and features on great buildings.

www.buildingconservation.com   UK

CONSERVING ASSETS
They claim to be the online information centre for the conservation and restoration of historic buildings, churches, gardens and landscapes; the site seems to live up to its billing providing plenty of quality information and links.

A

www.implosionworld.com   US

DEMOLITION

If watching buildings going down instead of up turns you on, then you should visit this site which offers videos and pictures of demolitions plus lots of information on explosive demolition. There's also an educational side to the site and an FAQ section covering the World Trade Centre disaster too.

Also check out the following sites:

www.aabc-register.co.uk – the register of architects accredited in building conservation.

www.archibot.com – US oriented news and forums dedicated to all things architectural.

www.archidose.org – an entertaining and informative weekly magazine devoted to contemporary architecture run by an American expert.

www.arcspace.com – photos, opinions and features on the most important architects and their work.

www.artandarchitecture.co.uk – an initiative to promote interaction between artists and architects. This site makes for interesting reading and whatever your opinions on the projects themselves, it certainly sparks debate and the imagination.

www.glasssteelandstone.com – a growing architecture encyclopedia with details of some 700 buildings.

www.retropolis.net – Art Deco architecture, a labour of love.

www.spab.org.uk – home of the charity The Society for the Protection of Ancient Buildings.

Art and the Arts

One of the best things about the Internet is the ability to showcase things that otherwise would be quite obscure or inaccessible. Now working artists are able to show their wares to excellent effect and we can view their art before we buy. In addition, we can now 'visit' some of the world's great galleries and museums. Here are the best sites for posters, online galleries, museums, cartoons, exhibitions, showcases for new talent and how to get the best clip art for your own use.

Resources and Encyclopedias

A

www.artlex.com
US

THE VISUAL ARTS DICTIONARY
From abbozzo to zoomorphic, there are over 3,600 definitions of art-related terms with links to related articles on other sites. The cross-referencing is excellent.

www.artcyclopedia.com
CANADA

THE FINE ART SEARCH ENGINE
A popular resource for finding out just about anything to do with art, it's quick, nicely designed and informative. At the time of writing they had indexed 1,800 leading arts sites and offer links to an estimated 150,000 works by 8,000 different artists.

www.accessart.org.uk
UK

MAKING ART ACCESSIBLE
A really good, colourful site dedicated to helping students, children and teachers get to grips with the art world and the meaning behind art. There are good online workshops on topics such as sculpture, use of colour and photography.

http://wwar.com
US

THE WORLD-WIDE ART RESOURCE
This is an effective search vehicle with links to artists, exhibitions, galleries and museums, it now offers over 91,000 works of art from over 22,000 'masters'. New for this edition is an art blogs section, should you feel tempted to have your say. Plenty of pop-up adverts spoil it though.

www.artchive.com
UK

MARK HARDEN'S ARTCHIVE
Incredible, but seemingly the work of one art fanatic, this superb site not only has an excellent art encyclopedia, but also the latest art news and galleries with special online exhibitions. The quality of the pictures is outstanding. There's also a section on theory, good links. For more links try **www.chart.ac.uk/vlib**

See also:
www.abcgallery.com – Olga's Gallery is hugely informative and well illustrated.
www.askart.com – a massive directory on art and artists, US-oriented.

A

www.ibiblio.org/wm – the web museum offers background and information on art movements and artists.

Art in the UK

www.culture.gov.uk
UK

THE GOVERNMENT'S VIEW
A dense site giving information on how the government is supporting the arts and museums. There are plenty of facts, figures and reports to download, as well as links and information on libraries, the creative industries and even sport.

www.design-council.org.uk
UK

PROMOTING THE EFFECTIVE USE OF DESIGN
This good-looking site effectively promotes the work of The Design Council through access to their archives of articles on design and details of their work with government; it also gives feedback on design issues.

www.artguide.org
UK

THE ART LOVER'S GUIDE TO BRITAIN AND IRELAND
Organised by artist, region, exhibition or museum with more than 4,500 listings in all. This site is easy to navigate with a good search engine and cross-referencing making it simple to find out about events in a particular region, aided by annotated maps.
See also **www.artsfestivals.co.uk** a good directory of the Arts Festivals in the UK.

www.artmovements.co.uk
UK

CONTEMPORARY ARTIST'S SHOWCASE
Promoting contemporary arts with portfolios of over 1,300 artists with a magazine, resources and good information on arts movements.

Art Styles, Periods, Schools, Most Popular Artists and Countries

www.impressionism.org
US

LEARN ABOUT IMPRESSIONISM
An overview of the movement with a tutorial all contained on a well-illustrated site.

A

www.surrealism.co.uk UK

ONLINE GALLERY

Not as way out as you'd expect, this site gives an overview of
surrealism and features contemporary artists. The online gallery
is OK without being that exciting, but as a showcase it works.

www.graffiti.org UK

THE WRITING ON THE WALL

If you're fascinated by graffiti, then here's the place to go –
it's got a gallery of the best examples, history and links to
other graffiti sites.

www.wga.hu HUNGARY

THE RENNAISANCE

The Web Gallery of Art is a virtual museum dedicated to
European painting and sculpture of the 12th-18th centuries. It is
nice to look at and contains a phenomenal number of paintings;
however, it takes a little time to get the knack of navigating the
site. There is the option to listen to related music while browsing.

www.the-artists.org UK

20TH CENTURY ART

This site is easy to use, with minimalist design and details
of every major artist of the last century.

www.dlc.fi/~hurmari/preraph.htm UK

PRE-RAPHAELITES

An exhaustive listing of sites and links to pages on the
Pre-Raphaelites, their paintings, lives and even those
who posed for them.

*For biographical information on a huge number of artists see
the entries under Resources and Encyclopaedias, the following
have pages devoted to the particular artists:*

http://arthistory.about.com/library/blartists.htm – biographies
of over 150 artists plus loads of art history information.

http://essentialvermeer.20m.com – Vermeer

www.chez.com/renoir/indexe.html – Renoir

www.daliuniverse.com – Dali

www.expo-degas.com – Degas

www.expo-klimt.com – Klimt

A

www.hansholbein.nl – Holbein
www.ibiblio.org/wm/paint/auth/rembrandt – Rembrandt
www.lucidcafe.com/library/96jun/gauguin.html – Gauguin
www.mark-rothko.com – Rothko
www.marmottan.com – Monet
www.mos.org/leonardo – Da Vinci
www.musee-matisse-nice.org – Matisse
www.okeeffemuseum.org – Georgia O'Keeffe
www.tamu.edu/mocl/picasso – Picasso
www.vangoghgallery.com – Van Gogh
www.warhol.org – Andy Warhol

Cultures

www.asianart.com   US
ART IN ASIA
All you need to know on Asian art. Basically, it covers all the major
cultures in four sections: exhibitions, articles, associations and
galleries. It's not very well cross-referenced which makes it hard
to navigate, although there is a pretty good search engine.

http://web-japan.org/webjapan/search/Culture_Fine_Arts_00.html
JAPANESE ART AND CULTURE
The Fine Arts section contains a virtual museum dedicated to
the art and culture of Japan. In addition to sections on fine art,
crafts and sculpture, there is information on flower arranging,
calligraphy, the tea ceremony, performing and martial arts as
well as architecture and gardens. Highly informative.

http://depts.washington.edu/chinaciv   US
CHINESE CIVILISATION
Essentially an educational resource, this site provides a good
general introduction to the arts and culture of China. Maps and
a good timeline help to make sense of it all. For a snapshot of
contemporary Chinese art visit www.newchineseart.com

www.latinart.com   US
THE LATIN AMERICAN ARTS SCENE
A magazine-style site dedicated to emerging and established
artists in Latin America. There is a guide to international
exhibitions showcasing Latin American art and some good
resources available on the site.

www.lonker.net/art_african_1.htm US

> AFRICAN ART
> A good-looking site dedicated to mainly sub-Saharan cave and
> rock paintings. It's well illustrated and authoritative, there's also
> a sister site on Aboriginal Art at
> **www.lonker.net/art_aboriginal_1.htm**

The Major Museums and Galleries

www.museums.co.uk UK

> MUSEUM SEARCH
> MuseumNet is a simple search engine which allows you to
> search either by subject or location, each entry has a short
> description and a map. There's also industry information and
> a jobs page for those who want to work in a museum.
> Unfortunately, the list of museums is still not comprehensive.

http://vlmp.museophile.com UK/US

> MUSEUMS WORLD-WIDE
> Provides links to the world's museums which have an online
> presence and indicates which languages they use. Information
> on galleries, museums and libraries is listed separately.

www.museumstuff.com US

> MUSEUM GATEWAY
> An outstanding portal devoted to American museums. There's
> information on virtually any topic you can name plus thousands
> of links to specialist sites and museums. They also provide a
> list of museum shops, chat rooms and forums plus links to the
> fun sections on museum sites.

www.24hourmuseum.org.uk UK

> OPEN ALL HOURS
> Run by the Campaign for Museums, this site aims to give high
> quality access to the UK's galleries, museums and heritage sites
> – and it succeeds. The graphics are clear, it's easy to use and
> really informative. There are a selection of online exhibitions,
> web features, a museum finder, links, news and a link to
> **www.show.me.uk** which is the excellent sister site for children.

A

www.tate.org.uk   UK

THE ARCHETYPAL GALLERY SITE
A real treat with excellent design and quality pictures, the site
covers all the Tate galleries and offers information about
exhibitions, relevant articles, webcasts and also a good shop.

www.nationalgallery.org.uk   UK

THE NATIONAL COLLECTION
A very comprehensive site, with sections on the permanent
collection and exhibitions. There's also a shop with a wide
range of books and gifts as well as information for schools and
the outreach programme. For access to the all the Scottish
National Galleries on a similar site, go to **www.natgalscot.ac.uk**
who have a similarly informative and enjoyable site.

www.thebritishmuseum.ac.uk   UK

ILLUMINATING NEW CULTURES
Whether you explore the world's cultures, take a tour, or just
browse the collection, this is a beautifully illustrated site. The
online shop stocks a selection of gifts and goods based on
museum artefacts. Delivery cost depends on weight of
purchases. Parents will appreciate the family online tour and
children's compass (a museum guide for children). They also
arrange museum tours and you can book for special events too.

www.npg.org.uk   UK

THE NATIONAL PORTRAIT GALLERY
With over 34,000 works on view, this is one of the biggest online
galleries. It shows the most influential characters in British history
portrayed by artists of their time. You can search by sitter or artist,
and buy the print. The online shop offers gifts plus pictures with
options on print size, framing and delivery, including overseas.

www.royalacademy.org.uk   UK

WHERE ART IS MADE, SEEN AND DEBATED
An interestingly designed and modern gallery site with all the
information you need on the Royal Academy as well as ticket
information and a shop. There's support for schools, colleges
and teachers, plus information and previews of exhibitions.

www.vam.ac.uk   UK

VICTORIA & ALBERT MUSEUM
The world's largest museum has a plain functional web site,

with information on visiting, learning and how you can help support the museum. The online shop offers gifts, reproductions and books. You can also explore the museum virtually, visiting most of the galleries plus back-up information explaining their exhibits with details of what they contain.

www.moma.org   US

THE MUSEUM OF MODERN ART IN NEW YORK
A comprehensive and minimally attractive site that covers the collection and offers much in the way of information on the works and artists. There's also an excellent gift shop, although shipping to the UK is expensive. It can be quite slow at times.

www.metmuseum.org   US

THE METROPOLITAN MUSEUM OF ART IN NEW YORK
A very stylish site, featuring lots of great ideas, with quality illustrations and photographs, you can view any one of 6,500 exhibits, have a taster by taking the director's tour, become a member, or visit a special exhibition. The shop offers a great range of products, many exclusive, and there's a handy gift-finder service. Delivery costs to the UK depend on how much you spend.

www.si.edu   US

THE SMITHSONIAN
A fairly cluttered site but once you get used to it there's a huge amount of information on every major aspect of art plus sections on science and history. The magazine is well worth a look, especially the journeys section.

www.courtauld.ac.uk   UK

COURTAULD COLLECTION
A minimally illustrated site with details of the collection plus educational resources and information on the gallery. The gallery's complete collection of 7,000 items is now available to view on their linked site A&A: **www.artandarchitecture.org.uk**
What's more, almost all the images on A&A are now available to buy as high quality photographic prints in a range of sizes with prices starting at a very affordable £1.

www.guggenheim.org   US

VANGUARDS OF ARCHITECTURE AND CULTURE
There is the promise of a unique virtual museum, but while we

A

wait, the five branches (Berlin, Bilbao, Venice, New York and Las Vegas) can be visited here. You can find out about exhibitions and collections, projects, tours, events and developmental programs, while membership entitles you to free entry and a store discount. The store is stocked with a wonderful selection of unusual goods and gifts, and is not bad value, though delivery to the UK is expensive.

www.louvre.fr   FRANCE
FRANCE'S TREASURE HOUSE
Similar to the UK's National Gallery site: there's a virtual tour where you can view the collection and learn about its history, you can also check out the latest exhibitions and buy advance tickets. The shop has some interesting items, delivery to the UK starts at 12.95 Euros.

www.hermitagemuseum.org   RUSSIA
THE STATE HERMITAGE MUSEUM
Another beautifully presented museum site with features on the highlights of the collection with a section of superb digital photographs, details of the museum itself, exhibitions and an education centre. There are some pretty extraordinary products for sale in the shop, but delivery begins at £18 and depends on weight, so it could be pretty costly if you place an order for the neo-classical bookcase.

Clip art

These sites are loaded with pop-ups and advertising which is really irritating, you may just try Google (www.google.co.uk) which has an excellent image search facility. If you know of a site that is ad free please let me know.

www.clipart.net   US
THE PLACE TO START IF YOU NEED CLIP ART
With this clip-art search facility you should quickly find the perfect image. Many linked sites have free art for use, otherwise cost varies enormously depending on what you want.

See also:
www.321clipart.com – some 12,000 images.
www.barrysclipart.com – a huge resource with hundreds of categories.

A

www.clipartcastle.com – sections on web graphics, photos and animation as well as clip art. Registration is a right pain though.

Cartoons and Drawing

www.cartoonbank.com   US
WORLD'S LARGEST CARTOON DATABASE
Need to find a cartoon for a particular occasion? Then there's a choice of over 20,000, mostly from New Yorker magazine. You can send e-cards and you can now get some products delivered to the UK with shipping starting at around £7. For a massive set of links to cartoon and humorous sites then try the excellent Norwegian search site **www.cartoon-links.com**

www.cartoon-factory.com   US
BUYING CARTOON CELS
Buy cartoon cels, mainly from Disney and Warner cartoons; you can search by subject or artist. Delivery is expensive, although they are flexible about payment.

See also the Open Directory Project's section on Animation. It offers nearly 16,000 links at **http://dmoz.org/arts/animation**

www.drawingpower.org.uk   UK
THE BIG DRAW
A bid to get us all drawing, the Big Draw happens every October and here you can get encouragement and details on events and programs.

Buying Art

www.eyestorm.com   UK

BUYING CONTEMPORARY ART
A really attractive and well-designed site which showcases contemporary art and photography, you can buy online as well.

www.whitecube.com   UK

WHITE CUBE GALLERY
This outstandingly designed site showcases top artists in an original way and highlights what can be done when web site

A

development technology is used at its best. Although this gallery is influential in developing the careers of some of the best artists working today, you can buy art here at reasonable prices too.

www.artnet.com
UK

FINE ART ONLINE
Possibly the largest gallery network featuring work from some 18,000 artists, the site is well put together and the information on offer is extraordinary with an encyclopedia, price database, links and a comprehensive directory.

Other online art showcase sites and stores worth visiting:
www.artandparcel.com – a messy site that shows the work of 120 artists.
www.artlondon.com – a well-designed art store with an emphasis on the UK, value for money and quality.
www.artprice.com – a subscription service that allows the subscriber to check on the value of the work from over 300,000 artists world-wide. There's also help and a good links section.
www.artuk.co.uk – a slightly confusing site but well worth a visit as there's some interesting art and articles.
www.axisartists.org.uk – a very good showcase site for contemporary artists with lots of content and information as well as links and exhibitions.
www.britart.com – a good-looking, well-stocked site concentrating on the work of British artists.
www.fineart.co.uk – the home of the Fine Art Trade Guild.
www.modernbritishartists.co.uk – a gallery and shop catering for those of us who love and covet the work of modern British artists, including those from early in the last century.
www.newartportfolio.com – another showcase site for new artists with an intriguing design, offering plenty of information and a money back guarantee – useful if you find you can't live with your purchase after all.

www.artloss.com
US

THE ART LOSS REGISTER
The register of stolen and lost art. Featured thefts and recoveries makes for interesting if rather sad reading.

Posters

www.artrepublic.co.uk   UK

BOOKS, POSTERS AND WHAT'S ON WHERE
A nicely designed, easy-to-use site with thousands of art
posters and prints to choose from. There is also an option to
have posters framed and free shipping world-wide. There is also
a glossary of art terms and biographical data on an impressive
number of artists. 'What's On World-wide' provides details of
the latest exhibitions, competitions and travel information for
over 1,250 museums around the world.

www.onlineposters.com   UK

POSTER SHOPS ONLINE
Simply a ranked list of shops that sell posters, from the
generalist to the very specialised retailers.

www.barewalls.com   US

INTERNET'S LARGEST ART PRINT AND POSTER STORE
This site backs its claim with a huge range, it's also excellent
for gifts and unusual prints and posters but be aware that the
shipping costs are high – $29 for the UK. There's also a gift
voucher scheme. See also **www.art.com** which is excellent and
does a great line in movie posters as well as art. They've
reduced shipping costs which are now as low as £4.60 for a
small print.

www.postershop.co.uk   UK

FINE ART PRINTS AND POSTERS
There are over 40,000 items to choose from, covering the work
of over 3,900 artists. There's also a framing service and a good
user-friendly search facility where you can search by subject as
well as artist. In the museum shop there's a range of art-related
gifts to choose from. Delivery costs £4 for the UK.

www.totalposter.com   UK

GET THE BIG PICTURE
Excellent poster store, specialising in photographic posters with a
very wide selection. Extra services include: printing up your own
photos to poster size, plus pictures of recent key sporting and
news events in their 'Stop Press' section. Delivery costs vary.

A

www.easyart.co.uk
UK
FINE ART PRINTS AND POSTERS
Excellent art shop selling posters, limited editions, photographs, etchings and now, canvas art too. They provide inspiration too with advice on the best place to hang art in your home and a custom art section where you can turn pictures of your friends into pop icons.

Creating Art

www.kurzweilcyberart.com
US
CYBER ART
Once you download the program, watch in fascination as art is created for you as a screen saver. It's free and great fun too.

www.saa.co.uk
UK
THE SOCIETY FOR ALL ARTISTS
Help, advice, forums, tuition and a good shop make this a useful site for any artist, amateur or professional. There's also a gallery if you're looking for art to buy. Additional services and discounts are on offer for those who join.

www.watercolor-online.com
US

ALL FORMS OF WATERCOLOUR
Very good site devoted to all aspects of watercolour painting; it has tutorials, advice, links and provides a good place to start when searching for information on the subject.

For more watercolour sites try:
http://painting.about.com/cs/watercolours/index.htm – pages of advice from the excellent **www.about.com**
www.wasp-art.skynow.co.uk – a simple online course by Peter Saw.

www.simplypainting.com
UK
FRANK CLARK
Learn how to paint with leading art teacher Frank Clark, the site has free lessons and tips plus a shop and gallery.

For more inspiration try:
www.codcottage.freeserve.co.uk – an introduction to calligraphy.

www.learn-to-draw.com – text dense, a bit American but sound. You have to pay about £10 to get the best out of it.
www.talens.com/stepbystep.html – good introduction of colours, learn to paint sunflowers step-by-step.

Astrology and Prediction

www.astrology.com   UK

ALL ABOUT ASTROLOGY
A very comprehensive site offering free advice from the stars, you can buy a personalised reading and chart, browse the general horoscopes and now you can get a tarot reading too. You can find celebrity horoscopes, and learn about the history and techniques of astrology. See also **www.horoscope.co.uk** home of *Horoscope Magazine*.

www.live-astro.com   UK

RUSSELL GRANT
Now is your chance to buy a horoscope from a real celebrity, costs range from £1.95 upwards. This site has been expanded to include dream interpretations, tarot and other astrological resources as well as the various horoscopes. If your dog appears a bit blue, you can organise psychic consultations for pets as well.

www.easyscopes.com   US

ASTROLOGY SEARCH ENGINE
Here you can get as many different free horoscopes as you can handle, the site contains direct links to the daily, weekly, monthly and yearly horoscopes for each zodiac sign. You just have to select your zodiac sign and you are presented with a large list of horoscopes to choose from. It's amazing how different they all are for the same sign!

www.lovetest.com   US

ARE YOU COMPATIBLE?
It's a bit long winded to use, but enter your birthday and your partner's and you get a compatibility score based on the star signs. There are also quizzes, chat, classified ads, links, not forgetting the love test thermometer.

See also:

www.astro.com – a comprehensive offering with every major aspect of astrology covered and explained.

www.astroadvice.com – one of the better astrology sites, well, in terms of design anyway.

www.astro-eclipse.co.uk – a basic site with an overview of the subject plus links.

www.freewillastrology.com – good-looking site with lots of predictions about future events, usual star signs and much more from astrologer Rob Brezsny.

www.tarot.com – tarot, astrology, numerology and the I Ching all on one site, all problems obviously.

www.thezodiac.com – a fairly amateur site but it's clear and easy to use with lots of fun astrological things to do.

Auctions and Classified Ads

Before using these sites be sure that you are aware of the rules and regulations surrounding the bidding process, and what your rights are as a seller or purchaser. If they are not properly explained during the registration process, then use another site. They should also offer a returns policy as well as insurance cover. Whilst there are plenty of bargains available, not all the products on offer are cheaper than the high street or specialist vendor; it's very much a case of buyer beware. Having said that, once you're used to it, it can be fun and you can save a great deal of money.

www.ukauctionhelp.co.uk
UK

HELP WITH USING AUCTIONS

A site dedicated to giving the low-down on auctions. It's informative and genuinely helpful – shame about the design, which makes it difficult to use and it's cluttered with lots of adverts.

www.bidxs.com
US

AUCTION SEARCH ENGINE

An attempt to allow you to search the auction sites for your wanted items, you can search by category, price or by item. It's quite slow but useful nonetheless.

www.ebay.co.uk UK

YOUR PERSONAL TRADING COMMUNITY
With millions of items listed, you are likely to find what you
want here. The emphasis is on collectibles and it is strong on
antiques of all sorts, although if it's sellable, it's sure to be here.
There is a 24-hour support facility, loads of online help and
automatic insurance cover on all items up to £250 using
PayPal. Previous clients have reviewed many of those who have
something to sell, so you can check up on their reliability.
See also **www.rummaging.org** which is an amusing blog run by
someone who keeps track of all the unusual stuff that ends up
on eBay.

www.ebid.co.uk UK

NO CHARGE TO LIST AN ITEM
Divided into auctions, wanted and swap sections. The auctions
can easily be accessed and browsed; its strengths are in
computing, electronics and music, although there has been a
great increase in the number of collectibles available. There is
a special section dedicated to raising money for charity if you
want to donate the proceeds of your auction.

www.icollector.com US

REDEFINING THE ART OF COLLECTING
An attractive site bringing together the wares of hundreds of
auction houses and dealers, icollector is an ambitious project
that works well. The emphasis is on art, antiques and
collectibles. Be sure that the auction house you're dealing with
ships outside the US.

www.qxl.com UK/EUROPE

A PAN-EUROPEAN AUCTION COMMUNITY
This wide-ranging site offers anything from airline tickets and
holidays to cars, collectibles and electronics (in several
languages). The quality of merchandise seems better than most
sites. Another site worth checking out is **www.CQout.co.uk** it
had almost 100,000 lots when we visited, a wide selection of
categories and a nice design.

A

www.sothebys.com
UK/US

QUALITY ASSURED
Details of their auctions and information on what they do, plus you can buy catalogues and search for items that may be coming up for sale.

www.christies.com
UK

FOR THOSE WITH DEEP WALLETS
Christies have a classic site with info on their programme of auctions and on how to buy and sell through them, but you can't carry out transactions from the site. The LotFinder service searches their auctions for that special item – for a fee. There's also a good specialist bookstore and lots of information on how to buy and sell.

www.bid-up.tv
UK

BID UP.TV
Linked to the TV channel of the same name, this site shows the auctions they have on TV, you can bid online or call their hotline.

www.ad-mart.co.uk
UK

AWARD WINNING
Excellent design and ease of use makes this site stand out; there are fourteen sections, all the usual suspects plus personal ads, boating and pets. See also **www.nettrader.co.uk** which is also really well designed and easy to use.

www.exchangeandmart.co.uk
UK

EXCHANGE & MART
Everything the paper has and more – great bargains on a massive range of goods found using a good search facility, all packaged on a bright, easy-to-use site. It is split into four major sections: home and leisure, motoring, business and, new this year, money.

www.loot.com
UK

FREE ADS ONLINE
A redesigned site with a clean look and access to thousands of classified ads in 12 categories, it has an excellent search engine and many bargains.

Beauty

Beauty product retailers are popular on to the Internet so we've featured a few of the best ones for advice, help and shopping. New for this edition is a listing for sites that specialise in organic or natural products.

www.beautyconsumer.com   UK

COMPLETE GUIDE TO SKINCARE

An excellent web site with help and information on all forms of skincare as well as beauty tips and product information there's even a section especially for men. Two people experienced in the field put it together and the information is very easy to access.

www.avon.uk.com   UK

AVON CALLING

A very good-looking and easy-to-use site selling a wide range of cosmetics. They also sell health products and lingerie, you can have a chat in the café and learn about their campaign against breast cancer.

www.lookfantastic.com   UK

LOOK FANTASTIC

A well-designed online retailer offering some really good discounts, and a wide range of products, it also offers advice guides on how to use make-up, shampoo and conditioners, in fact, virtually everything a girl needs – it's war out there after all. Shipping costs start at £2.65.

www.osmoz.com   US

ALL ON THE PERFUMES

An unusual site with an encyclopedia devoted to fragrances, reviews and analysis of the latest products. You can use a quiz to find your perfect perfume and there are also links to help you in your search.

www.fragrancenet.com   US

WORLD'S LARGEST DISCOUNT FRAGRANCE STORE

A massive range of perfumes for men and women, every brand is represented and there are some excellent offers. Shipping costs from America have been reduced and now begin at $10.95 for the first item. See also **www.perfumeshopping.com** who offer 1,000 perfumes and fragrances from a well-designed UK-based site and the eponymous **www.halfpriceperfumes.co.uk**

B

www.fragrancenet.com   UK

WIDE RANGE AND THE BEST PRICES

They claim to offer a wide range of perfumes with up to 90% off UK recommended retail prices plus other big brand name cosmetics. The site is quick and easy-to-use and the offers are genuine; however, delivery costs £3.95.

www.mankindonline.co.uk   UK

MALE GROOMING

Innovative and contemporary men's shaving, skincare and hair products. There's lots of help on understanding skin type, good advice and assistance in finding products for specific problems. There's a nice range of gifts both for him and for her, and they'll do the wrapping for you.

See also:

www.allbeautyproducts.com – excellent site from the Allcures camp.

www.beautybible.com – they claim to have the largest product directory plus good beauty advice, a newsletter and a selection of offers.

www.beautyexpert.co.uk – stocking a range of professional beauty products for home use.

www.benefitcosmetics.com – trendy cosmetics from the US, worth it to be different…

www.blackbeautyandhair.com – excellent site aimed at black and Asian folk, with a wide selection of products and a good regional directory.

www.buycosmeticsdirect.com – a wide range and lots of excellent offers, jewellery as well as cosmetics.

www.creativenailplace.com – specialist shop covering nail art and beauty.

www.magicmakeup.co.uk – great for special offers.

www.makeupalley.com – reviews, chat and products all on make-up.

www.skinstore.com – good-looking US site selling premium skincare products.

www.spacenk.co.uk – nicely designed store featuring their excellent cosmetics.

www.superdrug.com – you can't shop online, but you can compare their excellent prices and offers.

www.virgincosmetics.com – delicious products, shop online or arrange to have a party at home.

www.wellbeing.com – strong offering from Boots, easier to shop than the real store!

B

Hair

www.ukhairdressers.com   UK
HAIR STYLES DATABASE
Some 1,000 styles illustrated including celebrity styles and virtual makeovers, also with advice and fortune telling.

See also:
www.folica.com – great US site on hair care.
www.hqhair.com – magazine-style online store including tips on the products the celebrities use. Sells beauty products too.
www.salonweb.com – hair care products and advice.

Natural Beauty

www.lizearle.com   UK
NATURALLY ACTIVE SKINCARE
They select the best natural ingredients, organic wherever possible, to create award-winning beauty products. If you've ever wondered what frankincense is, there is a helpful guide to ingredients and they've included a few fact sheets too. Postage starts at £2.50.

www.bodynaturals.com   UK
DIVERSE SELECTION
An attractive all round natural beauty site with a reasonable range of products in all categories including shampoo for dogs. Free delivery available.

www.bodyshop.co.uk   UK
ISSUES, SELF-ESTEEM AND COSMETICS
Balancing the rights of the under-privileged with the demands of a commercial cosmetics company. There is good product information but you can't buy online.

www.lush.co.uk   UK
SOAP WITHOUT THE SCENT
Lush offer a wide range of soaps and associated products from

B

their site, it's easy to shop and if you like their soap but find the smell of the high street shops over powering, then it's perfect. Postage & packing starts at £3.95.

See also:
www.gentlebodycare.co.uk – for organic hair dyes, baby care and skin products, free delivery.
www.nealsyardremedies.com – working naturally with the body.
www.whiteginger.co.uk – good range of organic products.

www.acne-advice.com   UK
HELP IS AT HAND
A web site dedicated to advice on treating acne naturally. There is loads of information on acne, its causes and what you can do about it.

Blogging

Keeping a web log or 'blog' is one of the more recent and largest Internet crazes; it allows you to effectively set up your own site cheaply and to a high standard. Its commonest form is that of an online diary covering a specific interest, usually with lots of links to related web sites. Pages are added chronologically and there's usually a facility for visitors to leave comments; some blogs are very informative and entertaining. They are particularly useful for keeping up to date with friends and family.

Here are some sites that can help you on your way and give you all the advice you're likely to need.

www.blogger.com   US
THE MOST POPULAR
The original blogger's site, now owned by Google, it's easy-to-use and free, there are step-by-step instructions and plenty of support.

www.bloglines.com   US
ONE STOP BLOG SHOP
A search facility, subscription service and publishing tool all on one site. It's owned by ask.com so you can be sure it's a quality offering.

Other sites and software to help you on your way:

http://blogplanet.net and also **http://moblg.net** – blog services for people with mobiles, camera phones and PDAs.

http://blogsearchengine.com – search for content on blogs.

http://frassle.rura.org – create your own site directory and share it with others, give your opinions on sites and share them with your friends.

http://quacktrack.com – a massive database of blogs, some 135,000 in 1,500 categories.

http://radio.userland.com – easy to use and with lots of features, software for those lacking technical skills.

www.20six.co.uk – here you can even send photos to your blog via a mobile, the site is nicely designed but only the minimum service is free to use.

www.blogarama.com – a directory of almost 22,000 blogs.

www.blogwise.com – a directory listing in excess of 30,000 blogs.

www.guardian.co.uk/onlineblog formerly **www.onlineblog.com** – from the *Guardian*, a blog covering the latest in technology and the Internet.

www.livejournal.com – the most straightforward and communal of the blogging systems now with over 5 million users – that's 3 million more than last year!

www.moveabletype.org – one for the more advanced user but if you take the time to learn how to use it, it will offer some features for customising your blog.

www.typepad.com – a beautifully designed and easy-to-use blog service with lots of options to help you get your blog underway.

www.vidblogs.com – video blogs are said to be the 'latest thing', but it has to be said, most are just rubbish or plain boring. Be aware that there's adult content here.

Books and Booksellers

Books were the first products to be sold in volume over the Internet, and their success has meant that there are many online booksellers, all boasting about the speed of their service and how many titles they can get. In the main, the basic service is the same wherever you go, just pick the bookshop that suits you.

B

www.bookbrain.co.uk   UK

BEST PRICES FOR BOOKS

All you do is type in the title of the book and BookBrain will search out the online store that is offering it the cheapest (including postage). You then click again to get taken to the store to buy the book – simple.

See also:

www.bestbookbuys.com – a good US alternative to BrainBrain.
www.booktracker.co.uk – UK prices but some book information not always available and some of the information isn't that accurate. Hopefully this will be sorted as the site grows.
www.book-shops.net – a directory of internet bookshops.

Booksellers

www.amazon.co.uk   UK

MORE THAN JUST A BOOKSTORE

Amazon is the leading online bookseller and most online stores have followed their formula of combining value with recommendation. Amazon has spent much on providing a wider offering than just books and now has sections for music, gifts, travel, games, software and DVD/video. It also offers an auction service, there's an excellent kids' section aimed at parents, and you can download e-books to read on your PC or handheld computer. It also offers used goods for sale via third party retailers which can offer great value for money. For books, there are better prices elsewhere, although they have the odd very good offer. See also **www.waterstones.co.uk** who have abandoned their site in favour of Amazon, as has Borders **www.borders.com**

www2.uk.bol.com or www.bol.com   UK

THE EURO-BOOKSELLER

Owned by Bertlesmann, the German media giant, you can get access to books in five European countries and China. Slightly dull, it appeals to the true book lover with lots of recommendations, although it has plenty of offers. Like Amazon it has expanded to include music, video, DVD and games.

www.ottakars.co.uk   UK

E-MAIL A BOOKSTORE

Ottakars' site is clear and easy to use with some nice personal touches; it offers a mix of store information, recommendation, competitions and they offer free online magazines on a variety of genres that are very entertaining. There's a web page for each store giving information on the locale and events, and while there are no facilities to buy books from the site, you can e-mail your local store to see if they have the book you want.

B

http://bookshop.blackwell.co.uk
UK

NOT JUST FOR ACADEMICS
Blackwells are best known for academic and professional books, but their site offers much more, with the emphasis on recommendation and help finding the right book rather than value for money; however, there's free delivery on orders over £20. For more academic books, a good place to try is **www.studentbookworld.com**

www.bookfellas.co.uk
UK

GREAT BOOKS DELIVERED FOR LESS
Good, unfussy design, easy to navigate and well categorised too, with the promise of good service including order tracking. Free delivery on orders over £5.

www.swotbooks.co.uk
UK

LOW COST BOOKS FOR CLEVER DICKS
A fun bookshop aimed at students and young people that offers DVDs and music too. It also has one of the best e-bookshops around. There are cheaper alternatives though.

www.countrybookshop.co.uk
UK

YOUR LOCAL BOOKSHOP
It may not offer the cheapest books, but it's easier and more enjoyable to use than many sites and there's free delivery on orders over £25.

www.bn.com
US

THE WORLD'S BIGGEST BOOKSELLER
Barnes and Noble's site boasts more books than any other online bookseller. In style it follows the other bookshops with an American bias, and looks very similar to Amazon. It has a good out-of-print service; you can also buy software, prints and posters as well as magazines and music. Unusual features include an online university where you can take courses in anything from business to learning a language.

B

www.powells.com
US

MASSIVE

A huge and impressive site which is well designed and relatively
easy to use, Powells seems to occupy most of Portland in Oregon
and for once the cost of shipping isn't prohibitive for UK customers.
A good place to go if you're looking for something unusual.

www.thebookpeople.co.uk
UK

GREAT VALUE

The online version of this popular mail-order bookseller offers
the expected huge discounts and incentives. The range isn't
huge but enough to satisfy most book lovers.

Specialist Booksellers and Sites

The following sites specialise in one form or genre of book.
For science fiction and fantasy see page 389.

www.compman.co.uk – computer manuals.

www.crimetime.co.uk – good overview of what's going on in
the crime fiction world.

www.dancebooks.co.uk – if you need a book on dance here's
where to start.

www.firstbookshop.com – one of the few to offer book tokens.

www.gamblingbooks.co.uk – excellent selection from the High
Stakes bookshop.

www.greenbooks.co.uk – a specialist publisher on
environmental issues.

www.poems.com – home of Poetry Daily.

www.poetrybooks.co.uk – the poetry book society.

www.poetrybookshoponline.com – very good specialist
poetry shop.

www.soccer-books.co.uk – features over 1,000 books on football.

www.stanfords.co.uk – excellent site from the UK's leading
travel and map retailers.

Second-hand Books and Book Finding

www.abebooks.com
UK

ADVANCED BOOK EXCHANGE

A network of some 12,500 independent booksellers from
around the world claiming access to 60 million used, rare and
out-of-print books. Just use the excellent search engine to find
your book and they'll direct you to the nearest bookseller.

www.booklovers.co.uk   UK

QUALITY SECOND HAND BOOKS

If you can't find the book you want, then this is worth a try. There is an excellent search facility or you can leave them a request. They will then give you a quote if you want to sell a book or arrange a swap. There's also an events listing for book fairs.

www.greenmetropolis.com   UK

GOING GREEN

An interesting take on the bookselling theme, here all (mainly good condition second hand) books are one price £3.75 with free delivery and there's a donation towards planting a tree. You can sell your books at this site too. Great idea, we hope it catches on.

See also:

www.bibliofind.com – a search engine from Amazon devoted to second-hand and rare books.

www.bookfinder.com – a more detailed search facility than Bibliofind and you can use it in French, German and Italian.

www.hp-bookfinders.co.uk – UK-based book-finding service with an easy-to-use site.

www.shapero.com – a specialist in natural history and travel-related, second-hand books.

Audio Books

www.talkingbooks.co.uk also diverts from www.audiobooks.co.uk

THE TALKING BOOKSHOP

A talking website for these specialists in books on tape. They have around 6,000 titles in stock and can quickly get another 10,000. They also stock CDs but still no MP3 yet. Search the site by author or reader, as well as by title. There are some offers, but most stock is at full price with delivery being £2 per order. See also **www.isis-publishing.co.uk** who have thousands of unabridged audio books and more in the way of CDs.

See also:

www.audiobooksforfree.com – only free after $100 annual membership which does still represent good value.

www.payperlisten.com – a pay-as-you-go service which saves a huge amount on the usual audio book formats.

B

E-books

These are no longer the preserve of a few classical and out of copyright authors, there is a wide range of contemporary literature available, albeit not at the free sites. Many of the sites are online libraries and provide a useful source of information for educational and reference purposes.

www.free-ebooks.net   US
    E-BOOKS FOR FREE
    A straightforward site devoted to making the most of free e-
    books with recommendations and the encouragement to
    produce your own e-book. See also **http://ebookdirectory.com**

    See also:
    http://digitalmediastore.adobe.com – lots available but you
    have to have the Adobe reader to access them.
    http://onlinebooks.library.upenn.edu – over 20,000 books to
    download with a huge bias towards American titles; it's
    especially strong on history.
    www.bartleby.com/ebook – lots of classics and other free books
    to choose from. Also provides access to the encyclopedia as
    well as American dictionaries and thesauruses.
    www.fictionwise.com – a massive range of e-books from non-
    fiction to fiction and they seem to cover all the formats too.
    www.manybooks.net – a good selection of free e-books mainly
    taken from Project Gutenberg.
    www.netlibrary.com – awkward to use but a huge selection.
    www.questia.com – claiming to be the world's biggest online
    library with over 50,000 books and 399,000 journals and
    other articles, covering some 5,000 research topics. You have
    to subscribe though some content is free.

Literature and Authors

http://promo.net/pg/   US

    PROJECT GUTENBERG
    This is one of the most famous Internet projects ever and one of
    the first web sites to post free e-books. There are over 5,000
    listed. You can't do it justice in a small review, suffice to say it's
    well worth a visit for any book lover. If you're hooked on it, then
    there is the chance to become a volunteer proofreader too.

www.literature-awards.com   US
BOOK AWARDS
A comprehensive listing of the major book awards throughout
the world, why they exist and who won them. See also
www.artsfestivals.co.uk for a literature festival near you.

http://classics.mit.edu   US
THE CLASSICS ONLINE
A superb resource offering over 440 free books to print or
download, there's also a search facility and help with studying.
If that's not enough, try **http://etext.lib.virginia.edu** with 1,800
publicly-available e-books including classic British and
American fiction, major authors, children's literature, American
history, Shakespeare, African-American documents, the Bible.

Travel Abroad

The Good Web Site Guide's Top 10s of the Internet

1. **www.expedia.co.uk** – not always the cheapest but the best.
2. **www.fco.gov.uk/travel** – essential advice from the Foreign Office.
3. **www.xe.net/ucc** – the online currency converter.
4. **www.e-bookers.com** – reliable and good value especially
    for flights.
5. **www.baa.co.uk** – information on the major UK airports
    and flights.
6. **www.uk-airport-car-parking.co.uk** – book your parking
    in advance.
7. **www.lonelyplanet.com** – superb for independent travellers.
8. **www.mappy.co.uk** – get to where you're going.
9. **www.brochurebank.co.uk** – order your brochures and get
    them delivered to you.
10. **www.johnnyjet.com** – great travel portal.

B

www.wordswithoutborders.org   US

INTERNATIONAL LITERATURE
An attractive e-zine devoted to world literature with reviews,
recommendations and articles on books and writers. It's well
categorised, interesting and you're bound to find something new.

www.sacred-texts.com   US

HISTORICAL AND ANCIENT TEXTS
An amazing collection of historic documents and books
presented electronically, it covers mythology, religions, folklore
and the occult. Many have been translated into English and are
well presented with links to related sites and to Amazon.

www.william-shakespeare.info   US

COMPLETE WORKS
This is a straightforward site featuring historical and
biographical details plus a dictionary explaining the language
of the time.

See also:
www.bronte.org.uk – home of the Parsonage Museum in
Haworth with information about the place and an overview of
the Brontes and their lives.
www.ciconline.org/bdp1/ – a new look at Shakespeare,
excellent site design.
www.dickensmuseum.com – home of the Dickens Museum in
London with details about what you can see and links.
www.fidnet.com/~dap1955/dickens – a superb resource
dedicated to Dickens: a real labour of love.
www.janeausten.co.uk – the Jane Austen Centre in Bath with
a good online magazine offering information on everything from
fashion to biographical details.
www.hardysociety.org – The Thomas Hardy Society with good
contextual links.
www.lang.nagoya-u.ac.jp/~matsuoka/Bronte.html
– all you need to know about the Bronte sisters and more.
www.mss.library.nottingham.ac.uk/dhl_home.html
– DH Lawrence resources at The University of Nottingham.
www.pemberley.com – a pretty obsessive site devoted to
everything Jane Austen with discussion groups too.
www.yale.edu/hardysoc – award-winning site on Thomas Hardy.

Reading Groups

www.bookgroup.info   UK

READING GROUP GUIDE
An attractive and informative site on how run a book group and
choose titles with an archive of titles and how they've rated
them. There's also a forum, and a directory is promised.

See also:
http://readers.penguin.co.uk – run by Penguin books you can
get discounts for your group and use the directory, but you have
to register first.
www.readinggroupguides.com – an American site offering
information and guidance on books and how to run a
reading group.
www.readinggroups.co.uk – a neat site run by publisher
HarperCollins with news, advice and competitions.
www.thereadinggrouponline.co.uk – a good bookshop and
forum aimed at reading groups, run by The Book People.

Children's Books

www.cool-reads.co.uk   UK

CHILDREN'S BOOK REVIEWS
Books for 10- to 15-year olds, reviewed by 10- to 15-year
olds. An outstanding site both for its design and for its content.
The books are well categorised and reviewed using a star rating
system. If you're stuck for something to read, then a trip here
is well worthwhile. There are also games, quizzes and chat.

www.achuka.co.uk   UK

CHILDREN'S BOOKS
Achuka are specialists in children's books and offer a
comprehensive listing of what's available. There's plenty of
information on the latest news and awards as well as reviews,
author interviews, a chat section and links to booksellers.
For shopping you are directed to Amazon.

www.wordpool.co.uk   UK

FOR PARENTS, TEACHERS AND WRITERS
A very useful resource devoted to children's books with lots
of advice and recommendations. See also their sister site
www.ukchildrensbooks.co.uk, which is a list of links to sites
listed by author, illustrator, publisher and a miscellaneous section.

B

Other children's book sites:
www.carolhurst.com – good design and great for book reviews.
www.centreforthechildrensbook.org.uk – opening in 2005 in Newcastle.
www.childrensbookshop.com – very traditional site from a shop based in Hay on Wye.
www.myhomelibrary – Anne Fine encouraging children to build a library of their own (with the aid of charity shops) loads of bookplates to download.
www.redhouse.co.uk – a good site devoted to children's books with lots of discounts and recommendations.
www.ucalgary.ca/~dkbrown/ – home of the excellent Children's Literature Web Guide.
www.usbourne.com – good interactive site from this specialist publisher.
www.wordsofdiscovery.com – a children's bookshop that stocks books aimed at giving children a positive and more spiritual view on life.
www.worldbookday.com – find out about this great event that happens every March.

Resources for Writers

www.author.co.uk   UK

FOR AUTHORS EVERYWHERE
A good place to start if you think you've got a book in you (haven't we all?) with sections, articles and links to help. Worth a visit even for experienced authors. With a slightly messy site, **www.writersservices.com** offers just as much, if not more, help and advice.

See also:
www.thenewwriter.com – online magazine for writers.
www.theromancereader.com – lots of romantic reviews and links.
www.openinghooks.us – an entertaining site devoted to great opening lines, view the database and get inspired.

Best Publisher's Websites

www.bloomsbury.com – an attractive site, home of Harry Potter, Scott's Miscellany and more.

www.dk.com – excellent site from one of the leading reference publishers, some good offers too.

www.faber.co.uk – an interesting site from the most literary of publishers.

www.harpercollins.co.uk – now a word from our sponsors – a wide ranging site from the publishers of this book with sections on Tolkein and plenty of celebrities as well as fiction and reference.

www.madaboutbooks.co.uk – a cool site from Hodder Headline.

www.penguin.co.uk – a bright and breezy site from Penguin with plenty to see, information on author events and readers groups too.

www.randomhouse.co.uk – nice design from one of the biggest publishers, particularly good kids' section.

Other book-related sites worth checking out...

www.bookaid.org   UK

BOOKS FOR CHARITY

A charity dedicated to giving unwanted books to places where books are scarce and needed. Find out about their activities and how you can get involved.

www.bookcrossing.com   UK

RELEASE A BOOK

1. Read your book.
2. Say what you think about the book on the site with a reference number.
3. Release the book, give it to a friend or leave it somewhere. You can then get e-mails from anyone who reads the book.

Broadband

As access to ADSL or broadband becomes common, more and more sites are cropping up to cater for those lucky enough to have it. Here are some useful sites where you can start your broadband experience.

www.broadband-help.com   UK

ALL YOU NEED TO KNOW
A good place to start, here you'll find advice and reviews all dedicated to help you make the most out of your broadband experience. See also **www.adslguide.org.uk** which is just as informative albeit from a less attractive site.

www.broadbandchecker.co.uk   UK

BROADBAND AVAILABILITY
A neat and easy-to-use site; you just type in your postcode and phone number and the site will tell you whether broadband is available in your area. You can also compare providers, prices too.

www.jonnybroadband.com   UK

BROADBAND SEARCH
Broadband content, Jonny says 'I just love scouring the web to dig up the very finest broadband content around – the really cool stuff that makes it worth coughing up the cash for a fatter internet pipe in the first place and most of it is free, if you know where to look.' Useful and entertaining, although a bit messy, see also **www.razav.com** which is cleaner but less fun.

www.broadbandweek.com   UK

ALL THE LATEST DEVELOPMENTS
Keep abreast of all the latest technology and increasing download speeds at this business-like site.

www.broadband-television.com   US

STREAMING TV
A huge range of channels available to view including music as well as TV. You have to download the free software but the results are generally worth the effort, it's the choosing which is the difficult part.

www.btopenworld.com   UK
BRITISH TELECOM
Here you can establish whether you can get access to broadband
and, if not, they'll tell you more or less when it will be coming your
way. There are details of the various BT packages, other suppliers
and also information for business users too.

Other sites worth checking out are:
www.broadband4britain.co.uk – information from this
broadband pressure group.
www.ispreview.co.uk/broadband.shtml – informative pages
from the excellent ISP review.
www.low-cost-broadband.com – find the best deal in your area.
www.ntlhome.com/broadband – supplies most of the UK.
www.telewest.co.uk – supplies selected parts of the UK.
www.theregister.co.uk – the latest telecom and broadband news.

Browsers

We're often asked about alternatives to Internet Explorer, here are the best.

www.mozilla.org – home to Firefox, certainly one of the fastest
browsers and it works on all operating systems. It's easy to use
and set up too.
www.mozilla.org/products/camino/ – another Mozilla product,
here's an alternative to Apple's Safari browser.
www.netscape.com – the earliest real alternative to IE, it offers
a huge amount of content and plenty of extra features.
www.opera.com – another claimant for the fastest browser,
it's certainly flexible and easy on the eye and has lots of
features, there is a mobile version too.

Business

Here are a few essential and helpful business sites; see also the finance section on page 147 for share dealing and other related sites. Be aware that many official-looking sites offering advice are often companies out to make a profit or are part of a larger organisation, so may not be impartial.

www.economist.com   UK

THE ECONOMIST MAGAZINE
The airports' best-selling magazine goes online with a wide-ranging site that covers business and politics world-wide. You can get access to the archive and also their excellent country surveys. If you're in business, you need this in your favourites box.

See also:
www.better-business.co.uk – a helpful site from this magazine including tips on starting up and even what to do when things get boring.
www.businessweek.com – offering a wide range of business news and information.

www.businesslink.gov.uk   UK

THE NATIONAL BUSINESS ADVICE SERVICE
A government-run site which has a comprehensive set of helpful guides and links, backed up by a hotline. It has to be the first port of call for any small business needing advice or help.

See also:
www.dti.gov.uk – here you'll find a great deal of wide ranging information.
www.sbs.gov.uk – the government's small business service.

www.startinbusiness.co.uk   UK

AN ONLINE BUSINESS STARTER KIT
An excellent portal site on all things to do with business including a good guide to help you start a business. There are plenty of links plus listings of businesses for sale, property, services and potential opportunities. See also **www.startups.co.uk** which is a mess of a site but with a huge amount information, if you can find it. Excellent directory and links section.

www.businessadviceonline.org.uk   UK

BUSINESS ADVICE

An excellent resource whether you're starting out or want to improve an existing business. There are sections on choosing the right IT systems, contracts, selling techniques and much more.

See also:

www.bawe-uk.org – home of the British Association of Women Entrepreneurs.

www.bized.ac.uk – aimed at students and teachers but a great resource for business people too.

www.business-ethics.com – encouraging the right sort of corporate responsibility.

www.bvca.co.uk – the public face of venture capitalism.

www.clearlybusiness.com – offers the same information as above but is a more commercial affair.

www.ecademy.com – a messy business networking and community site.

www.fsb.org.uk – home of the Federation of Small Businesses.

www.iba.org.uk – contact a qualified business adviser.

www.linkedin.com – create your own business network.

www.payontime.co.uk – excellent advice on how to manage payment.

www.plaxo.com – a service devised to help you keep your business contacts up to date.

www.whichfranchise.com – a slightly messy site that offers the information you need on all the available franchises in the UK, and how to go about getting one.

www.hoovers.com   UK

COMPANY RESEARCH

Get basic information on any UK and US company plus related links and advice a very useful research tool.

See also:

www.carolworld.com – Company Annual Reports Online; a useful free service.

www.companies-house.gov.uk – a useful site if you want to research companies with access to information and guidance on most aspects of business and the regulations surrounding it. Here you can check-up on whether companies really exist or not.

www.uk.sage.com   UK

> BUSINESS SOFTWARE
> If you need accounting software to solve virtually any sort of
> problem or provide a new service, you should find it here.
> Sage has a good reputation for helping small businesses.
> See also **www.myob.com** who offer similar products.

Cars

*Whether you want to buy a car, check out your insurance or even
arrange a service, it can all be done on the Internet. If you want to
hire a car see page 526.*

Motoring Organisations, Campaigning Sites and Government Agencies

www.theaa.co.uk   UK

> THE AA
> A very comprehensive motoring site with a route planner, new
> and used car info, travel information, insurance quotes, shop
> and a car data checking facility.

www.rac.co.uk   UK

> THE RAC
> A much clearer site than The AA's, with a very good route
> planner and traffic news service. There's also information about
> buying a car, getting the best finance and insurance deals, and
> a small shop.

www.greenflag.co.uk   UK

> GREEN FLAG
> The usual route planner and car buying advice all packaged on
> a nice-looking and very green site, there's a particularly good
> section on European travel and motoring advice. See also
> **www.internationalbreakdown.com** who offer a wide range of
> cover across the UK and Europe.

www.dvla.gov.uk   UK

> DRIVER AND VEHICLE LICENSING AGENCY
> Excellent for the official line in motoring, the driver's section has

details on penalty points, licence changes and medical issues.
The vehicles section goes through all related forms and there's
also a 'What's New' page. It's clearly and concisely written
throughout and information is easy to find.

www.rmif.co.uk   UK

RETAIL MOTOR INDUSTRY FEDERATION
A rich source of information covering all aspects of buying and
selling cars for both industry and consumers alike. It's great as
a starting place if you want to find out about legislation and the
latest news, it also has an excellent links section.

www.smmt.co.uk   UK

SOCIETY OF MOTOR MANUFACTURERS & TRADERS
The SMMT support the British motor industry by campaigning and
informing the trade and public alike. Here you can get information
on topics like the motor show and the tax regime based on exhaust
emissions, as well as links to other industry sites.

For Sharing

The Good Web Site Guide's Top 10s of the Internet

1.   **www.flickr.com** – great for sharing photos.
2.   **www.friendster.com** – organise your social life.
3.   **www.furl.net** – save web pages and share them with
     your friends.
4.   **www.wikipedia.org** – share your knowledge.
5.   **www.dudecheckthisout.com** – put together your
     own set of favourites and share them with your network.
6.   **www.friendsreunited.co.uk** – get in touch with old friends.
7.   **www.feedster.com** – get the latest news, make it relevant
     to you and your friends.
8.   **www.kazaa.com** – share your talents with peer
     to peer technology.
9.   **www.linkedin.com** – create a business network.
10. **www.meetup.com** – share your interests with like
     minded people.

www.abd.org.uk
UK

CAMPAIGNING FOR THE DRIVER

The Association of British Drivers aims to be the lobbying voice of beleaguered drivers in the UK. Here you can find out about their campaigns against speed traps, speed limits, the environment and the road infrastructure.

www.rospa.co.uk/cms
UK

ROYAL SOCIETY FOR THE PREVENTION OF ACCIDENTS

An excellent site from ROSPA with loads of information about road safety with fact sheets available on most issues and problems that affect every driver and pedestrian. See also **www.cic.cranfield.ac.uk** where all the crash testing goes on.

www.roadpeace.org
UK

SUPPORT FOR CRASH VICTIMS

RoadPeace, the UK's national charity dedicated to supporting bereaved and injured road crash victims and the only national helpline for road victims. Join a campaign or use the extensive links section. Salutary.

www.secureyourmotor.gov.uk
UK

SECURITY TIPS FOR MOTORISTS

Pretty straightforward site detailing the best steps to guard against your car, bike or truck being stolen. You can take tests to see how secure your car is or test your security knowledge.

www.carclubs.org.uk
UK

RIDE SHARING

Join a car club and help the environment and aid congestion by sharing your journey with others. Here you can find a club in your area. See also **www.smartmoves.co.uk** and also **www.mystreetcar.co.uk**

www.cclondon.com
UK

LONDON CONGESTION CHARGES

All you need to know about the congestion charge and how to pay it.

www.speed-trap.co.uk
UK

THE SPEED TRAP BIBLE

While not condoning speeding, this site gives the low-down on speed traps, the law and links to police forces. There's even data on the types of camera used and advice on dealing with the courts and police. However, they are sponsored by a speed trap detector company. See also **www.speedcamerasuk.com**

www.parkingticket.co.uk   UK
  PARKING PROBLEMS
  This site gives details regarding parking and free advice on how
  to challenge a parking ticket that you feel has been issued unfairly.

C

Cheaper and Greener Fuels

www.est-powershift.org.uk   UK

  CONVERTING TO CLEANER FUELS
  A well-put-together and informative site aimed at encouraging
  drivers to shift to cleaner fuels such as LPG, you can find out
  how to convert your car, where the fuel stations are and the latest
  government information such as grants and future proposals.

www.spongecars.com   UK

  LPG CONVERSIONS
  Excellent overview and information site covering all aspects of
  converting a car to LPG, an explanation of what it is, how to
  get a conversion quote and the latest news.

  See also:
  www.bath.ac.uk/~en2bwp/gaspower.htm – learn about
  gas-powered cars.
  www.evuk.co.uk – not just milk floats and golf carts,
  it's serious stuff, the electric car business.
  www.honda.co.uk/IMA – Honda's greenest car.
  www.lpga.co.uk – information from the Liquid Petroleum
  Gas Association.
  www.toyota.co.uk/prius – home of the successful hybrid
  electrical petrol car.

Car Information and Buying Guides

www.autoindex.org   US

  WORLD CAR CATALOGUE
  An amazing directory of the world's car makers illustrated using
  thousands of pictures. There is detailed information on each
  manufacturer and what they produce. You can search by
  maker, country, and category or body style.

www.carsurvey.org   UK
  CAR REVIEWS BY THEIR OWNERS
  Don't let the basic design fool you; this is an impressive
  collection of reviews on hundreds of cars, by those most
  important people – their owners. It's easily searchable and
  genuinely useful if you're looking for unbiased opinion.

C

www.hoot-uk.com   UK
IT'S A HOOT!
A fun, simple site with a marque-by-marque news listing and
the latest headlines. There are also sections with car tests,
some good writing and chat at the aptly named 'Gas Station'.

www.parkers.co.uk   UK
REDUCING THE GAMBLE
The premier buying guide with a clear, readable site, this covers
all the information you'll need to select the right car for you.
However, these days you have to register to get the more
detailed information.

See also:
www.glass.co.uk offers similar information but their site
is poor and it costs £2.95 to get a valuation for your car.

www.jdpower.com   US
J.D.POWER RELIABILITY
It's only geared to the US market but some models are the
same and you can get a great deal of safety and reliability
information here.

Magazine and E-zine Sites

www.autoexpress.co.uk   UK

BEST MOTORING NEWS AND INFORMATION
Massive database on cars, with motoring news and features
on the latest models, you can check prices too. It also has
classified ads and a great set of links. You have to register to
get access to most of the information; lots of advertising makes
the site a bit annoying to use.

www.whatcar.co.uk   UK
WHAT CAR MAGAZINE
A neatly packaged, one-stop shop for cars with reviews and
data on every car. There's a cars for sale section and an
easy-to-use search facility.

www.autocarmag.com   UK

AUTOCAR MAGAZINE
A fine site from this popular weekly with plenty of interactive
features including videos and even a blogging service, there is
news, reviews, advice and shopping too.

www.carnet.co.uk   UK

ONLINE CAR MAGAZINE
Car Net is a well-designed and fun site with the latest news
and new car reviews as well as feature micro-sites and links to
deals on cars and insurance, statistics (on over 6,000 cars)
and classifieds. You can also visit the specialist forums and
have a go at the trivia quizzes.

www.carkeys.co.uk   UK

INFORMATION SERVICE STATION
A wide-ranging magazine-style site with lots of data on current
and new models as well as launch reviews and motoring news.

www.womanmotorist.com   US

MOTORING ISN'T JUST FOR MEN
A well-laid-out and interesting American magazine-style site
that dispels the myth that motoring is just for men. Lots of
advice, buying information, a glossary and car reviews.

TV Tie-in Sites

www.topgear.beeb.com   UK

TOP GEAR
A site to go along with the TV series, it has everything you'd expect
along with features on new and used cars, competitions, classifieds
and a shop. See also **www.bbc.co.uk/lifestyle/motoring/** which is
great for advice on buying and owning.

www.4car.co.uk   UK

DRIVEN
News, sport, reviews, advice, chat and games – it's all here,
and you can find out what's been and is being featured on their
main motoring programmes.

Traders and Car Finding Services

www.motortrak.com   UK

USED CAR SEARCH
A hi-tech site where, in theory, you can find the right used car.
Just follow the search guidelines and up pops your ideal car!
It's easy to use and very fast.

www.autobytel.co.uk   US/UK

WORLD'S LEADING CAR BUYING SERVICE
The easy way to buy a car online, just select the model you want
then follow the online instructions, they've improved information
on used and nearly new cars and will get quotes from local
dealers. All cars featured have detailed descriptions and photos.
There's also financial information and aftercare service.

www.oneswoop.co.uk   UK

SMART WAY TO BUY
Now owned by Norwich Union, a straightforward and very
popular site that concentrates on making the process of buying
a car as painless as possible. There are also some good special
offers and a finance section. It's very easy to use and faster
than most.

www.jamjar.com   UK

DIRECT LINE
Jam Jar is owned by Direct Line Insurance and they want to
make it work well. The design is OK, and if you persevere there
are some fantastic offers and they're also improving the service
by branching into other merchandise related to driving such as
personal leasing and insurance.

For more car buying information and cars for sale try:
http://cars.kelkoo.co.uk – the car price checking pages at Kelkoo
http://uk.cars.yahoo.com – the excellent Yahoo has a used car
search engine, car comparison facility and directory.
www.autolocate.co.uk – great for links, good new car guide
and review section, also good for used cars.
www.autopoint.ie – Ireland's leading online car retailer and
auction house.
www.autoseek.co.uk – thousands of cars for sale, great
for links.

www.autotrader.co.uk – claiming to be Britain's biggest car showroom with over 314,000 listed. Nice, clear design.

www.broadspeed.com – car import specialists with a nicely designed and fast site.

www.carseller.co.uk – free advertising if selling and good links.

www.carsource.co.uk – great for data and online quotes, thousands of cars for sale.

www.carsupermarkets.co.uk – a useful list of the UK's car supermarkets with lots of information and how to find them.

www.cartalk.com – a good US magazine site that is something of a cult stateside.

www.eurekar.com – lots of deals from this specialist importer.

www.fish4cars.co.uk – over 205,000 cars on their database, plus hundreds of other vehicles. Comprehensive.

www.new-car-net.co.uk – informative and well-illustrated car review site.

www.savemoneyoncars.co.uk – bright and breezy site with lots of deals and information on buying a car cheaply.

www.sellyourcarnow.co.uk – sell your car direct to the motor trade using this posting site.

www.showroom4cars.com – bright, brash and fast.

www.topmarques.co.uk – luxury vehicles only.

www.vanbuyer.com – vans and more vans of all shapes and sizes.

www.virgincars.com – good savings and speedy delivery and nice design.

www.wannavan.com – specialist in supplying vans for business and personal use.

www.hpicheck.com   UK

DON'T BE RIPPED OFF...
Before you buy a second-hand car it's wise to pay out £35.95 on an HPI check which will tell you about what mileage the car should have, whether it's been in an accident or damaged and also if there's any outstanding finance against it.

www.ukstolencars.co.uk   UK

ARE YOU DRIVING A STOLEN CAR?
A simple and free search of the UK stolen cars database offering helpful information and advice.

For Disabled Motorists

www.ddmc.org.uk   UK
DISABLED DRIVERS MOTOR CLUB
A campaigning site from the DDMC who are devoted to
improving the lot of disabled motorists. It has lots of useful
information and you can find out about and support their latest
campaigns. See also **www.dda.org.uk** home of the Disabled
Drivers Association who work along the same lines.

www.motability.co.uk   UK

GET MOBILE
UK
A scheme for helping disabled people get mobile by contract
hiring a car, the site is very clear and easy to use too.

See also:
www.aixam.co.uk – a leading supplier of quadricycles and
adapted cars.
www.dft.gov.uk – the Department for Transport.
www.motability.royalsun.co.uk/fullsite/index.html –
a motability scheme from an insurance company.

Car Registrations

www.dvla-som.co.uk   UK
CHERISHED AND PERSONALISED NUMBERS
Here's the first port of call if you want that special number
plate. They sell by auction but there's plenty of help and you
search for un-issued, select registrations in both new and old
styles. Order over the phone using their hotline.

For more sites offering car registrations try:
www.carreg.co.uk
www.newreg.co.uk
www.northumbrianumbers.com
www.regtransfers.co.uk

Insurance

Most of the general finance sites (page 147) and motoring organisations (page 62) will offer links to insurance companies, but these are worth a try.

www.easycover.com   UK

> CAR INSURANCE
> Quotes from a large number of insurance suppliers, you just fill in the form, and they get back to you with a quote.
>
> *See also:*
> **www.diamond.co.uk** and **www.girlmotor.co.uk** – specialists in insurance for women drivers who are statistically a safer bet.
> **www.cheapest-motor-insurance.co.uk**
> **www.eaglestar.co.uk**
> **www.swinton.co.uk**

Looking After and Repairing Your Car

www.ukmot.com   UK

> M.O.T.
> Find your nearest M.O.T. test centre, get facts about the test and what's actually supposed to be checked, there's also a reminder service. You can also run an HPI check from the site and find out about the foibles of specific models.

www.carcareclinic.com   UK

> LOOKING AFTER YOUR CAR
> If you need advice on car repairs or faults, then help is at hand here. There are discussion forums on all sorts of problems and, if you post a message or ask for advice, there's always someone to answer. They also provide a databank which is essentially a glossary of terms and a good set of links. See also **www.autosite.com/garage/garmenu.asp**, which is from a large American site, here you can find a maintenance encyclopedia.

www.haynes.co.uk   UK

> HAYNES MANUALS
> Unfortunately they've stopped the download service, so now you have to buy the books – there's 2,500 available so there should be one for you.

Car Accessories and Kits

www.halfords.com UK

DRIVING DOWN PRICES
A fairly wide range of products for your car and bike at good prices and sold from a very good site, there's advice and a store locator too.

www.autofashion.co.uk UK

ACCESSORISE YOUR CAR
An entertaining site where you can buy body kits and accessories for many makes of car, including custom made.

www.modify.co.uk UK

COMPREHENSIVE LISTING SERVICE
An outstanding source for information on those companies that can help you improve your car. There's a directory of specialists – everything from tuners to insurance, articles on how to modify your motor and lastly statistics on virtually very modern car.

See also:
www.autostore.co.uk – specialists in car storage solutions, slow site though.
www.caralarms-security.co.uk – every type of car alarm and security device.
www.gttowing.co.uk – for tow bars, roof racks and trailers, good site.
www.motech.uk.com – specialists in performance enhancement.
www.roofbox.co.uk – roof boxes and most other storage solutions.
www.saveanddrive.co.uk – for roof boxes, cycle carriers and radar detectors.

www.caraudiocentre.com UK

IN CAR AUDIO SYSTEMS
Here you can get loads of advice and offers on a wide range of stereos with a price promise and low delivery costs. See also **www.toade.com** who have a highly interactive site and can also supply security, multi-media and navigation equipment on top of audio.

www.mytyres.co.uk
UK

TYRES
A site where you can save money buying tyres for your car. It pays to know what you want but the prices appear competitive and they'll find a fitter for you too.

See also:
www.kwikfit.co.uk – very good site with mobile fitting service, although you can get cheaper deals by visiting them.
www.tyresafety.co.uk – home of the Tyre Industry Council with advice on safety.
www.tyres-online.co.uk – basic website but some good prices.

Specialist Car Sites

www.classicmotor.co.uk
UK

FOR CLASSIC CARS
By far the best classic car site. Design-wise it's a jumble (it's better to use the no frames version), but it's comprehensive, including clubs, classifieds and books; here you can buy anything from a car to a headlight bulb.

See also:
www.classic-car-directory.com – which is a well-categorised links site.
www.hireaclassiccar.com – classic car hire specialist.
www.kitcar.com – US-oriented and a messy site, but a huge amount of information.
www.kit-cars.com – home of *Kit Cars* magazine.
www.kitcars.org – UK site being redeveloped at time of our visit.
www.motorbase.com – a growing site with lots of potential, good for links but a little slow.
www.vintage-car-world.com – a German owned site offering news, event information and classifieds.

www.pistonheads.com
UK

SPEED MATTERS
Pistonheads is a British site dedicated to the faster side of motoring and is great for reviews of the latest cars and chat. It's passionate and very informative.

C

www.britishmm.co.uk   UK

HISTORY OF BRITISH CARS TO 1960
An amateur site with a good make-by-make history of the British
car industry, it includes a glossary and information on tax and other
historical references. Unfortunately it's not well illustrated.

www.conceptcar.co.uk   UK

AUTOMOTIVE DESIGN
A really interesting, comprehensive and well-laid-out site
devoted to car design and new concepts, it's great for links
and you can tell that it's used by the industry itself.

www.uglycars.co.uk   UK

UGLY CARS
There's been a spate of books published about the worst cars
sold in the UK and this site goes along with that trend and our
fascination with all things that are rubbish. Here you can relish
some of the worst excuses for car design and even suggest
some candidates to be added.

Learning to Drive

www.learners.co.uk   UK

LEARNER'S DIRECTORY
The point of this site is to help you find the right driving school.
Just type in your postcode and the schools will be listed along
with helpful additional information such as whether they have
a female instructor or whether they train for motorway driving.
There is plenty of supplementary information on things like
theory tests and how to buy a car.

www.2pass.co.uk   UK

THEORY AND PRACTICAL TESTS
A learner driver's dream, this site helps with your tests in giving
advice, mock exams plus other interesting snippets of information
such as why the British drive on the left. There are also articles on
driving abroad, on motorbikes and driving automatics. There's also
plenty of fun with top stories, quizzes and crash of the month.

www.driving-tests.co.uk   UK

THE DSA
Get the official line from the Driving Standards Agency where
you can now book both the theory and practical test online, get
advice for learners and instructors and learn about government
schemes to promote better driving. For the Highway Code
faithfully reproduced as a website and more theory tests go to
www.highwaycode.gov.uk

See also:
www.bsm.co.uk – one of the UK's biggest driving schools.
www.iam.org.uk – home of the Institute Of Advanced Motorists.
www.roadcode.co.uk – Highway Code for young people.

Celebrities

Find your favourite celebrities and their web sites using these sites.
A word of caution though – there are many celebrity search engines
available on the web and while it's easy to find your favourite, it's also
very easy to unwittingly access adult-orientated material through them.

www.celeblink.com   US

LINKS TO THE STARS
Just about the best celebrity directory in terms of lack of
advertising and dodgy links. There are also some good articles,
gossip and entertainment news.

www.celebhoo.com   US

FOR EVERYTHING CELEBRITY
A very good fan site directory plus information, birthdays,
chat and gossip.

www.thespiannet.com   UK

ACTORS AND ACTRESSES
Lots of actors and actresses listed with links and details including
e-mail addresses. It's also a good resource for aspiring thespians.

See also:
www.celebrity-link.com – over 10,000 celebrities listed and
links to 50,000 sites.
www.celebsites.com – huge listing of some 20,000 celeb sites.

www.celebrityemail.com   US

E-MAIL THE STARS
E-mail addresses to over 22,000 of the world's most famous
people. It's quite biased towards Americans but give it a try
anyway, you might get a reply.

C

www.debretts.co.uk   UK

POSH CELEBRITY GOSSIP
An excellent site from *Debretts* who have been tracking the
lives of celebrities for many years longer than the likes of *OK*
and *Hello*. There are sections on people in the news plus a
good celebrity search engine. There are also sections on the
royal family, a guide to the season, charities and a fun search
section where you can match birthdays.

www.hellomagazine.com   UK

THE WORLD IN PICTURES
Hello magazine's web site features pictures and articles from current
and previous issues with loads of celebrities. You can't search by
celebrity but you can have fun trawling through the pictures.

www.eonline.com   US

E!
Entertainment Online features all the latest gossip mainly oriented
towards the US and Hollywood in particular. It's fun and irreverent
and has a reputation for being first with the news.

www.glamourmagazine.co.uk   UK

LOSE YOURSELF IN GLAMOUR
Gossip, fashion, beauty tips, chat, competitions and, of course,
celebrities are the mainstay of *Glamour* magazine's site. Its main
function though is to plug the real magazine.

www.amiannoyingornot.com   US

VOTE FOR MOST ANNOYING CELEBRITIES
You can spend ages on this site; it's easy to vote and fun to
use. Each celeb gets a page with biographical details and
reasons why they could be annoying or not...

www.mugshots.com   US
WHEN IT ALL GOES WRONG
This could only happen in America, mug shots of the rich and
famous when, once in a while, they break the law. There's also
a serious side with sections covering national US events and
the FBI's most wanted list. Ghoulish but fascinating too.

www.thesmokinggun.com   US
FINDING THE SLEAZE – ALLEGEDLY
Devoted to finding skeletons in cupboards, Smoking Gun has
everything from confidential documents and incriminating
evidence to mug shots. If your favourite celeb has done
something wrong even a small thing, it'll be here.

www.bbc.co.uk/celebdaq   UK

CELEBRITY STOCK EXCHANGE
The BBC's celebrity stock exchange show now lives on in the
form of this web site. It monitors the rise and fall of many
celebrities and allocates a stock price to them – it's fun to see
who's on the up and who's on the slide. See also the
Hollywood Stock Exchange at **www.hsx.com**

Charities

*The Internet offers a great opportunity to give to your favourite charity
or support a cause dear to your heart. There are so many that we're
unable to list them all, but here are some top sites with directories to
help you find the ones that interest you. For charity cards see page
224 and for health-related charities see page 233.*

Charity Information

www.charitychoice.co.uk   UK

ENCYCLOPEDIA OF CHARITIES
A very useful and well-put-together directory of charities with a
good search facility and a list in over 30 categories. There's
also the excellent 'Goodwill Gallery' where you can post up a
service or a donation you're willing to give to charity.

www.caritasdata.co.uk   UK

> CHARITIES DIRECT
> A support site for charities with information on how to raise
> funds and run a charity, there's also a good directory of UK
> charities and you can rank them by expenditure, revenue and
> fund size.

www.charitycommission.gov.uk   UK

> THE CHARITY COMMISSION
> The Charity Commission's mission is to give the public
> confidence in the integrity of charities in England and Wales,
> and their site lists over 166,000 charities. There's also lots of
> advice for charities, a list of their publications and links to
> related sites.

www.charitynet.org   UK

> INFORMATION ON THE NON-PROFIT WORLD
> A useful database covering charities and non-profit
> organisations world-wide, it has sections on education,
> government, IT, legal issues and jobs too.
>
> *See also:*
> **www.bcconnections.org.uk** – businesses can find out how they
> can get involved in charity donations and charities can find out
> how they can get businesses involved in their work.
> **www.charities.org** – information about American charities.
> **www.helplines.org.uk** – the Telephone Helplines Association
> with useful search facility.

Giving

www.justgiving.com   UK

> GIVE EFFECTIVELY
> A newsy and informative site devoted to making the process of
> giving to charity as easy as possible whether you're an
> individual donor, charity or a company. The site is divided into
> three sections: Fundraise, Donate and Sponsor so you can go
> directly to the area that interests you. See also
> **www.allaboutgiving.org** which is especially informative about
> unusual ways of donating such as using tax and shares.

www.thehungersite.com   US

CLICK AND GIVE
Just one click and you'll donate a cup of food to the world's
hungry via registered sponsors, a brilliant idea and one that
works: last year the site funded nearly 44 million cups of food.
Sign up and they'll send you a reminder to visit every weekend.
There are also sister sites for breast cancer, saving rain forests,
animal rescue and child health. See also
www.freedonation.com which has similar aims and works
along the same lines.

www.careinternational.org.uk   UK

HELPING THE WORLDS POOREST
Care are all about helping the world's most stricken people,
here you can learn about their work and donate.

See also:
www.50ways.org – an outstanding American site devoted to
ways of giving money to save the world's children from
suffering.
www.buildaschool.org – just click to contribute to building
schools in developing countries.
www.charitychallenge.com – raise money for your chosen
charity by taking an adventure holiday through Charity
Challenge.
www.dec.org.uk – donate to the Tsunami appeal.
www.ecpat.net – working to eliminate all forms of child abuse.
www.givewater.org – help get water to where it's most needed.
www.sendacow.org.uk – get livestock to those who really need
it in East Africa.

Chat

There are literally thousands of chat sites and rooms on the web covering many different topics. However, this is the area of the Net that people have the most concerns about. There have been loads of cases where people have been tricked into giving out personal information and even arranged unsuitable meetings.

But at its best, a chat program is a great way to keep in contact with friends, especially if they live miles away. So chat wisely by following our top tips for keeping safe.

Chat – Our Top Tips

1. Be wary, just like you would be if you were visiting any new place.
2. Don't give your e-mail address out without making sure that only the person you're sending it to can read it.
3. People often pretend to be someone they're not when they're chatting; unless you know the person, assume that's the case with anyone you chat with online.
4. Don't meet up with anyone you've met online – keep your online life separate. Chances are they'd be a let down anyway, even if they were genuine.
5. If you like the look of a chat room or site, but you're not sure about it, get a recommendation first.
6. If you want to meet up with friends online, arrange a time and place beforehand.
7. If you don't like someone, just block 'em.
8. Check out the excellent **www.chatdanger.com** (see below) for more info on how to chat safely.

www.chatdanger.com   US

KEEP SAFE IN CHAT ROOMS
A great site devoted to the perils of using chat rooms, full of advice and sensible information, it can be a little slow though, but it's worth persevering.

The following are the major chat sites and programs:

www.aim.com   UK

AOL INSTANT MESSENGER
One of the most popular, it's pretty safe and anyway you can
easily block people who are a nuisance, or just set it up so that
only friends can talk to you.

http://web.icq.com   US

ICQ – I SEEK YOU
There are lots of chat rooms here. It's quick and easy to use
combined with a mobile phone. There are lots of features such
as games, money advice, music and lurve.

www.mirc.com   US

IRC – INTERNET RELAY CHAT
A straightforward chat program that is easy to use. Generally it's
been overtaken by the likes of AOL but some web sites may opt
to use it.

www.trillian.cc   US

COMMUNICATE WITH FLEXIBILITY AND STYLE
Trillian enables connections to all the major chat programs
through one interface. The reader looks good and you can
personalise it too.

www.paltalk.com   US

VERSATILITY
A feature-laden system with everything from video conferencing
to instant messaging – all free!

www.habbohotel.co.uk   UK

FOR UK TEENS
Lots of recommendations from users has meant the inclusion of
this site in the book, flexibility, fun graphics and an excellent
monitoring policy make it popular. This is the new UK site for
www.habbohotel.com the basics are free but additional
services have to be paid for.

www.there.com   US

3-D CHAT
Create your avatar or virtual identity, join in one of the
conversations or play a game with your new friends, it's
entertaining and best used in broadband.

Children

You can save pounds on children's clothes and toys by shopping over the Net; it's easy and the service is often excellent, the Internet is also a great way to educate and entertain children. They are fascinated by it and quickly become experts, often quickly overtaking their parents. We've put together a selection of the very best sites here but for ideas for days out with children see the British travel listings page 518, for educational sites see page 115 and for parenting concerns see page 346.

Shopping for Children

www.toy.co.uk   UK

FIND THAT TOY
A very useful toy search engine, you can search by type, company or age. Once searched, it lists the toys with details, price and where you can buy them online.

www.elc.co.uk   UK

EARLY LEARNING CENTRE
A well-designed and user-friendly site that offers a wide range of toys for the under-fives in particular, it's strong on character products and traditional toys alike. Delivery costs £3.95 per order (free over £75) and you can expect goods to arrive in 5 days.

www.hamleys.co.uk   UK

FINEST TOY STORE IN THE WORLD
Hamley's has improved its site and you can search for toys by gender, price or age. There's also an okay selection of character areas within the store as well as the more traditional range, which is their main strength. Children can leave a wishlist on the site and they do a birthday reminder service. Delivery starts at £6.99 for up to 20kg.

www.toysrus.co.uk   UK

NOT JUST TOYS
Good site with all the key brands and 'in' things you'd expect – you can even buy a mobile phone. Has links to key toy manufacturer's sites and a sister site called **www.babiesrus.co.uk** which covers younger children. Delivery is £3.90 for the UK.

www.thetoyshop.com   UK
THE ENTERTAINER
The online spin-off from the Entertainer high street stores; it
offers much in the way of bargains and this bright and breezy
site is easy to navigate. You can search by toy, age, price or
category. Shipping to the UK is £4 flat rate while international
rates vary.

www.newcron.com   UK
CHARACTER PRODUCTS
Newcron has taken over the Character Warehouse site to
produce an online store that offers a wide range of mainstream
and unusual character products. You can search by character,
product or price; delivery starts at £3.99. See also
www.shop4toys.co.uk which has a similar offer.

www.woodentoysonline.co.uk   UK
WOODEN TOYS
A wide range of wooden and innovative toys here covering
lots of categories and types, all on a well-categorised and
easy-to-use site.

www.outdoortoysdirect.co.uk   UK
LOW PRICES ON OUTDOOR TOYS
Excellent value for money with free delivery, a money back
guarantee, plus a wide range of goods. The selection consists of
everything from trampolines to swings, slides and play houses.
Free delivery on most goods. To complete your outdoor experience
you can always pay a visit to **www.kiteshop.co.uk** who offer a
wide range of kites and advice from an excellent site.

www.krucialkids.com   UK

ALL ABOARD THE KRUCIAL KIDS EXPRESS
This site specialises in developmental toys for children up to
eight years old, providing detailed information on the
educational value of each of the 200 or so toys. The site itself
can be slow, but the prices aren't bad so patience pays off.
Delivery begins at £1.95 and is free if you spend over £60.
For educational toys see also **www.mulberrybush.co.uk** who
specialise in toys for under 12s.

C

www.mailorderexpress.com   UK
SHOP IN THE COMFORT OF YOUR HOME
Excellent toy store with games and models too. Shop by brand or by category, with some good prices and special offers. The design is a little old fashioned but effective nonetheless.

www.bloomingmarvellous.co.uk   UK
MATERNITY, NURSERY AND BABY WEAR
Excellent online store with a selection of maternity, baby and nurseryware available to buy, or you can order their catalogue. Delivery in the UK is £3.95.

www.mothercare.com   UK
MOTHERCARE
An attractive site with a good selection of baby and toddler products, also clothing, entertainment and equipment. It's good value and there are some excellent offers, delivery is £3.95 for the UK. It's not all about shopping though, there are advice sections on baby care, finance, tips on how to keep kids occupied and chat rooms where you can share your experiences.

www.greenbabyco.com   UK
FOR GREEN BABIES
A good store where all products are environmentally friendly. There are clothes, nappies, toiletries, furniture, equipment, even laundry products amongst its many sections. Delivery is £3.99 for up to 15kg. For a similar site go to **www.ethosbaby.com** and also the attractive **www.gtexpectations.co.uk**

Other sites in this very competitive area that are worth a visit...
www.babycare-direct.co.uk – not the most attractive store but a wide range to choose from and some good offers.
www.babyhut.net – natural products for baby's and parents.
www.babyjunction.co.uk – an above average shop with a wide range of baby and toddler gear in lots of categories.
www.bibsandstuff.co.uk – great for all those hard-to-get things and equipment generally.
www.cheekyrascals.co.uk – a very good baby equipment store.
www.drtoy.com – a quirky American site run by someone who has reviewed and rated some 2,000 products for children, includes useful and intelligent 100 best toys of the year awards.

www.huggables.co.uk – specialists in teddies and other cute soft toys.

www.imaginarium.com – Amazon's toy store.

www.kiddicare.com – baby accessories and nursery.

www.mamasandpapas.co.uk – good-looking site, you can't buy online but you can order a catalogue.

www.modelmegastore.co.uk – excellent for models of all types, especially remote control cars, shipping is good value.

www.nurserydirect.co.uk – nursery products specialist with 1% of revenue going to charity.

www.orchardtoys.co.uk – specialists in fun, educational toys.

www.theoldtoyshop.com – mainly vintage and collectible toys.

www.totalrobots.com – all sorts of robots, probably one for dads really.

www.toycentre.com – a sparse site with some good prices, most brands represented.

www.toyopia.co.uk – a toy shop which has a fun design and a good range to choose from too.

www.toysdirecttoyourdoor.co.uk – good design, specialists in Brio among other things.

www.toywiz.com – an American site where you can get unusual and new toys, even those that are no longer produced, toys are generally cheaper but shipping is costly.

www.twinkleontheweb.co.uk – specialists in nappies, informative and helpful.

www.tyrrellkatz.co.uk – excellent upmarket range of clothes and stationery on a good-looking site, you have to fax or phone through orders though.

Products Other Than Toys

www.jojomamanbebe.co.uk   UK

FASHIONABLE MOTHERS AND THEIR CHILDREN
Excellent for everything from maternity wear and designer children's clothes to gifts for newborn babies. Also has sections on toys, maternity products and special offers. All the designs are tested and they aim to be comfortable as well as fashionable. Delivery costs £3.95, free if collected from the warehouse in Newport. For baby wear try **www.overthemoon-babywear.co.uk** who include a section on natural fibre clothing with free postage in the UK.

C

www.gltc.co.uk
UK

THE GREAT LITTLE TRADING COMPANY

A good-looking site offering a wide range of child safety products, furniture and baby equipment, you can search the site by age and by product category. Delivery starts at £4.95.

www.urchin.co.uk
UK

WORTH HAVING A BABY FOR

Urchin has a wide range of products and have won awards for their catalogue business. You'll find: cots and beds, bathtime accessories, bikes, clothes, travel goods, toys and things for the independent child who likes to personalise their own room. They boast a sense of style and good design, and they succeed. They also have a bargains section. Delivery is £4.50 per order with a next day surcharge of £3.

Things To Do

www.mamamedia.com
UK

THE PLACE FOR KIDS ON THE NET

This versatile site has everything a child and parent could want, there is an excellent selection of interactive games, puzzles and quizzes, combined with a great deal of wit and fun. Best of all it encourages children to communicate by submitting a message and gets them voting on what's important to them. There's a superb 'Grown-ups' section with information on getting the best out of the Net with your children.

www.bonus.com
US

THE SUPER SITE FOR KIDS

Excellent graphics and masses of genuinely good games make a visit to Bonus a treat for all ages. There are quizzes and puzzles, with sections offering a photo gallery, art resource and homework help. Access to the web is limited to a protected environment. Shame about the pop-ups and advertising.

www.show.me.uk
UK

SHOW ME

A vastly improved site specialising in picking out the best of what's going on in our museums and galleries and representing it online. There are games, what's on and special features with celebrities. It's educational without being overtly so and there are special sections for teachers and parents too.

www.yucky.com   US

THE YUCKIEST SITE ON THE INTERNET
Find out how to turn milk into slime or how much you know
about worms – yucky lives up to its name. Essentially this is an
excellent, fun site that helps kids learn science and biology.
There are guides for parents on how to get the best out of the
site and links to recommended sites.

www.wonka.com   SWITZERLAND

THE WILD WORLD OF WONKA
Ingenious site sponsored by Nestlé with great illustrations and a
fun approach, but it's one for the broadband owners really.
There's lots to see and do, with a store (aimed at parents), lots
of games, and other interactive features that change regularly.

www.fffbi.com   US

THE FIN, FUR AND FEATHER BUREAU OF INVESTIGATION
Outstanding activity site with lots of problem-solving crime
capers and games to play. The emphasis is on teaching
children about other cultures around the world, which it does
in a very entertaining and original fashion.

www.switcheroozoo.com   US

MAKE NEW ANIMALS
Over 6,500 combinations of animals can be made at this very
entertaining web site, you need Shockwave and a decent PC
for it to work effectively.

Other activity sites worth checking out:
http://web.ukonline.co.uk/conker – The Kids Ark – Join
Captain Zeb gathering material on the world, strange animals,
myths and facts – before it all disappears.
www.alfy.com – excellent with lots of games and plenty of
things to do and see.
www.badgeplanet.co.uk – a great site where you can buy and
also design your own badges.
www.ex.ac.uk/bugclub – bugs and creepy crawlies for all ages.
www.funschool.com – a bit commercial, but there's plenty to
do at this American activity come education site.
www.globalgang.org.uk – a Christian Aid sponsored activity
and magazine site mainly covering world issues.
www.headbone.com – part of Bonus with chat and games.

www.hotwheels.com/kids – a good-looking, but slow site from a model car maker that has some good features and games. Needs latest Flash Player to work.

www.kiddonet.com – download the interactive play area for games and surfing in a safe environment. Masses to do and good links. Largely aimed at girls.

www.kids.warnerbros.com – a links page to their children's productions, when you consider what they produce, it's a shame they can't do more.

www.kidscastle.si.edu – a pretty average kids' educational magazine site from the Smithsonian Museum. Useful for homework.

www.kidscom.com – play games, post a message on the message board and write to a pen friend (unfortunately the safe chat lines are open during our night-time). A bit dull.

www.kidsdomain.com – masses to download, from colouring books, music demos to homework help games. Split into three age ranges.

www.kidsjokes.co.uk – nearly 12,000 jokes...

www.kidskorner.net – great use of cartoons to introduce and play games – stealthily educational.

www.kidsreads.com – an American site all about kids' books, with games and quizzes. Good for young Harry Potter fans.

www.kzone.com.au – excellent activity site from Australia.

www.lego.co.uk – games, product information, adventures with their leading characters, lots of interactive features make this site something of a gem.

www.lemonadegame.com – how much lemonade can you sell? Learn about market forces in this oddly fascinating game.

www.matmice.com – create your own web site home page and add it to the internet the easy way.

www.missdorothy.com – the good-looking *Dot Comic*, which has loads of activities and is fun to use. Takes a while to download and you need the latest Flash downloads to get the best out of it.

www.neopets.com – look after a multitude of virtual pets, play games and even trade them.

www.noggin.com – an excellent American activity site for pre-school children.

www.puzzlepirates.com – a multi-player role-playing game for children, with excellent graphics and design.

www.roadcode.co.uk – take the road code and traffic light quiz and learn about road safety in the process.

Cookery for Kids

www.stickymitts.co.uk   UK

> JUNIOR CUISINE
> A site devoted to helping children get stuck in to cookery. It
> offers a series of courses which introduce the basics of cooking
> and also encourages children to have a go. The site itself is a
> little dull but the content is great. See also
> **www.coolmeals.co.uk**, which is a brighter affair with the
> emphasis on nutrition and food groups.

Magic

www.magictricks.co.uk   UK

> THE UK'S LEADING ONLINE MAGIC TRICKS STORE
> A magic store chock full of tricks, sets and accompanying
> equipment. You can send in suggestions for new tricks and
> even find a magician. There's also a section on TV magicians
> and a bookstore. P&P is free when you spend over £20.
>
> *See also:*
> **www.magicbypost.com** – magic tricks by mail order.
> **www.magictricks.com** – an American site which has lots
> of info and links.
> **www.magicweek.co.uk** – well-designed but quite adult.

TV, Book and Character Sites

www.citv.co.uk   UK

> CHILDREN'S ITV
> Keep up to date with your favourite programmes and talk to
> the stars of the shows. There's lots to occupy children here
> including chat with fellow fans, play games, find something
> to do, enter a competition, e-mail a friend and join the club.

www.nickjr.com   UK

> THE NICKELODEON CHANNEL
> Ideal for under-eights, this has a good selection of games and
> quizzes to play either with an adult or solo. The 'Red Rocket Store'
> has an excellent selection of merchandise, but beware of shipping
> costs. For activities aimed at a wider age range check out
> **www.nick.co.uk** where there is chat, gossip, games and plenty
> of background info on the shows.

C

www.sesamestreet.com UK
THE CHILDREN'S TELEVISION WORKSHOP
Enter Elmo's world which is very colourful, with lots to do.
There are games to play, art and music to create and friends
to talk to. There's plenty for parents too.

www.bbc.co.uk/cbbc UK
CHILDREN'S BBC
Lots of activities here, you can catch up on the latest news,
play games and find out about the stars of the programs. There
are also web guide links to other recommended children's sites.
See also **www.bbc.co.uk/cbeebies** which is for the very young
with printable colouring pages, stories and games.

www.bbc.co.uk/newsround UK
KEEP UP TO SPEED
One of the best bits of CBBC is Newsround, here you can get
all the latest news, do quizzes, chat and join their club.

www.disney.com US
WHERE THE MAGIC LIVES
1. Entertainment – details of films, activities and a Disney A–Z.
2. Kids Island – lots of games and music.
3. Playhouse – games and character sites for younger children.
4. Blast – the online kids' club.
5. Family fun – party planners, recipes and craft ideas.
6. Toontown – multiplayer games.
7. Destinations – Information on the theme parks.
8. Disney Direct – the Disney store, auctions and other
   sales opportunities.
9. Inside Disney – archives, newsletter and corporate info.

The British version **www.disney.co.uk** is more compact with
less about vacations and more emphasis on activity. Both sites
are very commercial and really more about selling Disney than
having fun.

www.cooltoons.com UK
RUGRATS, STRESSED ERIC AND MORE
Each character has their own section where you can find lots to
do and see. There's also an eight-step guide on how to become
an animator. The store has all the related merchandise.

www.foxkids.co.uk

UK

FOX TV

All the characters and shows are featured on this bright and
entertaining site with added extras like a games section,
competitions, a sports page and a magazine. There's also a
shopping facility where you earn Brix by using the site, they
can then be spent on goodies in the 'Boutik'. The graphics can
be a little temperamental.

www.aardman.com

UK

HOME OF WALLACE AND GROMMIT

This brilliant site takes a while to download but it's worth the
wait. There's news on what the team are up to, links to their
films, e-cards, a shop and an inside story on how it all began.

www.gosh.org

UK

HOME OF PETER PAN

A good site from Great Ormond Street Hospital's charity with a
section devoted to Peter Pan – all proceeds from the sale of the
books go to hospital. There's also lots to do on the site with
competitions, links and information about the hospital itself.

www.guinnessrecords.com

UK

GUINNESS WORLD RECORDS

An outstanding site that offers much in the way of
entertainment with footage of favourite records and informative
sections on key areas of record breaking such as sport, nature,
the material world and human achievements.

*Here's where the best children's characters from fiction,
cartoon and TV shows hang out:*

Favourites for Younger Children

Barbie – **www.barbie.com**
Bill & Ben – **www.bbc.co.uk/cbeebies/characterpages/billandben**
Bob the Builder – **www.bobthebuilder.org**
Boohbahs – **www.boohbah.com**
Fimbels – **www.bbc.co.uk/cbeebies/fimbles**
Ivor the Engine – **www.smallfilms.co.uk/ivor**
Letter Land – **www.letterland.com**

Mr Men – **www.mrmen.com**
Noddy – **www.noddy.com**
Teletubbies – **www.teletubbies.com**
Thomas the Tank Engine – **www.thomasthetankengine.com**
Tweenies – **www.bbc.co.uk/tweenies**

Cartoons and TV

Action Man – **www.actionman.com**
Asterix the Gaul – **http://www.asterix.tm.fr**
Bagpuss – **www.smallfilms.co.uk/bagpuss**
Batman – **www.batmantas.com** (animated series)
Batman – **www.batmanbeyond.com**
Beyblade – **www.beyblade.com**
Buffy – **www.buffy.com** and **www.buffyguide.com** and
www.bbc.co.uk/cult/buffy
Clangers – **www.clangers.co.uk**
Danger Mouse – **www.dangermouse.org**
Dragonball Z – **www.dragonballz.com**
Mary Kate and Ashley – **www.marykateandashley.com**
Pixar – **www.pixar.com**
Pokemon – **www.pokeland.yorks.net** or **www.pokemon.com**
Spiderman – **www.spiderman.sonypictures.com** or
www.spiderman.com
Thunderbirds – **www.thunderbirdsonline.co.uk**
Toontown – **www.toontown.com**
Yu-Gi-Oh – **www.yugiohkingofgames.com**

Favourite Characters From Children's Books

Angelina Ballerina – **www.angelinaballerina.com**
Animal Ark – **www.animalark.co.uk**
Artemis Fowl – **www.artemisfowl.co.uk**
Beano – **www.beano.co.uk**
Goosebumps – **www.scholastic.com/goosebumps**
Lemony Snicket – **www.lemonysnicket.com**
Paddington – **www.paddingtonbear.co.uk**
Roald Dahl – **www.roalddahlclub.com**
Tintin – **www.tintin.be**
Winnie the Pooh – **www.just-pooh.com** or
www.winniethepoohbear.net

Harry Potter

Harry Potter deserves a special mention and with loads of web sites springing up, here are the official and some of the best unofficial ones.

www.jkrowling.com   UK

JK ROWLING

The official site from the author of the Harry Potter books is original in design, cleverly enticing the visitor into exploring the site while guaranteeing they'll have fun. Catch up on the latest rumours and get an insight into what it's like to be the world's best-selling author. You need to switch off your pop-up blocker to use the site.

See also:

www.bloomsbury.com/harrypotter – find out all about the books, meet JK Rowling and join the Harry Potter club, send a Howler and more.

www.scholastic.com/harrypotter – here's the US publisher's site with wizard trivia, quizzes, screensavers, information about the books and an interview with JK Rowling, all on a fairly boring web site.

http://harrypotter.warnerbros.co.uk – an outstanding site offering the latest news on the films plus downloads and lots of other activities, you can chat, shop for Harry merchandise and play games.

www.mugglenet.com – an excellent fan site put together by some teenage fans, it has features on the books and the films plus links, games and the latest news. The Wall of Shame is particularly entertaining.

www.fictionalley.org – a good fan site that encourages Harry fans to have a go at writing and generally releasing their creativity.

Search Engines and Site Directories

www.yahooligans.com   US

THE KID'S ONLINE WEB GUIDE

Probably the most popular site for kids, yahooligans offers parents safety and kids hours of fun. There are games, articles and features on the 'in' characters, education resources and sections on sport, science, computing and TV. It has an American bias.

www.ajkids.com   US

ASK JEEVES FOR KIDS
A search engine aimed at children, it's simple, safe and is
excellent for homework enquiries and games.

www.fkbko.co.uk   UK

FOR KIDS BY KIDS ONLINE
Part on an EU funded project designed to make surfing the net
safe for children, it has chat, e-mail, surfing and search
facilities and the excellent design makes it easy to use too.

See also:
www.familyfriendlysearch.com – a simple search engine that
searches several of the major directories kids' sections.
www.infoplease.com – good for homework.
www.kidsseek.co.uk – a messily designed search engine that
allows UK only based searches.
www.kidtastic.com – safe search for kids.

Christmas

*Sites to give some seasonal cheer and also help you prepare for
the big day.*

www.happychristmas.com   UK

ONE STOP CHRISTMAS
Choose your gifts here and they'll transfer you to the retail site
for you to make your purchase. You can also get the family to
write a wish list, send e-cards, have a chat about Christmas, or
check the bulletin board for ideas. There are recipes, cocktails
and games to play in all the time that you've saved.

www.christmasarchives.com   UK

THE HISTORY OF CHRISTMAS
A curious site written by Christmas historians of noble birth.
There is masses of information on Christmas traditions
throughout the world although the site is not easy to navigate.
You can buy a traditionally decorated Christmas tree or even
one used on a film set, antique decorations and Christmas
related books.

www.christmas.com   US

CELEBRATING CHRISTMAS AROUND THE WORLD
A good directory of stores and sites devoted to all aspects of
Christmas, it has a strong American bias though.

Other Christmassy sites worth checking out:
www.christmas-carols.net – lyrics for all the best-known carols.
www.christmasrecipe.com – every Christmas recipe you're ever
likely to need.
www.emailsanta.com – too lazy to send a letter. Well, now you
can e-mail Santa.
www.howstuffworks.com/christmas – all your questions about
the advent season answered including the eternal question
'why is Christmas sometimes spelled Xmas?'
www.noradsanta.org – track Santa as he makes his way
around the skies.

Looking Things Up

The Good Web Site Guide's Top 10s of the Internet

1.   **www.a9.com** – a search engine that uses Google and many
     reference resources.
2.   **www.dmoz.org** – the most comprehensive site directory
     on the 'net.
3.   **www.mirago.co.uk** – great if you want a UK-biased result
     to your search.
4.   **www.refdesk.com** – information and links, very impressive
5.   **www.about.com** – fantastic, with expertly written pages on
     virtually any topic.
6.   **www.onelook.com** – access to almost 1,000 online dictionaries.
7.   **www.howstuffworks.com** – if it moves it's explained.
8.   **www.nationmaster.com** – information and stats on virtually
     every country.
9.   **www.wikipedia.org** – the people's encyclopedia.
10. **www.ehow.com** – instructions on how to do virtually anything.

C

www.northpole.com US

SANTA'S SECRET VILLAGE
A very good activity site for children and adults too, with
everything from educational activities to shopping.

www.christmastimeuk.com UK

CHRISTMAS SHOP
Selling all you could possibly need during the festive season,
this shop has a wide range and an e-mail service if you want
something specific. Delivery charges vary according to what you
buy and where you are. For another site featuring Christmas
related merchandise go to **www.xmastreesdirect.co.uk**

www.christmas.co.uk UK

RAISE FUNDS FOR CHARITY
A bright and entertaining site where you can give to certain
charities and shop for presents too.

*For Christmas related merchandise try these sites, see page
353 for sites specialising in parties.*
www.christmasdinnercompany.co.uk – everything you need
delivered to your door complete with instructions. Not cheap,
but high quality and hassle free.
www.kelly-turkeys.com – bronze turkeys delivered to the door.
www.lewisandcooper.co.uk – specialists in hampers and
plum puddings.
www.realfooddirect.co.uk – food gifts, hampers, condiments,
soft drinks and Christmas treats.
www.thecarvedangel.com – they make great claims for their
Christmas pudding, also supply foodie gifts.
www.thechristmaslightscompany.co.uk – a lights specialist
both indoor and out.

Competitions

www.loquax.co.uk UK

THE UK'S COMPETITION PORTAL
This site doesn't give away prizes but lists the web sites that
do. There are hundreds of competitions featured, and if you
own a web site they'll even run a competition for you. There are
daily updates and special features such as 'Pick of the Prizes'
which features the best the web has to offer, with links to the
relevant sites.

See also:
www.compaholics.co.uk – competitions and gambling too, heavy on the advertising.
www.myoffers.co.uk – which is a slow site, with, as the name suggests, lots of offers.
www.prizemagic.co.uk – humorous site from a person who has won over £100,000 in competitions.
www.theprizefinder.com – offer a wide range of prizes in lots of categories, you have to register, though they claim someone actually won £1 million there.
www.wincompetitionprizes.co.uk – a minimalist approach from this site, which appears to go for quality rather than quantity.

Computers

It's no surprise that the number one place to buy a computer is the Internet. With these sites you won't go far wrong, and it's also worth checking out the price checker sites on page 364 before going shopping and checking the software sites on page 412. Mac users should also check out the section on Apple Macs page 22.

Information and Reviews

www.itreviews.co.uk   UK
> START HERE TO FIND THE BEST
> IT Reviews gives unbiased reports, not only on computer products, but also on software, games and related books. The site has a good search facility and a quick visit may save you loads of hassle when you come to buy.

www.pcadvisor.co.uk   UK
> EXPERT ADVICE IN PLAIN ENGLISH
> A derivative from *PC Advisor* magazine, the site offers much in the way of reviews and information on how to find the best PC. It also allows you to pick up advice from experts on technical queries, download programmes and join forum discussions. You have to register, which is free, to gain access to the site.

> *See also:*
> **www.bbcworld.com/clickonline** – the technology pages from the BBC with some entertaining and interesting content.

www.byte.com – one for those who know something about computer technology.

www.compshopper.co.uk – good for reviews and information also links to Dabs (see below) for shopping.

www.computerweekly.com – fairly dull site but informative on all aspects of computing.

www.cnet.com – product reviews aplenty, also has downloads and shopping links.

www.streettech.com – opinions and personal reviews with attitude from several experts.

www.zdnet.co.uk – very good reviews section at this large and diverse site.

Stores

It's worth checking out price comparison sites such as
www.kelkoo.co.uk *but these stores specialise it PCs and consumables.*

www.pcworld.co.uk   UK

THE COMPUTER SUPERSTORE
A very strong offering from one of the leading computer stores with lots of offers and star buys. They sell a wide range of electronics from cameras to the expected PCs and peripherals.

www.simply.co.uk   UK

SIMPLY DOES IT
An award-winning site and company that offers a wide range of PCs and related products, their strengths are speed, quality of service and competitive prices. They also sell mobile phones.

www.dabs.com   UK

1,500,000 CUSTOMERS LATER...
One of the most successful online computer product retailers, with a very good reputation for service, there are loads of offers and a wide range of goods including home entertainment, digital photography equipment and mobile phones.

www.tiny.com UK

LATEST TECHNOLOGY AT UNBEATABLE PRICES
A business-like site that includes all the details you'd need on
their range of computers and peripherals for home and office
use. Tiny are the UK's largest computer manufacturer and have
a history of reliability and good deals. Shipping costs vary
according to what you buy and where you live.

See also:
www.ebuyer.com – good design and some excellent offers.
www.rankhour.com – huge range and competitive.
www.unbeatable.co.uk – very good prices and a wide range.

www.totalpda.co.uk UK

PERSONAL DIGITAL ASSISTANTS
Good-looking site specialising in PDAs and related products
with a wide range and some good bargains. See also
www.expansys.com who have some very good offers.

PC manufacturers' site addresses:
Apple – **www.apple.com**
Dell – **www.dell.co.uk**
Elonex – **www.elonex.co.uk**
Evesham – **www.evesham.com**
Gateway – **www.gateway.com/uk**
Hewlett Packard – **www.hp.com/uk**
Time – **www.timecomputers.com**
Viglen – **www.viglen.co.uk**

Computer Accessories

www.planetmicro.co.uk UK

ACCESSORIZE YOUR PC
Much in the way of add-ons for PCs and essential equipment
that can enable you to get more out of your computer, or keep
an old PC going. Good design and some good pricing too.

C

See also:
www.dreamdirect.co.uk – good-looking site mainly selling software but also with an OK range of PC accessories and equipment.

www.inksaver.com – a program that saves money on printing by allowing you to control the amount of ink your printer uses.

www.keytools.com – a great site devoted to providing equipment that is easy to use.

www.tonik.co.uk – excellent computer consumables store with free delivery in the UK.

www.cex.co.uk   UK

COMPUTER EXCHANGE

Computer Exchange buy and sell used electronics, computers and games. The process is pretty straightforward, so if you have an old PC give them a call.

Information on Repairing and Upgrading Your PC

The following sites are useful if you want to keep up with the latest developments, need help when your PC goes wrong or you just need to learn something.

www.pcmech.com   US

PC MECHANIC

Plain English explanations of all the bits that make up a computer, it's easy to follow and use with lots of background information and support. Excellent.

See also:
www.compinfo.co.uk – a bewildering number of computer-related links all set out in a large directory.

www.driverguide.com – advice on finding and installing the right drivers for your PC.

www.help.com – part of the high quality CNET site it has the most up-to-date information on new products and articles and advice. It assumes some knowledge.

www.maximumpc.co.uk – lots of tutorials, useful programs to download and reviews galore.

www.pcpitstop.com – a host of programs to get your PC running on top form. They can even test how well your PC is running and offer advice on how to improve its performance.

www.wired.com – all the latest news and product information.

Consumer Information and Advice

A new section following requests from readers, these sites help with the latest consumer law and provide answers or give guidance on what to do if you've been wronged.

C

www.which.net   UK

WHICH MAGAZINE
Excellent spin off from the magazine with everything from consumer advice to product reviews. You need to be a member to get the best out of it.

www.consumerdirect.gov.uk formerly www.consumers.gov.uk

THE CONSUMER GATEWAY
A consumer advice site run by the government that offers links and information across all the major areas where issues occur from cars to shopping to home improvements. A good place to start if you have issues you feel strongly about.

See also:
www.adviceguide.org.uk – the Citizens Advice Bureau offers a wide range of tips and advice on the most common problems and how to solve them, plus how to get in touch if you have specific issues.
www.bbc.co.uk/watchdog – lots of information on the back of the TV program with legal FAQs, example letters for complaints and specific features.
www.ciao.co.uk – independent product reviews on a wide range of categories.
www.consumer-rights.org.uk – handy hints and tips all designed to ensure that you get the best service.
www.consumerworld.org – an American site with a huge number of useful links.
www.ethicalconsumer.org – a UK-based site devoted to listing those companies whose environmental and social track records are less than envious.
www.howtocomplain.com – find out how to make a complaint at this easy-to-follow site, which even provides specially designed forms to make your complaint even more effective.
www.oft.gov.uk – home of the Office of Fair Trading.
www.streettech.com – honest reviews on the latest technology.

www.tomshardware.com – a popular and messy but very information-heavy site full of advice and help with the most common problems and issues facing the computer user.
www.tradingstandards.gov.uk – the Trading Standards site offers a wealth of information on safety and legislation for businesses, education establishments and consumers.
www.warrantyex.co.uk – extended warranties the easy way.

Crime

This section continues to expand. It is intended to be of help to victims of crime or it may even help solve one. Hopefully you won't need it.

www.police.uk   UK

THE POLICE ONLINE
Here you can notify the police of minor crimes and get essential information on the organisation and how it works. There are sections on specific crimes or appeals, recruitment and information on related organisations. The site is easy to navigate and use.

See also:
www.cia.gov – the Central Intelligence Agency.
www.crb.org.uk – Criminal Records Bureau helps employers with criminal records information amongst other services.
www.fbi.gov – the Federal Bureau of Investigation.
www.interpol.com – the fight against international crime.
www.nationalcrimesquad.police.uk – the fight against organised crime.
www.ipcc.gov.uk – Independent Police Complaints Commission formerly the Police Complaints Authority.

www.cjsonline.org   UK

THE CRIMINAL JUSTICE SYSTEM
A helpful site that tells what happens when someone gets arrested, and provides information about the trial procedure, how a court works and what you need to do if you're a witness. There's a guide to who does what in the legal profession and a section on related links. See also the Crown Prosecution Service at **www.cps.gov.uk**

www.crimestoppers-uk.org

UK

KEEP 'EM PEELED

Information on the Crimestoppers trust and how you can get
involved in their fight against crime with information on the latest
campaign and initiatives, links and, of course, their phone
number 0800 555 111. See also **www.crimereduction.gov.uk**
which has been set up by the government to become the
number one resource for the crime prevention practitioner.

www.neighbourhoodwatch.net

UK

NEIGHBOURHOOD WATCH

A directory of neighbourhood watch schemes by county with
advice on preventing crime and how you can set up a
neighbourhood watch scheme in your area. See also
www.crimeconcern.org.uk who give advice on helping to
reduce crime and also the fear of crime in local communities.

www.iwf.org.uk

UK

INTERNET WATCH FOUNDATION

The IWF works with the police to stamp out the use of
exploitative images of children, obscene and racist content that
is hosted by web sites based in the UK.

www.victimsupport.com

UK

VICTIM SUPPORT

An independent charity that supports the victims of crime throughout
the UK with help and advice. It also advises witnesses on the justice
system and campaigns for equal opportunities. You can also find out
about how you can help or give funds.

www.fraud.org

US

NATIONAL FRAUD INFORMATION CENTER

Find out about the many ways you can be defrauded and how
to spot a fraud on the Internet.

See also:
www.consumer.gov/idetheft – how to deal with identity theft
www.econsumer.gov – the EU's attempt to stop Internet fraud
and set up a process to deal with complaints.
www.fraudbureau.com – a consumer-oriented scam-listing
service, you can search for specific complaints and add your
experiences too.

www.quatloos.com – a listing of all sorts of scams and fraudulent practises; an entertaining and educational read.
www.privacyrights.org – how to protect your privacy.
www.scambusters.com – more help on scams and annoyances on the Internet.

www.dumbcriminalacts.com   US

THE STUPIDEST CRIMINALS
Here you can find out about the daftest criminal acts in history and have a good laugh at their expense, some are truly unbelievable and sadly it does lack a bit of credibility as it doesn't always list the source of the stories. See also **www.dumbcrooks.com** which is a bit low tech but the stories are more detailed.

Cycles and Cycling

See page 476 for cycling holidays and tours and page 427 for information on cycling as a sport.

www.cycleweb.co.uk   UK

THE INTERNET CYCLING CLUB
A great attempt to bring together all things cycling. Aimed at a general audience rather than cycling as a sport, it has masses of sections and links on everything from the latest news to clubs, shops and holidays.

See also:
www.bikemagic.com – forums on hot bike topics, reviews of equipment, buying advice, classifieds, the latest news, links and an events calendar.
www.bikeweek.org.uk – find out about Bike Week which is in mid-June.
www.ctc.org.uk – the National Cyclist's Organisation's site offers lots of information on all aspects of the hobby and the benefits associated with getting on your bike.
www.cycling.uk.com – great for cycling links.
www.newtocycling.co.uk – help from Izzy Sez for those who are new to cycling, with advice and links too.
www.procycling.com – a magazine devoted to professional cycling, pretty basic design but it covers all the latest news.

www.tandem-club.org.uk – a pretty basic site devoted to the world of the tandem with discussion groups, classifieds, buying advice, events and a newsletter.

Buying a Bike

www.bicyclenet.co.uk   UK

UK'S NUMBER 1 ONLINE BICYCLE SHOP
Great selection of bikes and accessories, there's also good advice on how to buy the right bike and assembly instructions on all that they sell. Delivery is free for bikes and orders in excess of £50.

See also:
www.cyclestuff.co.uk – a good range of accessories.
www.evanscycles.com – wide range, easy to navigate.
www.wiggle.co.uk – good name and good shop.

Travel UK

The Good Web Site Guide's Top 10s of the Internet

1. **www.visitbritain.com** – all you need to know about us.
2. **www.timeout.com/london** – probably the best guide to the capital.
3. **www.sightseeing.co.uk** – information on what to see and how to get there.
4. **www.nationaltrust.org.uk** – over 200 homes and gardens.
5. **www.ctc.org.uk** – the perfect site for cyclists.
6. **www.pti.org.uk** – all you need on public transport.
7. **www.walkingworld.com** – great for the UK and abroad.
8. **www.goodbeachguide.co.uk** – where best to put up your wind break.
9. **www.hebrides.com** – beautiful.
10. **www.knowhere.co.uk** – a warts and all overview of our islands.

Dance

Here are a few sites for those who dance or think they can...

www.danceart.com   US
DANCE!
A slightly messy but enthusiastic site centred on the dance
scene, it has lots of links, articles and interviews.

See also:
http://scarecrow.caps.ou.edu/~hneeman/dance_hotlist.html
– a hotlist of dance sites.
www.ballet.co.uk – magazine-style site with reviews,
interviews, biographies and blogging.
www.dancebooks.co.uk – where to go for specialist dance titles
also CDs, DVDs, videos and sheet music.
www.dancescape.com – a good Canadian dance magazine site.
www.dancesport.uk.com – the UK ballroom dancing
scene covered.
www.dancing-times.co.uk – *Dancing Times* and *Dance Today*.
www.folkdancing.org – home of the Folk Dance Association.
www.irishdancing.com – a cheery site from *International Irish
Dancing* magazine.
www.istd.org – home of the Imperial Society of Teachers
of Dancing.
www.pearldata.co.uk/dance/paul/cool.htm – good for dancing-
related links.
www.rad.org.uk – the Royal Academy of Dance.
www.the-ballet.com – a good e-zine all about ballet.
www.young-dancers.org – dedicated to helping teenagers learn
to dance.

Dating

*Using the Net has become an accepted means to meet people, but
be careful about how you go about meeting up; many people aren't
exactly honest about their details. If in doubt, err on the side of
caution. See also the new section on social networking on page 412.*

www.onlinedatingmagazine.com   US

AN AUTHORITATIVE INSIGHT
An excellent magazine site devoted to all aspects of dating with

site reviews, tips, articles and advice. It is well designed and up to date, there are even some cartoons and it's all written in a chirpy style.

See also:
www.dating-agencies-uk.co.uk/dating-tips.htm – good advice all round.
www.topdatingtips.com – attractive site with lots of articles on dating.
www.wildxangel.com – old site but sage advice.

www.thedatingportal.com   US
DATING LINKS
A portal devoted to dating sites; they are well categorised but it is geared towards the US market. See also **www.datingbind.com** and for the UK **www.dating-agencies-uk.co.uk**

www.uksingles.co.uk   UK

FOR ALL UK SINGLES
Not just about dating, this site is devoted to helping you get the most out of life. There are several sections: accommodation, sport and activities, holidays, help for single parents, and listings for matchmaking and dating services. All the companies that advertise in the directories are vetted too.

www.faceparty.com   UK
BIGGEST PARTY ON EARTH
A combination of dating agency, party organiser and chat site. You download your details and photo to create your own profile, then just join in.

Here are some additional sites, there's not much to choose between them, it's all a matter of taste. All are secure and allow you to browse and participate in relative safety:
www.dateline.co.uk – 30 years of experience at the dating game gives Dateline lots of credibility and it's a good site too, easy to use and reassuring.
www.datingdirect.com – claims to be the UK's largest agency with over 1 million members, the site is not as sophisticated as some, though they seem to have lots of success stories.
www.dinnerdates.com – one of the longest established and most respected dining and social events clubs for unattached single people in the UK; find out how you can get involved here.

www.directdating.com – one of the most popular dating sites with over 1.5 million members.

www.idealpartner.net – a personality profiling approach to finding a partner.

www.ivorytowers.net – where unattached alumni and undergraduates from the 'leading' universities get together.

www.lavalife.com – one of the larger dating companies, not great site design though.

www.love-exchange.co.uk – upmarket profiles for busy professionals, you can chat without revealing your proper e-mail address.

www.match.com – leading site in the US which now has a UK branch, get your profile matched to someone or join in the chat, there's an excellent magazine too.

www.nomorefrogs.com – find your perfect partner using psychometric testing.

www.singles121.com – good site, easy to use with, on the whole, good quality photos.

www.speeddater.co.uk – the latest dating craze covered for the UK and especially London.

www.udate.com – US site for over 25s only, an attractive site with a good search facility.

www.rom101.com   US
ROMANCE
If you need romance in your life and tips on what to say to the opposite sex, try here for pick up lines, finding your perfect partner and so on, just don't take it too seriously...

www.soyouvebeendumped.com   UK
HOW TO COPE...
An interesting way to help yourself after you've split up, lots of advice and help to get you through it all.

Death – Support and Advice

When faced with the death of a loved one, there are a bewildering number of things to be done and decisions to be made at a time of emotional stress and confusion. These sites help you to find your way through this minefield and provide both practical and emotional support.

www.ifishoulddie.co.uk UK

EVERYTHING YOU NEED TO KNOW
Written in response to the confusion felt following a close death,
this site takes you through all that you need to know including
all the legalities, organ donation, funeral arrangements, wills,
inheritance tax and coping with life-threatening illness and
bereavement. There is a helpful section on the various funeral
arrangements for the major religions although the site itself is
careful not to take a religious stand. If you still need help, join
in the forum and there are excellent links for more support.

www.funeralsuk.com UK

LOCAL DIRECTORIES
Very good listings for everything you need from funeral directors, to
printers, to monumental masons and florists. The 'Topics' section
also provides help and links to other related services such as
repatriation, wills, an online obituary service and even pet funerals.

Other related sites:
www.argonet.co.uk/body – British Organ Donation Society.
www.gatesofrememberance.com – a site for online tributes.
www.humanism.org.uk – British Humanist Association,
providers of non religious funeral ceremonies.
www.naturaldeath.org.uk – helps arrange inexpensive,
family-run and environmentally-friendly funerals and provides
information on burials on private land.
www.the-bereavement-register.com – to remove the names
and addresses of people who have died from databases and
mailing files.
www.ves.org.uk – Voluntary Euthanasia Society with guidelines
on writing a living will.

Legal and Financial Advice

www.courtservice.gov.uk/cms/2971.htm – legal advice and
information on probate without recourse to a solicitor.
www.inlandrevenue.gov.uk/leaflets/iht.htm – the Inland
Revenue's downloadable leaflets on inheritance tax.
www.lawontheweb.co.uk – jargon-free guide to wills, power
of attorney, probate and what happens after a death. Pity about
the design.
www.mypersonalfinances.co.uk/life-iht.asp – use the
inheritance tax calculator to assess the damage.

Emotional Support

www.befriending.net – volunteers who befriend those facing terminal illness and their carers on a long-term basis.

www.crusebereavementcare.org.uk – the leading charity in the UK specialising in bereavement.

www.samm.org.uk – emotional support to those bereaved through murder and manslaughter.

www.tcf.org.uk – support for bereaved parents and their families with local help groups and literature.

www.winstonswish.org.uk – helps bereaved children and young people rebuild their lives after a family death.

Disability Help and Information

In this expanded section you'll find sites that may help if you are disabled or care for someone with a disability. It's worth checking your local council's site as they tend to have good local information on the help that is available in your area.

Information and Advice

www.disability.gov.uk   UK

THE GOVERNMENT'S VIEW

Information and help on rights for the disabled with links to related departments. You can't help thinking that there could have been more information across a broader spectrum. See **www.dwp.gov.uk/lifeevent/discare** for an index of benefits and services available.

www.bcodp.org.uk   UK

THE BRITISH COUNCIL OF DISABLED PEOPLE

An action-oriented site that has information on how the council works, useful articles and helpful information. It shows how you can get involved whether you are disabled or not, and most importantly, how you can contribute.

www.disabilityview.co.uk   UK

DISABILITY VIEW

Inspired by the magazine of the same name, this site sets out to be the best source of information for all those who have to cope with a disability, and it largely succeeds. There are loads of links and useful sections such as travel, guides, sports and an events guide.

For more advice check out the following sites:

www.abilitynet.org.uk – excellent regional database offering help whatever your situation.

www.dialuk.info – the Disability Advice Network.

www.disabilitynow.org.uk – great magazine site dealing with issues and offering advice.

www.disabilityresources.org – an American site devoted to resources available on the Internet.

www.makoa.org – another US site, not a good design, but a huge number of links all the same.

www.youreable.com – great for news, features and jobs.

Independent Living

www.dlf.org.uk   UK

THE DISABLED LIVING FOUNDATION
A charity devoted to helping people who need equipment to live life to the full. This excellent site has information on how to choose the best equipment, masses of links to self-help groups, a bookshop, training information and of course a section on how you can contribute.

See section on motability under cars page 70 as well as:

http://disabledaccessories.com – excellent range and good value make this store stand out.

www.disabledgo.info – a directory of places that have good access and businesses that are sympathetic to disabled people.

www.e-accessibility.com – a monthly newsletter largely aimed at people with sight problems, it concentrates on various aspects of technology and computing.

www.inclusive.co.uk – a plethora of gadgets and useful educational tools to help life and learning easier.

www.independentliving.co.uk – equipment and advice on making life easier.

www.keytools.com – an excellent site from a company specialising in providing computer accessories.

www.mobilitywarehouse.com – excellent range of products and an attractive and user-friendly site.

www.motability.co.uk – the scheme that helps you contract hire a car or powered wheelchair or scooter.

www.sunrisemedical.com – a wide range of products and links, some only available abroad, the site is slow too.

www.wheelchair-travel.co.uk – self-drive wheelchairs and cars for hire.

Children

www.ncb.org.uk/cdc   UK

>COUNCIL FOR DISABLED CHILDREN
>From the National Children's Bureau, this site is basically a
>forum devoted to helping parents and children cope with
>disability. It's a good starting point if you need information, but
>it's not an easy site to navigate so patience is required.
>
>*See also:*
>**www.cafamily.org.uk** – find advice and support on caring for
>a disabled child.
>**www.cforat.org** – a charity devoted to helping disabled children
>integrate into the school curriculum.
>**www.childcarelink.gov.uk** – excellent government-run children's
>information service site.

Students and Education

www.techdis.ac.uk   UK

>HELP FOR STUDENTS WITH A DISABILITY
>A site containing masses of help and information designed to
>enable disabled students to have the opportunity to learn
>effectively. Most of it is free, so an excellent resource. See also
>**www.skill.org.uk** who help promote opportunities for post-16
>year olds in education **and www.nasen.org.uk** the National
>Association for Special Educational Needs.

Jobs

www.jobability.com   UK

>LEADING JOB SITE FOR DISABLED PEOPLE
>Now integrated with Totaljobs.com and Leonard Cheshire this is
>a straightforward site designed to help disabled people find
>employment; it covers the UK by region plus opportunities in
>the rest of the world. There's also advice on careers and how
>to find a job.

See also:
www.rehab.ie/uk – training and support to help people with disabilities into the workforce.
www.remploy.co.uk – provides employment opportunities for disabled people all over the UK and in their own factories.
www.shaw-trust.org.uk – training and work opportunities for the disadvantaged.

Rights and Having your Say

www.drc-gb.org   UK
DISABILITY RIGHTS
A helpful site offering links and views on rights issues for the disabled. The site doesn't always load properly and it's not easy to find your way around, but useful nonetheless – at least there's a search facility.

www.radar.org.uk   UK
RADAR
A campaigning organisation devoted to the social inclusion of disabled people. There's lots of information on the campaigns and how you can get involved.

www.webequality.org.uk   UK
DISABILITY EQUALITY TRAINING
Working with employers to enable disabled people to get employed and stay employed. There's masses of practical advice and even a quiz to start you off.

www.chooseability.org   US
CHOOSE ABILITY
A US-based community site which offers blogging and issues forums plus news and articles, it has a great feel and attitude although the site itself is a bit clunky.

For Carers

www.carers.gov.uk   UK

> FOR THOSE WHO CARE
> A barely useful resource from the government for carers, there
> are links and details of their policies concerning care. See also
> **www.caringmatters.dial.pipex.com** which has articles, chat
> and useful links.

Keeping in Touch

www.disabledunited.com   UK

> THE MEETING PLACE
> A sort of Friends Reunited, but much more as it offers
> information on travel, links, chat, forums and, lastly, dating.

Travel

www.disabledholidaydirectory.co.uk   UK

> HOLIDAY INFORMATION
> Very useful directory site devoted to providing holiday
> information and contacts for disabled people. They have a wide
> range of holidays and offer sensible advice on how to get the
> best out of your holiday.

See also:
www.abletogo.com – a very wide range of holiday options.
www.access-able.com – poorly designed site but lots of useful
information.
www.allgohere.com – a directory of hotels that offer facilities
for the disabled.
www.disabilitytravel.com – experienced agent and good if
you're confined to a wheelchair.
www.tripscope.org.uk – a charity devoted to helping disabled
travellers.

(Do-It-Yourself is now under Home and DIY on page 257.)

Education

Using the Internet for homework or study has become one of its primary uses; these sites will help enormously, especially alongside the reference and encyclopedia sites listed on page 371. There is also a section aimed at students on page 450 and search engines for children are on page 93.

Homework Help

www.bbc.co.uk/education   UK

GET EQUIPPED FOR LIFE
Good-looking site covering learning at school, college and adult education. Each section tends to be tied to a particular programme rather than subject, but there is masses here and the quality of content is particularly good. The revision sections are excellent.

www.brainpop.com   US

LEARN BY ANIMATION
A wonderful example of how the Internet should be used. Here you can download animations that cover and explain specific aspects of maths, health, technology, science, English and more. The site is American but very useful for UK students too though only a few topics are available for free; subscription to the whole site is around £50 per year. See also **www.funbrain.com** which is free.

www.cln.org/int_expert.html   US

ASK AN EXPERT
This site lists almost a hundred sites by subject, including somewhere you can ask an expert your homework question – what a doddle! North American bias though. See also the American **www.sparknotes.com** who offer some of their study guides free to use online and a helpful forum if you're stuck.

www.discoveryschool.com   US

ANSWERS TO HOMEWORK, FREE
Go to 'Homework Helper' to access a number of study tools and games including links to over 700 reference sites with the provision to ask questions too. Layout has been improved and you can more easily access the information, it also has an excellent clip art gallery.

E

www.happychild.org.uk
UK

PROJECT HAPPY CHILD

A mess of a site but one that aims to provide an index of educational resources for schools, parents and children. There's loads to see and do, and it does a good job of highlighting charities, for example, but the poor design gets in the way of its objectives. Well worth a visit, but be patient.

www.homeworkelephant.co.uk
UK

LET THE ELEPHANT HELP

Rightly considered one of the top educational sites with some 5,000 resources and straightforward layout, all aimed at helping children achieve great results. There's help with specific subjects, hints and tips, help for parents and teachers. The agony elephant is great if you get really stuck. It's constantly being updated, so worth checking regularly.

www.homeworkhigh.co.uk
UK

LEARN WITH CHANNEL 4

Split into six learning sections: history, geography, science, maths, English and languages. There's also news and a chat room plus a personal help section that covers topics like bullying. They even provide teachers online for live sessions to help you out. You can ask questions, track down lots of information and chat with fellow homework sufferers. All in all, this is one of the better-looking homework sites. Excellent.

www.kevinsplayroom.co.uk
UK

AWARD-WINNING PORTAL

An excellent site which is put together with the heavy involvement of pupils. It's won numerous awards and is a favourite among teachers and pupils alike. It has over 2,000 approved sites and they are well categorised and reviewed. There's also a translation service and a links page for teachers.

www.learningalive.co.uk
UK

FOR PRIMARY AND SECONDARY

The 'Living Library' is a useful resource for homework help for both primary and secondary students; you can either browse by topic or use the search facility. It can also be accessed directly on **www.livinglibrary.co.uk** The 'Pathways' section provides over 4,000 links to a variety of reference sites. There are loads of resources for teachers too. If you are still short of information, try the children's section of the Internet Public Library **www.ipl.org/div/kidspace**

www.schoolzone.co.uk   UK

UK'S TOP EDUCATIONAL SEARCH ENGINE
With over 40,000 sites and bits of resource all checked by teachers, Schoolzone has masses of information. It is clearly designed and easy to use with all the sites summarised and reviewed. There is free software to download, plus homework help, career advice, teacher support (they do need it apparently) and much more. Don't be put off by the confusing layout; it's worth sticking with. See also **www.ukeducationguide.co.uk** who offer hundreds of links, **www.thelighthouseforeducation.co.uk** and the American **http://northvalley.net/kids**

www.skool.ie   IRELAND

INTERACTIVE LEARNING
An excellent site covering the Irish curriculum but with lots of free resources and information, it's well laid out and easy to navigate.

www.topmarks.co.uk   UK

EDUCATIONAL PORTAL
Developed by a school teacher, this site steers pupils, parents and teachers to some of the best educational web sites. Search for sites by topic or by age from early years to higher ed.

Pre-school and Infant Education

www.under5s.com   UK

WEB RESOURCE FOR PRE-SCHOOL
Loads of things to do and see here, from games and activities to download, to help and advice for parents. Like the best educational sites, its educational bias is not obvious or overwhelming, the tone is just right, it's also simple to use and fast.

www.enchantedlearning.com   UK

FROM APES TO WHALES
It's messy, uncool and largely aimed at young children, but there's loads of good information and activities hidden away, especially on nature. Use the search engine to find what you need.

www.thebigbus.com   UK

HOORAY FOR THE BIG BUS!
Excellent animation and content make this stand out, it can be a
little slow and you have to subscribe to the CD magazine to get
the best out of it (you get a free demo one as a trial). Excellent for
younger children but caters for primary children too.

See also:
www.mousing.co.uk – a fun a free way to learn how to use
and develop skills with a mouse – the computing kind
of course.
www.pre-school.org.uk – home of the Pre-school Learning Alliance.

Primary

www.parentlink.co.uk   UK

HELPING YOUR CHILD
A site written by teachers aimed at helping parents to help their
children by preparing them for the classroom. Very useful
although it concentrates on numeracy and literacy.

www.dfes.gov.uk/parents/discover   UK

HELP YOUR CHILD DISCOVER
For primary parents who want to be proactive in their child's
education, the Department for Education and Skills has
produced a series of helpful online leaflets on a range of
curricular areas to enable you to support your child at home.

www.primarygames.com   US

GAME-BASED LEARNING
This site is packed full of educational games, some better than
others, but there's loads to do and masses to learn. Check on
'curriculum guide' to find games that match your child's
interests or level. **www.funschool.com** is a similar site.

www.bbc.co.uk/schools/revisewise   UK

HELP FOR KEY STAGE 2 SATS
The BBC's excellent interactive site to support 10- to 11-year
olds as they prepare for their Key Stage 2 National Curriculum
Tests in English, Maths and Science.

Here are several subscription only sites which may be of interest, they stand out in terms of quality and content, they may well be used at your school.

www.atschool.co.uk   UK

PRIMARY EDUCATION

Specialising in Key Stage 1 and 2, this site is fun as well as educational and, while the content is strong, you do have to subscribe. Rates start at £9.99 for a quarterly subscription. This site does seem quite slow, so probably one for the broadband users.

www.edontheweb.com   UK

HELP WITH SATS

Written by a teacher, this site is designed to help children pass their SAT exams. It's lively and well written with lots of activities too. Subscription costs £9.99 per year.

www.gridclub.com   UK

FOR 7- TO 11-YEAR OLDS

An excellent site which is backed by the government and several high-profile contributors including Channel 4. It uses entertaining educational games to do most of its tutoring but there are links to the more traditional stuff available too. It's been built with safety in mind and it encourages children proactively. All in all, what an educational site should be – unfortunately it costs £29.99 per year for home use.

Secondary

There are so many brilliant educational support sites it is impossible to list them all here. Use extra-curricular or homework help sites to search for the ones that best suit your needs or use the following to get you started. If you can't find what you are looking for here, don't forget our sections on Art, English usage, History, Nature and environment, Reference, Religion, Science and Space all of which are extremely helpful when it comes to homework.

www.examaid.co.uk   UK

THE NON-ACADEMIC SIDE

Not a great web site and a bit of a misnomer, but it does give an insight into how students cope with exams (or not) and how to help get through them successfully. The resources section is useful for those non-exam concerns such as relationships and bullying.

Extra-curricular

www.courseworkbank.co.uk
UK

ESSAY HELP

Claiming to be the UK's largest database of quality essays by
students from 14-year olds to those at university, they cover a
wide variety of subjects and there's no charge but beware that
teachers are familiar with this resource too! If that's not enough
www.coursework.info has another 63,000 academic
documents to view.

www.s-cool.co.uk
UK

FOUR STEPS TO REVISION

Well written and presented, this revision site covers GCSEs, AS and
A level exams in four steps: principles, a quick learn guide, trial
questions and revision summary. There is an interactive careers
guide, discussions, a teacher's page and a great magazine with
masses of information and advice aimed at young people.

www.studyzones.com
UK

ONLINE TUTORS

Fabulous resource mainly for GCSE and A level students, you
can ask a question related to your studies and they'll get back
to you within 24 hours. Submit your essays and they'll grade
them and comment on how to improve it. You can search
through 7,500 archived answers but to have yours answered
you'll have to register, it's free.

www.samlearning.com
UK

EXAM REVISION

SAM stands for self-assessment and marking, on this brilliant
site you can do just that, it has mock exams covering every
major subject and key stage plus GCSE and A level. There are
top tips on taking exams and the chance to win some great
prizes when you register. There is a 14-day free trial then there
are various payment options. See also **www.courseshop.co.uk**
who offer a wide range of courses from GCSE upwards.

English

www.englishresources.co.uk   UK

ENGLISH

Hundreds of free resources available here, it's very useful for
revision and for teachers too with a good search engine and
sections aimed at each secondary school age range. See also
our section on English usage on page 129.

History

www.schoolhistory.co.uk   UK

HISTORY REVISION

An excellent site devoted to helping students learn and revise
history with quizzes and many free resources. Also has lessons
and worksheets for teachers. See also
www.learningcurve.gov.uk which covers key stages 2 to 5
using information from the National Archives.

For Older Children

The Good Web Site Guide's Top 10s of the Internet

1.   **www.yahooligans.com** – excellent guide to what's on the web.
2.   **www.fkbko.co.uk** – safe surfing.
3.   **www.girland.com** – no boys here.
4.   **www.mykindaplace.com** – very popular site for young teens.
5.   **www.dubit.co.uk** – needs patience but the 3-D graphics
      are great.
6.   **www.mindbodysoul.gov.uk** – health for teens.
7.   **www.globalgang.org.uk** – see what children around the
      world are up to.
8.   **www.young–money.co.uk** – a fun way of learning about
      finance – honest.
9.   **www.neopets.com** – virtual pets, better than the real thing!
10.   **www.jkrowling.co.uk** – the official Harry Potter site.

Languages

www.frenchrevision.co.uk   UK

FRENCH REVISION
Lots of interactive exercises at most levels of French for students
aged 11 to 18. There are also useful links and past papers to
try out. See also our language section on page 282.

Maths

http://mathworld.wolfram.com   US

MATHS WORLD
An outstanding site devoted to the world of mathematics. It
explains the complexities really well and is great for homework.
It also has sections on chemistry, physics and astronomy. See
also the comprehensive **http://tcaep.co.uk/maths/index.htm**
and also **www.mathsisfun.com**

http://nrich.maths.org   UK

MATHS ENRICHMENT
A stimulating offering from Cambridge University that provides
challenging mathematical problems for pupils of all ages. You'll
find a good search facility, interesting graphics, discussion
forums, a mathematics thesaurus and a course finder service.

Science

www.zephyrus.co.uk   UK

INTERACTIVE EDUCATION
Aimed at children aged between 8 and 14, there is a wealth of
information, simply written with good graphics. For more of the
same try **www.wpbschoolhouse.btinternet.co.uk** with lots of
science materials for all secondary levels; particularly good for
chemistry A level. For a more folksy approach, there's
www.ftexploring.com with more quality information.

www.exam.net   UK

A LEVEL BIOLOGY
Good site with all you're likely to need to pass this A level, it
has lots of interactive features including video clips.

Post 16 and adult education

www.ngfl.gov.uk   UK

> THE NATIONAL GRID FOR LEARNING
> The official government education site with sections on every
> aspect of learning. There's something for everyone, whatever
> your needs. It is particularly good for info on further and adult
> education. There are also details on school web sites, a features
> section that covers news and events, plus advice on Internet
> safety. See also **www.lsc.gov.uk** home of the Learning and
> Skills Council which provides education for over 16-year olds
> and **www.lifelonglearning.co.uk** aimed at helping people with
> further education ambitions.

www.learndirect.co.uk   UK

> ADULT LEARNING
> A government backed site which aims to bring education to
> everyone whatever their needs. The site explains the
> background to the initiative plus details of courses and how you
> can find one that meets your requirements. There's also help for
> businesses and a jobs advice section.

www.icslearn.co.uk   UK

> ONLINE COLLEGE
> A great alternative to school or college, enrol in an online
> course in a wide variety of subjects at GCSE or A level.
> Alternatively, they offer professional qualifications in such
> subjects as business, beauty, childminding and IT or certificate
> courses in a range of 'leisure' subjects, such as gardening and
> art. Courses vary in fees.

> *See also:*
> **www.city-and-guilds.co.uk** – vocational qualifications with over
> 500 from which to choose.
> **www.niace.org.uk** – a non-governmental organisation formed to
> 'support an increase in the total numbers of adults engaged in
> formal and informal learning in England and Wales; and at the
> same time to take positive action to improve opportunities and
> widen access to learning opportunities for those communities
> under-represented in current provision'.
> **www.support4learning.org.uk** – a wide-ranging resource aimed
> at helping people support their education needs in a more
> holistic way.

E

www.wea.org.uk – the Worker's Educational Association helps provide learning opportunities for everyone but especially those who had missed out or been disadvantaged in some way.

National Curriculum, Government Policy and Support

www.nc.uk.net   UK

NATIONAL CURRICULUM REVEALED
Very detailed explanation of the National Curriculum and prescribed standards.

See also:
www.ace-ed.org.uk – help for parents at the Advisory Centre for Education.
www.becta.org.uk – information on technology and ICT education.
www.dfes.gov.uk – the Department of Education and Skills' site if you want a more overall picture on education.
www.he-special.org.uk – support for people who have children with special educational needs.
www.ngfl.gov.uk – National Grid for Learning, outstanding for links. Some very good content too.
www.ofsted.gov.uk – the Office for Standards in Education, check out the standards of your local schools.
www.parentcentre.gov.uk – well, more information from the government on supporting children's learning.
www.qca.org.uk – more information on the National Curriculum.
www.sqa.org.uk – for information on the Scottish education system.

Specialist Education Publishers

Below are listed some of the key education publishers, they often have competitions, online help and free books.

www.activerevision.com – from HarperCollins, at this site you can test yourself to see how likely you are to pass your exams. It then recommends which books would help you to get a pass.
www.cgpbooks.co.uk – a basic online shop with details of their popular study guides, which you can buy online.
www.hoddereducation.co.uk – one of the biggest education publishers offers a fairly staid but useful site. Teachers can order inspection copies of their books.

www.letts-education.co.uk – excellent site with lots of resources, news and explanatory notes about their books. Plus the Letts Challenge for schools, and shop.
www.nelsonthornes.co.uk – a typical publishing site with good background on their titles and how to order them. Some books are available as online resources if you register.

Teacher Resources

www.theteachernet.co.uk   UK

ALL A TEACHER NEEDS
An excellent site that pulls together all the education resources that a teacher is likely to need from advice on how to use the Internet to getting a job and, of course, forums; there's even a certificate generator.

See also:
http://edujourney.net – resources, links and ideas for primary teachers.
www.byteachers.org.uk – a collection of useful web sites created by teachers for teachers.
www.darvill.clara.net – online science resources, lots of quizzes.
www.eteach.com – recruitment for teachers.
www.everythingeducation.org – like an education swap shop this site brings education and business together. A great place to find equipment for schools at a decent price.
www.learninginfo.com – excellent site aimed at helping those with learning disabilities.
www.literacymatters.co.uk – a good resource site for teachers on literacy from pre-school to year 7.
www.primaryresources.co.uk – excellent place to go for free lessons, ideas and worksheets.
www.primaryworksheets.co.uk – a straightforward site listing work sheets for primary school teachers.
www.qualityteachingresources.co.uk – similar to the Teacher Net but aimed at primary-school and student teachers.
www.teachingtables.co.uk – work sheet generation and times table help.
www.tes.co.uk – educational resources and news from the *Times Educational Supplement.*

These sites might also be of interest to anyone interested in schools:
www.fundraising.co.uk – helpful ideas.
www.governornet.co.uk – government advice on school governance.
www.ngc.org.uk – the National Governors Council.

Home Education

It's becoming more common for children to be fully educated at home, here are a few sites that offer support.

www.heas.org.uk   UK
> HOME EDUCATION ADVISORY SERVICE
> A good place to start, here you'll find advice and publications covering the topic, subscription costs £12 per annum.

> *See also:*
> **www.choiceineducation.org.uk** – a magazine devoted to home education.
> **www.education-otherwise.org** – a site run by a home education support charity.
> **www.schoolhouse.org.uk** – home education help in Scotland.

Electrical Goods, Gadgets and Appliances

This section covers stores that sell the usual electrical goods but also offer a bit more in terms of range, offers or service. There's also the odd spy camera and gadget shop.

www.comet.co.uk   UK
> ALWAYS LOW PRICES, GUARANTEED
> A pretty messy site these days with masses of offers on the front page, having said that it's a great place to view the widest range of goods at excellent prices.

www.dixons.co.uk   UK
> OFFERS GALORE
> The Dixons site has plenty of offers and reflects what you'd find in their stores very well. It has a similar but slightly wider product range to Comet, with an additional photographic section. Delivery costs vary.

www.richersounds.com UK

LOWEST PRICES GUARANTEED
Despite the fact this site wouldn't win design awards, bargain
hunters will want to include this site on their list, it's similar to
the other electrical goods retailers but with a leaning towards
music and TVs, with plenty of offers and advice. There is a
search facility and the products are obviously good value,
delivery charges vary depending on what you buy, although
products are delivered within 10 working days.

www.maplin.co.uk UK

ELECTRONICS CATALOGUE
Maplin is well established and it's a bit of an event when
the new catalogue is published. Now you can always have
access to the latest innovations and basic equipment at this
well-put-together site. It features the expected massive range
with free delivery for orders over £35.

www.electricshop.co.uk UK

BETTER PRODUCTS, BETTER PRICES
A good-looking but slightly messy site with a huge range of
electrical goods with offers too. The site is easy to use and has
a good search facility and it's a combination of all these factors
that make it stand out.

See also:
www.24-7electrical.co.uk – which is well designed and looks
strong on customer service judging by the number of times they
ask you to contact them.
www.be-direct.co.uk – some very good offers and a wide range.
www.discount-appliances.co.uk – excellent range of kitchen
appliances but awful site design, having said that product
pictures are good.
www.electricaldiscountuk.co.uk – a pretty straightforward site
with some good offers and a wide range.
www.empiredirect.co.uk – a busy-looking site with lots of
offers and a wide range.
www.hughesdirect.co.uk – a solid offer from this well-
established retailer.
www.rtwodesign.ndirect.co.uk – good-looking site from this
kitchen specialist.
www.searchappliance.co.uk – well-illustrated store from
another kitchen appliance specialist.

www.vacuumcleanersdirect.co.uk – some 200 models to choose from and a range of other goods besides, some great prices too.

www.we-sell-it.co.uk – is also worth a visit for good prices on kitchen and other domestic appliances.

www.appliancespares.co.uk   UK

FIX IT YOURSELF

Ezee-Fix has thousands of spare parts for a massive range of products, nearly all illustrated, including fridges, cookers, microwaves, vacuum cleaners, etc. All it needs is online fitting instructions, and more details on the products and it would be perfect.

www.bull-electrical.com   UK

FOR THE SPECIALIST

Fascinating to visit, this mess of a site offers every sort of electronic device, from divining rods to radio kits and spy cameras. There are four basic sections:

1. Surplus electronic – scientific and optical goods, even steam engines.
2. Links to specialist shops – such as spy equipment and hydroponics.
3. Free services.
4. Web services – shopping cart technology, for example.

www.innovations.co.uk   UK

NEW TECHNOLOGY

Several hundred innovative, unusual or just plain daft items for sale, all on a neat web site, the best bit is probably the gift wizard, which helps you find the perfect gift when you're stuck for something to buy. Other places for technology geeks to get their kicks are **www.gadgetshop.co.uk** who have free delivery on orders over £50 and a free returns policy, and **www.firebox.com** for a really wide range of gadgets amongst other boy's toys.

www.simplyradios.com   UK

RADIOS SPECIALIST

An excellent site devoted to radios and the first place to go if you want something groovy or the latest thing in digital. For specialists in digital radio go to **www.pure-digital.com**

English Usage

With the success of the book Eats, Shoots and Leaves, *English grammar, punctuation and usage have come under the spotlight and it seems there's even more pressure to get it right. If you're not sure where apostrophes go or what a noun or pronoun is, then these sites can help. If it is a dictionary you're after, those are found on page 375.*

www.learnenglish.org.uk   UK

LEARNING ENGLISH
An excellent site from the British Council primarily aimed at those for whom English is a second language but it has a huge amount of information for students and those who just want to brush up.

See also:
www.apostrophe.fsnet.co.uk – learn how to use and misuse them at the home of the Apostrophe Protection Society.
www.askoxford.com/betterwriting – grammar, spelling, letter writing and effective communication.
www.cogs.susx.ac.uk/local/doc/punctuation/node00.html – a guide to punctuation from Sussex University.
www.dailygrammar.com – grammar lessons and quizzes.
www.englishclub.net – learn and teach English with the help of this comprehensive site; you have to register, but it's free.
www.english-zone.com – an American site and directory devoted to learning English; it's useful, but you have to register, around £20 p/a.
www.gramster.com – a free 'light' programme to help with your grammar; however, the full programme is quite expensive.
www.plainenglish.co.uk – the Plain English Campaign and their fight to make everything clear. Check out the free guides, which are most helpful.
www.soundofenglish.org – English pronunciation.
www.stpt.usf.edu/pms – punctuation made simple.
www.ucl.ac.uk/internet-grammar – a free online course about English grammar aimed at university undergraduates but useful nonetheless.
www.usingenglish.com – a solid English language learning site.
www.vocabulary.co.il – excellent site for building vocabulary using simple word games such as hangman and wordsearch.
www.whoohoo.co.uk – confused by your English dialects? Here's a translation service!

E-mail

Here's a selection of the best free e-mail providers, there are hundreds to chose from, but hopefully these sites should help you find the one that's right for you, whether you're after efficiency or a trendy @ moniker.

www.fepg.net   US

FREE E-MAIL PROVIDERS GUIDE
Here's the place to start, it lists over 1,400 providers in 85 countries, including over 40 from the UK, so it's pretty comprehensive. It tends to just list them with a few details but there are recommended sites too. There's also a news section and forums.

www.sneakemail.com   US

SNEAK E-MAIL
Sneak e-mail provides an e-mail protection service whereby you can maintain a level of anonymity, stop spam or unsuitable e-mails getting to you, avoid unwanted soliciting or prevent others from selling your e-mail address to marketing companies, for example.

www.twigger.co.uk   UK

ANYWHERE IN THE WORLD
An excellent service that enables you to use your chosen e-mail address wherever you may be. One advantage is that you can see attachments before you download them onto your PC. The service is subscription based.

www.emailaddresses.com   US

E-MAIL ADDRESS DIRECTORY
A useful directory of e-mail services and programs to help you manage your e-mail and mail to your site if you own one, there are also tips on how to find an e-mail address and a directory of address directories. See also **www.web-email-addresses.com** a very good directory with site and software reviews

www.spamcop.com   US

STOP SPAM
Spam is a term used to describe unsolicited commercial e-mail, we all get bombarded by it and at this site you can download a useful little program that will help you minimise it. See also **www.qurb.com** and **http://spamarrest.com** and **www.spaminspector.com**

See also...

http://gmail.google.com – one to watch, this is Google's e-mail project, it offers lots of memory and flexibility.

www.cloudmark.com – a highly recommended e-mail security program, $19.95.

www.didtheyreadit.com – a program that offers an automatic receipt so that you can tell when someone has opened the mail you sent them.

www.havetheyreadityet.com – this program inserts chosen images into your outgoing e-mails and then tells you when and where they have been read.

www.pocomail.com – a well-recommended-flexible and secure e-mail program.

Ethical and Green Topics

Ethics is a difficult subject but if you are concerned about the effect you are having on the environment, want to live a greener lifestyle or are concerned about the origins and manufacture of what you buy, then this listing will help. Some of the sites are already reviewed in other sections of The Good Web Site Guide.

www.alotoforganics.co.uk   UK

LEAN, GREEN SEARCH MACHINE
UK search engine for everything organic including facts, news, events, gifts, food, alternative therapies, finance and shops. For an alternative try **www.greenchoices.org** which is comprehensive.

Animals and Plants

www.forestry.gov.uk – Forestry Commission has details of its work and how you can help sustain our woods and forests.

www.fsc-uk.info – Forest Stewardship Council UK, an international non-governmental organisation promoting the responsible management of the world's forests.

www.futureforests.com – a UK organisation working to protect the earth's climate. They will calculate your CO_2 emissions and advise on ways to neutralise your carbon debt.

www.ifaw.org – home of the International Fund for Animal Welfare.

www.rspb.org.uk – the Royal Society for the Protection of Birds.

www.rspca.org.uk – the Royal Society for the Prevention of Cruelty to Animals.

www.traffic.org – a campaigning site working against the illegal and sometimes appalling trade in animals throughout the world.

www.ufaw.org.uk – improving animal welfare using scientific knowledge.

www.wwf.org.uk – WWF site with detailed information for conservationists on habitats, areas of global importance, endangered wildlife and the latest campaigns.

Energy

www.eaga.co.uk – the Energy Action Grants Agency.

www.energysaving.me.uk – energy saving products.

www.energywatch.org.uk – independent energy watchdog.

www.est.org.uk – home of the Energy Saving Trust.

www.greenelectricity.org – sign up for a greener tariff.

www.natenergy.org.uk – energy-saving advice from the UK charity for energy efficiency, the National Energy Foundation.

www.ofgem.gov.uk – the UK's electricity and gas regulation body.

www.switchandgive.com – switch suppliers and give the savings to charity.

www.uswitch.com – switch to a green energy supplier.

Environment

www.airquality.co.uk – air quality information across the UK.

www.bbc.co.uk – for the latest news and reports on environmental issues.

www.cat.org.uk – Centre for Alternative Technology offering practical solutions to environmental problems.

www.defra.gov.uk – the Department for Environment, Food and Rural Affairs.

www.eco-portal.com – massive portal site covering all things green.

www.emagazine.com – the *Environmental Magazine* online.

www.envirolink.org – environmental community site with lots of info and links.

www.environment.about.com – information on environmental issues.

www.environment-agency.gov.uk – Environment Agency's site offers information on the latest initiatives and news.

www.environmentwebsites.co.uk – a portal for environmental sites.

www.ewg.org – the Environmental Working Group, dedicated to the fight against pollution; US-oriented.

www.foe.co.uk – Friends of the Earth.

www.greenpeace.org – find out about their latest activities and how to get involved.

www.lowimpact.org – Low Impact Living Initiative, a non-profit organisation protecting the global environment.

www.planetdiary.com – monitoring world environmental events.

www.projectearth.com – recognising the damaging effect man has on the environment and pointing the way towards a better future.

www.scorecard.org – the facts on local pollution from this US-oriented but informative site.

www.wen.org.uk – Women's Environmental Network. A campaigning organisation covering environmental and health issues.

www.wri.org – World Resources Institute promoting effective campaigning for a far better world.

Fashion

www.cleanclothes.org – improving conditions for those working in the garment-making industry.

www.ethicallyme.com – fashionable clothes produced ethically.

www.ethicalthreads.co.uk – clothing not made in sweatshops.

www.furisdead.com – anti fur campaigning.

www.iftf.com – the fur trade's organisation for the opposite view.

www.labourbehindthelabel.org – campaigning for worker's rights with a list of good traders and retailers.

www.nosweat.org.uk – join the fight against sweatshop owners.

Finance

www.abcul.coop – Association of British Credit Unions.

www.co-operativebank.co.uk – banking with a conscience; also **www.smile.co.uk** their online bank.

www.ecology.co.uk – the Ecology Building Society which is a mutual society promoting sustainable housing and communities.

www.eiris.org – the Ethical Investment Research Service offers independent research into corporate behaviour.

www.ethicalinvestment.org.uk – ethical savings.

www.invest-trees.com – invest in trees.

www.letslinkuk.net – Local Exchange Trading Schemes.

www.switchwithwhich.co.uk – switch bank accounts.

www.triodos.co.uk – Triodos Bank offers environmentally sound savings accounts.

www.uksif.org – UK Social Investment Forum, the UK network for socially responsible investment.

Food

www.ciwf.org.uk – Compassion in World Farming web site, campaigning for farm animal welfare, includes the Eat Less Meat initiative.

www.crueltyfreeshop.com – the animal-friendly superstore.

www.earthsave.org – promotes vegetarianism by helping you choose the right way to eat.

www.farmersmarkets.net – find your nearest Farmers' Market.
www.foodag.com – food additives.
www.freedomfood.co.uk – RSPCA site on farm animal health.
www.goodnessdirect.co.uk – supermarket with over 4,000 items including good range of grocery, fresh and frozen products.
www.organicdelivery.co.uk – a good organic food retailer.
www.organicfood.co.uk – news and links on all things organic.
www.soilassociation.org – the Soil Association web site with masses of information on organic food, farming and education resources.
www.sustainweb.org – the Alliance for Better Food and Farming site with lots of information and links on sustainable farming, seasonal food and reducing food miles.
www.swaddles.co.uk – a wide range of organic food including meat.
www.vegansociety.com – the Vegan Society web site.
www.whyorganic.org – a Soil Association site covering a variety of issues about organic versus non-organic produce.

Home and Gardening

www.allotments-uk.com – all you need to know about owning an allotment.
www.communityrepaint.org.uk – a UK network to reuse old paint and redistribute to charities, voluntary organisations and local groups.
www.ecosolutions.co.uk – safe water-based paint and varnish removers.
www.greenbuildingstore.co.uk – green building products online.
www.greengardener.co.uk – specialists in biological and organic pest control.
www.hdra.org.uk – the Henry Doubleday Research Association, the leading authority on organic gardening.
www.just-green.com – natural pest control with advice and products.
www.nsalg.org.uk – National Society of Allotment and Leisure Gardeners.
www.organiccatalogue.com – a comprehensive store related to the HDRA.
www.pan-uk.org – the Pesticide Action Network who are working to eliminate the hazards associated with pesticides.
www.salvo.com – reclaim old furniture.

Miscellaneous

www.idealswork.com – compare and find out about the ethical track records of major companies.

www.naturaldeath.org.uk – The Natural Death Centre's site, covering woodland burials and green funerals.

www.who.int – the World Health Organisation, the UN specialist agency with comprehensive information on every aspect of health.

www.willaid.org – draw up a will and support charity at the same time.

Recycling

www.cartridges4charity – charity recycling inkjet cartridges, toner cartridges and mobile phones.

www.cleanaway.co.uk – recycling specialists.

www.crn.org.uk – the Community Recycling Network.

www.fonebak.com – mobile phone reuse and recycling.

www.letsrecycle.com – waste management company directory.

www.keepwalestidy.org – environmental charity in Wales.

www.oilbankline.org.uk – find your nearest waste oil recycling site.

www.oxfam.org.uk/what_you_can_do/recycle/phones.htm – mobile phone recycling. including school and corporate schemes.

www.paper.org.uk/info/recycling.htm – Confederation of Paper Industries.

www.paperchain2000.org.uk – information on recycled paper campaigns.

www.recoup.org – national charity developing plastics recycling.

www.rethinkrubbish.com – the best ways to recycle your rubbish.

www.vao.org.uk – Vision Aid Overseas, international charity which recycles spectacles.

www.wastewatch.org.uk – nationwide organisation promoting action on waste reduction and improved recycling and reuse.

www.webdirectory.com/recycling – general information on recycling.

www.wrap.org.uk – The Waste and Resources Action Programme, creating markets for recycled products.

Shopping

www.afrigoods.org – quality gifts from Africa with profits going to the artists who made them.

www.cardaid.co.uk – charity Christmas cards.

www.crueltyfreeshop.com – a wide range of products on sale all of which are guaranteed not to have involved any animal cruelty or exploitation in their production.

www.ecozone.co.uk – online shopping for environmentally friendly household products.

www.ethicalconsumer.org – *Ethical Consumer Magazine,* ethical information behind the big brand names.

www.fairdealtrading.com – Fair Deal Trading Partnership for footballs and trainers.

www.fairtrade.org.uk – home of the Fair Trade Foundation which exists to enable poor artists and workers to get a better deal.

http://shopping.guardian.co.uk/ethicalshopping – useful advice and links.

www.getethical.com – who have a wide range of ethically produced and sourced products plus advice, links, holidays and a magazine.

www.goodgifts.org – online charitable alternative gifts catalogue.

www.goodshoppingguide.co.uk – ethical shopping reference book.

www.greatgifts.org – World Vision charity website offering alternative, online gifts catalogue.

www.greenshop.co.uk – online shop selling hundreds of environmentally friendly products including paint and household cleaners.

www.naturalcollection.com – comprehensive range of products from clothing to food and cosmetics.

www.onevillage.org – shop specialising in ethnic products and using the Fair Trade system.

www.surefish.co.uk – Christian Aid web site with information on ethical living including shopping, gifts and energy.

www.traidcraftshop.co.uk – good selection of crafts, foods and other goods from around the world.

Tourism

www.changingworlds.co.uk – worthwhile working holidays.
www.coralcay.org – 'providing resources to help sustain livelihoods and alleviate poverty through the protection, restoration and management of coral reefs and tropical forests'.
www.ecoafrica.com – the wonders of Africa for the ecologically minded.
www.ecoclub.com – a network providing a wealth of information about all aspects of ecotourism.
www.eco-tour.org – Eco Tourism directory.
www.ecotourism.org – the International Ecotourism Society.
www.ecotravel.com – good all-round travel site from US.
www.ecovolunteer.com – if you want to give your services to a specific animal benefit project.
www.responsibletravel.com – eco-friendly and ethically responsible holidays.

Transport

www.carclubs.org.uk – CarPlus charity site looking at responsible car use, car clubs and car sharing.
www.eta.co.uk – the Environmental Transport Association.
www.liftshare.com – car sharing web site.
www.smartmoves.co.uk – the largest UK car club operator.
www.sustrans.org.uk – nation-wide charity encouraging alternative methods of transport.
www.transportenergy.org.uk – a division of the Energy Saving Trust.

Volunteering

www.btcv.org.uk – the British Trust for Conservation Volunteers, including UK and global projects and Green Gyms.
www.csv.org.uk – Community Service Volunteers, the UK's largest volunteering and training organisation.

Water

www.hippo-the-watersaver.co.uk – water-saving device.
www.ofwat.gov.uk – the government regulator for the water industry.
www.wateraid.org.uk – international non-governmental organisation dedicated to the provision of safe water and sanitation.
www.waterconserve.info – general information on water conservation.

E-zines

E-zines are the magazines of the web and there are millions of them, some with great content and quality writing. Here are some of the best reviewed along with a couple of sites that can help you find one that you like. You should be aware that many contain adult or pornographic material.

http://zinos.com   US
E-ZINE DIGEST AND DATABASE
A well-categorised site with information and reviews of some of the worlds' best e-zines, it's attractive and makes it easy to find what you're looking for but not that comprehensive.
See also **www.ezine-dir.com** who offer almost 3,000.

http://ezinearticles.com   US
FOR WRITERS AND PUBLISHERS
Writers are able to post articles on the site, while publishers in need of content can search the database for ready-to-wear content. Free trial membership.

Some of the Best

www.salon.com   US

SALON
An outstanding magazine offering a wide range of articles and topics with quality contributors and excellent writing. It's entertaining and witty covering the latest news and in depth features on current topics.

www.theregister.co.uk   UK

THE REGISTER
An opinionated and newsy e-zine devoted to the technology and computing worlds – it describes itself as 'biting the hand that feeds. It's not an easy read but it's very authoritative.

www.theonion.com   US

AMERICA'S FINEST NEWS SOURCE
A great send-up of American tabloid newspapers, this is one of the most visited sites on the Internet and easily one of the funniest.

www.fray.com   US
   STORYTELLING
   A great site offering up true stories which, on the whole, are
   pretty well written. It's well designed, very accessible and free.

Fashion and Accessories

*The big brands have never been cheaper. Selling fashion and
designer gear is another success story for the internet as customers
flock to the great discounts that are on offer and get access to the
latest fashion trends. Many people still prefer to try clothes on before
buying but the good sites all offer a convenient returns policy.*

Fashion

www.fuk.co.uk   UK
   FASHION UK
   All you ever need to know about the latest in UK and world fashion,
   updated daily. There's a good links library, competitions, chat and,
   of course, shopping. It's all packaged into a really attractive site,
   which initially looks cluttered but is OK once you get used to it.

www.vogue.co.uk   UK
   THE LATEST NEWS FROM BRITISH VOGUE
   An absolute must for the serious follower of fashion. There's the
   latest catwalk news and views, and a handy who's who of
   fashion. There's also a section on jobs, and you can order a
   subscription too. For a similar experience try **www.elle.com** or the
   slightly less fashion-oriented but more fun **www.cosmomag.com**

www.ftv.com   FRANCE
   FASHION TV
   The 24-hour fashion station, so popular in gyms and bars, has
   a good site offering the latest from around the world. Features
   include video clips, radio interviews with designers plus links,
   gossip and horoscopes.

www.net-a-porter.com   UK
NET A PORTER
A great-looking site that is easy to use with information on the latest fashions, plus catwalk reports and shopping where you can browse by designer or product type. Delivery costs vary according to what you buy.

www.fashionmall.com   US
FASHION STORE DIRECTORY
A huge number of stores listed by category, packed with offers and the latest new designs. Most stores are American and their ability to deliver outside the US and delivery charges vary considerably. The site is well designed and easy to browse.

www.fashion.net   US
GUIDE TO FASHION
A good fashion search engine and directory with the added advantage that it carries the latest fashion news too.

www.yoox.com   UK

TOP DESIGNERS
A great-looking site with top offers from the top designers. It's well laid out and easy to navigate with a good returns policy. You can search by designer or category and the quality of the photos is good. Offers range from a few pounds to massive discounts.

www.haburi.com   UK
CUT-PRICE DESIGNER CLOTHES FOR MEN AND WOMEN
Not a big range of clothes but excellent prices. Clear, no-nonsense design makes the site easy to use.

www.apc.fr   FRANCE
FRENCH CHIC FROM A.P.C.
Unusual in style and for something a little different, APC's site is worth a visit. Delivery is expensive in line with the clothes, which are beautifully designed and well presented. For more of the French look go to **www.redoute.co.uk**

www.gap.com   US
FOR US RESIDENTS ONLY
A clear, uncluttered design makes shopping here easy if you live in
the United States! For UK residents it's window-shopping only.

www.next.co.uk   UK
THE NEXT DIRECTORY
The online version of the Next catalogue is available including
clothes for men, women and children as well as products for
the home. Prices are the same as the directory, next day
delivery is £3.50 and return of unwanted goods is free. You can
order the full catalogue for £3.50.

www.extremepie.com   UK
EXTREME FASHION FOR EXTREME SPORTS
A brand-led selection of clothes from the world of BMX, surf,
skate and other so-called sports. The site is excellent with
clear visuals and delivery costs start at £2.95.

For Young Children

The Good Web Site Guide's Top 10s of the Internet

1. www.mamamedia.com – great for encouraging
   communication skills.
2. www.bonus.com – excellent, great looking and fun.
3. www.yucky.com – learn about science the fun way.
4. www.nickjr.com – a superb site from Nickelodeon.
5. www.sesamestreet.com – still going strong.
6. www.bbc.co.uk/cbeebies – great for the very young.
7. www.disney.co.uk – despite the overt commerciality
   it's still worth a visit.
8. www.barbie.com – heaven for 5-year-old girls.
9. www.lego.co.uk – a little gem featuring the little bricks.
10. www.citv.co.uk – more games and programme links.

www.pop-boutique.com UK

BUY SOMETHING THAT'S ALREADY OUT OF DATE!
A fantastic site devoted to fashion chic from the 60s, 70s and 80s,
it can be a little slow but worth the wait if you're into the period.
It also sells accessories and offers a good set of related links.

See also:
www.kitschshop.co.uk – who offer lots beside just clothes.
www.retrorebels.co.uk – quirky and streetwise.

www.badfads.com US

IT SHOULD NEVER HAVE HAPPENED...
An entertaining site featuring the Bad Fad Museum full of clothes,
events and collectibles that maybe we'd be better off not
remembering. The whole is a fun reminiscence of the 70s and 80s.

Other fashion sites worth a peek:
www.colette.fr – an eclectic collection of quirky products and
fashion items, we can't work out if the web site is brilliantly
designed or just plain annoying...
www.east.co.uk – they don't sell from the site but the clothes
look great.
www.fashionangel.com – excellent directory and portal for
fashion-related links.
www.fashionguide.com – US-oriented fashion gossip and tips.
www.fashionplanet.com – New York-oriented fashion magazine
and store.
www.firstview.com – be among the first to see the latest from
the fashion shows, you have to subscribe though.
www.girlonthestreet.com – home to a New York trend agency
with some top tips and a sneak preview on what's coming up.
www.girlprops.com – another New York-based site with masses
of accessories to choose from. Delivery is expensive to the
UK though.
www.gofugyourself.com – a very amusing blog devoted to the
worst fashions worn by the stars. It introduces the word Fugly,
meaning 'frightfully ugly'...celebrities beware!
www.hintmag.com – a well-designed fashion e-zine with regular
features, news and links. The photography is especially good.
www.japanesestreets.com – the latest on Japanese street fashion.
www.lucire.com – another fashion magazine, this one is well
thought of and it covers everything from catwalk style to skincare.
www.monsoon.co.uk – good illustrations and online store.

www.ntgi.net/ICCF&D/textile.htm – an encyclopedia of textiles and materials used in fashion and tailoring.

www.oasis-stores.com – good-looking site with information on the latest trends, also see the vintage collection not available in many stores.

www.toastbypost.co.uk – good mail-order catalogue with the latest designs.

Top Designers

www.alexandermcqueen.net – Alexander McQueen
www.armaniexchange.com – cheap Armani
www.bensherman.co.uk – Ben Sherman
www.chanel.com – Chanel
www.christian-lacroix.fr – Christian Lacroix
www.dior.com – Dior
www.gucci.com – Gucci
www.hugo.com – Hugo Boss
www.jpgaultier.fr – Jean Paul Gaultier
www.karenmillen.com – Karen Millen
www.kenzo.com – Kenzo
www.paulsmith.co.uk – Paul Smith
www.tedbaker.co.uk – Ted Baker
www.tommy.com – Tommy Hilfiger

General Clothes Stores

www.arcadia.co.uk   UK

THE UK'S LEADING FASHION RETAILER
The Arcadia Group has over 1,200 stores in the UK and the web sites are accessible, easy to use and offer good value for money. Each site has its own personality that reflects the high street store. Delivery charges vary.

www.burton.co.uk – Burton
www.dorothyperkins.co.uk – Dorothy Perkins
www.evans.ltd.uk – Evans
www.missselfridge.co.uk – Miss Selfridge
www.outfitfashion.com – Outfit
www.topman.co.uk – Topman
www.topshop.co.uk – Topshop
www.wallis-fashion.com – Wallis

www.zoom.co.uk   UK

> MORE THAN JUST A SHOP
> This is an excellent magazine-style site, with lots of features
> other than shopping, such as free Internet access and e-mail.
> Shopping consists of links to specialist retailers. You can enter
> prize draws and there are a number of exclusive offers as well.
> Not always the cheapest, but an entertaining shopping site.

Catalogues

www.kaysnet.com   UK

> KAYS CATALOGUE
> Massive range combined with value for money is the formula
> for success with Kays. While they lead with clothes there are
> plenty of other sections outside of that: jewellery, home
> entertainment, toys, etc. They offer free 48-hour delivery,
> £2.95 for next day delivery.

www.freemans.co.uk   UK

> FREE DELIVERY IN THE UK AND GOOD PRICES
> A similar site to Kays, not the full catalogue but there's a wide
> range to choose from, including top brands. They offer free
> delivery for UK customers. There are also prizes to be won,
> special features on topical themes and information on how to
> get the full catalogue. For another version of the same web site
> see **www.grattan.co.uk** for Grattan's catalogue online.
>
> *See also:*
> **www.aboundonline.com** – a catalogue site with a very good
> choice, which also offers a style guide and outfit finder service.
> **www.littlewoods-online.com** – wide selection from across
> the range.

Specialist Clothes Stores

www.asseenonscreen.com   UK

> BUY WHAT YOU SEE ON FILM OR TV
> Now you can buy that bit of jewellery or the cool gear that
> you've seen your favourite TV or film star wearing, As Seen on
> Screen specialises in supplying just that. You can search by star
> or programme, it isn't cheap but you'll get noticed. They also
> have a handy gift ideas section if you're looking for inspiration.
> See also **www.celebfashion.co.uk**

www.enokiworld.com   US

VINTAGE CLOTHES FOR MODERN WOMEN
A nicely designed site with a wide range of vintage clothing.
Prices and delivery costs vary according to what you buy.

www.bloomingmarvellous.co.uk   UK

MATERNITY WEAR
The UK's leading store in maternity and babywear has an
attractive site that features a good selection of clothes and
nursery products. There are no discounts on the clothes, but
they do have regular sales with some good bargains. Delivery
in the UK is £3.95 per order.

Shoes

www.shoe-shop.com   UK

EUROPE'S BIGGEST SHOE SHOP
A massive selection of shoes and brands to chose from. The site
is nicely designed with good pictures of the shoes, some of which
can be seen in 3-D, a facility they are expanding. Delivery is
included in the price and there's a good returns policy.

See also:
www.britfoot.com – home of the British Footwear Association
for hard-to-find footwear.
www.cosyfeet.com – a good site devoted to extra roomy
footwear and socks!
www.elephantfeet.com – stylish shoes in larger sizes.
www.immortalsole.co.uk – excellent site devoted to retro trainers!
www.magnusshoes.com – another large size specialist, with a
good site.
www.office.co.uk – neat site design from this High Street retailer.
www.shoesdirect.co.uk – straightforward with some good offers.
www.shoetailor.com – a huge range from this popular specialist.
www.tallsmall.com – a shopping directory devoted to online
shoe shops.
www.voodooshoes.com – great name and quite fashion oriented.

www.centuryinshoes.com   UK

SHOE HISTORY
An interesting and very well-designed site devoted to the
development of the shoe from 1900 to the present day, each
shoe and boot is available to view in three dimensions and
you can get into the detail easily.

Underwear and Lingerie

www.figleaves.com   UK

MORE THAN JUST A FIG LEAF
Fig Leaves has become a big Internet success with a huge
range of lingerie from most major designers with plenty of offers
and on an easy-to-use site. The site now hosts the upmarket
brand **www.rigbyandpeller.com** which used to have its own
site. There is free delivery on orders over £25 and a free return
option too.

www.amplebosom.com   UK

ITS ALL IN THE NAME
One of the media's favourite Internet success stories, Sally sells
bras for everyone, including large and small sizes, mastectomy,
nursing and maternity bras.

See also:
www.assetsco.co.uk – for men's underwear.
www.kiniki.com – more men's underwear.
www.lasenza.co.uk – good selection for ladies and reasonable
prices includes glamour, character, nightwear and swimwear.
www.legsonline.com – a UK specialist with a wide range.
www.littlewomen.co.uk – solutions for little women.
www.nicolajane.com – good selection of feminine mastectomy
bras and swimwear.
www.victoriassecret.com – for designer style, but beware high
shipping costs.

Accessories and Jewellery

www.jewellers.net   UK

THE BIGGEST RANGE ON THE NET
Excellent range of products, fashion jewellery, gifts, gold and
silver, the watch section is particularly strong. There is also
information on the history of gems, the manufacturers and
brands available. Delivery to the UK is free for orders over £50,
and there is a 30-day no quibble returns policy.

Also check out:
www.geraldonline.com – a wide range of jewellery and watches from Gerald Ratner and associates.
www.jewellerycatalogue.co.uk – guaranteed low prices.
www.madaboutjewellery.com – costume jewellery with designer style.
www.tateossian.com – great contemporary jewellery and accessories.

www.topbrands.net   UK

WATCH HEAVEN
A large range of watches including Swatch, Casio, G Shock, Baby G and Umbro are available here. The site is fast and easy to use, but a better search facility would save time. Delivery is free for the UK, but prices appear to be similar to the high street.

Finance, Banking and Shares

The Internet is proving to be a real winner when it comes to personal finance, product comparison and home share dealing, with these sites you will get the latest advice and may even make some money.

General Finance Information Sites, Directories and Mortgages

www.fsa.gov.uk   UK

FINANCIAL SERVICES AUTHORITY
The regulating body that you can go to if you need help with your rights or if you want to find out about financial products; it will also help you to verify that the financial institution you're dealing with is legitimate. See also **www.oft.gov.uk** for the Office of Fair Trading and its informative site.

www.financial-ombudsman.org.uk   UK

FINANCIAL OMBUDSMAN SERVICES
When you have a complaint about a financial service this is a good point of call for sensible advice and help on how to go about getting a fair hearing.

F

www.find.co.uk   UK

INTERNET DIRECTORY FOR FINANCIAL SERVICES
Access to thousands of financial sites; split into nine sections:
loans, credit cards, insurance, mortgages, investment, banking
and savings, life and pensions, advice and infomation, business
services and some hints on best buys. Superb. See also
www.financelink.co.uk

www.ft.com or www.ftyourmoney.com   UK

FINANCIAL TIMES
FT.com offers up-to-date news and information. The 'Your
Money' section is biased towards personal finance. Although it
looks daunting, it is easy to use and provides sound,
independent advice for everyone.

www.fool.co.uk   US/UK

THE MOTLEY FOOL
Finance with a sense of fun. The Fool is exciting and a real
education in shrewdness. It not only takes the mystery out of
share dealing but gives great advice on investment and personal
finance. You need to register to get the best out of it.

www.thisismoney.com   UK

MONEY NEWS AND ADVICE
Easy-to-use site with reliable 24-hour financial advice from
the Daily Mail group. It has loads of information on all aspects of
personal finance and is particularly good for comparison tools,
especially mortgages, and there's a good 'Ask the Experts' section.

www.iii.co.uk   UK

INTERACTIVE INVESTOR INTERNATIONAL
Now known as Ample, the emphasis is on investment and
share dealing with some personal finance thrown in. It retains
the interactivity of the original site but with some additional
investment information. Also at **www.ample.com**

www.moneynet.co.uk   UK

IMPARTIAL AND COMPREHENSIVE
Rated as one of the best independent personal finance sites, it
covers over 100 mortgage lenders, has a user-friendly search facility
plus help with conveyancing and financial calculators. It now also
covers banking, refused credit and life insurance.

For other similar sites go to:

www.advfn.com – a really ugly site but comprehensive, if you can put up with the design.

www.adviceonline.co.uk – independent financial advice on a logically designed site.

www.bbc.co.uk/yourmoney – outstanding and ever changing site from the BBC, best for keeping up to date with the latest financial news.

www.digitallook.com – one of the leading providers of financial information, excellent site.

www.financialplanning.org.uk – help from the Institute of Financial Planning.

www.financial-planning.uk.com – a wide range of advice available but the site could be better organised and accessible.

www.fsa.gov.uk/consumer/compare – one of the best comparison sites with lots of useful tables and excellent common sense advice.

www.marketplace.co.uk – 'independent' advisers from Bradford and Bingley help you make the right financial choices from mortgages to investments and pensions.

www.moneybrain.co.uk – a slick site offering a wide range of financial products and independent advice.

www.moneyfacts.co.uk – a no-nonsense information site which shows the cheapest and best value financial products with lots of authority, it's also a comparatively fast site and less tricky than some. It also covers annuities and offshore banking.

www.moneysupermarket.com – a very good all-rounder with help in most of the important areas of personal finance; good site layout and lots of practical advice add to the package.

www.unbiased.co.uk   UK

FIND AN INDEPENDENT FINANCIAL ADVISER

A good independent financial adviser is hard to come by if you need one. But here's a good place to start. Just type in your postcode and the services you need and up pops a list of specialists in your area. See also **www.financialplanning.org.uk** for the Institute of Financial Planning and **www.sofa.org** for the Society of Financial Planners, both sites give information on how to get a financial adviser and plan your finances.

www.quote-engine.com   UK
>BEST VALUE CREDIT
>A guide to help you find the best deals on credit cards and
>loans. It's easy enough to use and there are online forms as
>well as links. It also covers insurance and household bills.

Mortgage Specialists

www.charcoalonline.co.uk   UK
>JOIN CHARCOAL
>This established mortgage adviser owned by Bradford & Bingley
>offers over 500 mortgages from over 45 lenders. There are also
>sections on pensions, investments and insurance.

>*It's worth shopping around, so check out these sites too:*
>**www.endowmentaction.co.uk** – from *Which* magazine here
>you can find out what to do if you think you've been miss-sold
>an endowment policy – but hurry time is running out.
>**www.mortgageman.co.uk** – aimed at the self-employed or
>those having difficulty getting a mortgage from the usual
>lenders, or with CCJs.
>**www.mortgagepoint.co.uk** – geared towards first-time buyers
>and those with a less than perfect credit history.
>**www.mortgageshop.com** – independent financial advice about
>which is the best mortgage for you, a somewhat messy site though.
>**www.mortgages-online.co.uk** – good independent source
>of information.
>**www.yourmortgage.co.uk** – *Your Mortgage* magazine.

Insurance

www.insurancewide.com   UK

>HOME OF INSURANCE ON THE WEB
>Claim to have a unique system that gives you personalised
>comparative quotes from most UK insurance providers. They
>offer a wide range of insurance policies covering life, travel,
>motor, home, small business as well as sections for students,
>young people, women and lifestyle.

www.easycover.com UK

UK'S BIGGEST INDEPENDENT INSURANCE WEB SITE
Here you can get a wide range of quotes just by filling in one
form. The emphasis is on convenience and speed.

www.warrantydirect.co.uk UK

EXTENDED WARRANTIES
Here you can get cover for the important things in life: your car,
appliances and your computer.

Other sites worth checking out:
www.eaglestardirect.co.uk – a sparse but useful site from one
of the market leaders.
www.elephant.co.uk – instant quotes on a wide selection of
policies although they mainly specialise in car insurance.
www.inspop.com – choose the specially selected policy and
buy online.
www.insurance.co.uk – another comparison site backed by
Lloyds TSB.
www.morethan.com – hyped with the 'Where's Lucky' ads, this
site is from Royal Sun Alliance and it's good for quotes in most
areas including pets.
www.quotelinedirect.co.uk – quotes on a wide range of
insurance areas.
www.soreeyes.co.uk – a wide range of policies and options.
www.theaa.com/services/insuranceandfinance – AA Insurance
covers travel, cars and home.
www.theidol.com – a wide range of insurance options
available here.
www.ukinsuranceguide.co.uk – a good place to find specialist
insurers.

For advice on insurance or problems with insurance:
www.abi.org.uk – Association of British Insurers, lots of advice
on all aspects of insurance plus industry information.
www.gisc.co.uk – General Insurance Standards Council, where
to go if you have a problem, it is responsible for a code of
conduct amongst insurers. Some sections are available in Welsh.

Investing and Share Dealing

www.investmentguide.co.uk   UK

FOR THOSE WHO GO IT ALONE
An outstanding site that gives you access to three books from Harold
Baldwin which are regularly updated and contain high-quality
information regarding share dealing and other investments; suitable
for beginners or experts. Some information is by subscription.

See also:
www.aitc.co.uk – an excellent guide and advice site to
Investment Trusts.
www.citywire.co.uk – advice and analysis from a well-regarded
source, some information is subscription only.
www.hargreaveslansdown.co.uk – a wide-ranging site with
lots of investment options and advice on where to put your
hard-earned cash.
www.investmentuk.org – home of the Investment Management
Association where you can find some useful advice and learn
how the investment industry is managed and how it works
with government.
www.investopedia.com – described as the investment
education site, it's packed with information and helps to
navigate the investment minefield.
www.londonstockexchange.com – guide to the exchange,
how it works plus information on stocks and shares.

*Any of the following are worth checking out when it comes to
dealing in shares. They are all good sites, each with a slightly
different focus, just find the one that suits your needs:*
www.apcims.co.uk – home of the Association of Private Client
Investment Managers and Stockbrokers and a usefully
informative site to boot.
www.barclays-stockbrokers.co.uk – good value for smaller
share deals and possibly the best for beginners.
www.cofunds.co.uk – have more control over your investments
and savings.
www.deal4free.com – unusual and highly rated dealing site
offering spread betting, share dealing and currency trading. You
need a good understanding of finance to get the best out of it.
www.earningswhispers.com – the latest hot stock picks and
earnings news.

www.ethicalinvestment.org.uk – if you want to invest your money in business that has a moral conscience, then here's the site that will lead you in the right direction.

www.etrade.com – a well-designed share trading site.

www.e-traderuk.com – a directory of investment and related financial sites.

www.freequotes.co.uk – an all singing and dancing site with the latest share information, tips and links to related and important sites.

www.fundsnetwork.co.uk – an online investment superstore with a huge range of options.

www.gni.co.uk – award-winning trading and investment site, good design.

www.hedgeworld.com – a guide to the seemingly complex world of hedge funds.

www.hemscott.com – one of the more comprehensive offerings with good use of other technologies such as SMS.

www.hoovers.com – good for background information; provides comprehensive company, industry and market intelligence on 40,000 of the world's top businesses.

www.investorschronicle.co.uk – this established magazine offers a useful site for share information and dealing, especially good for data on medium-sized and large companies.

www.invest-trees.com – profits from investing in woodlands.

www.itsonline.co.uk – a well-designed site that concentrates on explaining and campaigning for investment trusts.

www.morningstar.co.uk – a very dense site with huge amounts of information, part of its service is to collate and interpret the output of financial journalists, which must be a job in itself.

www.nsandi.com – National Savings and Investments.

www.sharepeople.com – owned by American Express, it has a nice design and is easy to use with lots of explanation on how it all works. Costs vary depending on the size of trade.

www.sharexpress.co.uk – the Halifax share dealing service that is a good beginner's site and charges competitively.

www.tdwaterhouse.co.uk – slightly more expensive than Barclays, but still quite good value, well designed with good information to back it all up.

www.trustnet.co.uk – all you need to know about investing in trusts.

Pensions

www.investmentguide.co.uk

UK

FIND A PENSION
Excellent site if you need help around the pensions minefield, with lots of jargon-free and independent information. It tells you how to buy one, how much you should be paying and advice on what you should be saving if you want a golden retirement.

www.pensionguide.gov.uk

UK

KNOW YOUR OPTIONS
A newly designed web site that provides an impartial guide to pensions from the government, which aims to help you choose the right option, there's also information for employers and current pension holders. Also check out
www.thepensionservice.gov.uk – the Department for Work and Pensions represents the government line on pensions and gives good advice and the latest news.

www.essentialpensions.co.uk

UK

FREE GUIDE TO UK PENSIONS
While the site wouldn't win any design awards, it is very useful and offers a comprehensive overview of most types of pension plus a calculator and a service that traces old and neglected schemes.

For more information on pensions see:
www.dwp.gov.uk – the government's advice site from the Department of Work and Pensions with information on benefits and services.
www.opas.org.uk – the Office of the Pensions Advisory Service helps when things go wrong.
www.opra.gov.uk – the Occupational Pensions Regulatory Authority ensures pension schemes are run properly.
www.pensioncalculator.org.uk – a useful and detailed site on calculating your pension.
www.pensionsnetwork.com – good site dedicated to bringing you the best value stakeholder pensions. It's easy to use and comes with a good pensions calculator.
www.sippdeal.co.uk – advice on how to invest your pension in a Self Invested Personal Pension.
www.sipp-provider-group.org.uk – informative site on SIPP.

Banks and Building Societies

Despite various concerns and scandals surrounding the security of some banking sites, internet banking is here to stay and is a very popular and useful way of keeping track of your finances.

Common sense is the key to good security. Never e-mail bank information, card, PIN or account numbers under any circumstances; it's also a good idea not to have the information stored on your PC as there are programs capable of obtaining that information without your knowledge. See our security section on page 397 for more on how you can keep safe but also check out www.banksafeonline.org.uk where you'll find a great deal of relevant information and help.

www.bankfacts.org.uk   UK
BRITISH BANKER'S ASSOCIATION
Answers to the most common questions about banking, advice about Internet banks, the banking code and general information. There's also a facility that helps you resurrect dormant accounts. See also **www.bankingcode.org.uk** where you can find details of the standards of service that all the banks have signed up to. For information on building societies go to the Building Society Association at **www.bsa.org.uk** and also the portal site **www.buildingsocieties.com** which offers a useful regional guide.

Here are the high street and Internet banks, building societies and the online facilities they currently offer:
www.abbey.com – offers a wide range of online financial services on a very red site. For their trendy internet bank go to the sharper designed Cahoot at **www.cahoot.com,** which offers similar services.
www.alliance-leicester.co.uk – a bright, comprehensive service offering mortgages. Insurance and banking.
www.banking.hsbc.co.uk – straightforward and easy-to-use site offering online banking alongside the usual services from HSBC. Like most other big banks, they've also launched a trendier Internet bank called **www.firstdirect.co.uk** which offers all the expected features plus WAP banking from an impressive site.
www.barclays.co.uk – one of the original innovators in Internet banking, they offer an exhaustive service covering all aspects of personal and small business banking.

www.citibank.co.uk – very impressive site with a complete Internet personal banking service with competitive rates. Citibank have few branches and this is their attempt at a bigger foothold in the UK.

www.co-operativebank.co.uk – acknowledged as the most comprehensive of the banking sites – it's easy to use and has an ethical ethos. Excellent, but they have also launched the trendier and more competitive Smile banking site **www.smile.co.uk** which is aimed at a younger audience.

www.egg.co.uk – a new-look site with banking, insurance, investment advice and even shopping.

www.halifax.co.uk – comprehensive range of services via an easy-to-use and well-designed site. You'll find a great deal of advice and information all clearly explained. Their Internet-only banking offshoot is called Intelligent Finance, which is excellent and can be found at the memorable **www.if.com**

www.lloydstsb.co.uk – combined with Scottish Widows, Lloyds offer a more rounded and comprehensive financial service than most. The online banking is well established and efficient. They provide help for small businesses and some Welsh language support too.

www.nationwide.co.uk – a much slicker design than the old Nationwide site, they offer a complete online banking service as well as loans and mortgages.

www.natwest.com – NatWest offer both online and share dealing, with good sections for students and small businesses. It's got a nice design, and it's straightforward to use.

www.newcastlenet.co.uk – a nice-looking and easy-to-use site from one of the smaller banking/building societies, offering all the usual services including online mortgage applications.

www.standardchartered.com – good-looking and user-friendly site from this small bank.

www.thechelsea.co.uk – a competent site from the Chelsea Building Society.

www.virgin-direct.co.uk – access to Virgin's comprehensive financial services site featuring a share dealing service, pension advice, banking, mortgages and general financial advice. There's help for the visually impaired as well.

www.woolwich.co.uk – online banking plus all the other usual personal financial services make the Woolwich site a little different.

www.ybs.co.uk – a good all-rounder from the Yorkshire Building Society.

www.switchwithwhich.co.uk   UK

SWITCH BANK ACCOUNTS EASILY
Which? magazine's site devoted to a campaign to encourage
people to switch to less costly bank accounts. There is advice
on the best account for you and how to move your account
to the recommended one painlessly.

Tax

www.inlandrevenue.gov.uk   UK

TALK TO THE TAXMAN
The Inland Revenue has a very informative site where you can
get help on all aspects of tax. You can even submit your tax
return over the Internet and there's a good set of links to other
government departments.

www.tax.org.uk   UK

CHARTERED INSTITUTE OF TAXATION
A great resource, they don't provide information on individual
questions but they can put you in touch with a qualified
adviser. It's a good place to start if you have a problem with
your tax.

www.taxbuddies.com   UK

TAX ADVICE
A pretty comprehensive effort with a huge amount of data,
information and advice on aspects of taxation both personal
and business.

http://listen.to/taxman   UK

THE TAX CALCULATOR
Amazingly fast, just input your gross earnings and your tax and
actual earnings are calculated.

See page 60 for our expanded business section.

Credit Checking

www.checkmyfile.com   UK

IS YOUR CREDIT GOOD?
For £18.95 you can get a basic online credit rating on yourself, or if
you pay more, they'll send you a more detailed report. Very useful
and informative, they even keep updating your file for a yearly sum.
You can also work out your likely credit score using their online
calculator for free. They also offer identity fraud services and will
check out car details. Data protection is guaranteed too.

See also these sites that offer similar information and services:
www.callcredit.plc.uk – online consumer credit reference
agency with a variety of services.
www.equifax.co.uk – get a full detailed credit report for
£11.75 online.
www.experian.co.uk – get a credit report sent for £2.

Debt Management

www.ncab.org.uk   UK

CITIZENS ADVICE BUREAU
Often the first port of call for people with debt issues, the site
offers useful information and the latest campaigns. There's a
search facility to find your nearest office and a link to
www.adviceguide.org.uk, which contains basic advice and
information on your rights.

See also:
www.cccs.co.uk – a charity dedicated to helping people get out
of debt.
www.debtcounsellors.co.uk – specialists in advising people
on what to do if they get into financial difficulty and dealing
with creditors.
www.nationaldebtline.com – a free debt help service with
useful links.

Miscellaneous

www.young-money.co.uk   UK

ONLINE MONEY GAME SHOW
Combines general knowledge and financial games aimed at
turning the little ones into the financial whiz-kids of the future.

There's a lot that most adults can learn from the site as well –
it's a fun way of learning about the world of finance. You need
Shockwave for it to work. See also **www.moneychimp.com** who
offer a basic explanation on most aspects of finance.

www.ifs.org.uk   UK
INSTITUTE OF FISCAL STUDIES
Independent analysis of all things financial especially the tax
system, surprisingly interesting but a pretty dull site.

www.paypal.com   UK

SEND AND RECEIVE MONEY ONLINE
A genuinely useful service, especially for small businesses and
online auction junkies, it's very easy and straightforward to use.
There's a directory of over 42,000 web sites that use PayPal
and details of how your site can get involved. See also
www.worldpay.com

www.moneysavingexpert.com   UK

SAVE ON EVERYTHING
Saving money guides to almost everything we pay out on, from
credit cards to utilities, this is an extremely useful site from TV
and radio pundit Martin Lewis.

Finding Someone

*Following the success of Friends Reunited, there's been a massive
explosion of sites dedicated to finding old friends and colleagues.
Here we've listed all the best sites, and also the place to go to find
a phone number, contacts for business and the home.*

Directory Sites

www.yell.co.uk   UK

UK BUSINESS DIRECTORY
Basically a search engine and directory devoted to businesses.
The online Yellow Pages is a very handy site to have in your
favourites list, it's easy to use and you can download the
toolbar on to your browser to make it even more convenient.
You can even get your search results shown on a map.
See also **www.bigyellow.com** for the US.

www.scoot.co.uk   UK
THE SIMPLE WAY TO FIND A BUSINESS
Register, type in the person's name or profession then hit the
scoot button and the answer comes back in seconds. Oriented
towards finding businesses but useful nonetheless. There's also
a cinema finder.

www.thomweb.co.uk   UK
THE ANSWER COMES OUT OF THE BLUE
Thomson's offer an impressive site and provide local directories
online. It's divided up into the following major categories:
1. Business finder – search using a combination of name, type of
   business or region.
2. People finder – track down phone numbers and home or e-mail
   addresses.
3. Comprehensive local information – available on the major cities
   and regions.

www.bt.com/directory-enquiries   UK
BRITISH TELECOM DIRECTORY
The way to cut those bills to directory enquiries. You're given
free access to 10 enquiries per day, but you can have another
200 free searches per month if you register. For a full overview
of BT services including checking up and paying your phone
bill go to **www.bt.com**

See also:
www.addresses.com/intl-directories.php – another list of
international directories.
www.anywho.com – straightforward American-oriented search
site with an international section.
www.infospace.com – another good search engine with yellow
(business) and white (people) pages sections, it offers much
more though including a good web directory.
www.royalmail.co.uk – this site offers a useful address and
postcode finder and you can track your recorded deliveries too.
www.ukphonebook.com – simple to use, quick with a no-
nonsense design, also has mapping, a business finder and lots
of adverts.

www.192.com   UK

THE UK'S LARGEST DIRECTORY SERVICE
Plenty available for no fee such as people and business finders,
directories and route planning. There are also various subscription
options, providing access to other databases such as the electoral
role and a range of business services. For a fee, they'll even try
to track down individuals you've lost contact with.

Finding Old Friends

www.friendsreunited.co.uk   UK

THE ONE STOP SITE TO REUNITE
Once the UK's most visited web site, a phenomenal success story
and millions of people have made contact with old friends using
the site. The read-only service is free, but access to the full
service costs £7.50. For that you get access to the schools and
workplace database and the ability to contact people through the
site. It's very easy to use and you'll quickly lose yourself.

See also:
www.disabledunited.com – dedicated to uniting disabled people.
www.friend-ships.com – find that person you met on a cruise.
www.gradfinder.com – good site covering many of the world's
schools and universities.
www.reunitelostfriends.co.uk – a nicely designed site with some
unusual sections such as 'lost sweethearts' and 'mothers groups'.
www.scoutsreunited.co.uk – find your old scouting buddies here.

*Some similar sites dedicated to re-uniting old service
colleagues:*
www.armedforcesfriends.co.uk
www.forcesreunited.org.uk
www.servicepals.com

Try also:
www.ariadne.ac.uk/issue20/search-engines/#lycos
– another page of tips, advice and links on finding people using
the Internet.
www.arielbruce.com – Ariel Bruce is an ex-social worker with
a good track record of finding missing people.
www.find-someone.com – a very commercial US site offering
software for sale that may help track someone down.

www.journalismnet.com/people – a tips sheet that contains links and advice on how to find people.

www.missing-you.net – free message posting designed to help find lost friends thought to be in the UK.

www.peopletracer.co.uk – people traced for a fee – from £24.95.

www.reunite.org – helping families who have suffered the trauma of child abduction.

www.andys-penpals.com   UK

FIND A PENPAL

A site devoted to penpals around the world. It's easy to use and free; there are also links to similar sites and a chat room.

Flowers

Sending Flowers

www.interflora.co.uk   UK

TURNING THOUGHTS INTO FLOWERS

Interflora can send flowers to over 140 countries, many on the same day as the order. They'll have a selection to send for virtually every occasion and they offer a reminder service. The service is excellent, although they are not very up front on delivery costs, which can be high. If you can't get what you need here then try www.teleflorist.co.uk who offer a similar service.

www.flyingflowers.com   UK

EUROPE'S LEADING FLOWERS BY POST COMPANY

Freshly picked flowers flown from Jersey to the UK from £8.99. All prices include delivery and you save at least £1 on all bouquets against their standard advertised off-line prices. They'll also arrange next day delivery in the UK. The site is simple and there's a reminder service just to make sure you don't forget anyone.

www.clareflorist.co.uk   UK

STYLISH BOUQUETS AND PRETTY PICTURES

Easy-to-use site with good customer services and free delivery to UK with surcharge for same day delivery. Cost reflects the sophistication of the flowers. For a similar service try www.daisys2roses.com

Flower Arranging

www.paula-pryke-flowers.com   UK

LIVE YOUR LIFE IN COLOURS
A bright and well-laid-out site from one of the UK's premium
flower arrangers. There are details of her books and designs,
which you can order.

See also:
www.jane-packer.co.uk – another top celebrity with a site
offering limited information; however, it does come with a
contact e-mail.
www.nafas.org.uk – informative, if dull, site from the National
Association of Flower Arrangement Societies.
www.silkflowerarranging.com – learn how to arrange silk
flowers successfully.
www.thegardener.btinternet.co.uk – details on how to achieve
the perfect flower arranger's garden.

Food and Drink

*Whether you want to order from the comfort of your own home, indulge
yourself, find the latest food news or get a recipe, this collection of sites
will fulfil your foodie desires. It features supermarkets, online magazines
and information sites, specialist food retailers, vegetarian and organic
stockists, drinks information and suppliers, where to go for kitchen
equipment and help in finding the best places when eating out.*

Supermarkets and General Food Stores

www.iceland.co.uk   UK

FROZEN FOOD SPECIALIST DELIVERS
Iceland's online service is considered one of the best with nearly all
of the UK covered. Easy to navigate, but can be ponderous to use.
Your order is saved each time, which then acts as the basis for your
next order. Information on the products is good, and there's a wide
range available; orders must be £40 or more. They also offer deals
on home appliances.

www.waitrose.com UK

IF YOU ARE REALLY INTO FOOD

Waitrose is offering a very good, comprehensive and well-designed site that oozes quality, so it's a pleasure to do your grocery shopping online. You can buy wine, gifts, organics and some John Lewis products. In addition it also has all the features you'd expect from an ISP: articles and recipes in their *Illustrated Food* magazine including information on food-related campaigns and organic issues; an excellent gift shop; plus party, flowers and travel sections and even one on competitions and puzzles.

www.ocado.com UK

AWARD WINNING

In partnership with Waitrose, Ocado offers a supermarket delivery service to mainly the south of England but their range is expanding all the time. Hopefully the site will be a success as it's easier to use than most of the other supermarket sites.

www.tesco.co.uk UK

THE LIFESTYLE SUPERSTORE

This functional site has a comprehensive offering, there's a wide range of goods on offer though, including electrical goods, clothes and books. There's also a section on personal finance, other shops, parenting advice and healthy living. Offers now abound with some great savings all aimed at capturing your e-mail address and future custom. As if echoing Tesco's movement away from selling just food, groceries do not seem to be the major function of this site anymore.

www.sainsburys.co.uk UK

NOT JUST GOOD TASTE

Sainsbury's site has more emphasis on good food, cooking, recommendation and taste, and of course the Nectar loyalty card. The facility to place an advance order at their Calais store, which you can then pick up and pay for in France, will appeal to those who wish to save time on their booze run.

www.somerfield.co.uk UK

MEGADEALS

The emphasis is firmly on offers but there's also a recipe finder, wine guide and essential food facts. Delivery covers most of the UK and it's free if you spend more than £25, provided you live near enough to the store.

www.asda.co.uk   UK

> PERMANENTLY LOW PRICES
> There's lots of information about the company and what it
> stands for plus links to its online shop. There are also sections
> on financial services, health and offers. Delivery is £4.25.

Alternatives to Supermarkets

www.homefarmfoods.com   UK

> DELICIOUS FROZEN FOOD DELIVERED FREE
> Good selection of frozen foods and huge range of ready meals
> with a good use of symbols indicating whether the product is
> low fat, microwavable, vegetarian etc. With free delivery, it's
> especially good value, and there is no minimum order. See also
> **www.foodhall.co.uk** who have a good selection of specialist
> stores to choose from.

www.farmersmarkets.net   UK

> NATIONAL ASSOCIATION OF FARMERS' MARKETS
> A farmers' market sells locally produced goods. Locate your
> nearest market or get advice on how to set one up.

www.freedomfood.co.uk   UK

> RSPCA FARM ASSURANCE
> Details of a scheme from the RSPCA to improve conditions
> for farm animals. The site shows where you can buy these
> products, lists producers and has some recipes too.

www.goodnessdirect.com   UK

> HEALTHY PRODUCTS
> A wide ranging health food store that offers advice and
> information alongside a broad selection of products, it also
> offers body and haircare products alongside the foods.

> *The remainder of the food section is alphabetically arranged
> by topic.*

African Cuisine

www.betumi.com   UK

> TRADITIONAL AND CONTEMPORARY
> Recipes, information and links on Africa and its food, it also
> has some charitable aspects.
>
> *See also:*
> **http://africafood.tripod.com** – some recipes at this site
> promoting an African cookery book.
> **www.afrol.com/Categories/Culture/recipes.htm**
> – West African recipes.
> **www.boykie.co.uk/south-african-cuisine.htm**
> – South African cuisine.
> **www.khound.com/topics/africanr.htm** – a bit of a mess but
> a good overview of African cookery by country and region plus
> information on its derivatives too.

Asian and Indian Cookery

www.curryhouse.co.uk   UK

> EVERYTHING YOU NEED TO KNOW ABOUT CURRY
> Curryholics can get their fill of recipes, recommendations,
> taste tests, interviews with famous chefs and a restaurant
> guide, good for links too.
>
> *See also:*
> **www.curryguidenet.co.uk** – a good-looking site with a good
> range of recipes and restaurants.
> **www.currypages.com** – an Indian Restaurant guide.
> **www.currysauce.com** – get all the sauces delivered and still
> win a year's supply.
> **www.gcosta.co.uk/curryclub** – join Pat Chapman's famous
> curry club, access recipes and buy his range of ingredients.
> **www.redhotcurry.com/food_and_drink/index.htm** – excellent
> food and drink section from the well-known British Asian portal.
> **www.simplyspice.co.uk** – buy authentic ingredients, including
> spices, oils, pulses and package mixes, at very low prices.

www.straitscafe.com   SINGAPORE
RECIPES FROM SINGAPORE
A straightforward site with lots of recipes not only from
Singapore, but from Southeast and East Asia including Japan
and China, there's also a good set of links and a useful glossary
at the 'pantry'. For Indonesian cooking go to the enjoyable
Henks Hot Kitchen, which can be found at **www.indochef.com**

www.japanweb.co.uk   UK
JAPANESE CUISINE
An interesting and growing site covering the basics of Japanese
cooking along with recipes and a UK restaurant guide. It also
has a glossary and tips on etiquette. 'Itadakimasu' as they say.

See also:
www.bento.com – a good-looking site with lots of information
on Japanese food and eating out.
www.sushilinks.com – links to all things sushi!
www.yosushi.com – a hi-tech site which features their
restaurants and a sushi ordering service to selected areas.

www.thaicuisine.com   US
RECIPES AND RESTAURANTS
This site offers recipes and ingredient information,
though the restaurant list is only for the US, see also
http://thai-uk.org/food.html which has good background
information on Thai food, and **www.importfood.com** who
offer up some 135 recipes.

www.chinavoc.com/cuisine/index.asp   US
CHINESE COOKERY
Lots of tips and background information on Chinese cookery
with advice on techniques and recipes.
www.chinavista.com/culture/cuisine/recipes.html is worth
checking out for its list of regional recipes. Also
www.chinatown-online.co.uk is dedicated to what's going on
in London's China Town; it has an excellent food section.

See also:
www.asianonlinerecipes.com – some 2,000 recipes and useful
for links too.
www.asiarecipe.com – a messy, but well-intentioned site with
a range of recipes and ingredients covering the whole of Asia.

Barbecues

www.barbecuen.com   US
BARBECUES
In the unlikely event that our weather will be good enough to
have a barbecue, then here's a site with all you need to know
on the subject. See also the musically enhanced
www.britishbarbecue.co.uk with 2,250 recipes.

British and Irish Cookery

F

www.greatbritishkitchen.co.uk   UK
BRITISH FOOD TRUST
This has an extensive recipe collection, history, chat from
celebrity chefs and a kids' recipe collection, which makes this
a much improved site. Unfortunately the site is currently not
being updated while the Trust is undergoing a review.

See also:
http://pages.eidosnet.co.uk/cookbook/index.html – a tribute
to British cooking with some fifty recipes, the site is pretty
dated though.
www.recipes4us.co.uk – have over 2,000 recipes although
some are international.
www.regionalfoodanddrink.co.uk – a regional guide to the
UK's food specialists.

www.rampantscotland.com/recipes   UK
A WEE FEAST
A very simple site listing a good selection of traditional Scottish
recipes. **www.ifb.net/webit/recipes.htm** and
www.scottishrecipes.co.uk also have a small collection of
Scottish recipes.

www.tasteofireland.com   UK
A TASTE OF IRELAND
Recipes, a restaurant guide and a shop all in one, it's not that
comprehensive and the site isn't that reliable but well worth
a visit nonetheless.

www.red4.co.uk/recipes.htm   UK

> ### WELSH RECIPES
> Here are over 120 traditional recipes including lava bread,
> wines, cawl and Welshcakes. See also
> **www.hookerycookery.com/welsh-menu.htm** where there's
> a similar list.

Celebrity Chefs and TV Food Shows

*If you can't find what you're looking for on their dedicated web sites,
checkout* **www.bbc.co.uk/food** *where you'll find a list over 40
TV cooks and presenters.*

www.delia.co.uk   UK

> ### DELIA SMITH
> The queen of British cookery has a clean, well-designed site with
> lots of recipes, which can be accessed by the good search facility. If
> you join, you get added features such as daily tips, competitions and
> the chance to chat to Delia. There's also a section on what Delia is
> up to and you can ask questions and get advice at the cookery
> school. This is increasingly becoming a lifestyle site with sections on
> travel, gifts, gardening and homeware.

www.jamieoliver.net   UK

> ### WHAT HE'S ABOUT
> The official site mainly dedicated to Jamie's diary but there's
> also advice on school dinners and links to his restaurant,
> charity and kitchenware. In addition you can buy a limited
> selection of clothing and other bits and bobs, join in the forums
> and even see his moblog. The small recipe collection continues
> to grow and, of course, there's an opportunity to buy the books.

www.nigella.com   UK

> ### DOMESTIC GODDESS
> A disappointing offering that promotes her books, her Living
> Kitchen range and herself. There is a forum for discussion and
> recipes, though sadly these come from visitors to the site, not
> from the doyen herself.

www.rickstein.co.uk   UK

> ### PADSTOW, STEIN AND SEAFOOD
> Information on Rick, his restaurants and cookery school all
> wrapped up in a tidy web site. You can also book a table or
> a room as well as order products from the online deli.

www.uktvfood.co.uk   UK

UK FOOD
Very attractive site from this specialist TV channel with lots
of recipes, tips and features based on their programming.

www.foodtv.com   US

FOOD NETWORK
A rather strange but quite appealing site devoted to American
TV cooks. It has some video footage and a search engine that
covers 20,000 recipes, plus some good articles.

Cheese

www.cheese.com   US

IT'S ALL ABOUT CHEESE!
A huge resource site with information on over 700 types of cheese.
There's advice about the best way to eat cheese, a vegetarian
section, a cheese bookshop and links to other cheese-related sites
and online stores. You can even find a suitable cheese searching by
texture, country or type of milk. For more cheese information try the
attractive Cheesenet site at **http://65.61.15.248/cheesenet** it has
an excellent search facility, or the American Dairy Association's
www.ilovecheese.com which also offers a cheese guide and lots
of recipes.

www.cheesemongers.co.uk   UK

OPULENT SITE FROM UK'S OLDEST CHEESEMONGERS
Paxton and Whitfield, the royal cheesemongers, provide a very clear
and easy-to-use online shop but charge £10.00 to ship goods.
A superb selection of cheese and luxury produce, with hampers,
cheese kitchen, accessories and wine. A pleasure to browse and
it's tempting to buy; you can also join the Cheese Society. See also
the British Cheese Board at **www.britishcheese.com** where you
can learn about our cheeses, get some recipes and general
cheese propaganda.

www.teddingtoncheese.co.uk   UK

BRITISH AND CONTINENTAL CHEESEMONGERS
Much-acclaimed site offering over 130 types of cheese at
competitive prices. The sections are split by country and there's
a good system for showing whether the cheese is suitable for
vegetarians, pregnant women, etc. There is also an

encyclopedia, a selection of wine and other produce; you can even design your own hamper. When buying you can stipulate how much cheese you want in grams (150 minimum), shipping from £7.99 for the UK.

www.fromages.com   FRANCE
TRADITIONAL FRENCH CHEESE
French cheese available to order and delivered within 24 hours along with wine recommendations and express shipping from France. Delivery is included in the price but if you're worried about cost you probably shouldn't be shopping here.

Confectionery, Cake and Chocolate

www.hotelchocolat.com   UK
DEDICATED TO GOOD CHOCOLATE
An excellent and well-illustrated site from an experienced retailer, they also offer lots of choice and a wide range of chocolate-related gifts and you can even buy in bulk! There's a really good selection facility and the chocolate tasting club. Delivery to UK included in the price and they will guarantee that it's delivered by a specified date. Formerly called **www.chocexpress.co.uk**

www.chocaid.com   UK
HELP THE HUNGRY
A great site where you can give to charity when you buy gourmet chocolates. They have a good selection and you can choose which good cause your donation goes to.

www.thorntons.co.uk   UK
WELCOME TO CHOCOLATE HEAVEN
Thorntons offer a comprehensive and easy-to-use site, with an emphasis on gifts. The range is extensive and they supply world-wide – at a cost (£4.50 for the UK). There are product sections for continental, premier, gifts and hampers plus flowers and wine. For handmade chocolates try the tempting selections at **www.handmadechocolates.co.uk**

See also:

www.bettysbypost.co.uk – a wide selection of goodies from this well-known Harrogate confectioner.

www.cadbury.co.uk – where you can learn all about chocolate plus lots of recipes and play games.

www.chocolate.co.uk – home of the Chocolate Society.

www.cocoaura.com – high-class chocolatier with some very original handmade recipes.

www.hersheys.com – tour the famous American factory, good for recipes too.

www.lamaisonduchocolat.com – excellent chocolate shop with lots of gift options.

www.prestat.co.uk – hand-made chocolates delivered to your door the next day.

www.virtualchocolate.com – where you can send virtual chocolate, read chocolate-inspired stories and poems.

www.thecakestore.com   UK

CAKES, CAKES AND MORE CAKES

Very good online cake store with a huge selection, good prices and you can order a tailor-made cake too. Sadly they only deliver in London and parts of the South East. See also **www.clickthecookie.co.uk** who offer a wide range of cookies and gift options; particularly useful if you want to send themed fortune cookies or a tube of fortune cookie insults.

www.janeasher.co.uk   UK

JANE ASHER CAKES

A pretty workman-like affair, you can order personalised cakes (London orders only delivered or collected by customer), select from a range of mail-order cakes and you can buy equipment too. For another source of sugarcraft paraphernalia try **www.squires-shop.com**

www.pastrywiz.com   US

PASTRY HEAVEN

A general food site with the emphasis on pastry in all its forms, there are plenty of recipes and links to keep all cake fans happy. See also **www.flourbin.co.uk** and get any number of different types of flour here.

www.oldsweetshop.com   UK
SWEETS THE WAY THEY USED TO BE...
Sweets from an old-fashioned sweet shop, stacked with
favourites like Dolly Mixtures, sugared almonds and Parma
violets, a visit here is a nostalgia trip as much as anything.
Delivery is according to weight. See also **www.sugarboy.co.uk**
who offer a wide range of goodies, **www.cybercandy.com** and
also **www.aquarterof.com** which is great for old favourites.

Diet and Nutrition

www.eatwell.gov.uk   UK
NANNY KNOWS BEST
A well-meaning and informative attempt by the Food Standards
Agency to improve the British diet. There are sections on healthy
diet, ages and stages, health issues, food safety and labelling.

www.3fatchicks.com   US

THE SOURCE FOR DIET SUPPORT
The awesome Three Fat Chicks have produced one of the best food
web sites. It's text heavy but entertaining and informative about
dieting or trying to stay healthy. There are food reviews, tips on how
to live on fast food, recipes, links to other low fat sites, a section for
chocoholics, diet tips and a 'tool box', which has calorie tables and
calculators; also sections on getting started, on losing weight and
how to get free samples. Check out the fast-food guide to get the
nutritional low-down on your fast-food chain favourites.

www.cookinglight.com   US
THE BEST FROM *COOKING LIGHT* MAGAZINE
One of the world's best-selling food magazines, their slow site
offers a huge selection of healthy recipes and step-by-step
guides to cooking. There are also articles on healthy living.

www.weightwatchers.co.uk   UK
WELCOME TO WEIGHTWATCHERS UK
A much improved site with more information on how to lose
weight, keep motivated, keep fit, chat and, of course, where
to find your local group. There's also a shop where you can
buy specially selected foods and related diet products – delivery
starts at £3.50, free on orders over £60.

http://atkins-uk.com   UK
DR ATKINS
The world's best-selling dietician offers a site that gives the
background to his low-carbohydrate diet and how you can lose
weight and get healthy on it. You can shop for Atkins supplements
and foods, delivery begins at £4.95. For another approach
try **www.low-carb.com**

www.mynutrition.co.uk   UK

ONLINE GUIDE TO HEALTHY EATING
Find out what you really should be eating from this cool British
site, which has been put together by a professional nutritionist.
Its features include an A–Z of ailments and diseases, dietary
advice, newsletter, relevant articles and of course shopping.
Delivery is £1.50 for the UK.

www.weightlossresources.co.uk   UK
FAD-FREE TOOLS FOR HEALTHY WEIGHT LOSS
Excellent place to go for information on weight loss and diets;
you can keep a weight loss diary, find out about exercise, get
advice on what to eat and catch up on the latest research. You
can also share your experience with others too, you have to
register to get the best out of it.

www.realslimmers.com   UK
NEVER VISIT THE SUPERMARKET AGAIN
Let someone else do the cooking for you, order a set menu for a
week, or construct your own. The food is relatively inexpensive,
from under £50 per week for everything including breakfast,
snacks, main meals and delivery.

www.hungry-girl.com   US
TIPS & TRICKS FOR HUNGRY CHICKS
A great design combined with useful information all presented
in 'bite sized' articles, some is geared towards US readers but
it's still useful and enjoyable to use.

See also:
http://lowfatcooking.about.com – a well-presented and
informative section from the About.com web site.
www.caloriecontrol.org – low fat information from the Calorie
Control Council.

www.caloriecounter.co.uk – a good site with a diet based on counting calories and exercise.

www.cyberdiet.com – a good all rounder with a wide range of advice, including specialist diets.

www.dailydiettracker.co.uk – a popular and well-put-together site that enables you to track what you eat and monitor your progress.

www.fatfree.com – almost 5,000 recipes all fat free or very low fat.

www.fatfreekitchen.com – Indian vegetarian, low fat recipes and healthy eating info.

www.foodsubs.com – a useful food thesaurus with the added benefit that it offers up low fat substitutes to fatty foods.

www.nutrition.org.uk – home of the British Nutrition Foundation, a site with masses of advice and information, especially useful for parents.

www.rosemary-conley.co.uk – all about Rosemary and her healthy lifestyle.

Special Dietary Needs

Also refer to the section on health, page 225.

www.diabeticgourmet.com   UK

DELICIOUS FOR DIABETICS

Lots of recipes and ideas to make food palatable without endangering your blood sugar levels from *Diabetic Gourmet* magazine, see also **www.diabetic.com/cookbook** where there's a great archive of recipes.

www.nutritionpoint.co.uk   UK

GLUTEN FREE

Their mission is to expand the range of gluten-free products available in Britain. They also provide a helpful checklist indicating which of their products are available on prescription; failing that you can buy goods through a link to an online shop **www.goodnessdirect.co.uk** For more information try **www.coeliac.co.uk** or the US sites **www.gfcfdiet.com** and **www.celiac.com**

www.foodag.com   UK

E-NUMBERS MADE CLEAR

The food additives guide with information on what additives are bad for you and which are derived from animals. The ingredients section provides a list of E-numbers in common food groups indicating the nasties to be avoided.

www.foodallergy.org   US
ALLERGY AND ANAPHYLAXIS
A useful site with information and links on food allergies and
their reactions, it's very much oriented to the US so also try
www.anaphylaxis.org.uk which is also very helpful and
UK based.

French Food

http://frenchfood.about.com   US
FRENCH CUISINE
About.com have created a superb resource at this site with
a huge amount of data, articles and recipes. Every aspect of
French cooking seems to be covered from the ingredients to
the shops and presentation.

See also:
www.afrenchkiss.com – make your own gourmet meals with
this fun French recipe-creation program.
www.goodfrance.com – a wide range of French food available
to buy, with good regional sections and hampers too.
www.hertzmann.com/index.php – French recipes from an
obsessive...
www.manoir.com – world-class recipes from Raymond Blanc
as well as details of his hotels and restaurants.
www.paniers.com – high-quality French food online, for a price.

Halal

www.halalfoodauthority.co.uk   UK
HALAL FOOD
Information on Halal food and the regulations that surround it; it
explains what Halal means and offers support to suppliers too.

Holland

www.typicaldutchstuff.com   HOLLAND
DUTCH PRODUCE
A wide range of food available here, though mainly oriented towards
confectionary. Delivery costs vary according to how heavy the order
is. For your Dutch cheese fix go to **www.gestam.com**

Hygiene and Food Safety

www.foodsafety.gov/~fsg/fsgadvic.html UK
FOOD SAFETY
A government site with basic advice on handling foods in all
sorts of situations from product-specific advice to helping those
with special needs; there are also good links to related topics.

See also:
www.food.gov.uk – home of the Food Standards Agency who
have lots of information on what is safe to eat.
www.ourfood.com – an overview of food science and hygiene.

Italian Food

www.halalfoodauthority.co.uk UK

EAT WELL
An award-winning site that covers everything to do with Italian
cookery. Its aim is to give a grand tour of Italian cuisine – and it
succeeds, including some 600 recipes in the English language
section, but over 1,600 overall.

See also **http://italy1.com/cuisine** which has good regional
cooking and food information as well as lots of recipes and if
that's not enough, **www.italianfoodforever.com**

www.savoria.co.uk UK
TRUE TASTE OF ITALY
There will be no problem fulfilling the minimum order of £50 at
this wonderful deli full of culinary indulgences. Delivery is
£11.70 or free if your order is £100 (ex-VAT) or more.
Alternatively, try **www.esperya.com**, which sends produce
direct from Italy starting at €20. At **www.dolcevita.com/cuisine**
you'll find produce, recipes and a survival kit for Italian cuisine.

www.ilovepasta.org US
US NATIONAL PASTA ASSOCIATION
250 recipes, tips, fast meals and healthy options all wrapped
up in a clear and easy-to-use site. There's also information on
the different types of pasta and advice on the right sauces to
go with them.

www.getoily.com UK
OLIVE OIL
All you need to know about olive oil, cooking with it, health
benefits and history, oh and you can buy it too, along with a
good selection of other Mediterranean products.

www.dominos.co.uk UK
PIZZA DELIVERY
Order your pizza online and get it delivered to your home
providing you live near enough to one of their outlets that is.
It's a nicely designed site, which also has a few games if you
get bored waiting.

Kitchen Equipment

www.lakelandlimited.co.uk UK
EXCELLENT CUSTOMER SERVICE
Lakeland pride themselves on service and it shows, they aim to
get all orders dispatched in 24 hours and delivery on orders
over £45 is free, otherwise they charge £3.50. The product
listing for both kitchen and homeware is comprehensive too.

www.urbanbar.com UK

GLASS AND CLASS
A very attractive site from this glass specialist, the range isn't
large but it's well presented and there are recipes, links and
special offers too.

See also:
www.7day-chef.com – wide range of equipment and kitchen
accessories and some excellent offers on top brands too.
www.alessi.com – a tour round the kitchen design powerhouse that
is Alessi, the best bit is that you can now buy from this site too.
www.cucinadirect.com – a very wide range of kitchen
equipment and related products, delivery starts at £4.95.
www.divertimenti.co.uk – Divertimenti are also worth a look,
they go for quality and they are good for gifts.
www.kingsofhagley.co.uk – excellent cookware shop with lots
of choice and a personal service.
www.kitchenware.co.uk – have a good range, with postage for
the UK being £3.95 per order.
www.pots-and-pans.co.uk – Scottish company offering kitchen
equipment through a good online store; it's good value but
delivery charges may vary.

Kosher Cookery

www.koshercooking.com UK

JEWISH CUISINE
Lots of recipes and links covering all forms of kosher cookery
and occasions.

www.totallyjewish.com/food UK

J-FOOD
Part of the lively Totally Jewish site which has a
magazine-style approach to modern Jewish cookery including
a message board, restaurant guide, chef's questions and
features. For another more personal recipe collection go
to **http://screamingmeemies.com/eats**

Luxury Food, Deli and Gift Sites

www.allpresent.com UK

GIFTS FOR THE DISCERNING
An Amazon-style shop offering gifts in the form of chocolates,
drinks and bakery items, such as cakes and biscuits, all
beautifully boxed. They also sell flowers and cards; delivery
costs vary according to what you buy.

www.fortnumandmason.co.uk UK

EXQUISITE GIFTS
A wide range of gift chocolates, hampers and more from one of
the leading luxury stores, UK residents have a wider choice
including condiments, teas and wines. Carriage is £7 for UK
residents unless you're an F&M account holder then it's free
when you spend £50.

See also:
www.champershampers.co.uk – family-run hamper business.
www.fifthsense.com – odd design but a wide range and
good value.
www.hamper.com – good design and a wide range of products
and you can create your own.
www.hampers.uk.com – a wide range of hampers, large and small.
www.lewisandcooper.co.uk – they've been producing hampers
for many years and here you can create your own or order one
of their range.
www.valvonacrolla-online.co.uk – lots of special food from this
Edinburgh retailer.

Meat and Fish

www.traditionalbutcher.co.uk   UK

A TRADITIONAL BUTCHER
John Miles is based in Herefordshire and knows a thing or two
about meat. You can buy meats and deli products online.
There's a good range and delivery is charged at cost. They
seem to take a great deal of care on quality.

See also:
www.donaldrussell.co.uk – a butcher who offers a wide range
of other produce as well as meats. The site is well illustrated
and there are recipes too.
www.meat-at-your-door.com – who offers a wide range of
meats; delivery cost is £29.38 for up to 20kg in weight.
www.swaddles.co.uk – organic butchers, with other produce
for sale from a good-looking site.

www.fresh-fish-online.co.uk   UK

FRESH FISH DELIVERED
A Devon company who own their own trawlers and will deliver
overnight so that your fish is very fresh. They also deliver frozen
fish, shellfish and smoked fish. They claim to subsidise delivery
costs, so there's a minimum charge of £10. Be aware that this
is a speaking web page, so turn off your sound if you want a
silent visit.

www.martins-seafresh.co.uk   UK

SOMETHING FISHY
You can order your fish fresh from this messy site which also
has recipes and helpful information on things fishy including
dealing with shellfish. For reputedly excellent oysters check out
www.kellyoysters.com

Mediterranean Food

www.belazu.com   UK

> CAPTURING THE MED
> This attractive site covers the cuisine of Spain, Italy, Greece
> and Morocco, there's a shop and a list of recipes too.

Middle Eastern Cookery

www.al-bab.com/arab/food.htm   UK

> MIDDLE EASTERN CUISINE
> An excellent overview of Arab cuisine from Arab Gateway with
> links to key sites covering all the major styles.

www.arabicslice.com   UK

> STEP-BY-STEP ARABIC CUISINE
> A well-designed and well-written cookery site featuring the best
> of Arabic food with simple step-by-step recipes, lots of
> explanation and illustrations.

Miscellaneous Food Sites

www.reluctantgourmet.com   US

> GOURMET COOKING FOR BEGINNERS
> Basically a beginner's cookery book, it's well designed and easy
> to follow with a glossary, guide to techniques, equipment, tips
> and recipes.

www.cheftalk.com   UK

> THE FOOD LOVER'S LINK TO PROFESSIONAL CHEFS
> Excellent site for articles and discussion about food with tips
> and advice from the top chefs. There's a good links section,
> recipes and a recommended restaurant guide.

www.expatboxes.com   UK

> FOOD PARCELS FOR THOSE LIVING ABROAD
> OK so you miss HP sauce, childhood sweet favourites and proper
> salad cream, relief is at hand here. You can get your rations in the
> form of specially selected hampers or they will tailor make and shop
> the high street for you. Delivery costs are high. For the Scottish
> equivalent try **www.scottishfoodoverseas.com**

www.hardtofindfoods.co.uk   UK

FOR SOMETHING SPECIAL

A great selection of the scarce and unusual from spices to oils to beans. You can learn a lot just by browsing, although that turns out to be an expensive thing to do. Delivery is free on orders of £100 or more.

www.edible.com   UK

YOU CAN EAT IT, HONEST!

All sorts of insects, unusual meat and bugs you can eat, often mixed with something exotic, the food available here is only for the culinary brave. The site design is excellent though some people might find the intro faintly disturbing... See also the listings at **www.weird-food.com**

Other unusual sites to check out:
www.egullet.com – a messy e-zine devoted to food that has some good articles if you can be bothered to wade through the site.
www.exploratorium.edu/cooking – discover the science of cookery at this site which makes fascinating reading.
www.gti.net/mocolib1/kid/food.html – a timeline marking the history of cookery through the ages, with links and background information.
www.topsecretrecipes.com – discover what really goes into America's big brand-name foods.

Recipes, General Food Sites and Magazines

www.kitchenlink.com   US

WHAT'S COOKING ON THE NET

A bit clunky to use, but it has so many links to other key foodie sites and food-related sections that it has to be the place to start your online food and drink experience. The design can make it irritating to use and it's got a little slow, but persevere and you'll be rewarded with a resource that is difficult to beat.

Other sites worth checking out are these, all have loads of recipes and it's just a matter of finding one you like:
www.chef2chef.net – outstanding professional cookery portal site with masses of links.
www.cookeryonline.com – very messy design but pretty comprehensive.

www.cyber-kitchen.com – excellent for links and specialised subjects.
www.goodcooking.com – another excellent food site with some good food writing.
www.ichef.com – good search facility, nice design.
www.meals.com – good for meal planning and recipes.
www.mealsforyou.com – recipes for solutions: healthy, tasty, nutritional and so on.
www.netcooks.com – hundreds of recipes submitted by the public.
www.recipes4us.co.uk –over 2,500 British and international recipes.
www.recipezaar.com – the world's smartest cookbook.
www.ucook.com – the ultimate cookery shop with recipes added.
www.yumyum.com – good fun.

www.tudocs.com   US

THE ULTIMATE DIRECTORY OF COOKING SITES
The main difference with Tudocs is that it grades each cookery site on its site listing. The listing is divided up into 19 sections, such as meat, beverages, low fat and ethnic. British cookery is in the ethnic section. See also **www.cookingindex.com**

http://epicurious.com   US

FOR PEOPLE WHO EAT
Owned by Condé Nast, this massive site combines articles from their magazines with information generated by the Epicurious team, the site has been tidied up but there's still plenty of advice with recipes, cooking tips, TV tie-ins, restaurant reviews, live chat, forums, wine and kitchen equipment. It's fast, easy to navigate and international in feel.

www.allrecipes.com   US

THE HOME OF GREAT RECIPES
This site gets its own review because it's not overly cluttered, it's just got loads of recipes which can be found easily and each is rated by people who have cooked them.

http://cookbook.rin.ru   RUSSIA

COOKERY ART
Really interesting cookery site with all the usual recipe sections but some unusual ones including exotic and erotic!

www.cookingbynumbers.com   UK

COOK WITH WHAT YOU HAVE

It's not a new idea to click on a list of ingredients and for a site to come up with a list of recipes, but here it's done particularly well. There's also help for beginners with some excellent step-by-step guides.

Spanish Food

www.spanish-kitchen.co.uk   UK

SPANISH CUISINE

What looks like a thorough walk though of the cuisine with recipes and explanations of what to expect when you go there.

www.tenstartapas.com   UK

TOP TAPAS

An exercise in the creation of the best ever tapas by several of the UK's top chefs. The whole point of it though is actually to get you interested in Sherry of all things. Still the site looks great.

See also:
www.catacurian.com – enjoy Catalan cuisine here.
www.culinaryweeks.com – Spanish food course in hilariously bad English.
www.donquijote.org/culture/recipes – some good recipes from this primarily language-learning site.
www.spanishhampers.co.uk – a great selection of Spanish food for sale, recipes are pretty good too.

Spices

www.apinchof.com   US

HERBS AND SPICES

A bit of a mess but it's very informative about a whole range of herbs and spices with articles from chefs and gardeners. It has recipes and lots of links to help you out.

See also:
www.ringoffire.net – a diverse web ring devoted to all that is hot and spicy.
www.seasonedpioneers.co.uk – recipes and spicy foods from all around the globe.

www.spiceadvice.com – useful spice encyclopedia from this
American spice retailer who doesn't ship outside the US.
www.thespicebazaar.com – a good-looking and well-laid-out
spice store that also sells dried fruits and herbs.

Vegetarian and Organic

www.organicfood.co.uk   UK

A WORLD OF ORGANIC INFORMATION
A very informative site which gives the latest news on organic
food. There are sections on why you should shop organic,
recommendations on retailers, lifestyle tips, shopping and chat.
There are also links to key related sites.

See also:
www.crueltyfreeshop.com – the animal-friendly superstore who
sell a wide range of products but a limited amount of foodstuffs.
www.helenbrowningorganics.co.uk – buying advice, recipes
and an online shop from this Wiltshire organic farmer.
www.organicdelivery.co.uk – a good organic food retailer with
some good offers. London delivery only.
www.sustainweb.org – a farming site with lots of information
and links on sustainable farming.
www.swaddles.co.uk – a wide range of organic food
including meat.

www.freshfood.co.uk   UK

THE FRESH FOOD COMPANY
Another combined supermarket and information site with a
wide range of produce to choose from, this one has a recipe
section too. They have a subscription system, which delivers
your chosen goods on a regular basis. Delivery is covered by a
box scheme, which is like a regular subscription; prices vary
according to your commitment.

www.vegsoc.org   UK

THE VEGETARIAN SOCIETY
An informative and attractive site with advice and help on going
vegetarian, a business section and recipes; also covers the
Cordon Vert cookery school and there's a good education
section for teachers and young people.

www.vegweb.com   US

VEGGIES UNITE!
If you're a vegetarian this is a great place, though not a great
design. There are hundreds of recipes, plus features, chat and
ideas in the VegWeb newsletter.

www.vegansociety.com   UK

AVOIDING THE USE OF ANIMAL PRODUCTS
The official site of the Vegan Society, promotes veganism by
providing information, links to other related sites and books.
There is a limited selection of goods in the shop, mostly books
and personal items. For a wider shopping experience go to
www.veganstore.co.uk who offer over 800 suitable products.

See also:
www.ciwf.org.uk – campaigning for farm animal welfare and
includes the Eat Less Meat initiative.
www.earthsave.org – a worthy organisation which promotes
vegetarianism by helping you choose the right way to eat.
www.living-foods.com – devoted to the subject of eating only
raw foods.
www.veggieheaven.com – UK restaurant guide for vegetarians
and vegans with over 185 listed.

Drink: Non-alcoholic

www.whittard.co.uk   UK

SPECIALITY TEAS DELIVERED WORLD-WIDE
An excellent site dedicated to their selection of teas and coffees;
it's easy to use and they will ship throughout the world.
Delivery varies according to weight for the UK – free if you
spend £50 or more.

See also:
www.coffeegeek.com – an American site covering coffee, it's
very comprehensive.
www.englishteastore.com – a well-designed site and online
shop devoted to all things tea.
www.pgmoment.com – all you need to know about PG tips.
www.realcoffee.co.uk – coffee delivered to your door the day
after roasting from the Roast and Post Coffee company.

www.redmonkeycoffee.com – modern online coffee retailer with free UK delivery.

www.tea.co.uk – great-looking site from the Tea Council with lots of facts and reasons given why we should drink more of the stuff.

www.twinings.com – information on tea and their products too.

Drink: Beer

wwww.camra.org.uk   UK

THE CAMPAIGN FOR REAL ALE STARTS HERE

A comprehensive site that has all the news and views on the campaign for real ale. Sadly, it only advertises its Good Beer Guide and local versions, with only a small section on the best beers. Includes sections on beer in Europe, cider and festivals.

www.realbeer.com   US

THE BEER PORTAL

Over 150,000 pages dedicated to beer, with articles, reviews, links and shopping all wrapped up in a well-designed site.

See also:

www.beerhunter.com – a very good site, home to expert Michael Jackson author of the *World Beer Guide*.

www.beersofeurope.co.uk – a beer store who offer a huge range not just from Europe, but from all over the world.

www.protzonbeer.com – aficionado Roger Protz gives his views on beer and pubs.

Drink: Wine and Spirits

There are many web sites selling wine and spirits, the quality of the information in this section is very high. These are some of the best.

www.berry-bros.co.uk or www.bbr.co.uk   UK

THE INTERNET WINE SHOP

This attractive and award-winning site offers over 1,000 different wines and spirits at prices from £4 to over £4,000. There is a great deal of information about each wine and advice on the different varieties. You can also buy related products such as cigars. Delivery for orders over £180 is free; otherwise it's £10 for the UK. They will deliver abroad and even store the wine for you.

www.winecellar.co.uk   UK

NOT JUST WINE AND GOOD VALUE
They also sell spirits as well as wine and, while the choice isn't
as good as some online wine retailers, Wine Cellar are good
value. Use the search facility to find the whole range which
isn't obvious from the home page. Delivery is £5.99.

www.wine-lovers-page.com   US

ONE OF THE BEST PLACES TO LEARN ABOUT WINE
Highly informative for novices and experts alike, this site has it
all. There are categories on learning about wine, reading and
buying books and tasting notes for some 80,000 wines. Also
within the site there's a glossary, a label decoder, a list of
Internet wine shops, wine writers archive, wine search engine
and much more.

www.winespectator.com   UK

THE MOST COMPREHENSIVE WINE WEB SITE
From *Wine Spectator* magazine you get a site packed with
information. There's news, features, a wine search facility,
forums, weekly features, a library, the best wineries, wine
auctions and travel. The dining section has a world restaurant
guide, tips on eating out, wine matching and a set of links to
gourmet food.

www.wine-pages.com   UK

A GREAT BRITISH NON-COMMERCIAL WINE SITE
Most independently written wine sites are poor; however, wine
expert Tom Cannavan has put together a strong offering, which
is updated daily. It's well written, informative and links to other
good wine sites and online wine merchants.

www.wineanorak.com   UK

THE WINE ANORAK
For another good British independent wine site, try the Wine Anorak,
it's just a great wine zine, with lots of advice, articles, issues of the
day and general information on wines and regions.

www.jancisrobinson.com   UK

TV WINE EXPERT
Jancis Robinson has a bright site with wine news, tips, features
on the latest wines and information on her books and videos.

www.ozclarke.com   UK
OZ ON OZ
Lots about Oz and what he's up to plus information on how to get his books and CD-ROM. There are also recommended wines and merchants of the month, tips on tasting and information on how to access his mobile wine guide for when you're out and about.

www.superplonk.com   UK
MALCOLM GLUCK
Excellent site from Malcolm Gluck, the author of the Superplonk books, there are offers and tips on where to buy good-value high-quality wines. For full access you have to subscribe.

Other wine sites worth checking out are:
www.booths-wine.co.uk – claims to sell imaginative and distinctive wines.
www.cephas.co.uk – superb images of wines and vineyards around the world.
www.internetwineguide.com – a good, if advert laden, all rounder.
www.laithwaites.co.uk – no-nonsense site with lots of offers and a money back guarantee. All wines are illustrated with a picture of the bottle.
www.majestic.co.uk – lots of offers and a well-designed site.
www.vintageroots.co.uk – excellent for organic wines, spirits and beers.
www.wineontheweb.com – good wine magazine with audio features.
www.wine-searcher.com – a wine search engine, type in the wine you want and up pops a selection from various retailers from around the world and UK, all suppliers are vetted for quality and service. Pricey.

www.idrink.com   US

DRINK RECIPES AND COCKTAILS
With over 6,000 drinks recipes you're almost bound to find something to your liking, you have to be a member to get the best out of it though. See also **www.cocktailtime.com** and the comprehensive **www.webtender.com**

www.barmeister.com
US

THE ONLINE GUIDE TO DRINKING
Packed with information on everything to do with drink, there are
over 2,000 drink recipes available and about 500 drinking games.
If you have another, then send it to be featured in the site.

www.whiskyweb.com
UK

A WEE DRAM
A comprehensive site for the whisky lover featuring history,
information on how whisky is made, links to all the distilleries
by region, a list of events and, of course, a shop (phone for
delivery rates according to purchase). For a whisky trail around
the Spayside distilleries go to **www.ifb.net/webit/whisky.htm**

Eating Out

www.goodguides.com
UK

HOME OF THE GOOD PUB GUIDE
Once you've registered it has an easy-to-use regional guide to
the best pubs, which are rated on food, beer, value, good
places to stay and good range of wine. You can also get a
listing by award winner. The site hosts the Good Guide to
Britain, which is a good resource for what's on where. See also
www.greatbeer.co.uk one man's passion and guide to over 200
pubs in the UK.

www.dine-online.co.uk
UK

UK-BASED WINING, DINING AND TRAVEL REVIEW
A slightly pretentious, but sincere, attempt at an independent
eating out review web site. It has a good and expanding
selection of recommended restaurants, covers wine and has
some well-written feature articles. It relies heavily on reader
recommendation, so there's a good deal of variation in coverage
and review quality and some were written some time ago. Not
very user friendly, no search by area.

www.theaa.com/getaway/index.html
UK

AA RESTAURANT SEARCH
Nestled away in the AA site is a little known gem in its hotel section
– an excellent regional restaurant guide to the UK. Each of the
4,000 listed is graded and there are comments on quality of food,
ambience, an idea of the price and, of course, how to get there.

www.viamichelin.co.uk   UK

MICHELIN
A site from Michelin with the emphasis on route finding, but
including a good restaurant finder and hotel guide.

Other restaurant review sites worth looking at before you go out are:
www.conran.com/eat – a guide to Terence Conran's restaurants
with online booking and some special offers, nice design too.
www.cuisinenet.co.uk – book online at selected restaurants,
nice design.
www.grabameal.co.uk – a pretty comprehensive directory of
takeaways and restaurants in the UK, with some 23,500 listed.
www.local-restaurant.com – good restaurant finder for cities,
not so good for country areas.
www.squaremeal.co.uk – newsy guide to London's restaurants,
it also covers selected ones in the UK.
www.toptable.co.uk – co-ordinates free booking at over 1,100
restaurants, nice design too.

Free Stuff

*Free stuff is exactly what the term suggests, and these are sites
whose owners have trawled the Net or been offered free services,
software, trial products and so on. It's amazing what you can find.*

www.freeinuk.co.uk   UK

JUST THE UK

Not just free stuff but also excellent Internet offers from British
sites, good design, but not that easy to navigate. The Top ten
section is great.

*Other sites worth looking into are these listed below, but most
are American so some offers may not apply for the UK.*

www.1freestuff.com – one of oldest and probably best categorised.
www.find-a-freebie.co.uk – very well-categorised and
extensive selection
www.freeandfun.com – the usual long list, don't see what's fun
about it though.
www.freebielist.com – a well-categorised listing of web-based
freebies – easy to use and good links.

www.freestuffpage.com – some really esoteric ones here.
www.thefreesite.com – more web stuff, nice layout.
www.thefreezone.co.uk – an excellent collection of link pages.
www.totallyfreestuff.com – massive selection.

Furniture see under Home and DIY page 267.

Gambling and Betting Sites

Gambling sites abound on the Internet and they often use some of the most sophisticated marketing techniques to keep you hooked. For example new screens pop up as you click on the close button tempting you with the chance to win millions. All the gaming sites are monitored by gaming commissions but above all be sensible, it's easy to get carried away. You should be aware that some carry spyware, programs that monitor your online activity.

Gambling and Gaming

www.betgambling.net   US

THE GAMBLER'S PORTAL
A useful gambling directory, which also offers forums and guides to the various games and sites. Its design isn't great but it is quite comprehensive. See also the less cluttered **www.winner.com**

www.gamblehouse.com   UK

YOUR ONLINE GAMBLING GUIDE
A very good place to start. They review online casinos and rank them according to whether they are licensed, make payments quickly, offer good odds. The variety and quality of games and lastly customer service. There are lots of pop-up adverts though.

These are the casinos and gambling sites we liked:
www.24ktgoldcasino.com – good graphics and fast response times make this great fun, but you need a decent PC to download the software. There are 40 or so games and you can play either for fun or for money.
www.888.com – claims to be the world's most popular online casino, great design.

www.betasyouclick.com – a directory with links to web sites from around the world, which offer, among other things sports books, casinos, poker rooms, lotteries and competitions.
www.galagames.co.uk – good graphics, lots of games and less fussy than most.
www.gamble.co.uk – a good directory and review site.
www.intercasino.com – easy to use and they've over 80 games to choose from.
www.pogo.com – from EA Games, lots to choose from, lots of prizes to play for.

Betting

www.settle-a-bet.co.uk   UK

BETS EXPLAINED
If you can't tell the difference between a trixie or a yankee and thought spreadbetting was something that went on toast, then this is the site for you. It has (not always simple) explanations of virtually every conceivable type of bet.

www.oddschecker.co.uk   UK

COMPARE THE ODDS
A great way to ensure you get the best deal from the online bookmakers, you just choose the sport and the event, then you get a read-out of the latest odds given by a selection of bookies – you can click on the bookmaker of your choice to place your bet. It's continually being updated; the site's a must for the committed gambler.

www.ukbetting.com   UK

LIVE INTERACTIVE BETTING
Concentrating on sports betting, this is a clear, easy-to-use site; take a guest tour before applying to join. You need to open an account to take part, using your credit or debit card, minimum deposit £10. The popular **www.bluesq.com** also offers a similar but possibly slightly broader service, and special bets on things like soap operas and political elections. Also worth a visit is **www.bet365.co.uk** who cover a wide variety of areas and offer some good deals.

www.mybetting.co.uk   UK

FREE BETTING

My betting works as a collation site for free bets and offers from
bookmakers around the Internet. It takes a minute or so to get
used to the design but once you're on board it's easy to get
yourself a few free bets, albeit at the price of a registration or two.

www.racingpost.co.uk   UK

THE RACING POST

A combination of news, racing and betting on a clear,
well-designed site. Also features greyhounds and information
on bloodstock.

www.ladbrokes.co.uk   UK

UK'S NUMBER 1 BOOKMAKER

Ladbrokes offer a combination of news, information and sport-
related betting with excellent features on racing, golf and the
other major sporting events. There's also a casino, lotteries,
a specials section where you can bet on politics or big events
and, of course, the now ubiquitous poker game.

www.willhill.com   UK

THE MOST RESPECTED NAME IN BOOKMAKING

The best online betting site in terms of speed, layout and design,
it has the best event finder, results service and betting calculator.
The bet finder service is also very good and quick. All the major
sports are featured and there is a specials section for those out-
of-the-ordinary flutters. Betting is live as it happens.

See also:

www.paddypower.com – a strong site from Ireland's biggest
bookmaker with betting on horses, football and other top sports
– even politics.
www.sportingindex.com – excellent and wide-ranging
spreadbetting site with offers and competitions.

www.totesport.com   UK

THE TOTE

The Tote has reinvented itself and become a general betting site
with casino and instant reward games. It covers a wide range of
sports but is especially strong on horse racing where you'll find
lots of useful information to back up your betting decisions.

www.thedogs.co.uk   UK

GONE TO THE DOGS
Everything you need to know about greyhounds and greyhound racing. You can adopt or get advice on buying a dog, find the nearest track, get the latest results and learn how to place bets. You can't gamble from the site but they provide links.

Miscellaneous

www.national-lottery.co.uk   UK

IT COULD BE YOU
Find out about Lotto and even play online, there's info on how to play and results of Euromillions and instant win games too. They also tell you about the good causes that the National Lottery supports. If you want to know whether your premium bonds are worth anything try **www.nationalsavings.co.uk** (you need your bondholder number handy).

G

For Men

The Good Web Site Guide's Top 10s of the Internet

TOP 10

1. **www.sharpman.com** – odd but essential advice on staying sharp.
2. **www.menshealth.co.uk** – excellent magazine site.
3. **www.firebox.com** – the place to find boys' toys.
4. **www.fathersdirect.com** – advice and support.
5. **www.kiniki.com** – the best underwear.
6. **www.clareflorist.co.uk** – because you're bound to need a florist at some stage.
7. **www.realbeer.com** – 150,000 pages devoted to beer…perfect.
8. **www.hard2buy4.co.uk** – when you need help buying a gift.
9. **www.sportzine.co.uk** – a portal for the sports obsessive.
10. **www.askmen.com** – a great e-zine full of information.

www.highstakes.co.uk   UK
HIGH STAKES BOOKSTORE
Books on virtually every aspect of gambling at this minimalist
site. It also offers selected links and you can order online too.

www.gamblersanonymous.org.uk   UK
WHEN THE STAKES GET TOO HIGH...
Where to go when it all gets too much, a straightforward site
listing crucial phone numbers and information on how to deal
with the compulsion.

See also:
www.gamanon.org.uk – help and advice for addicted gamblers
and their families.
www.gamcare.org.uk – an authority on the provision of
information on gambling, with advice and practical help in
addressing its social impact.

Games

*There's a massive selection of games on the Internet, here are just some of
the very best ones; from board games to quizzes to your everyday 'shoot
'em up' type. There are more games for Macs listed on page 24.*

*It's worth remembering that before downloading a game from a site it's
wise to check for viruses. If you've not got anti-virus software on your PC,
then check out our section on virus management on page 397.*

**Parents should be aware that some games are quite violent or contain
sexual references, so it's as well to check them out before letting your
child loose on them.**

Finding Games

http://gamespotter.com   US
GAMES SEARCH ENGINE
A really handy site where you can get links to virtually every
type of game whether it be a puzzle or action. Alternatively, you
can use the search facility to find something. Each game on the
list is reviewed as well.

Games Magazines and Information

www.avault.com   US

THE ADRENALINE VAULT
A comprehensive games magazine with demos, reviews
and features on software and hardware – good looking too.
There's also a good cheats and hints section.

www.gamespy.com   US

GAMING'S HOMEPAGE
Lots here, apart from the usual reviews and features. There are
chat and help sections and links to the arcade section with
hundreds of demos plus free games to play. See also
www.gamespot.co.uk which offers lots of info as well.

www.gamers.com   US

A MOMENT ENJOYED IS NOT WASTED
A great-looking site with all the features you'd expect from a
games magazine but it has more in the way of downloads and
games to play. There is also a chat section and competitions.

www.happypuppy.com   US

GAMES REVIEWED
Happy Puppy has been around a while now reviewing games in
all the major formats. Each is given a thorough test, then it's
rated and given a review. There are also links to related games
sites. It's all packaged on a really good web site which is quick
and user-friendly.

www.gamefaqs.com   US

GAMES FREQUENTLY ASKED QUESTIONS
All information is free and donated, there are FAQs and tip sheets
on any number of games, and it seems to be regularly updated.

www.game-sector.co.uk   UK

FOR THE GAMERS BY THE GAMERS
A very good games review and news site with an interesting
design. There are sections for each type of game player as well
as feedback and forums too.

http://vgstrategies.about.com   US

ABOUT GAMES
A set of information pages from the excellent About.com with articles and links covering all the likely strategies needed for gaming.

See also:
http://games.slashdot.org – described as News for Nerds, it looks the part and seems very comprehensive with the latest games news by format.
www.eurogamer.net – another newsy site, this is better laid out than most but there's still a lot to take in.
www.gamestudies.org – an intellectual and scholarly approach to games with articles and emphasis on the cultural, aesthetic and communicative value of gaming.
www.gaming-age.com – more news and reviews.
www.spong.com – the Internet Video Games Archive has a massive amount of information on games. Their intended objective is to archive every game, they have some 30,000 listed.

Games to Play

www.boxerjam.com   UK

ONLINE GAMESHOW
Excellent site devoted to giving the user access to original and traditional games played online, for cash and prizes.

www.classicgaming.com   US

GAMING THE WAY YOU REMEMBER IT
Probably one for older gamers but there's some good stuff on here so it's at least worth a look and it's amazing how new some of the games are.

www.gamehippo.com   US

OVER 1,000 FREE GAMES
Enough to keep you occupied for hours with games of every type from board to action to puzzles and sports. It's worth checking out **www.freeloader.com** which has a more modern selection available, but you have to register and jump through a few hoops to get them.

See also the oddly designed **www.download-game.com** who also offer a large number including old favourites, and Sean O'Connor's site **www.windowsgames.co.uk** where there's a small selection of high-quality games to download.

www.gamearchive.com   UK
PINBALL MACHINES
A site devoted to pinball machines and similar games put together
by real fans. There's also a selection of video games and links to
similar sites, however, there are no console games. See also
www.videogames.org for The History of Videogames Museum.

www.gamebrew.com   US
CHOOSE YOUR GAME
Gamebrew specialises in Java games and there are some
brilliant ones to download and play here, you choose from six
categories from puzzles to casino to arcade.

http://games.yahoo.com   US
YAHOO!
This popular search engine has its own games section. Here
you can play against others or yourself online. The emphasis is
on board games, puzzles and quizzes.

www.graalonline.com   UK
THE GRAAL KINGDOMS
Set in a mythical realm, this is a good multi-player game with lots
of levels and a high degree of interactivity and customisation.

www.worldogl.com   US
ONLINE GAMING LEAGUE
Join a community of gamers who play in leagues for fun. You can
play all the major online games and compete in the leagues and
ladders if you like. To quote them: 'What matters is that people are
meeting and interacting with other people on the Internet via our
services and their game'.

www.planetquake.com   US
THE EPICENTRE OF QUAKE
Quake is the most popular game played on the Internet, and
this slightly slow site gives you all the background and details
on the game. It's got loads of links and features as well as
reviews and chat.

www.shockwave.com   US

SHOCKWAVE GRAPHICS
Shockwave's fantastic site offers much in the way of high
definition games for both action fans and those who prefer to
test their minds a bit; the site also offers films and other useful

programs. You can also subscribe to their online gaming section with over 60 games choose from .

www.lysator.liu.se/tolkien-games   SWEDEN

LORD OF THE RINGS
Get immersed in Tolkien's Middle Earth with some 100 games. It's got action games, quizzes and puzzles, strategy games and, of course, role playing games.

www.wireplay.com   US

THE GAMES NETWORK
A good online games resource, the site encourages the players to interact, it has chat rooms and forums and also organises competitions.

www.zone.com   US

MICROSOFT GAMES ZONE
With over 100 games to choose from you shouldn't be disappointed. They range from board and card games to multi-player strategy and simulation games to playing for cash. It's a shame they've done away with what was a good children's section.

www.orisinal.com   US

JUST FOR FUN
A selection of high-quality silly and funny games using a very original and text-free format and design.

www.spaceinvaders.de   GERMANY

SPACE INVADER SHRINE
A fun homage to the original game with history, trivia, tips and of course you can play the game too.

www.popcap.com   US

100% JAVA
An excellent site with very high-quality games to download onto the PC, palm or Mac and also to play on the web.

www.sodaplay.com   UK

BUILD YOUR OWN...
A really interesting and different gaming experience. Here you can design your models and send them to the 'zoo' for display and use by others. You can race them and exchange them with friends too.

Game Manufacturers and Console Games

www.dreamcast.com   US

> DREAMCAST FROM SEGA
> Under reconstruction when we visited but you can get the latest
> information on what's coming, try it out or play online.

http://cube.ign.com   US

> GAME CUBE
> Dedicated to the format, there are lots of reviews, previews and
> the latest information on what's coming too.

www.hasbro.com/games   US

> HASBRO GAMES
> A commercial site from one of the biggest manufacturers with
> a useful list of what they produce.

Visual Treats

The Good Web Site Guide's Top 10s of the Internet

1. **www.nationalgeographic.com** – beautiful photography
    and writing too.
2. **www.apple.com/uk** – proving that computers need not be dull.
3. **http://uk.fmagazine.com** – the gorgeous *Forum* music
    magazine.
4. **www.scifi.com** – makes the best of all those effects.
5. **http://hubblesite.org** – stunning pics from the Hubble space
    telescope.
6. **www.musicplasma.com** – information on any artist graphically
    presented and linked.
7. **www.noggin.com** – great for young kids.
8. **www.thebanmappingproject.com** – stunning site on the history
    of Thebes and the Pharoahs.
9. **www.yoox.com** – make fashion shopping a pleasure.
10. **www.edible.com** – unusual food, not for all, but the site
    is cool!

www.nintendo.com   US
OFFICIAL NINTENDO
Get the latest news from Nintendo and its spin-offs – N64,
Game Boy and Game Cube. There's also information on the
hardware and details of the games new and old. For a site with
wider Nintendo info go to the excellent **www.nintendojo.com**

http://uk.playstation.com   US
OFFICIAL PLAYSTATION SITE
Looks good with games information, information on the
hardware, previews, new release details and a special features
section with reviews by well-known gamers. There's also a chat
section and a shop.

Also check out:
www.absolute-playstation.com
www.playstation.com
www.psxextreme.com

www.pocketgamer.org   UK
GAMES FOR POCKET PCS
OK so you've bought your handheld PC, you've impressed the boss,
now, what do you really use it for? Oh yes, play games! There's a lot
here for most different types of operating systems, if not, then there
are links to related sites. Try also **www.handango.com**, which is not
a specialist site, but the games section has been expanded and the
design is much improved.

www.gamespy.com/xbox   US
XBOX
Part of the Gamespy network, this site gives background on
Microsoft's toy, with the latest game news, reviews, demos and
previews too. See also **www.xbox.com** and the annoying to
load **www.xboxemea.com/playtogether** who offer some
exclusive previews. Formerly **www.planetxbox.com**

www.station.sony.com   US

SONY ONLINE GAMES
Sony have put together an exceptional site for online gaming,
and with over 6 million members, it's one of the most popular.
The site is well designed and easy to use and there are lots
of games to choose from. Providing you can put up with the
adverts, it's a real treat to use.

www.sega-europe.com   EUROPE

SEGA

Get the latest news on the latest games and buy them at the
store. The site is well designed but it can be irritating waiting
for stuff to load if you're on a normal modem.

Fantasy League and Strategy Games

www.fantasyleague.com   UK

FANTASY FOOTIE

Be a football manager, play for yourself, in a league, or even
organise a game for your workplace or school. Get the latest team
news on your chosen players and how they're doing against the rest.

www.thedugout.net   UK

CHAMPIONSHIP MANAGER

An excellent site devoted to Championship Manager and soccer
gaming, you can discuss the game, get up to speed with the
latest tactics, get the low-down on the players and generally
join in. There are also links to related sites.

www.primagames.com   US

PRIMA

The largest fantasy game publisher offers a site packed with reviews,
demos and articles. You can also buy a book on virtually every
strategy game. See also **www.strategy-gaming.com** which is
pretty comprehensive.

www.gamesworkshop.com   UK

WAR GAMING

A comprehensive offering covering war games including
collecting, painting and gaming itself, there are also forums,
chat and links to the major games. See also
www.wargames.co.uk, which is pretty comprehensive.

Cheats, Hints and Tips

www.computerandvideogames.com   US

THE CHEAT STATION

Select the console or game type that you want a cheat on, then
drill down the menus until you get the specific game or cheat
that you want. There are cheats for thousands of games so you

should find what you're looking for. If you can't, check out
www.xcheater.com who have a smaller selection, but you never
know your luck.

See also:
www.cheatextreme.com – great for Play Station cheats.
www.cheatheaven.com – a one-stop site for cheats in over
2,000 games covering most consoles. Good search facility, but
some annoying adverts and pop-ups.
www.playstation2-cheats.co.uk – cheats for PS2.

Games Shops

*If you know which game you want, then it's probably better to use a
price checker such as Kelkoo (http://uk.kelkoo.com) to find the best
price on the game. They will put you through to the store offering the
best all round deal. If you want to browse, then these are considered
the best online stores for a wide range of games:*

www.chipsworld.co.uk – good for Sega and Nintendo.
www.game.uk.com – a good comprehensive offering with daily
and weekly offers.
www.gameplay.com – Gameplay is one of the most visited games
sites. Once a magazine site, it's now transformed into a well-
designed store, browsable by platform and good value.
www.streetsonline.co.uk – follow the link to 'gamestreet' for
one of the top shops on the Internet. Parents will be sorry that
the kids' section has gone. Delivery costs start at £1. Good
value too.
www.telegames.co.uk – around 5,000 types of game in stock,
covering all makes. Also has a bargain section.
www.ukgames.com – excellent range and good prices.

Miscellaneous

www.etch-a-sketch.com   UK
REMEMBER ETCH-A-SKETCH?
For those of you who don't remember back that far, Etch-a-
Sketch is a rather annoying drawing game. It's been faithfully
recreated here and it's still just as difficult to do curves. There
are also a few other simple games and some links to children's
games sites.

www.hangman.no   NORWAY

HANG MAN

A great hangman game, you can play in many categories,
thankfully you can also turn the music off.

www.there.com   US

THE ISLAND GETAWAY

I'm not sure whether this should be categorised under dating,
chat or games but it's here, so choose your avatar, give them
some personality and play cards!

Card and Board Games

www.tradgames.org.uk   UK

TRADITIONAL GAMES

A history and a guide to traditional games, including board
games, table games, pub games and lawn games too.

www.playsite.com   US

EASY TO PLAY

A collection of straightforward multi-player online games,
specialising in cards, word puzzles and board games.

www.chess.co.uk   UK

ULTIMATE CHESS

Massive chess site that's got information on the game, news
and views, reviews and shopping. There are lots of links to
other chess sites and downloads. Also info on backgammon,
go, poker and bridge.

See also:
www.bcf.org.uk – for the British Chess Federation.
www.chessclub.com – for the Internet Chess club who had
over 2,000 players online when we visited, including 19
grandmasters.

www.gammon.com   US

BACKGAMMON

If you like backgammon, here's the place to start. There are
links to live game playing and masses of related information.
Also check out **www.bkgm.com**

www.msoworld.com US

BOARD GAMES, PUZZLES AND QUIZZES
The ultimate site of its type, there are over 100 board games
and masses of quizzes and tests.

www.monopoly.com US

MONOPOLY
A pretty boring site, it offers a history plus information on where you
can buy, along with tips on how to play and how you can get
involved in tournaments. See also **http://uk.mymonopoly.com** where
you can create your own personalised game to order.

www.thehouseofcards.com US

LOADS OF CARD GAMES
Huge number of card games to play and download with sections on
card tricks, history, links and word games – there's not much
missing here. See also **www.pagat.com** for an alternative.

www.solitairegames.com US

SOLITAIRE
Play online or download a game onto your PC, there are plenty
to choose from and it's quick. There's also a good set of links to
other online card games.

http://bridge.ecats.co.uk UK

BRIDGE RESOURCE
A good place for information on bridge from a software
company associated with the game at a high level. See also
www.bridgemagazine.co.uk

Crosswords, Puzzles and Word Games

www.cluemaster.com UK

CROSSWORDS AND WORD PUZZLES
A collection of crosswords and word searches. You have to
register to get access to the free puzzles, otherwise it costs
£1.50 to download 50 puzzles.

www.crosswordsite.com UK

ALL CROSSWORDS
Hundreds to chose from, with the option either to print off or fill
in online. There are four levels of difficulty with the hardest
being quite tough. See also **www.crossword-puzzles.co.uk**

www.fun-with-words.com   US
>
> THE WORDPLAY WEBSITE
> Dedicated to amusing English, the Fun with Words site offers
> games, puzzles and an insight into the sorts of tricks you can
> play with the language.
>
> *Other crossword and puzzle sites worth checking out are
> listed below:*
> **http://crosswords.about.com** – links and tips from this giant
> reference site.
> **www.canopia.com** – odd design but a good choice of puzzles
> and crosswords.
> **www.download.com** – the games section here has masses of
> choice, some free.
> **www.lovatts.com.au** – plenty to chose from at this Australian
> magazine.

Quizzes and General Knowledge

www.thinks.com   UK
>
> FUN AND GAMES FOR PLAYFUL BRAINS
> Massive collection of games, puzzles and quizzes with
> something for everyone, it's easy to navigate and free.

www.trivialpursuit.com   UK
>
> TRIVIAL PURSUIT
> A massive disappointment; this is a purely commercial site
> geared to selling the various versions of the official game.

www.playwithyourmind.com   UK
>
> MIND GAMES AND IQ TESTS
> More than 20 mind-stretching games including word, maths,
> card and logic puzzles, the design isn't great but the games
> are good.

www.mensa.org.uk   UK
>
> THE HIGH IQ SOCIETY
> Mensa only admit people who pass their high IQ test – see if
> you've got what it takes. The site, which has been upgraded,
> has a few free tests and, if eligible, you can join the club.

www.queendom.com US

SERIOUSLY ENTERTAINING

It's not entirely free but an excellent site for all sorts of brain tingling tests, the major difference is that it also offers personality profiles and psychometric tests which may help you in getting on in your career or just keeping your brain healthy see also **www.emode.com**

Check out these sites:
www.coolquiz.com – several different types of quiz from sports to movies and quotes. Nice wacky design.
www.funtrivia.com – a massive trivia site with over 650,000 questions.
www.quiz.co.uk – a couple of hundred questions in several unusual categories including kids, nature, food and sport.
www.quizyourfriends.com – a fun quiz creation site.

G

Gardening

There are lots of high-quality British gardening sites, but some sites are based in America, so bear this in mind for tenderness, soil and climate advice. Due to regulations on the importation of seeds and plants, these can't be imported from outside the UK.

www.gardenworld.co.uk UK

THE UK'S BEST

Described as the UK's best garden centre and horticultural site. It includes a list of over 1,000 garden centres, with addresses, contact numbers and e-mail addresses. Outstanding list of links to other sites on most aspects of gardening, very comprehensive with sections on wildlife, books, holidays, advice, societies and specialists, it now also has the addition of a link to the RHS plant finder service and Latin name converter – excellent.

www.gardenweb.com UK

GARDEN QUESTIONS ANSWERED

Probably the best site for lively gardening debate; it's enjoyable, international, comprehensive and has a nice tone. There are several discussion forums on various gardening topics, garden advice, plant dictionary and competitions. Using the forums is easy and fun, and you're sure to find the answer to almost any gardening question.

www.kew.org.uk   UK

ROYAL BOTANIC GARDENS

Kew's mission is to increase knowledge about plants and
conserve them for future generations. This site gives plenty of
information about their work, the collections, features and events.
There are also details of the facilities at the gardens, conservation,
educational material and lots of links to related sites.

www.rhs.org.uk   UK

ROYAL HORTICULTURAL SOCIETY

An excellent site from the RHS which features a plant-finder
service covering some 70,000 plant types, a garden finder
and an event finder. There's also advice and information about
the RHS, an opportunity to buy advance tickets to their shows
and a seed catalogue.

*Other gardening advice and information sites well worth
trying are:*

www.carryongardening.org.uk – award-winning site with all
the usual features plus some celebrity input. Good for links and
the idea exchange feature.

www.gardenforum.co.uk – outstanding gardening forum site,
good if you're a novice to using forums and chat sites.

www.gardenguides.com – a useful American resource site with
loads of information on every aspect of gardening. It has lots
of tips, handy guides, and a free online newsletter.

www.gardenlinks.co.uk – links to gardening sites in over 40
categories, a good place to start searching for something specific.

www.gonegardening.com – nice design, wide-ranging
magazine and shop.

www.plants-magazine.com – very good garden magazine,
broad in scope but particularly strong on new plants, a vehicle
for selling the magazine itself.

Allotment Gardening

www.allotments-uk.com   UK

ALLOTMENT ADVICE

Lots of links, advice and tips, plus a forum to discuss all your
allotment problems. See also **www.nsalg.org.uk** home to the
National Society of Allotment Gardeners, which isn't a great site
it has to be said.

Gardening Stores

www.greenfingers.com   UK

COMPREHENSIVE GARDENING
A gardening superstore with many categories and some good
offers. There's also plenty in the way of advice and tips, plus an
ask the gardener facility.

www.crocus.co.uk   UK

GARDENERS BY NATURE
A good-looking site full of ideas enhanced by excellent
photographs, there are some good articles and features, but it's
basically a gorgeous shop with thousands of plants and
products to choose from and some good offers. Delivery to
England and Southern Scotland starts at £5.95 (£1 for seeds).
If you live elsewhere you need to contact them to see whether
delivery is possible for a surcharge.

www.blooms-online.com   UK

ONE-STOP GARDENER'S RESOURCE
A beautiful site that will supply all your garden needs and
desires. In addition to ordering your seeds and buying your
garden furniture, there's a great plant search where you can
find plants of specific size and colour for that difficult hole in
the border. There are DIY projects, a design service, a
gardener's club and advice. Delivery cost depends on your
order. Alternatively, you can pick up at their nearest store.

www.gardentrading.co.uk   UK

GARDENING GIFTS
A well-presented site from a company that specialises in gift
products associated with gardening from furniture to lighting to
small gifts.

Other gardening shops worth checking out are:
www.burncoose.co.uk – nice design, searchable plant
catalogue with some good offers.
www.gardentrading.co.uk – less about gardening more about
accessorising your patch.
www.glut.co.uk – the Gluttonous Gardener provides unusual
presents for every gardener.
www.rkalliston.co.uk – excellent for gardening accessories
and gifts.

Garden Design

www.thegardenplanner.co.uk   UK

THE GARDENER'S DIRECTORY
Everything you need to plan your perfect garden, this excellent
directory is the place to start.

See also:
www.bali.co.uk – the home of the British Association of
Landscape Industries, here you can find a company qualified to
do the work you want.
http://gardendesign-uk.com – a good directory of garden
designers.
www.gardendesigner.com – a serious American site with in-
depth advice.
www.sgd.org.uk – Society of Garden Designers to find a
landscape gardener.

Organic and Environmentally Friendly Gardening

www.hdra.org.uk   UK

HENRY DOUBLEDAY RESEARCH ASSOCIATION
The leading authority on organic gardening. Their site offers a
superb resource if you're into gardening the natural way. It's
particularly good if you're growing vegetables and includes fact
sheets and details on why you should garden organically.

See also:
www.greengardener.co.uk – specialists in biological and
organic pest control and wormeries.
www.just-green.com – natural pest control with advice
and products.
www.organiccatalogue.com – a comprehensive store related
to the HDRA.
www.pan-uk.org – the Pesticide Action Network who are
working to eliminate the hazards associated with pesticides.
www.recyclenow.com formerly **www.rethinkrubbish.com** –
the best ways to recycle your rubbish.
www.soilassociation.org – for advice on growing organic food
plus the latest news on their campaigns.

British Wildflowers and Plants

www.nhm.ac.uk/science/projects/fff   UK

FLORA AND FAUNA
Using the postcode search, find out which plants are native to your
area, where to get seeds and then how to look after them once
they're in your garden. Sponsored by the Natural History Museum.

www.british-trees.com   UK

FORESTRY AND CONSERVATION
Comprehensive information on British trees plus a good set of
links and a list of books and magazines. For more information
on how to care for trees go to **www.trees.org.uk**

www.wildflowers.co.uk   UK

BRITISH WILDFLOWERS
An online store specialising in British wildflowers with advice on
how to grow them; there's also a search engine where you can find
the plants you need using common or Latin names. If you want a
wildlife-friendly garden try **www.wildlifegardening.co.uk** which is a
basic but informative site.

See also:
www.meadowmania.co.uk – another specialist but also offers
bulbs and plug plants.
www.wildseeds.co.uk – specialist suppliers of wild seeds
and grasses.

Specific Plants, Societies and Specialists

www.alpinegardensociety.org   UK

ALPINES
An informative site on Alpines with articles from the society
magazine, seed exchange, newsletter and shop. You can also
find out about their tours to the best Alpine territories.

www.discoveringannuals.com   UK

ANNUALS GALORE
Based on the successful book, this site offers information on
hardy annuals, half-hardy annuals, biennials and seed-raised
bedding plants of all kinds. There's an A–Z listing on the plants
and it tells you where you can buy them.

www.thecgs.org.uk
UK

COTTAGE GARDEN SOCIETY

The place to go if you want the picture-perfect cottage garden.
The site is quite basic but there's plenty of information to get
you started plus a seed exchange service via their magazine.

www.hardy-plant.org.uk
UK

HARDY PLANT SOCIETY

A society devoted to conserving the older, rare and unusual
garden plants. There's information about how you can get
involved, where their fairs are, plus a seed list and limited plant
information.

www.herbnet.com
US

G

GROWING AND COOKING HERBS

An American network specialising in herbs, with links to
specialists, and to trade and information sites. It can be hard
work to negotiate, but there's no doubting the quality of the
content – although the quality of the music is up for debate.
See also **www.herbsociety.co.uk**, which isn't a great site but
does contain some useful info.

www.nccpg.com
UK

CONSERVING PLANTS AND GARDENS

The National Council for the Conservation of Plants and
Gardens is responsible for maintaining the national plant
collections of which there are over 600. Here you can find out
about the NCCPG's conservation work and plant database and
how you can get involved.

www.rareplants.co.uk
UK

RARE PLANT NURSERY

A site developed by a specialist nursery, which is well illustrated,
and pretty comprehensive, it offers information on the plants and
can supply plants world-wide. Delivery costs vary.

www.rosarian.com
UK

ROSES

If you love roses or just need information on them, drop in here
for a good, long browse. See also **www.davidaustinroses.com**
the outstanding rose specialist and also the Royal National Rose
Society at **www.rnrs.org**

www.vegetable-gardening-club.com   UK
GROWING VEG
Lots of advice and help on growing most types of vegetables, with links and information on what tools to use, for seeds try **www.vegetableseedwarehouse.com** who offer a wide choice.

www.windowbox.com   US
CONTAINER GARDENING
A really good American site which is well worth a look if you're into container gardening in any form. It's well laid out and very well written with great ideas for unusual plant combinations. Worth a long browse.

Other specialists worth a look:
http://lockyerfuchsias.co.uk – good mail-order service from this Bristol-based company, supplying fuchsias.
www.brogdale.org – basically all you need to know about fruit grown in the UK.
www.citruscentre.co.uk – the place to go for your lemons, limes and more.
www.oaklandnurseries.co.uk – a specialist in showy but tender plants.
www.orchid.org.uk – home of the North of England Orchid Society with a well-illustrated site.
www.orchids.uk.com – attractive site and home of specialist grower Burham Nurseries and you can buy orchids online.
www.topiaryart.com – an online course with background on the subject.

Seed Specialists

www.chilternseeds.co.uk   UK

SEED SPECIALIST
Choose from over 5,000 different types of seeds with many unusual plants including organically grown seeds. Very easy to find the right plant, excellent.

See also:
www.suttons-seeds.co.uk – comprehensive offering with a money back guarantee and an easy-to-use site.
www.thompson-morgan.com – huge range, good advice and good value too.

Gardening Peripherals and Equipment

www.lawnmowersdirect.co.uk   UK
BUY A LAWNMOWER ONLINE
A retailer specialising in mowers and other power tools. You can browse the site by make and it's quick and easy to use, if a little basic. Delivery within the UK is free if you spend more than £50.

www.lightingforgardens.co.uk   UK
LIGHT UP YOUR GARDEN
A specialist that offers advice, ideas and a wide range of products to light up your garden, all on a nicely designed site.

www.agriframes.co.uk   UK
GARDEN STRUCTURES
An improved site, from probably the UK's leading supplier, which now shows off their wide range of non-plant garden products to good effect. There's everything here from pergolas, fruit cages, watering cans and lighting, plus information on their made-to-order service too.

www.simplygardeningtools.co.uk   UK
GARDEN TOOLS
A messy, bright site offering a wide range of tools and equipment and free delivery in the UK, plus a money back guarantee. See also **www.fredshed.co.uk** for reviews of the best products.

www.garden-sheds-online.co.uk   UK
SHEDS!
A company that is passionate about sheds. There is information to help you pick the right one and a good selection to choose from. For the lighter side of life in garden sheds, you should check out the bizarre but excellent **www.readersheds.co.uk**

www.watergardening-direct.co.uk   UK
WATER GARDENING PRODUCTS
Not a great web site, but it all works and there is a good range. You can order online and ask for advice too.

See also:
www.giantgamesales.co.uk – specialists in giant garden games.

TV Tie-ins and Celebrities

www.bbc.co.uk/gardening   UK
GARDENING AT THE BEEB
A set of web pages from the BBC site which offer a great
gardening magazine, featuring celebrities but mixed with helpful
advice and sections such as design inspiration, plant profiles,
ask the expert and today in your garden. You can sign up for
their free newsletter.

www.barnsdalegardens.co.uk   UK
GEOFF HAMILTON'S GARDEN
To many people the real home of Gardener's World, this site
tells you all about Barnsdale and has features about the garden,
Geoff and his work. There's also an online store selling a
limited range of products and a good set of gardening site links.

www.alantitchmarsh.com   UK
ALAN TITCHMARSH
Part of the Expert Gardener site with competitions, biographical
details, sponsored events and some gardening details.

Other important and well-known gardeners:
www.bethchatto.co.uk – find out about her garden and shop
for plants too.
www.gertrudejekyll.co.uk – devoted to the work of this
amazing woman.
www.kimwilde.com – news about what Kim has been up
to and what projects she's working on.

Visiting Gardens and Garden History

www.gardenvisit.com   UK
GARDENS TO VISIT AND ENJOY
With over 1,000 gardens listed world-wide, this site offers
information on all of them and each is rated for design, planting
and scenic interest with Sissinghurst scoring top marks. There's
also information on the history of gardening, tours and hotels
with good gardens.

See also:
http://hcs.osu.edu/history – from Ohio State University, the history
of horticulture through biographies of the most famous gardeners.

www.edenproject.com – for the grandest garden scheme of them all.

www.gardenhistorysociety.org – an overview of what the society is about and information on what they're up to, but little in the way of history bar a few articles.

www.greatbritishgardens.co.uk – good regional reference and guide that includes biographies of great British garden designers.

www.museumgardenhistory.org – based in Lambeth, this site offers details of the museum and the famous Tradescant family.

www.nationaltrust.org.uk – offering information on their gardens and places of interest.

www.ngs.org.uk   UK

NATIONAL GARDEN SCHEME

This is basically the famous yellow book converted into a web site with details on over 3,500 gardens to visit for charity and the work they undertake with the money they earn from your support. See also **www.gardensofscotland.org** which operates a similar scheme.

Gardeners With Special Needs

www.thrive.org.uk   UK

NATIONAL HORTICULTURAL CHARITY

This charity exists to provide expert advice on gardening for people with disabilities and older people who want to continue gardening with restricted mobility. The site gives information on how the charity works and links to related sites. See also **www.gardenforever.com** who offer lots in the way of horticultural therapy.

Gay and Lesbian

www.rainbownetwork.com   UK

LESBIAN & GAY LIFESTYLE

A very well thought out magazine-style web site catering for all aspects of gay and lesbian life. It primarily covers news, fashion, entertainment and health, but there's a travel agency as well. There are also forums and chat sections, classified ads as well as profiles on well-known personalities.

www.gayscape.com US

GAY SEARCH ENGINE
This isn't going to win design awards, but it is a useful and well categorised directory of over 102,000 sites. See also **www.queery.com** and for the UK only try the well-put-together **www.gayindex.co.uk**

For other good gay/lesbian sites try:
www.aegis.com – an excellent site giving the latest information on combating AIDS and HIV.
www.gaybritain.co.uk – excellent graphics, a gay portal site.
www.gaylifeuk.com – well-rounded magazine site with support and advice sections.
www.gaysports.com – wide-ranging sports site.
www.gaytravel.co.uk – gay travel guide, UK-oriented but with some good world-wide information.
www.glinn.com – the gay gateway to the web.
www.lesbianuk.co.uk – a good information site.
www.navigaytion.com – a travel specialist.
www.outintheuk.com – an excellent gay community site.
www.planetout.com – a good all-round magazine site.
www.proudparenting.com – interesting site aimed at helping gay and lesbian parents and their children.
www.stonewall.org.uk – campaigning for justice and equality for gay and lesbian people.
www.uk.gay.com – British page from the big American magazine site.

Genealogy

www.sog.org.uk UK

THE SOCIETY OF GENEALOGISTS
This is the first place to go when you're thinking about researching your family tree. It won't win awards for web design, but it contains basic information and there is an excellent set of links you can use to start you off. See also the excellent **www.cyndislist.com** where you'll find over 240,000 links in 150 categories to help with your family research.

www.pro.gov.uk UK

PUBLIC RECORD OFFICE

To quote them 'The Public Record Office is the national archive of England, Wales and the United Kingdom. It brings together and preserves the records of central government and the courts of law, and makes them available to all who wish to consult them. The records span an unbroken period from the 11th century to the present day'. The site is easy to use and the information is concisely presented and easy to access. See also **www.familyrecords.gov.uk** which can help enormously with tracing your family tree; the links selection is excellent.

www.census.pro.gov.uk UK

1901 CENSUS

You can search the database for free but for detailed information you have to pay using a rather odd system. Mapping is also available from the site to help with place names or boundary changes.

www.bbc.co.uk/history/familyhistory UK

WHO DO YOU THINK YOU ARE?

Loads of fascinating material on how to find out more about your family's history, plus articles on other people's journeys of self-discovery. Based on a radio series, there is also a useful factsheet on how to trace your ancestors at **www.bbc.co.uk/education/beyond/factsheets/surnames/surnames_intro.shtml**

www.origins.net UK

DEFINITIVE DATABASES

This site has information provided from the Society of Genealogists' records from Scotland going back to 1553 and from England going back to 1568, and unlike many other sites in this area, it's also well designed and easy to use. There are also search tips, access to discussion groups and a new section devoted to Ireland.

www.brit-a-r.demon.co.uk UK

THE OFFICIAL BRITISH ANCESTRAL RESEARCH SITE

For £435 they will research one surname or line, for £785 two or for £185 they will do a minimum of 7 hours' work. They guarantee results to four generations. Not as much fun as doing it yourself though.

www.genuki.org.uk   UK

> VIRTUAL LIBRARY OF GENEALOGICAL INFORMATION
> An excellent British-oriented site with a huge range of links to
> help you find your ancestors. There is help for those starting
> out, news, bulletin boards, FAQs on genealogy and a regional
> search map of the UK and Ireland.
>
> *Other useful sites that may help in your family research:*
> **www.achievements.co.uk** – a research outfit who have a track
> record working with TV companies, but who will also give you
> a quote to research your family tree.
> **www.britishorigins.com** – information from an excellent
> database for people tracking their relatives, some free access,
> but the full service costs.
> **www.familysearch.org** – The Church of Jesus Christ and the
> Latter-day Saints' excellent research site with good step-by-step
> information.
> **www.genealogypro.com** – a very comprehensive genealogists
> and genealogy services directory.
> **www.genfair.com** – a bookshop specialising in family history books.
> **www.gengateway.com** – claims to have the number one family
> tree making software.
> **www.historicaldirectories.org** – a collection of digitally reproduced
> directories for England and Wales from 1750 to 1919.
> **www.ihgs.ac.uk** – the Institute of Heraldic and Genealogical
> Studies offer information and help to research your family –
> a good place to start.
> **www.landsearch.me.uk** – find out who owned what property
> for a price.
> **www.morrigan.com** – specialist in Irish genealogy.
> **www.nla.gov.au/oz/genelist.html** – a starting point for Australians.
> **www.tartans.com** – resources for Scottish genealogists.

American Genealogy Sites

*Genealogy is a big deal in the US; here are some of the best and
most useful.*

www.accessgenealogy.com   US

> GENEALOGY WEB PORTAL
> A massive number of links and access to web rings from a
> number of different countries give this site 'must check out'
> status. It is biased towards an American audience but it's very
> useful nonetheless. See also another portal site
> **www.genealogyportal.com** which is less cluttered.

www.ancestry.com   US
NO 1 SOURCE FOR FAMILY HISTORY
This US-oriented site has 1 billion names and access to 3,000
databases. It's especially good if you're searching for someone
in the US or Canada. It offers some information for free, but for
real detail you have to join. How much you pay to find out
about your ancestors depends on what you wish to know.
Linked to this is the chat site **www.familyhistory.com** where
you can visit surname discussion groups.

www.surnameweb.org   US
ORIGINS OF SURNAMES
A great place to start your search for your family origins. On top
of the information about your name, there are thousands of
links and they claim 2 billion searchable records.

See also:
www.ellisislandrecords.org – records of all who entered the US
via Ellis Island.
www.genforum.com – a huge number of forums devoted to
specific family names, US oriented.
www.rootsweb.com – free genealogy site supported by
Ancestry.com with interactive guides and research tools.

Government

www.direct.gov.uk   UK

THE ENTRY POINT FOR GOVERNMENT INFORMATION
A massive portal for public service information. You can browse
information by topic 'Info about' or by audience group 'Info
for...'. Alternatively, you can use the 'Quick find' section to find
information on government services online, local councils,
statistics, public records and jobs. The newsroom service gives
the latest headlines on the public sector.

http://parliament.uk   UK

UK PARLIAMENT
A good site giving information on how parliament works, what's
on in the House of Commons, Hansard and a directory of MPs
and Peers, should you want to write, as well as links and
a glossary.

Other key links:

http://www.scottish.parliament.uk – for Scottish issues; to see live broadcasts of the parliament in action to go to **www.scottishparliamentlive.com**

http://younggov.ukonline.gov.uk – a good site aimed at explaining the workings of government to 11- to 18-year olds.

www.cabinet-office.gov.uk – how the Civil Service supports the government.

www.clicktso.com – The Stationery Office bookstore.

www.electoralcommission.org.uk – managing and modernising the electoral process in the UK.

www.localegov.gov.uk – the office of the Deputy Prime Minister and his projects.

www.number-10.gov.uk – send an e-mail to the Prime Minister or learn about the history of No.10 Downing Street.

www.parliamentlive.tv – the workings of Parliament broadcast live. Comes with a calendar of events too.

www.royal.gov.uk – for the monarchy.

www.ukmps.info – a definitive non-political portal for United Kingdom Members of Parliament.

www.wales.gov.uk – the National Assembly for Wales.

The Major Political Parties

www.conservatives.com – Conservative party.

www.labour.org.uk – Labour party.

www.libdems.org.uk – Liberal Democrats.

Foreign Governments and Political Bodies

http://europa.eu.int – the European Union.

www.congress.org – an excellent overview of the US. Congress and how it works.

www.europarl.eu.int – how the European Parliament works.

www.politicsonline.com – a messy and dense site with an overview of US politics.

www.ukmeps.info – information on Members of the European Parliament.

www.un.org – United Nations.

Activist and Monitoring

www.epolitix.com – an excellent political news site with lots
of links and the latest policy announcements.
www.fistfulofeuros.net – a blog site devoted to the goings on in the
Eurozone, with lots of contributions and some good writing too.
www.hrc.org – home of the Human Rights Campaign.
www.hrw.org – Human Rights Watch identifies corrupt
governments and provides information on where they are going
wrong.
www.liberty-human-rights.org.uk – Liberty, protecting human
rights and civil liberties.
www.spinwatch.org – an excellent guide to the murky world
of spin and corporate garbage.
www.theyworkforyou.com – everything MP's say is recorded,
find it here alongside a great deal of background information.
www.ukpol.co.uk – a good fortnightly political magazine.
www.writetothem.com – the easy way to contact your MP
or MEP, there's background information on them too.
www.yougov.com – get involved in polling and take part.

Greetings Cards

*What used to be free on the Internet is now largely charged for, and
most of the e-card sites now follow the trend, which wouldn't be so
bad except that you often have to search through a lot of rubbish to
get to the good ones...*

www.worldwidecards.com   UK
REAL CARDS TO REAL PEOPLE
Create your card and message and they'll send it for you, all for
£2.95 but virtual cards are free. For a similar service go to
www.moonpig.com who have personalised humorous cards to
create and buy.

www.bluemountain.com   US
E-CARDS
Blue Mountain has thousands of cards for every occasion; it's
easy to use but you have to subscribe to get the best designs.
There are all sorts of extras you can build in like photos, music,
cartoons and even voice messages.

See also:

www.egreetings.com – big range, busy design that gets on your nerves after a while.

www.greencardcompany.co.uk – Christmas cards on recycled paper, can provide bespoke designs.

www.greeting-cards.com – massive range and geared to the American market, not all free, masses of adverts.

www.jimpix.co.uk – excellent site for unusual and free e-cards, everything from interactive flash cards to ones with an anti-war message.

www.regards.com – nice design and the best bit is that it's free!

www.web-greeting-cards.com – massive selection and well categorised too.

http://cards.webshots.com   US

PHOTOS INTO CARDS

Part of the Corbis site, there's a great deal to choose from in the form of photographic and general cards.

www.nextcard.co.uk   UK

3-D CARDS

Send free three-dimensional cards using this site, there are great pictures of animals, sunsets and mountain scenery to choose from.

www.charitycards.co.uk   UK

 CONTRIBUTIONS TO CHARITY

Buy your cards here and give money to charity, this is traditionally a Christmas thing but Charitycards have turned it into an all-year-round possibility. They will also design and personalise Christmas cards. There are also discounts available and free postage if you buy in quantity, and they also sell stamps.

www.what2write.co.uk   UK

WHAT TO WRITE

A fairly cheesy site that offers suggestions for those situations where you can't think what to write in your card, you can also make suggested entries and send e-cards too.

Health and Fitness

Here are some of the key sites for getting good health advice,
featuring online doctors, fitness centres, nutrition and sites that try to
combine all three. As with all health sites, there is no substitute for
the real thing and if you are ill, your main port of call must be your
doctor. Dietary advice sites are listed on page 173, specialist sites
aimed at men on page 289 and for women on page 541. The advice
for parents, page 342 and teens, page 453 may also be useful.

General Health

www.nhsdirect.nhs.uk   UK

NHS ADVICE ONLINE
NHS Direct is a telephone advice service and this is the Internet
spin-off, it comprises of an excellent guide to common ailments with
the emphasis on treating them at home and a superb selection of
NHS-approved links covering specific illnesses or parts of the body.
There's also health information and an A–Z guide to the NHS.

www.nelh.nhs.uk   UK

NATIONAL ELECTRONIC LIBRARY FOR HEALTH
This programme is working with NHS Libraries to develop a
digital library for NHS staff, patients and the public; it is an
outstanding resource already and can only get better. It should
be the first port of call when researching.

See also:
www.avma.org.uk – an organisation working for better safety for
patients. If something goes wrong then this site is worth a visit.
www.doh.gov.uk – for the Department of Health's informative site.
www.helpthehospices.org.uk – information on how you can
support hospices and where to find one.
www.npsa.nhs.uk – the NHS Patient Safety Agency.
www.patients-association.com – an organisation campaigning
for patients' rights.

www.self-help.org.uk   UK

THE SELF-HELP DATABASE
A portal site devoted to providing a searchable database of self-help
and patient organisations in the UK. There are currently over
1,000 on file. You could also check out **www.ukselfhelp.info**
for similar information.

www.dipex.org   UK

PATIENT EXPERIENCES
An award-winning site devoted to showing you a wide variety
of personal experiences of illness, which covers over 100 from
cancers to mental health. The idea is to use Internet technology
to share information and experiences and to help fellow
sufferers get through their illness.

www.healthfinder.com   US

A GREAT PLACE TO START FOR HEALTH ADVICE
Run by the US Department of Health, this provides a link to
more or less every health organisation, medical and fitness site
you can think of. In several sections you can learn about hot
medical topics, catch the medical news, make smart health
choices, discover what's best for you and your lifestyle and use
the medical dictionary in the research section. The site is well
designed, fast once it's fully downloaded and very easy to use.

www.patient.co.uk   UK

FINDING INFORMATION FROM UK SOURCES
This excellent site has been put together by two GPs. It's
essentially a collection of links to other health sites, but from here
you can find a web site on health-related topics with a UK bias.
You can search alphabetically or browse within the site. All the
recommended sites are reviewed by a GP for suitability and
quality before being placed on the list. For a second opinion you
could visit **www.surgerydoor.co.uk**, which is more magazine-like
in style with up-to-the-minute news stories. It's comprehensive
and has an online shop. Also try the well-designed
www.netdoctor.co.uk who describe themselves as the 'UK's
independent health web site' and offer a similar service.

www.embarrassingproblems.co.uk   UK

FIRST STEP
An award-winning and much-recommended site that works
well; it's what the Internet should be about really. The site helps
you deal with health problems that are difficult to discuss with
anyone; it's easy to use and comprehensive. Younger people
and teenagers should also check out **www.coolnurse.com**
which is an excellent American site with similar attributes.

H

www.drkoop.com   US

THE BEST PRESCRIPTION IS KNOWLEDGE

Don't let the silly name put you off, Dr C Everett Koop is a
former US Surgeon General and is acknowledged as one of the
best online doctors. The goal is to empower you to take care of
your own health through better knowledge. The site is very
comprehensive covering every major health topic and is aimed
at all, including both young and old.

www.mayohealth.org   US

RELIABLE INFORMATION FOR A HEALTHY LIFE

Mayo has a similar ethic to Dr Koop but is less fussy and very
easy to use. However, the amount of information can be
overwhelming, as they claim the combined knowledge of some
2,000 doctors in the 21 'centers'. Essentially it's a massive
collection of articles that combine to give you a large amount of
data on specific medical topics. There are also guides on how
to live a healthy life, first aid and a newsletter, plus information
on specific medical conditions and diseases.

www.cellscience.com   UK

MEDICAL DICTIONARY

The dictionary covers Aids, HIV, cancer, cystic fibrosis and
diabetes. It's easy to use and contains listings for links,
hospitals and charities as well as other essential information.

www.quackwatch.com   US

HEALTH FRAUD, QUACKERY AND INTELLIGENT DECISIONS

Exposes fraudulent cures and old wives tales, then provides
information on where to get the right treatment. It makes
fascinating reading and includes exposés on everything from
acupuncture to weight loss. Use the search engine or just
browse through the site; many of the articles leave you amazed
at the fraudulent nature of some medical claims. See also the
National Council Against Health Fraud at **www.ncahf.org**

www.kidshealth.org   US

KIDS' HEALTH

An engaging American site with three areas, one for parents,
one for kids and one for teenagers with each having their
content adjusted and focused accordingly. The kids' section is
particularly effective with even quite complex illnesses and
personal issues explained well.

H

www.stjohnsupplies.co.uk   UK

FIRST AID AND MORE
Here at the St John's Ambulance Brigade shop you can buy
several first aid kits and all the health and safety equipment
you're ever likely to need.

For more health information:
http://medlineplus.gov – a health information centre from the
US National Library of Medicine.
www.24dr.com – a site from a UK doctor, lots of help with self
diagnosis and what appears to be a good medical encyclopedia.
www.bbc.co.uk/health – good all rounder covering lots of
topics, good links.
www.drugscope.org.uk – how to get information on drugs.
www.e-med.co.uk – 'your doctor wherever you go' is the strap
line for this site; it costs £20 to join then £15 per consultation.
www.gmc-uk.org – home of the General Medical Council, the
place to go if you have a problem with a doctor.
www.healthcyclopedia.com – a straightforward health portal
with comprehensive coverage.
www.hospitalweb.co.uk – an excellent medical search engine.
www.medterms.com – a straightforward glossary of medical terms.
www.nice.org.uk – the National Institute of Clinical Excellence
provides 'robust and reliable guidance on current health
best practise'.
www.studenthealth.co.uk – written by doctors, sensible and
funny with some good competitions.
www.vh.org – lots of information at the Virtual Hospital.

Private Health

www.bupa.co.uk   UK

BUPA HOMEPAGE
Health fact-sheets, special offers on health cover, health tips
and competitions are all on offer at this well-designed site. You
can also find your nearest BUPA hospital and instructions on
referral. See also **www.ppphealthcare.co.uk** who have over
150 fact-sheets available on a wide range of health conditions
located in the 'Health' section found in 'You and Your Family'.
See also **www.privatehealth.co.uk** a portal site devoted to all
things related to private health.

Medical Tourism

www.medicaltourism.co.uk   UK

MEDITOURISTS...
An interesting twist on the issue of hospital waiting lists, here
you can find out how to have your operation abroad and even
combine it with a holiday. See also **www.medplex.org**

Medicine and Pharmacy

www.allcures.com   UK

UK'S FIRST ONLINE PHARMACY
After a fairly lengthy but secure registration process you can shop
from this site which has all the big brands and a wide range of
products. There are also sections on toiletries, beauty, alternative
medicine and a photo-shop. You can arrange to have your
prescriptions made up and sent to you with no delivery charge.

See also:
www.boots.com – for prescriptions go to the 'pharmacy' then
use the free postal delivery service. There's also an A–Z of
common conditions and info on embarrassing problems.
www.mhra.gov.uk – the government department that deals
with safety in medicines.
www.mypharmacy.co.uk – good basic health site from a
real pharmacist, with a shop stocking a relatively wide range
of products.
www.pharmacy2u.co.uk – who have lots of offers and cover
lots of health areas, even a section on embarrassing problems.
Prescription service available.
www.postoptics.co.uk – eye-care products and contact lenses
by post.

Fitness and Exercise

www.netfit.co.uk   UK

DEFINITIVE GUIDE TO HEALTH AND FITNESS
Devoted to promoting the benefits of regular exercise with a
dedicated team who put a great deal of effort into the site. You can
gauge your fitness plus there's information on some 200 exercises,
tips on eating and dieting, nutrition advice and links to useful
(mainly sport) sites. If you don't like going it alone, they will even try

to link you up with a training partner in your area. For those hooked on the idea, they've introduced a membership scheme which promises to sculpt your body into shape – for $52 per year.

www.hfonline.co.uk   UK
HEALTH & FITNESS MAGAZINE
A spin-off site from the magazine, which offers the latest health news and advice; it's attractive and it's quite comprehensive.

www.fitnessonline.com   US
PROVIDING PERSONAL SUPPORT
This good-looking site is from an American magazine group. It takes a holistic view of health offering advice on exercise, nutrition and health products. In reality what you get is a succession of articles from their magazines, all are very informative but getting the right information can be time-consuming.

The following sites also offer good advice and information:
www.exercise.co.uk – a good health equipment store with information on exercise and choosing the right equipment.
www.exercisegroup.com – natural body building.
www.fitnesspeak.co.uk – the best prices for gym equipment but hard on the eyes.
www.thefitmap.com – a portal site for the UK's health and fitness clubs, find your nearest one.

Alternative Medicine and Therapies

www.altmedicine.com   US

ALTERNATIVE HEALTH NEWS
Keep up to date with the latest therapies and trends with articles and features from some of the key figures in the world of alternative medicine. The site is supplemented by an excellent medical search engine, an overview of the major philosophies and associated healing techniques plus a good set of related links.

www.therapy-world.co.uk   UK
THERAPY WORLD MAGAZINE
A well-put-together magazine covering many different types of therapies with a good overview of all of them and some interesting articles.

www.medical-acupuncture.co.uk
UK
ACUPUNCTURE
A good-looking site with information from the British Medical
Acupuncture Society on the nature of acupuncture and where
to find a practitioner in your area. There are also good links and
information on courses. See also **www.acupuncture.org.uk**
and also **http://accupuncture.com**

www.drlockie.com
US

HOMEOPATHY MADE EASY
An interesting, clear and simple site that offers sensible advice at all
levels. Click on any of the medicine jars to get to the relevant
sections on everything from basic information, products and links.

www.armaweb.com
US
AROMATHERAPY
A good information site on aromatherapy with lots of articles,
recipes and oil profiles.

H

Services

The Good Web Site Guide's Top 10s of the Internet

1. **www.businesslink.gov.uk** – if you're in business there's
    no site more helpful.
2. **www.uswitch.co.uk** – find the best household deals.
3. **www.flickr.com** – easy-to-use photo-sharing service.
4. **www.nhsdirect.nhs.uk** – if you're feeling unwell go here
    and get help.
5. **www.newsnow.co.uk** – outstanding news feed service.
6. **www.which.co.uk** – independent consumer advice.
7. **www.skype.com** – free internet telephony.
8. **http://eurekster.com** – a good place to check on your
    PC's vulnerability.
9. **www.over50.gov.uk** – invaluable resource for oldies.
10. **www.ottakars.co.uk** – have a conversation with your local
    book store.

www.thinknatural.com   UK

THINK NATURALLY
A nicely designed site with a mass of information on every
aspect of natural health including a comprehensive shop with
loads of special offers and a very wide range of products.

See also:
http://nccam.nih.gov – home of the US National Centre for
Complementary and Alternative Medicine, it's a good place
for research.
www.alternativemedicines.co.uk – use the ailment search to
find the right alternative products.
www.drweil.com – the vitamin guru has a site that offers much
in advice and his own brand of balanced living.
www.homeopath.co.uk – attractive site but still only partly
functional when we visited, good directory of homeopaths though.
www.homeopathyhome.com – slightly confusing but
comprehensive.
www.homeopathy-soh.org – home of the Society of Homeopaths.
www.interconnections.co.uk – up-to-date information on
living holistically.
www.internethealthlibrary.com – a good directory for
alternative health sites.

Yoga

www.yogauk.com   UK

YOGA
Welcome to the yoga village where you can get information on
yoga in the UK, subscribe to their magazine, or browse the
links section, which has a comprehensive list of stores.

See also:
www.bwy.org.uk – the British Wheel of Yoga.
www.calmcentre.com – calming experiences from Paul Wilson
and take the stress test.
www.iyengaryoga.org.uk – all about Iyengar yoga techniques.
www.mydailyyoga.com – simple yoga exercises.
www.yogaplus.co.uk – who offer courses and workshops.
www.yogatherapy.org – using yoga to cure.

Sites Catering For a Specific Condition or Disease

*Here is a list of the key sites relating to specific diseases and ailments, we have not attempted to review them, but if you know of a site we've missed and would like it included in the next edition of this book please e-mail us at **goodwebsiteguide@hotmail.com**. There is a separate section on cancer which follows our list. For sites relating to children see the section on parental concern on page 346.*

Acne
www.acne-advice.com
www.acne.org
www.m2w3.com/acne

AIDS and HIV
www.avert.org
www.hivstopswithme.org
www.tht.org.uk

Alcohol and Drug Abuse
www.al-anon-alateen.org
www.alcoholconcern.org.uk
www.alcoholics-anonymous.org

Allergies
www.allergy.co.uk
www.allergy-info.com (sponsored by Zyrtec)
www.allergyfoundation.com

Alzheimers and Dementia
www.alzheimers.org.uk
www.dementia.ion.ucl.ac.uk

Anxiety
www.anxieties.com
www.healthanxiety.com
www.anxietynetwork.com

Arthritis
www.aboutarthritis.com
www.arc.org.uk

Asthma
www.asthma.org.uk

Autism
www.nas.org.uk

Back and Spinal Problems
www.backpain.org
www.chirohelp.com
www.spinalnet.co.uk

Blindness
www.rnib.org.uk
www.sense.org.uk

Bowels and Bladder
www.continence-foundation.org.uk
www.digestivedisorders.org.uk
www.ibsnetwork.org.uk
www.incontact.org

Brain Disease and Injury
www.bbsf.org.uk
www.headway.org.uk

Breast Cancer Campaign
www.bcc-uk.org

Bullying
www.bullying.co.uk

Cancer
See page 238.

Cerebal Palsy
www.scope.org.uk

Chiropdy
www.drfoot.co.uk
www.feetforlife.org

Crohns Disease and Colitis
www.crohns.org.uk
www.nacc.org.uk

Deafness

www.britishdeafassociation.org.uk
www.rnid.org.uk
www.thehearingaidcouncil.org.uk

Death and Suicide

www.med.uio.no/iasp/
www.naturaldeath.org.uk
www.suicide-helplines.org
www.uk-sobs.org.uk

Dental

www.bda-dentistry.org.uk
www.dentalwisdom.com
www.gdc-uk.org

Depression

http://www.depressionalliance.org

H

Dermatology

www.skinhealth.co.uk

Gossip

The Good Web Site Guide's Top 10s of the Internet

1. www.popbitch.com – the first stop for conjecture.
2. www.salon.com – excellent and up-to-the-minute e-zine.
3. www.hollywood.com – over 1 million pages to choose from.
4. www.aintitcoolnews.com – the latest film gossip and reviews.
5. www.bollywoodworld.com – all you need on the world's
    biggest film industry.
6. www.celebhoo.com – find all the info on your favourite star
    at this directory.
7. www.debretts.co.uk – posh celebrity gossip.
8. www.thesmokinggun.com – if it's sleaze you're looking for,
    it's probably here.
9. www.mykindaplace.com – gossip and celebrity news
    for teenagers.
10. www.teamtalk.com – sports gossip.

Diabetics
www.diabetes-insight.info
www.diabetes.org.uk

Digestion
www.digestivecare.co.uk

Donation
www.blood.co.uk, www.scotblood.co.uk,
www.welsh-blood.org.uk, www.nibts.org
blood and bone marrow donation
www.uktransplant.org.uk – organ donation

Drugs
www.acde.org
www.drugs.gov.uk
www.release.org.uk

Eczema
www.eczema.org

Epilepsy
www.epilepsynse.org.uk
www.epilepsy.org.uk

Eyes
www.moorfields.org.uk

Fertility
www.ifconline.org
www.infertilitynetworkuk.com

Fibromyalgia
www.ukfibromyalgia.com

Gambling
www.gamblersanonymous.org.uk

Heart
www.bhf.org.uk
www.heartuk.org.uk
www.riskscore.org.uk

High Blood Pressure
www.hbpf.org.uk

Kidney Problems
www.kidney.org.uk

Liver Problems
www.britishlivertrust.org.uk

Lupus
www.lupusuk.com

Meningitis
www.meningitis-trust.org

Mental Health
www.mentalhealth.com
www.mind.org.uk
www.rcpsych.ac.uk
www.youngminds.org.uk

Migraine
www.migraine.org.uk
www.migrainetrust.org

Multiple Sclerosis
www.mssociety.org.uk

Older People
www.elderabuse.org.uk

Osteopathy
www.osteopathy.org.uk

Pain Management
www.pain-talk.co.uk

Plastic Surgery
www.baaps.org.uk

Psoriasis
www.psoriasis-association.org.uk

H

Repetitive Strain Injury
www.rsi.org.uk

Sexually Transmitted Diseases (STDS)
www.playingsafely.co.uk

Smoking
www.ash.org.uk
www.givingupsmoking.co.uk

Social, Personal and Emotional Support
www.samaritans.co.uk
www.shyness.com

Spina Bifida
www.asbah.org

Stress
www.isma.org.uk
www.stressrelease.com

Stroke
www.differentstrokes.co.uk
www.stroke.org.uk

Cancer

www.cancerhelp.org.uk   UK
   CANCER RESEARCH
   An overview of what causes cancer, its treatments and the
   latest news. You can also find out how to donate and details of
   ongoing clinical trials. See also the sister site at
   www.cancerresearchuk.org which has more information.

   See also:
   www.bowelcancer.org – a good overview with advice on
   prevention and what to do if you have the symptoms.
   www.breastcancercare.org.uk – very informative on breast cancer.
   www.breakthroughgenerations.org.uk – details of a major
   study on breast cancer.

www.cancerfacts.com – detailed information on most forms
of cancer.
www.cancer.gov – excellent site from the US health department.
www.goingfora.com – excellent site covering what happens
in oncology and radiology.
www.leukaemiacare.org.uk – useful support for sufferers of
the blood cancers including leukaemias, Hodgkin's and other
lymphomas.

History and Biography

*The Internet is proving to be a great storehouse, not only for the latest
news but also for cataloguing historical events in an entertaining and
informative way, here are some of the best sites.*

General History Sites

www.thehistorychannel.com   US

THE BEST SEARCH IN HISTORY
Excellent for history buffs, revision or just a good read, the
History Channel provides a site that is packed with information.
Search by key word or timeline, by date and by subject, get
biographical information or speeches. It's fast and easy to get
carried away once you start your search.

www.historyworld.net   UK

HISTORY WORLD
An outstanding site containing timelines, articles, quizzes and
tours all designed to educate and bring history to life in an
engaging and stimulating way, and it's successful. The OCEAN
historical index which was once part of this site has gone it
alone and now contains more than 35,000 precise links to
external sites. It can be found at **www.oceanindex.net**

www.historytoday.com   UK

WORLD'S LEADING HISTORY MAGAZINE
Contains some excellent articles from the magazine, but
probably the most useful bit is the related links section, which
offers many links to other history sites.

www.newsplayer.com   UK

RELIVE THE LAST CENTURY
Relive the events of the past hundred years, witness them at
first hand as they happened. A truly superb site with real
newsreel footage worth the £4 annual subscription fee. See
also the BBC's excellent site **www.bbc.co.uk/onthisday** where
you can see what happened on a particular day in history.
Strongly biased to the 20th century with film clips and eye
witness reports.

www.ukans.edu/history/VL   US

HISTORY LINKS
The folks at the University of Kansas love their history and have
put together a huge library, organised by country and historical
period. It's got an easy-to-use search engine too. For modern
history go to **www.fordham.edu/halsall/mod/modsbook.html**

http://history.about.com   US

HISTORY AT ABOUT.COM
A massive archive notably bringing history to life through the
use of eyewitness accounts of people who were actually there.
This site is excellent for most periods of history.

www.bl.uk   UK

THE BRITISH LIBRARY
An overview of who they are and what they provide, on the site
you can get information about the library and see some of their
key treasures such as the Magna Carta. Access the 'Turning the
Pages' project where you can virtually 'turn' the pages of
digitised manuscripts. There are several already available
including Leonardo's notebook, a charming Jane Austin text
and the Lindisfarne Gospels and more are planned.

www.nationalarchives.gov.uk   UK

DOWNLOAD YOUR HISTORY
From the Public Record Office, this site gives you the chance to
see digitised versions of over 1 million wills, ancient documents
and other important academic papers. You can also pre-order
documents for your visit to the centre in Kew.

www.pbs.org/commandingheights   US
GLOBAL ECONOMY
An outstanding site devoted to the explanation of how the global economy works, great for students of politics and history alike.

For more general history sites try these:
www.eyewitnesstohistory.com – containing a large catalogue of historical recollections both ancient and modern, takes the 'history through the eyes of those who lived it' approach.
www.historyhouse.com – excellent for history trivia and odd facts.
www.historylearningsite.co.uk – great for school, it covers Key Stage 3 and upwards.
www.sbrowning.com – create your own history timelines at this innovative site.
www.spartacus.schoolnet.co.uk – a useful history encyclopedia.
www.thehistorynet.com – a good resource from a US magazine site.

Listed here are a selection of specific sites or pages from larger university sites that cover specific periods in time, events or regions, they may not win design awards but the information they contain is usually comprehensive or sufficient to enable you to access more from elsewhere.

UK History

www.bbc.co.uk/history   UK
HISTORY INTERACTIVE
Part of the outstanding BBC site, here you can find sections covering all the important bits of British history. The site uses technology well and there are some good articles too. It also shows what's on TV and radio that's history related.

www.visionofbritain.org.uk   UK

BETWEEN 1801 AND 2001
A well designed and truly informative site which, using maps and statistics, tracks the development of Britain through 200 years. Just type in your postcode and you get access to lots of background information on your area such as industry, population, work and poverty. Excellent for schools and for those interested in local history.

See also:
www.britannia.com – an American site devoted to British History that offers a good overview of the subject.
www.britarch.ac.uk – a portal for British Archaeology.
www.british-history.com – a site offering sections on Roman Britain, 100 Year War, Wars of the Roses, English Civil War, Napoleonic Wars and the Second World War.
www.britainunlimited.com – biographies of 250 people who shaped Britain.
www.enrichuk.net – links to local and regional history projects throughout the UK.
www.history.uk.com – excellent directory and portal featuring some 28,000 sites.
www.lib.byu.edu/~rdh/eurodocs/uk.html – documents through history.
www.livinghistory.co.uk – effectively a portal site for those who love to re-enact history.

Royalty

www.royal.gov.uk   UK
THE BRITISH MONARCHY
A comprehensive and entertaining site with a very good overview of the history of the British monarchy. For more see also **www.royalty.nu** which is a bit of a mess but does offer information on other royal families.

Middle Ages and Before

www.netserf.org   US
MEDIAEVAL LIFE
Excellent and well-categorised portal site covering every conceivable aspect of life in the Middle Ages.

See also:
www.darkagestrust.org.uk – an attempt to recreate England as it was 1,000 years ago.
www.learner.org/exhibits/middleages – a good educational resource.
www.pastforward.co.uk/vikings – a directory of all things Viking.
www.postroman.info – a good overview of early mediaeval Britain.
www.regia.org – Anglo-Saxons, Vikings and Normans.

www.suttonhoo.org – information on the ship burial.
www.the-orb.net – who also cover European history in
mediaeval times.
www.vikingsword.com – a sword expert's view, not only of Viking
weaponry but also of swords generally, good links section.

www.essentialnormanconquest.com   UK

THE NORMANS
A good-looking site from Osprey Publishing, which features a
1066 timeline, and blow-by-blow account of the conquest. It's
got some good maps and a quiz too.

See also:
www.bayeuxtapestry.org.uk – a scene-by-scene explanation
of the Bayeux Tapestry.
www.normanconquest.co.uk – an old site being updated but
still useful.
www.wsu.edu:8080/~dee/ma/normans.htm – a dry overview.

The Tudors to the Georges

www.warsoftheroses.com   UK

WARS OF THE ROSES
Excellent site covering the period 1450 to 1490 with all its
turmoil and politics, it also has a good timeline and links.

www.tudorhistory.org   UK

TUDOR FAMILY TREE
A basic but informative site with a who's who of Tudor times
with background information on what it was like to live then.

See also:
http://tudors.crispen.org – a period-by-period overview, turn
the sound off if you don't like Tudor music.
www.elizabethi.org – a great biographical site with a good deal
of background on Elizabethan life as well.
www.renaissance.dm.net – the Renaissance was an amazing
time and, while this site doesn't cover it that well, it does have
a good links section; it's also very oriented towards England.
www.tudorgroup.co.uk – re-enacting Tudor and Elizabethan times.

www.pepysdiary.com

UK

DIARY OF SAMUEL PEPYS

Put together by an aficionado of Pepys, this is updated daily
with an entry from the diaries on the day he wrote them over
340 years ago. Apart from the fascinating social history there's
lots of annotation, explanation and cross referencing too, as
well as audio readings, which all help you to picture the scene.

See also:

www.cannylink.com/history17thcentury.htm – a list of articles
on important 17th century events.
www.gunpowder-plot.org – interesting site devoted to the
happenings that surround the Gun Powder Plot of 1605.

www.olivercromwell.org

UK

OLIVER CROMWELL

A detailed biography of the man and his times. There's
background on the civil wars too and a guide to places linked
with him that you can visit.

See also:

www.ecwsa.org – the English Civil War Society of America
with a good site with lots of detail, articles and links.
www.open2.net/civilwar – detailed information on the English
Civil War.

www.georgianindex.net

UK

ALL THINGS GEORGIAN

A scrappy site but one with a wide range of information on
Georgian times, what it was like to live then and what events
took place.

See also:

http://dspace.dial.pipex.com/mbloy/c-eight/18chome.htm
– a very detailed site on George III and what events took place
during his reign.
http://regencygarderobe.com – regency fashion.
www.elizabethpowell.net – a good overview of the Regency
Period via the Regency ring.
www.royal-stuarts.org – the placing of the Stuart monarchy
in history with a strong Scottish bias.

The Victorians and Empire

www.victorianweb.org   UK

VICTORIANS EXPLAINED
Background on events, social and political history, biographies
and even entertainment, it's all here.

See also:
http://victorianresearch.org – a scholarly site but with
excellent material.
www.hiddenlives.org.uk – essentially a graphic account of the lives
of the children looked after by the Waifs and Strays Society but it's
also an incredibly interesting insight into Victorian Britain.
www.victorians.org.uk – for information on the daily lives of
the Victorians.
www.victorianstation.com – everything from architecture
to shopping.

www.britishempire.co.uk   UK

THE BRITISH EMPIRE
A thorough walk through the Empire with articles, maps and
sections on science, arts and military power that round
everything off. It also has a useful timeline, just to put
everything in context.

See also:
http://homepage.ntlworld.com/haywardlad – a slow but pretty
comprehensive site on the rise and fall of the Empire.
http://regiments.org – an overview of the land forces who
served the Empire and Commonwealth.

The 20th Century

*There doesn't seem to be one really good site dedicated to the UK's
20th century history although many of the larger history sites major
on the 20th century anyway. Those listed below do a great job in
bringing history to life whilst informing us about the historical details.*

www.1940.co.uk – remembering the 40s, a nice site and shop.
www.bbhq.com/sixties.htm – a very ugly site but lots of info
on the 60s.

www.bergen.org/AAST/Projects/ColdWar/index2.html – a chilling
reminder of what it was like to live through the Cold War.
www.britishpathe.com – Pathe films covered most of the major
events of the century and you can buy and see clips here.
www.fiftiesweb.com – entertaining overview of the decade's
events and culture.
www.greatwar.co.uk – a well-laid-out site on the 1914–18 war.
www.holnet.org.uk – the history of London.
www.movinghere.org.uk – a history of migration to England.
www.sixties.net – a bright and breezy stroll through the 60s.

World History

Ancient History

www.ancientsites.com   US

ANCIENT SITES
Seven key times and sites are featured and you must subscribe
to get the best out of it. The whole thing is a little long winded
although worth the faffing around as you get access to lots of
background information and social history. You can also chat to
fellow members.

www.ancientcivilisations.co.uk   UK

INTERACTIVE HISTORY
An outstanding site design from the British Museum. You choose a
theme from the map: cities, religion, buildings, technology, writing or
trade; this provides you with a short overview plus a timeline which
you can stop at any point to get the information you need. If you
want real detail, then go to a specialist site; however, this site
provides sufficient information to start you off.

www.anthro.net   US

ANTHROPOLOGY
Masses of links in this well-categorised site which covers
everything from Ancient Egypt to Ethnomathmatics!

Africa

www.thebanmappingproject.com   US

THEBES AND THE VALLEY OF THE KINGS
A great and genuinely interesting site devoted to life in ancient

Thebes in what is now Egypt, with over 200 interactive maps, narrative tours and 3-D features. Excellent.

See also:
http://royalafricansociety.org – the Royal African Society promotes the continent and its many causes, useful for links and current affairs.
www.africainformation.net – a useful site with plenty of links to help when researching African history.
www.columbia.edu/cu/lweb/indiv/africa/cuvl – Columbia University's comprehensive African studies pages.
www.eternalegypt.org – excellent and accessible site covering 5,000 years of Egyptian history with lots of interaction and information too.
www.fordham.edu/halsall/africa/africasbook.html – excellent database of sources and links covering African history from the Ancient Egyptians to Nelson Mandela.
www.newton.cam.ac.uk/egypt – the excellent Egyptology resource.

Asia

http://coombs.anu.edu.au/WWWVL-AsianStudies.html

ASIAN STUDIES
Basically a selection of links that cover the whole of Asia by country, region and centre.

See also:
http://depts.washington.edu/chinaciv – lots of information on China with an excellent timeline.
http://sun.sino.uni-heidelberg.de/igcs – more links on China than you'll ever need.
http://web.uccs.edu/history/globalhistory/japan.html – Japanese history covered.
www.1421.tv – interesting site from people who have proved that the Chinese 'discovered' and mapped the world before the Europeans.
www.asianinfo.org/asianinfo/korea/history.htm – an outline of Korean history.
www.asterius.com/china – a good basic overview of Chinese history.
www.fordham.edu/halsall/india/indiasbook.html – excellent overview of India's history.

Australasia

www.academicinfo.net/histaus.html   AUSTRALIA

AUSTRALIA

A pretty good directory of sites relating to Australian history
ancient and modern. There's an explanation and review of each
site featured.

See also:

www.awm.gov.au – Australian war memorials.
www.enzed.com/hist.html – useful overview of
New Zealand's past.
www.pvs-hawaii.com/history.htm – a history of Polynesia from
the Polynesian Voyaging Society.

Europe

www.hartford-hwp.com/archives/60   UK

EUROPE AS A WHOLE

A directory of links and articles covering the whole of Europe
and its history, the selection can be a bit disparate, but there
is a search facility on the main site.

France

http://chnm.gmu.edu/revolution – the French Revolution
explored, this site offers a huge amount of information.
www.napoleonguide.com – an outstanding site on Napoleon
and his times, with lots of background information and links to
related subjects.
www.napoleonic-literature.com – a very good site about
Napoleon and the effect he had on Europe, with background on
the battles and his writing.

Germany

www.tau.ac.il/GermanHistory/links.html – a chronological set of
links and articles covering German history from ancient times.

Greece

www.ancientgreece.com – an excellent site devoted to all
aspects of Ancient Greece.
www.mythweb.com – all the Greek myths illustrated in a fun
and entertaining way.

Ireland

www.irelandstory.com/today/main.html – from prehistory to
the Anglo-Irish agreement.
www.ucc.ie/celt – excellent resource on Irish historical events,
literature and politics too.

Italy

www.arcaini.com/italy/italyhistory/ItalyHistory.html – a good
chronological history of Italy from pre-history to the 20th century.
www.roman-empire.net – excellent site covering all aspects
of the Roman Empire with a good kids' section.

Russia

www.barnsdle.demon.co.uk/russ/rusrev.html – an interesting
site covering the events surrounding the Russian Revolution.
www.departments.bucknell.edu/russian/history.html
– complete overview and chronology of Russian History,
and they've taken the trouble to make the site look good too.

Spain

www.sispain.org/english/history – a chronology of Spanish
history with links.
www.users.dircon.co.uk/~warden/scw/scwindex.htm
– the Spanish Civil War.

Turkey

www.friesian.com/turkia.htm – a dense, text-heavy overview
of the Ottoman Empire.

Latin America

http://users.snowcrest.net/jmike/latin.html   US

LATIN AMERICAN LINKS
An outstanding collection of links, categorised by country and region
covering Latin and South America and also the Caribbean.

http://users.snowcrest.net/jmike/latin.html   US

ANCIENT MEXICO
A beautifully illustrated site covering ancient Mexico and the
Mayan and Aztec empires; there are also similar sister sites on
Chile and Peru.

Middle East

www.albany.edu/history/middle-east   US

HISTORY IN THE NEWS
A very good resource site with lots of documents, articles and
links plus a chronology and social background on the Middle
East and its tormented past.

See also:
www.al-bab.com/arab/history.htm – a good overview of Arab
history with links and articles.
www.fordham.edu/halsall/ancient/asbook05.html – all you
need on ancient Persia.
www.prc.org.uk/palestine%2048/history.html – an account of
Palestinian history.

www.hum.huji.ac.il/dinur   US

JEWISH HISTORY RESEARCH CENTRE
This site is a little difficult to navigate and use but it does offer
some 6,000 links which are well categorised, it covers biblical
history too. See also **www.cjh.org** the Center for Jewish History:
well illustrated with a US bias.

http://yadvashem.org   ISRAEL

THE HOLOCAUST
A moving and well-put-together site from the Holocaust Martyrs
and Heroes Remembrance Society. There are thousands of
photographs and accounts, all of which make a visit here pretty
moving, to say the least.

North America

http://americanhistory.about.com   US

ABOUT AMERICA
Just about all you'll be needing on American history from the
ever excellent About.com; it's well categorised with links and
related articles too.

See also:
http://earlyamerica.com – the chronicling of the early history
of America.
http://memory.loc.gov/ammem – excellent collection of articles,
micro-sites and links from the American Library of Congress.

www.brightmoments.com/blackhistory – excellent African American history site.

www.historybuff.com – entertaining site that uses old. newspaper coverage to illustrate aspects of US history.

www.historyplace.com – good for articles, features and links.

www.timearchive.com – *Time* magazine's archive is excellent but you have to subscribe.

Biography

www.biography.com   US

FIND OUT ABOUT ANYONE WHO WAS ANYONE
Over 25,000 biographical references and some 4,000 videos make this site a great option if you need to find out about someone in a hurry. There are special features such as a book club and a magazine. There is a shop but at the time of going to press they don't ship to the UK.

See also:

http://almaz.com/nobel/nobel.html – a fascinating site about the people who have won the Nobel prize.

www.fordham.edu/halsall – a messy site presenting copies of history source books that are freely available for use.

www.royalty.nu – the world of royalty: historical and recent.

www.rulers.org – an amazing database providing a list of the rulers of every country going back to 1700.

www.s9.com/biography – a biographical dictionary covering the lives of over 28,000 people!

www.who2.com – a good biography portal site that covers celebrities as well as the historically famous.

www.whosaliveandwhosdead.com – basically a list of celebrities cross referenced by what they did. It shows who's alive, who died and when. Morbidly fascinating.

Visual History

www.francisfrith.co.uk   UK

HISTORY IN PHOTOGRAPHS
This remarkable archive was started in 1860 and there are over 365,000 photographs featuring some 7,000 cities, towns and villages. The site is very well designed with a good search facility. You can buy from a growing selection of gifts, photos, maps and now aerial shots too; different sizes are available and

it's pretty good value too. See also **www.photolondon.org.uk** where you'll find an excellent photo archive of the capital.

www.old-maps.co.uk   UK

OLD MAPS

Access to mapping as it was between 1846 and 1899, just type in your town and you get a view of what it looked like in those times. The quality is variable but it's fun to try and spot the changes. See also **www.alangodfreymaps.co.uk**

www.museumofcostume.co.uk   UK

COSTUME THROUGH THE AGES

Excellent site showing how the design of costume has changed through the ages. There's a virtual tour and links to other museums based in Bath.

Other History-related Sites

www.findagrave.com   US

FIND A GRAVE!

Find graves of the rich and famous or a long-lost relative, either way there's a database of over 3 million to search. It really only covers the US.

www.the-reenactor.co.uk   UK

TAKE PART IN A BATTLE

OK so you feel the urge to play at being a Viking for the day, well here's where to start. The site lists some 90 societies to join and play a part in. It is divided into sections according to time period and you can find out where re-enactments are taking place, plus the latest news.

www.uchronia.net   US

ALTERNATIVE HISTORIES

A bibliography and review site featuring almost 2,500 books that in some way or another scope out alternative histories. It makes interesting reading – the 'what if' scenario fascinates most historians after all.

Hobbies

www.yahoo.co.uk/recreation/hobbies   UK

IF YOU CAN'T FIND YOUR HOBBY THEN LOOK HERE
Hundreds of links for almost every conceivable pastime from
amateur radio to urban exploration, it's part of the Yahoo
service (see page 396). Also try **www.about.com/hobbies**,
who have a similarly large list but with an American bias.

See also:
www.allcrafts.net – a wide-ranging directory covering all the
major crafts and many minor ones. Very good links pages.
www.hobbywebguide.com – a modest list with some good
hobby sites.

www.save-on-crafts.com   US

SAVINGS EVERYWHERE YOU LOOK
An excellent craft supply and interiors store covering an
extensive range of crafts and merchandise. It's well worth a
browse and good for the unusual but shipping is expensive.

www.cass-arts.co.uk   UK

ONE STOP SHOP FOR ART MATERIALS
A huge range of art and craft products available to buy online,
also hints and tips and step-by-step guides for the novice. There
is an online gallery and a section of art trivia and games. The
shop has a decent search engine which copes with over 20,000
items, delivery is charged according to what you spend.

See also:
www.artdiscount.co.uk – good value and a wide range on offer.
www.pictureframes.co.uk – show off your masterpiece to
best effect.

www.codcottage.freeserve.co.uk   UK

CALLIGRAPHY
A good introduction into calligraphy with lots of advice and help
as well as links to related sites. See also **www.calligraphy.co.uk**
who also have lots of links.

www.hobbycraft.co.uk   UK
ARTS AND CRAFTS SUPERSTORE
A nice retro feel to this site with a wide selection of inspirational
ideas and information on what they sell and where their shops
are, sadly you can't buy online.

www.sewandso.co.uk   UK
SHOP AT THE SPECIALISTS
This site offers a huge range of kits and patterns for cross-stitch,
needlepoint and embroidery. In addition, there's an equally large
range of needles and threads, some 20,000 products in all. There
are some good offers and delivery starts at £1 for the UK, but the
cost is calculated by weight. It's also worth checking out the
specialist pages at About.com **http://knitting.about.com** and
http://sewing.about.com and if you're a quilter seeking inspiration
visit **www.fatquartershop.com**

www.whaleys-bradford.ltd.uk   UK
FANTASTIC FABRICS
Whether you're looking for a simple cotton lawn, a shot taffeta,
or fabrics for the theatre, Whaley's have it all – and they will
send you up to 10 samples free of charge. There is a useful
A–Z of fabrics and a good search facility. There is a choice of
delivery options. Also see **www.online-fabrics.co.uk** who also
have a good selection.

www.horology.com   UK
THE INDEX
The complete exploration of time, this is essentially a set of
links for the committed horologist. It's pretty comprehensive, so
if your hobby is tinkering about with clocks and watches, then
this is a must.

www.jigboxx.com   CANADA
JIGSAWS
Excellent for jigsaw enthusiasts, there's a wide range, a search
facility, plus loyalty scheme and you can be kept abreast of the
latest designs too. Delivery charges vary.

www.royalmint.com   UK

THE VALUE OF MONEY
The Royal Mint's web site is informative, providing a history of

the Mint, the coins themselves, plus details on the coins they've issued. You can buy from the site and delivery is free.

See also:
http://coins.to – US coins and much more from the Austin Coin Collecting Society.
www.coinclub.com – good for information and links.
www.coinlink.com – a good directory devoted to all things numismatic.
www.tclayton.demon.co.uk/coins.html – Tony Clayton's informative home page on coins.
www.telesphere.com/ts/coins/faq.html – commonly asked questions about coin collecting.
www.tokenpublishing.com – owners of *Coin News.*

www.stanleygibbons.com   UK

STAMPS ETC.
The best prices and a user-friendly site for philatelists. You can buy a whole collection or sell them your own. Their catalogue is available online and you can take part in auctions.

See also:
www.corbitts.com – auctioneers for stamps, coins, notes and medals.
www.duncannon.co.uk – for accessories and albums.
www.postcard.co.uk – home of the Postcard Traders Association.
www.robinhood-stamp.co.uk – for good prices and range.
www.stamp.co.uk – excellent resource for all stamp collectors.
www.stampsatauction.com – a good auction site devoted to stamps.
www.ukphilately.org.uk/abps – information on exhibitions and events at the Association of British Philatelic Societies.

www.themodelmakersresource.co.uk   UK

MODEL MAKING MATERIALS
A wide range of tools, materials, kits and other modelling essentials here, plus lots of information and links, some good prices too.

www.towerhobbies.com   US

EXCITING WORLD OF RADIO-CONTROLLED MODELLING
An excellent, clearly laid out site offering a vast range of radio-

controlled models along with thousands of accessories and parts. The delivery charge depends on the size of the order.

See also:
www.ehobbies.com – large US retailer with an international division where you'll find a wide range of models, kits and radio-controlled cars
www.fusionhobbies.com – for cars and tanks.
www.otherlandtoys.co.uk – radio-controlled gifts and gadgets too.
www.rchobby.co.uk – British-based shop with plenty of choice to buy by mail order.

www.brmodelling.com   UK
BRITISH RAILWAY MODELLING
A high-quality magazine site devoted to model railways, it includes a virtual model set for you to play with and articles on specific types of trains and railways. There's also a forum where you can chat to fellow enthusiasts.

See also:
www.corgi.co.uk – home of the leading model car maker.
www.modelboats.co.uk – a model boat magazine.
www.toysoldier.freeuk.com – informative site devoted to toy soldiers.
www.ukmodelshops.co.uk – a directory, mainly railways oriented.
www.wingsandwheels.co.uk – model aircraft specialists.

www.ontracks.co.uk   UK
MODEL AND HOBBY SUPERSTORE
They sell over 35,000 models and hobby items, but it's tricky to find what you want as the site is a bit messy with lots of annoying graphics. Having said that there are some good special offers and delivery prices are reasonable.

www.woodworking.co.uk   UK
WORKING WITH WOOD
A good amateur site offering loads of information about all aspects of woodworking. There's a gallery of work from featured craftsmen plus advice for beginners. The home page contains a link to **www.toolpost.co.uk** where you can get all your tools.

Home and Do-It-Yourself

The web doesn't seem a natural home for do-it-yourself, but there are some really useful sites, some great offers on tools and equipment and plenty of sensible advice.

Superstores

www.diy.com   UK

THE DIY SUPERSTORE
> B&Q has a bright and busy site with lots of advice, inspiration, tips and information on projects for the home and garden. It also has an excellent searchable product database. There are also plenty of offers and the store has a good selection of products covering all the major DIY areas. Delivery costs vary according to how much you buy and how fast you want it. Returns can be made to the stores. You need to be able to accept cookies before the site can operate effectively or before you place an order.

www.wickes.co.uk   UK

> DIY SPECIALISTS
> Good ideas, inspiration and help are the key themes for this site; it's easy to use and genuinely helpful with well laid out project details. You can visit their showrooms for product information and download leaflets on a wide variety of domestic jobs. There's a handy calculator section where you can work out how many tiles or rolls of wallpaper you may need.

www.focusdoitall.co.uk   UK

> FOCUS DO-IT-ALL
> A functional site, which attempts to put over lots of ideas and inspiration, it also carries a wide range of products at good prices. Delivery is £4.99 on most items and you can return unwanted goods to your nearest store.

> *Other DIY stores worth checking out are:*
> **www.buildbase.co.uk** – good site for the professional.
> **www.decoratingdirect.co.uk** – functional and easy-to-use site that concentrates on home décor products at excellent prices.
> **www.homebase.co.uk** – site was being redeveloped at time of writing (as indeed it was last year) but there is plenty of information on their product ranges.

www.jewson.co.uk – Jewson's site is more corporate than anything but it does have a small section on each part of the house and how they can help.

Buying Tools and Equipment

www.screwfix.com   UK

PRODUCTS FOR ALL DIY NEEDS

Rightly considered to be one of the best online stores, Screwfix offer excellent value for money with free delivery on orders over £45 and wholesale prices on a massive range of DIY products.

www.cooksons.com   UK

TOOLS A-PLENTY

An award-winning site from this Stockport firm, it has a huge number of tools and related products available, with free delivery on orders over £45. There are plenty of special offers and a loyalty scheme for regulars.

www.draper.co.uk   UK

QUALITY SINCE 1919

An attractive site that is easy to use, the only downside being that you have to have the latest downloads for it to work effectively. If you're a regular visitor and know the stock number of the item you want there's a good fast-track service too.

www.diytools.co.uk   UK

MORE TOOLS

Another well-designed and extensive tool store with a huge range of products, there's also free delivery for orders over £50. Also check out **www.blackanddecker.co.uk** who have lots of advice on how to use power tools correctly, and also the slow but thorough **www.worldofpower.co.uk** who also supply garden equipment, plus quad bikes and other motorised toys.

Tool Hire

www.hss.co.uk   UK

WHERE YOU CAN HIRE ALMOST ANYTHING

A useful site where you can organise the rental of a huge range of tools and equipment, it's great for those one-off jobs.

Trade Information

www.fmb.org.uk   UK

THE FEDERATION OF MASTER BUILDERS
Get advice on avoiding cowboys and on getting the best out of a
builder. There's information and articles on most aspects of home
maintenance, plus hints on finding reputable help.

See also:
www.buildersguild.co.uk – who also offer much in the way
of information.
www.qualitymark.org.uk – covering the government's scheme
to ensure the reliability of tradesmen and search for those
willing to work in your area.

Advice and DIY Encyclopedias

www.hometips.com   US

EXPERT ADVICE FOR YOUR HOME
American the advice may be, but there is plenty here for every
homeowner. The site is well laid out and the advice good.
Alternatives are **www.naturalhandyman.com** which is fun,
or the extensive **www.doityourself.com** which is very detailed.

www.diyfixit.co.uk   UK

ONLINE DIY ENCYCLOPEDIA
Get help with most DIY jobs using the search engine or browse
by room or job type. The information is good especially now
they've added more illustrations.

See also:
www.diyfaq.org.uk – practical information form this UK-based
forum site.
www.diynot.com – a good all-rounder, encyclopedia, forums
and DIY help.
www.diystickit.co.uk – from a glue manufacturer using glues
to solve problems.
www.finddiy.co.uk – a list of DIY sites.
www.fourwalls.co.uk – DIY sites listed and reviewed.
www.freddyfixit.co.za – DIY help from South Africa.
www.homedoctor.net – an American site with lots of homey tips.
www.ukdiyguide.co.uk – a useful DIY site listing.

Building and Improving on Your Home

For further information and advice on finding and using an architect, refer to the section on Architecture, page 25.

www.ebuild.co.uk   UK

BUILD YOUR OWN HOUSE
All the information and contacts you need if you're thinking of buying that plot of land and getting stuck in. There's also a continually updated list of what plots of land are available and where.

The following sites will also prove useful if you're out to build your own:
www.bricksandbrass.co.uk – the place to go if you have a period home to renovate.
www.builditthisway.co.uk – a good overview from a retired builder on what it takes to build your own house.
www.bwpda.co.uk – home of the British Wood Preserving and Damp Proofing Association, with a 'find a contractor' service.
www.homebuilding.co.uk – a spin off from a magazine, lots of resources and information.
www.planning.odpm.gov.uk – the Office of the Deputy Prime Minister has information on the latest government initiatives on planning.
www.planningportal.gov.uk – a huge and very useful resource about planning regulations, with advice and a guide to the process.
www.plotfinder.net – find a spot to build your dream home but you have to subscribe.
www.selfbuildcentre.com – a pretty annoying design but lots of links and advice make it worth a visit.
www.selfbuildit.co.uk – help for first timers.

Salvage

www.salvo.co.uk   UK

SALVAGE AND RECLAMATION
Salvo provides information on where to get salvaged and reclaimed architectural and garden antiques. The site is comprehensive and easy to use with interesting information such as what buildings are due to be demolished and when, so you can be ready and waiting.

Conservatories

www.conservatoriesonline.co.uk   UK

ALL YOU NEED TO KNOW ABOUT CONSERVATORIES
A good portal site which offers links and advice on conservatories,
sunrooms, garden rooms and solariums. There's a buyer's guide
plus information on materials, styles, even on pools and orangeries.

See also:
www.advisoryservice.co.uk – home of the Conservatory and
Windows Advisory Service, a good place to go for getting advice
on the right sort of materials to use.
www.conservatories-direct.co.uk – a good, comprehensive site
from this specialist.
www.diy-conservatories-uk.co.uk – all you need if you want to
erect your own.

Plumbing, Bathroom and Kitchen

www.plumbworld.co.uk   UK

AN ONLINE PLUMBING SHOP
Good selection of plumbing tools at competitive prices. Not
exactly the most informative site as you have to assume much,
for example, there's very little information about shipping
which, incidentally, is free to most of the UK when you spend
£50 or more.

See also:
www.plumbers.co.uk – if you need to find a plumber try the
directory of plumbers.
www.plumbnet.com – for information on how to do work yourself.
www.registeredplumber.com – home of the Institute of
Plumbing with a member directory and their code of practise.

www.bathroomexpress.co.uk   UK

BETTER BATHROOMS
A wide range of bathrooms and accessories are available at
decent prices, with some interesting luxury items such as
après-shower driers and some unique toilet seats. Delivery is
based on how much you spend. See also **www.bathroom-
association.org** and **www.thebathroomaccessoryshop.com**

www.alarisavenue.co.uk   UK

KITCHENS AND CANE
A beautifully designed store that offers much in the way of
inspiration and quality products for the kitchen.

www.toppstiles.co.uk   UK

TILES
You can't get tiles delivered but there's a shop-finder service
and details of available ranges including floor tiles.

See also:
www.digitile.co.uk – find out about how to get custom-made tiles.
www.taylortiles.co.uk – a wide range and sample ordering service.
www.tiles.org.uk – home to the Tile Association and full of
good advice.

Doors

www.handlesdirect.co.uk   UK

HANDLES GALORE
A functional site where you can buy, well, handles. It's also got
a selection of locks, switches and sockets that match certain
handles. The emphasis is on contemporary style, and there's a
good advice section which shows you how to fit them. See also
www.diytools.co.uk who offer a wide range including security
products in their 'knobs and knockers' section.

www.doorsdirect.co.uk   UK

DOORS AND HANDLES
Features replacement doors for kitchens and bathrooms, you
can order made-to-measure or standard and there's a selection
of fittings as well.

www.locksmiths.co.uk   UK

FINDING A LOCKSMITH
A useful site where you can get help to find a locksmith in your
area and some advice on home security.

Paint and Wallpaper

www.decoratingdirect.co.uk UK

DECORATING MATERIALS
A really well-designed store offering a very wide range of
decorating products, it's simple to use and fast. Orders are free
when you spend more than £50 and it will save a trip to one
of those huge DIY stores, or is it just me that hates them?
Check out the refund policy before you buy though.

www.dulux.co.uk UK

DULUX
A good-looking, interesting but slow site from Dulux, with a
'mouse painter' that you can use to redecorate a number of
pre-selected rooms, there's also product information, and top
tips on painting techniques. You can't buy from the site
although there is a list of stockists. Crown has a similar but less
interactive site that can be found at **www.crownpaint.co.uk**

www.farrow-ball.co.uk UK

TRADITIONAL PAINT AND PAPER
Excellently designed web site featuring details on how their
paint and paper is manufactured – something they obviously
take pride in. You can also order from the site or request
samples. For that traditional Mediterranean look try
www.casa.co.uk who have a good selection and a nice site.

www.paintquality.co.uk UK

PAINT QUALITY INSTITUTE
A very attractive site from a company that specialises in testing
paints. There's information on choosing the right type of paint
with decorating tips, a calculator and glossary.

www.sanderson-online.co.uk UK

CLASSIC, CONTEMPORARY AND TRADITIONAL STYLE
Find out about the company, its heritage and what designs they
have – new and old. You can also order a brochure and visit
the Morris & Co pages where they have all the favourite
designs. For more information on William Morris try visiting
www.morrissociety.org

www.wallpaperdirect.co.uk   UK

BUY WALLPAPER

A good store offering a wide range of wallpapers, sampling service, advice and free delivery if you order more than £150 worth.

www.thedesignstudio.co.uk   UK

GET THE RIGHT DESIGN

This is an excellent database of wallpaper and fabric samples which is easy to use and good fun. Once you've selected your swatch you can then find the nearest supplier. You need some patience, as it can be quite slow and you have to register to use the service.

www.communityrepaint.org.uk   UK

REUSING OLD PAINT

Not a great web site but a very useful service. The site highlights a number of schemes across the country that take reusable paint and redistribute it to those who can't afford to buy their own.

www.photo-furnishings.com   UK

YOUR PHOTOS ON YOUR FURNISHINGS

Outstanding use of web design to sell a novel service, here they will put your photos onto soft furnishings or wallpapers. You have to apply for prices. See also **www.artmeetsmatter.com** who offer all sorts of products.

Lighting

www.lightsaver.co.uk   UK

SAVE ON LIGHTING

With lots of savings and a wide range to choose from this site is worth a visit, it's not the epitome of great web design but it's effective nonetheless. You should also check out **www.thelightingsuperstore.co.uk** and **www.lighting-direct.co.uk** who both offer good alternatives.

Inspiration, Design and Interiors

www.design-gap.co.uk   UK

DESIGNER DIRECTORY

A directory of UK-based designers and manufacturers with some 300 pages to browse through. They are arranged alphabetically by first name or company name as well as by category. The illustrations are excellent. See also **www.designdirectory.co.uk** which is a listing of design consultants.

www.design-online.co.uk   UK

NEED A DESIGNER?
Design Online's mission is to put buyers and suppliers in touch with each other and to use the Internet to promote the use of well-designed products and services. You just search for the service you want and a list of suitable suppliers with contact details quickly appears. Could do with some illustrations and examples of the work that they are trying to promote.

See also:
www.bida.org – home of the British Interior Design Association.
www.britishdesign.co.uk – a showcase site for British talent.
www.tribu-design.com/en – an encyclopedia of 20th century design and decorative arts.

www.bhglive.com   UK

BETTER HOMES AND GARDENS
There's more to this than DIY, but superb graphics and videos give this site the edge. There's lots of help on design and decorating and the 'how-to encyclopedia' under 'home improvement' is excellent. It's American, so some information isn't applicable to the UK.

www.geomancy.net   UK

FENG SHUI
What a mess of a site! Considering that it's supposed to promote the principles of light and harmony, it isn't very well designed. However, there's an excellent set of links and you can learn all you need to know about Feng Shui. See also **www.rising-dragon.co.uk** which is slow but better designed.

Stores for Design

www.habitat.net   UK

HABITAT STORES
An information-only site with lots of details on their product range. It's all wrapped up in a funky design, which is a little jerky with a normal modem and needs the latest version of Flash to work. You

can't order online although you can check store availability. See also the US store **www.crateandbarrel.com** who offer similar products but shipping is very expensive.

www.ikea.com   UK

IKEA STYLE
You can't buy from the site but you can check whether a store has the item you want to buy in stock before you go (it would be great if more stores did this). Otherwise the site is more the usual store fare with plenty of ideas, articles and product lists.

www.maelstrom.co.uk   UK

CONTEMPORARY SELECTION
A wide selection of contemporary gifts, accessories, gadgets and furniture on a good-looking site. Delivery is 10% of the value of the order with a flat charge of £10 if you spend more than £100.

www.next.co.uk   UK

NEXT HOME WARE
A good selection of Next homeware as well as the usual products on a fairly impractical site.

www.bluedeco.com   UK

DESIGN ONLINE
This site offers a selection of designer products for the home, from furniture to ceramics, with free delivery to the UK. Unfortunately, returns have to go to Luxembourg.

www.pier.co.uk   UK

THE PIER
A very good offering from the Pier. Eclectic and always interesting, there's a wide range to choose from. Delivery charges vary according to the type of product you buy.

www.pussyhomeboutique.co.uk   UK

DESIGNER BOUTIQUE
An eccentric and slightly kitsch range of products, furniture, home accessories and wall panels. Delivery charges vary.

See also:
http://sawitfirst.co.uk – excellent shop featuring contemporary designer furniture and home accessories.

www.afternoah.com – great for the unusual and the eclectic.
www.interiorinternet.co.uk – a well-illustrated and unusual
selection of designer furniture .
www.oceanuk.com – a wide range and some good prices too.

Soft Furnishing

www.simplyfurnishings.com   UK

SOFT FURNISHING
All you need to know about making and buying soft furnishing
with plenty of advice for all levels and a good store directory.

See also:
www.clarissahulse.com – gorgeous leafy designs on soft
furnishings, and wall paper too.
www.crowsonfabrics.com – nice products but no online ordering.
www.monkwell.com – beautiful ranges but you can't buy online.

Furniture

www.mfi.co.uk   UK

MFI HOMEWORKS
MFI offer a nicely designed site with all the best aspects of
online shopping and a wide range of surprisingly good furniture
for home and office available for order online or via a hotline.
Delivery is included in the price.

www.furniture123.co.uk   UK

SMART PLACE TO BUY FURNITURE
This company has a well laid out web site offering a good range
of furniture, many offers, tips and free delivery.

www.heals.co.uk   UK

STYLISH CONTEMPORARY DESIGN
Heals has a beautifully designed web site which gives
information about the store and inspiration for the home.
There's an online store which stocks primarily gifts and home
accessories, but there's a special services section where you
can get information on furniture and interior design.

www.conran.com   UK

TERENCE CONRAN STYLE

As well as information on all his restaurants, this site has an online shopping facility that allows you to buy Conran-designed accessories as well as stuff for the home including a good range of furniture and kitchen products.

www.ancestralcollections.co.uk   UK

REPRODUCTIONS FROM THE BEST HOMES

A web site that has developed well with a wide range of high-quality beds and furniture on an attractive site with good pictures and descriptions of the products. They've expanded into gifts too and offer good value for money.

Other furniture retailers and sites that may be worth a virtual visit are:

www.bfm.org.uk – a useful directory of British furniture makers.

www.cjfurniture.com – contemporary furniture.

www.connectedlines.com/styleguide – a basic guide to furniture styles.

www.davidlinley.com – posh contemporary classics.

www.furniturebusters.com – a wide range and masses of offers too.

www.mufti.co.uk – more posh, beautifully designed furniture.

www.new-heights.co.uk – simple, stylish solid wood.

www.pinesolutions.co.uk – a very well-designed furniture store, they also sell sofas and oak furniture.

www.sofaweb.co.uk – good value sofa and sofa bed shop.

www.sofaworkshopdirect.co.uk – well designed with quality photos of the sofas and what looks like a good online service.

www.thebedshed.net – worth a visit just for the jaw-droppingly bad jingle, there's also a decent product range and store directory.

www.twelvelimited.com – beautiful recycled furniture and home accessories.

TV and Celebrity Designers

www.llb.co.uk   UK

> LAURENCE LLEWELYN-BOWEN
> Join the fan club, view Laurence's designs from greeting cards
> to cutlery to wallpaper, then find out how to buy them. There's
> lots here, even competitions. See also **www.bbc.co.uk/homes**
> with lots of ideas and helpful hints, in particular, go to
> 'Changing Rooms' which has top tips, articles and biographies.

www.ukstyle.tv/homesandproperty   UK

> UK STYLE TV
> A bright and breezy site packed with ideas from the TV shows
> and features on the various projects and aspects of the home.
> There's an 'ask the expert' section and a guide full of practical
> ideas and tips too.

Miscellaneous

www.howtocleananything.com   CANADA

> STAIN REMOVAL PAR EXCELLENCE
> A group of cleaners have got together to produce a site that
> contains over 1,000 cleaning tips for outside or inside the
> house or the car – except for curry!

www.thistothat.com   US

> GLUE
> A site that helps you work out which is the right glue to use.
> Just input the two things you want to glue together and the site
> makes a recommendation…what could be easier!

Humour

*The Internet has become home to an amazing array of funny sites.
Here's just a few of the best. You should be aware that most aren't
suitable for children.*

Jokes, Links and Directories

www.comedy-zone.net   UK

COMPLETE COMEDY GUIDE
Excellent and wide-ranging comedy site with lots of links and
competitions, alongside quotes, jokes and chat.

For other comedy portals and loads of jokes go to:
http://uk.dir.yahoo.com/entertainment/humour – Yahoo's
excellent listing devoted to humour and bizarre sites.
www.bored.com – a great directory of humour sites.
www.funnybone.com – huge database with lots of rude jokes.
www.funnymail.com – lots of jokes and well categorised with
good features such as tests, top 10 jokes of all time, newest
jokes and so on.
www.humorlinks.com – massive portal for all things funny.
www.humournet.co.uk – categorised jokes, links and
funny pictures.
www.jokecenter.com – hundreds of jokes, vote for your favourites.
www.jokepost.com – hundreds, all well categorised.
www.jokes2000.com – e-mail you the latest jokes.
www.jokes.com – typical jokes directory but these are rated,
tame, racy etc…
www.kidsjokes.co.uk – 12,000+ jokes, great for the family.
www.weirdwebbed.com – a directory of the weirdest web sites.

www.uebersetzung.at/twister   AUSTRIA

TONGUE TWISTERS
An international collection of tongue twisters, over 2,000 in 87
languages when we last visited, nearly 400 in English –
'Can you can a can as a canner can can a can?' as they say.

Multi-media

www.funny-downloads.com   US

THE BEST IN MULTI-MEDIA HUMOUR
What used to be Olley's Place has transformed into a subscription
only site costing €10 per annum. For that you get access to a
superb selection of funny video clips and comedy downloads, there
is some free content though and you should be aware that most of
it is adult oriented.

Other sites offering video clips, viral e-mails and generally daft adult-oriented entertainment:

http://uk.news.yahoo.com/promo/office/index.html – Yahoo's excellent Office Attachments page.

www.b3ta.com – a particularly silly and very popular e-zine.

www.boreme.com – excellent collection of video clips.

www.cyberparodies.com – a mixed bag of song parodies.

www.ebaumsworld.com – good but a pain to use.

www.gagreport.com – a messy site with a huge collection of humorous videos and jokes.

www.jengajam.com – a daily listing of photos, games, trivia and videos.

www.spongi.com – over designed but there's some fun stuff here if you can be bothered to find it.

Stand-up Comedy

www.chortle.co.uk   UK

GUIDE TO LIVE COMEDY IN THE UK
Chortle provides a complete service, listing who's on, where and when – also whether they're any good or not. There's also a comic's A–Z so that you can find your favourites and get reviews on how they're performing, or not, as the case may be. See also **www.jongleurs.co.uk** whose entertaining site has audio clips and details of what's on and when at their clubs.

Comedy Magazine and Satirical Sites

www.theonion.com   US

AMERICA'S FINEST NEWS SOURCE
A great send-up of American tabloid newspapers, this is one of the most visited sites on the Internet and easily one of the funniest. See also the equally good Framley Examiner at **www.framleyexaminer.com** and also **www.thespoof.com** a great spoof news site.

www.private-eye.co.uk   UK

PRIVATE EYE
A pretty average effort really considering the wealth of material that must be available, there are a few of the best cartoons and features, but it's only updated every couple of weeks or so.

H

www.punch.co.uk   UK
PUNCH MAGAZINE
A new look and more commercial approach from *Punch* with
plenty of cartoons and some of the best of *Punch* available to
browse and buy.

www.viz.co.uk   UK
NOT FOR CHILDREN
A very good reflection of what you get in the real thing with lots
of games and downloads, you can even contribute to Roger's
Profanisaurus.

www.thespark.com   US
TAKE THE SPARK TESTS
The Spark is actually a spin-off from the Spark notes revision
guides. Its best feature, and the reason why millions visit, is the
tests. From the popular personality test, through bitch and
bastard tests to the wealth test, all are good for a laugh and, of
course, very accurate. Dare you take the 'death test' or the
'unintelligence test' though?

www.bizarremag.com   US
BIZARRE MAGAZINE
The magazine is devoted to 'life in the extreme' and the site
reflects this with a selection of pictures and stories. It's all
geared to getting you to subscribe. Be aware that the content is
adult oriented.

www.whitehouse.org   US
THE WHITE HOUSE
A great micky-take on the US presidency, very clever and
vicious too.

www.nicecupofteaandasitdown.com   UK
TAKE A BREAK
Put your feet up and while away some time here, review your
favourite biscuit or not…take your time…make tea….lovely

www.lazystuff.co.uk   UK
HOW TO WASTE TIME
Lots of pointless and time-wasting things to do, but it's all so
interesting and there's the top 50 lazy gifts to choose from.

TV Comedy

www.bbc.co.uk/comedy   UK
BBC COMEDY
An outstanding site with a comedy guide and lots to see and
do. There are features on each major program and even a
comedy blog, also links to associated sites, clips to watch and
radio features to download.

www.comedycentral.com   US
THE HOME OF SOUTH PARK AND MORE
Great for South Park and selected American TV shows, but also
with clips and background information and stand-up comedy too.

www.thesimpsons.com   US
HOME OF THE SIMPSONS
The official site with biographies, background, quizzes and
more, plus the ever-present merchandise store. If you are a real
fan then go to the Simpsons archive at **www.snpp.com**

See also:
www.britishcomedy.org.uk – a poor site but good background
on some classic radio comedy.
www.britishcomedyhelpdesk.moonfruit.com – any questions
about British and TV comedy, ask the helpdesk...
www.phill.co.uk – a comprehensive directory of TV comedy.

Urban Legends, the Unlikely and the Unloved

www.snopes2.com   US
URBAN LEGENDS
An outstanding collection of all those stories and myths that have
that edge of unlikely truth about them. Well categorised and with a
good search facility, it's easy to find your favourites. See also
www.thisistrue.com which is full of unlikely but true stories.

www.darwinawards.com   US
FATAL MISADVENTURES
The Darwin Awards have been going several years now and
their site is packed with stories, urban legends and personal
accounts of those who have 'improved our gene pool by
removing themselves from it in really stupid ways'.

www.halfbakery.com   US

INVENTIONS OR NOT

A fun catalogue of useless inventions and ideas, some real, most not; it's very silly really and it's a shame that there are not more illustrations.

www.craptowns.com   UK

OUR CRAP TOWNS

The site that spawned a best-selling book. Here's an eclectic collection of towns in the UK and US that have been awarded the status of being crap, most for no apparent reason. Irreverent and pretty funny, there are some very angry people out there.

www.iusedtobelieve.com   US

CHILDHOOD BELIEFS

A catalogue of childhood misconceptions and beliefs, you can rate them and even add your own. It's the sort of site that makes you smile and you can't help joining in.

Cartoons

www.bcdb.com   US

THE BIG CARTOON DATABASE

A catalogue covering all the major producers of cartoons, the main characters and of course the cartoon series themselves. It has an American bias but it's pretty comprehensive and you can rate your favourites too.

www.weebls-stuff.com   UK

WEEBLS

An award-winning site and one of our favourites. It's home to the Weebl and Bob cartoons as well as many other cartoons and includes the unforgettable tune that is 'Everyone loves Magical Trevor'.

www.joecartoon.com   US

FREAKY CARTOONS

Follow the gruesome, messy adventures of Joe, download the cartoons and send them to your friends and buy the T-shirt – he's a legend after all. Superb animation and very funny, but you need patience for the downloads.

www.emilystrange.com

ENTER THE WORLD OF EMILY STRANGE
Another animated site with outstanding illustrations that's worth
a visit just to look at the design, if nothing else. Emily is a
popular icon with teenagers and here you can participate in her
freaky adventures.

See also:
www.cartoonbank.com – outstanding New Yorker cartoons for
sale in various formats and guises.
www.cartoonstock.com – a database of over 50,000 cartoons.
www.justfunnycartoons.com – an odd site with lots of animated
adverts but there are some funny cartoons to be found.
www.marsdencartoons.com/directory.htm – a comprehensive
directory of cartoonists with links.
www.nonstick.com – home of Warner Brothers cartoons with
some available to download, plus links and background
information on those involved.
www.tomandjerryonline.com – all you need to know about the
awesome Tom & Jerry.
www.unitedmedia.com/comics/peanuts – home of Charlie
Brown and Peanuts.

www.super-jam.com

UK

YOU BE THE DANCING QUEEN...
Pick a digital photo of yourself or your friend, crop and
download, pick a body and start dancin'...

Miscellaneous and Just Weird

www.strangereports.com

US

PRANKS ONLINE
Play pranks on your friends using the service available here,
with trick web sites and fake news reports it's almost
irresistible, but beware their revenge... See also
www.computerpranks.com and also **www.prank.org** both of
which contain classics.

http://officeolympics.net

US

THE OFFICE OLYMPICS
OK so it's a slow day at the office, you've got nothing to do,
well you could follow the example set here and set up your own
Office Olympics...with events such as cubicle hurdles and chair
hop, you can't go wrong.

www.freakydreams.com   US

DREAM INTERPRETED
You just type in the description of your dream and an 'accurate' interpretation pops up in seconds.

www.20q.net   US

TWENTY QUESTIONS
Pick something and the site will guess what it is within twenty questions, it's amazingly accurate and very time consuming as you try to beat it without cheating.

www.user-error.co.uk   UK

EXCUSE GENERATOR
Apart from the excellent excuse generator which is very handy, there's also a virtual makeover section, articles on the unusual universe we live in and, if you're in a disagreement with someone over some fact or other, they'll help you settle your bet.

www.museumofhoaxes.com   UK

HOAXES
The world's greatest hoaxes and April Fools are catalogued here. It makes entertaining browsing and is sometimes unbelievable.

www.smalltime.com/dictator   UK

GUESS THE DICTATOR
You think of a dictator or TV sit-com character, answer the questions put to you and the site will guess who you are thinking of…it's spookily accurate.

www.optillusions.com   US

OPTICAL ILLUSIONS
A good selection of optical illusions to download, plus links to other similar and funny sites. The visit is completely spoiled by the large amount of adverts both pop-ups and banners. See also **www.grand-illusions.com**

www.emotioneric.com   US

EMOTIONAL ERIC
A cult site in the US. Eric will act out any emotion in any situation, you just have to place your request.

www.snapbubbles.com   US
VIRTUAL BUBBLE WRAP
How comforting, when you have the urge to pop and there's no
bubble wrap to hand, just come here for the nearest substitute.

www.engrish.com   US
MISTAKEN ENGLISH
This site started off as a list of humorous mistakes that the
Japanese made with English; it's now expanded slightly to take
in other cultures and it's very funny.

www.pickthehottie.com   US
PICK THE HOTTIE!
Probably the best of many sites where people post photos of
themselves and their friends (or enemies) the idea being that
you vote for the hottest-looking people and the ugliest too.

*While we're on the subject of the unattractive, check out these
sites listed below...*
www.badfads.com – home of the Bad Fads Museum, fashion
victims galore...
www.mulletmadness.com – in celebration of the haircut and
culture.
www.mulletsgalore.com – more mullets!
www.uglydress.com – Bridesmaids' dresses from hell, dare you
to look at this without putting your hand over your mouth...
www.uglyfootballers.com – yes we well remember them...

www.faceanalyzer.com   US
AUTOMATED FACE READER
Download your picture onto the site and get an analysis and
score based on a number of indicators, it will estimate how
honest you are, or intelligent or even tell if you are gay or not.

Internet Service Provision

There are so many Internet Service Providers (ISPs) that it would be impossible to review them all and it's moving so fast that any information soon becomes outdated. However, help is at hand and here are some sites that will help you chose the right one for you.

www.net4nowt.com   UK

THE PLACE TO START LOOKING FOR THE BEST ISP
This is a directory of Internet service providers offering news and advice on the best ones. There is an up-to-date critique on each ISP with comments on costs and reliability. There is also a good summary table featuring all the ISPs, which proves useful for comparisons.

www.ispreview.co.uk   UK

INTERNET NEWS
Find out what's really going on at this impressive site – they are especially good at exposing the worst performers. There's plenty in the way of news, offers and a top 10 ISP list.

See also:
www.cisas.org.uk – home of the Communications and Internet Services Adjudication Scheme, which aims to solve disputes between ISPs and customers.
www.ispa.org.uk – Internet Service Providers Association with an informative site.
www.thelist.com – the ISP providers guide from the US.

Jobs and Careers

There are several hundred sites offering jobs or careers advice but it's largely a matter of luck if you come across a job you like. Still, it enables you to cover plenty of ground in a short space of time without trawling the newspapers. These sites offer the most options and best advice.

Career Guidance

www.careerguide.net   UK

ONLINE CAREER ADVICE RESOURCE
This is a comprehensive service with many sections on job hunting, vacancies, CVs, careers advice and professional institutions that can help.

www.careers-portal.co.uk
UK

AWARD-WINNING CAREERS SERVICE
An excellent portal site that is part of the National Grid for Learning, with lots of advice on universities, jobs and how to apply. There's a very useful careers directory and it's all geared to helping you choose the right career. However, it also involves buying their guides.

www.careers-gateway.co.uk
UK

THE CAREERS GATEWAY
Great advice and lots of information, for example, how to launch a proper career, evaluate your options and read articles to help you decide what you can do with your life. There's a virtual career show, quizzes designed to help and advice for HR professionals too.

www.reachforthesky.co.uk
UK

CAREERS ADVICE FROM SKY TV
Sky has put together a great web site that doesn't just look good. However, it's developed into more of a teen magazine, but there is a good deal of advice here plus some fun too.

www.careersolutions.co.uk
UK

HELP TO GO FORWARD
A good place to start if you're not sure what you want to do next with your career, don't know where to start or you've been made redundant. Using the site enables you to narrow your options and clarify things. The list of links is logically laid out and very helpful.

Job Finders

www.transdata-inter.co.uk/jobs-agencies
UK

DIRECTORY OF JOB SITES
Don't let the long URL put you off, this is an excellent place to start on your search. The Directory lists all the major online employment agencies and ranks them by the average number of vacancies, the regions they cover, whether they help create and store CVs and what industries they represent. Clicking on the name takes you right to the site you need.

www.jobs.co.uk   UK

JOB SEARCH ENGINE
With this facility you can search all the major job sites in one
go, it's easy to use and quite accurate providing you have a
defined job title. They also offer all the usual features such as
CV help and advice. See also **www.jobsearch.co.uk**

www.gisajob.co.uk   UK

SEARCH FOR YOUR NEXT JOB HERE
The largest of the UK online job sites with over 44,000
vacancies. You can search by description or sector or get
advice on your career. It's good for non-senior executive types.

www.workthing.com   UK

IT'S A WORK THING
One of the best-looking job sites with a reputation to match,
this site must be one of the first to visit when job hunting
across a wide range of industries. Registered users can set up
an e-mail alert when a job matching their search criteria
appears. There is also help for businesses trying to improve
their people skills and recruitment. There is also advice on
training and personal development too.

www.monster.co.uk   UK

GLOBAL JOBS
With thousands of jobs available in 26 countries, there are
plenty to choose from. The site is well designed and easy to use
with the usual help features. At the time of writing there were
over 36,000 UK jobs listed in over 20 categories.

www.stepstone.co.uk   UK

EUROPEAN INTERNET RECRUITMENT
Regarded as one of the best, Stepstone has a huge number of
European and international vacancies. It's quick, easy to use
and offers lots of time-saving cross-referencing features. You
can also register your CV. For other overseas jobs see
www.overseasjobs.com

Other job finder and career sites worth checking out:
www.deskdemon.com – jobs and resources for secretarial
and support staff.
www.doctorjob.com – graduates only need apply.

www.jobserve.co.uk – a well-categorised job search engine covering the major industries, good design.

www.reed.co.uk – some 210,000 vacancies from a wide range of categories.

www.thegumtree.com – jobs in London.

www.totaljobs.co.uk – 60,000 jobs listed in a wide range of sectors.

These government-run sites might also be useful:

www.aimhigher.gov.uk – how to get the qualifications to get the job you really want.

www.connexions.gov.uk – an advice service aimed at 13- to 19-year olds.

www.dfes.gov.uk – the Dept of Education has lots of helpful advice.

www.jobcentreplus.gov.uk – information about job centres and how to go about finding a job.

www.worktrain.gov.uk – jobs, training, voluntary work, it's all here.

J

Ten of the Best

The Good Web Site Guide's Top 10s of the Internet

1. **www.bbc.co.uk** – for TV, news and many free services.
2. **www.google.co.uk** – not just a search engine.
3. **www.amazon.co.uk** – not just a book store anymore.
4. **www.apple.com** – an absolute must for all Apple users.
5. **www.24hourmuseum.org.uk** – access to all our galleries and museums.
6. **www.ebay.co.uk** – for some a way of life, for others the best online auction site.
7. **www.imdb.com** – if anyone has appeared on screen they're listed here at the Internet Movie Database.
8. **www.shockwave.com** – for games and graphics, they don't come any better.
9. **www.howstuffworks.com** – if you want to find out how something works, start here.
10. **www.wikipedia.org** – the people's encyclopedia.

Other Careers and Related Sites

www.i-resign.com/uk   UK
THE INS AND OUTS OF RESIGNATION
Pay a visit before you send the letter, it offers a great deal of
advice both legal and sensible. The best section contains the
funniest selection of resignation letters anywhere. There are also
jobs on offer, links to job finder sites and a career guide service.

www.homeworking.com   UK
WORKING FROM HOME
A site full of advice and information for anyone considering or
actually working from home. There are links and directories as
well as forum pages where you can share experiences with
other home workers.

www.eoc.org.uk   UK
EQUAL OPPORTUNITIES COMMISSION
A very informative site and it's where to go if you think you are
being discriminated against.

www.adastra-cm.com   UK
CAREERS ADVICE
An excellent site from a career management consultancy with
some really sound careers advice within their newsletters,
which is written in a very accessible style.

Online Practise Tests

www.queendom.com   UK

SERIOUSLY ENTERTAINING
Apart from the fun tests there's a serious side to this site that
allows you to take the sort of tests you're likely to face when
applying for a job. See also **www.emode.com**

Language: Learning and Translation

*In this new section you'll find a selection of sites that will help you
learn a language, whether it's in depth or for a short trip. There's also
help if you just want some text translated.*

www.ilovelanguages.com   US
LANGUAGE LINKS
A directory of language-learning sites; it's US oriented but a
good place to start. The list is pretty comprehensive, featuring
some 2,000 sites.

www.bbc.co.uk/languages   UK
LEARN WITH THE BBC
Featuring the BBC's extensive list of language courses, it covers
all the major European languages plus Chinese and Japanese.
There are lots of features and the site is well integrated with the
books and TV programs.

See also:
www.csulb.edu/~txie/online.htm – the place to start if you
want to learn Chinese.
www.elanguage.com – language-learning software to buy.
www.ethnologue.com – excellent resource regarding the
history of the 6,800 major languages of the world.
www.eurocosm.com – excellent free resources for the major
European languages and cultures.
www.ielanguages.com – basic tutorials for nine European
languages.
www.indianlanguages.com – a good introduction to Indian
languages.
www.languageguide.org – tries to pull together language
resources using volunteers; it is a bit of a mess but you may
find something useful.
www.learn-japanese.info – basic course in Japanese for
English speakers.
www.linguascope.com – interactive language-learning
resources, unfortunately not free.
www.parlo.com – learn about the culture as well as the language.
www.usingenglish.com – excellent range of resources for English
as a second language for students and teachers.

Translation Services

*Listed below are a few sites that are helpful if you just want to
translate a short piece of text.*

http://babelfish.altavista.com/tr – one of the originals, easy
to use and good for the major European and Far Eastern languages.

http://dictionaries.travlang.com – some 35 language dictionaries to choose from.
www.foreignword.com – lots of links and dictionaries, good for the less widely used languages.
www.freetranslation.com – very good for short phrases, also offers professional services.
www.langtolang.com – more links, services, e-books and software to download.
www.smartphrase.com – a helpful online phrase book.

Sign Language

Not all language can be heard...
www.british-sign.co.uk – a sign dictionary, help and discussion forums.
www.britishsignlanguage.com – a visual dictionary.
www.handspeak.com – good site on international sign language.
www.learnbsl.org – excellent and well-designed virtual guide to British Sign Language.

Legal Advice and the Law

We all need help with certain key events in life: marriages, moving house, making a will or getting a divorce. Maybe you need advice on lesser issues like boundary disputes or problems with services or property? Here are several good sites that could really make a difference. There's more on divorce and separation in the section on problem relationships, page 345.

www.advicenow.org.uk   UK

INDEPENDENT LAW AND RIGHTS ADVICE
A great site designed to keep up with and explain the law in layman's terms. It's well designed and information is easy to find; it also offers links to the relevant site if required. Excellent.

www.compactlaw.co.uk   UK

LEGAL INFORMATION FOR ENGLAND AND WALES
An extremely informative and useful site that covers many aspects of the law in a clear and concise style, there are usable documents – you can download some free, others to buy, case histories, news, tips and plenty of fact-sheets. Formerly
www.lawrights.co.uk

www.uklegal.com   UK

LEGAL RESOURCES AT YOUR FINGERTIPS
This site offers a superb selection of links to everything from
private investigators to barristers to legal equipment suppliers.

www.family-solicitors.co.uk   UK

FAMILY LAW REFERENCE
Excellent resource for everyday legal issues covering everything
from wills to neighbourhood disputes. Great for links too with
an excellent search facility for finding a family law solicitor near
you. See also **www.solicitors-online.com** for the Law Society's
advice on lawyers. Another site that will help you find a lawyer
is the well-put-together **www.lawyerlocator.co.uk**

www.desktoplawyer.net   UK

THE UK'S FIRST ONLINE LAWYER
This site is quite straightforward if you know what you need
and have read through the instructions carefully. First you
register, then download the software (Rapidocs) enabling you to
compile the document you need. The legal documents you
create will cost from £2.99 upwards depending on complexity.
The range of documents available is huge and there are more
being added. See also **www.everyform.net** who have some
1,800 free forms to download.

www.legalservices.gov.uk   UK

GOVERNMENT ADVICE
The replacement for legal aid, this is the official line on legal matters
with guidance on how to access legal assistance, where to get
information and news on latest changes to the Community Legal
Service and Criminal Defence Service. It could be a lot more user-
friendly. For Scottish legal aid go to **www.slab.org.uk**

See also:
www.clsdirect.org.uk – free legal advice from the Community
Legal Service.
www.courtservice.gov.uk – information on how the court
service works.
www.divorce-online.co.uk – fast-track divorces and good advice.
www.emplaw.co.uk – the low-down on British employment law.
www.feedmelegal.com – an interesting American legal blog site.
www.findlaw.com – an American law portal.

www.freelawyer.co.uk – a London-based legal services shop.
www.infolaw.co.uk – a legal document search engine.
www.lawassure.co.uk – subscribe to excellent personal legal advice and related services.
www.lawpack.co.uk – legal book specialist.
www.lawscot.org.uk – the Law Society of Scotland.
www.lawsociety.org.uk – the Law Society of England and Wales.
www.lawsoc-ni.org – the Law Society of Northern Ireland.
www.legaladvicefree.co.uk – excellent all-rounder that provides the answer to many legal questions.
www.legalpulse.com – well-designed site along the lines of Desktop Lawyer although not as comprehensive.
www.legalshop.co.uk – affordable solutions to your legal problems; a good site, with a business section too.
www.multikulti.org.uk – legal documents and other helpful information for new citizens and minorities available in many languages.
www.officer.com – site for American law enforcement officers; some interesting reading.
www.oldbaileyonline.org – interesting site offering up the proceedings of the Old Bailey from 1674 to 1834.

L

www.dumblaws.com   US

THE DAFTEST, STUPIDEST LAWS
Did you realise that in England placing a postage stamp that bears the Queen's head upside down is considered treasonable, or that in Kentucky it's illegal to fish with a bow and arrow? These are just a couple of the many dumb laws that you can find on this very entertaining site. It's now been expanded to include dumbest criminals, dumbest warnings and place names.

Linux

Linux is a free operating system that competes with Windows; it has a reputation for stability and is gaining popularity. Here are some informative sites to help you.

www.linuxlinks.com   US

LINUX DIRECTORY
A Yahoo style directory with over 28,000 links, forums and articles. It's well categorised and a good place to start.

See also:
http://beginnerslinux.org – a personal guide for beginners.
www.linux.com – authoritative site with good tutorials.
www.linux.org – a Linux community site, good once you've learnt a bit.
www.redhat.com – a company with its own version of Linux, lots of support.

Magazines and Newspapers

Where to buy and subscribe to your favourite magazines, see also our news section on page 333.

www.newsstand.co.uk   UK

A GIFT THAT LASTS ALL YEAR
A wide range of titles that are available by subscription, on a well-categorised site. It has a strong British bias, a pity there are not more overseas and foreign language magazines available.

www.zinio.com   US

DIGITAL MAGAZINES
You have to download the bespoke viewer and subscribe, but here are a large selection of magazines for you to read on your PC – the American editions anyway. The quality is good and it allows you to turn the pages realistically; however, it's best viewed on a wide-screen PC.

See also:
www.actualidad.com – newspapers of the world and links to their sites.
www.magazinecity.com – large selection of subscriptions, you pay in dollars.
www.subscription.co.uk – a good range of UK magazine subscriptions.
www.whsmith.co.uk – some good offers on subscriptions which are available to UK addresses only.

M

Men

Here are a few sites especially for blokes, lads and real men.

Magazines

www.fhm.co.uk   UK
FHM MAGAZINE
A good reflection of the real thing, with sections on everything
from serious news to the lighter side, with the usual blokey
features, it suffers from lots of advertising though.

www.gqmagazine.co.uk   UK
GENTLEMEN'S QUARTERLY
A stylish site, which gives a flavour of the real magazine, it contains
a few stories, competitions, fashion tips and the odd feature.

www.sharpman.com   UK
SHARP!
While a little odd, it's good fun and there's some useful advice.
Split into seven key sections: dating, with tips on conversation and
repartee; toys, from fitness gadgets to snowboards; work, getting the
best out of the Internet; travel, staying sharp abroad; grooming,
looking the part; toys – the best advice on windsurfing; tips (a new
section), a motley selection of articles on how to make yourself even
sharper.

www.fathersdirect.com   UK
A MAGAZINE FOR FATHERS
Written by fathers for fathers, this entertaining e-zine has all the
advice and support you need if you're a new dad or you're
trying to fit in both work and kids. There are competitions, a
rant section where you can let off steam and a games room.
Rather twee graphics let it down somewhat.

See also:
http://theladsmag.co.uk – reviews from all the best men's
magazines; slow site.
www.askmen.com – a very good American men's magazine
covering almost every topic you're likely to need.
www.dullmen.com – the dullest web site from the National
Council for Dull Men, very funny too.

www.modernman.com – nicely designed men's magazine site from the US with loads of interesting articles and features.
www.nutz.co.uk – a portal site featuring men's interests; some adult content.

Health

www.menshealth.co.uk   UK

MEN'S HEALTH MAGAZINE
Lots of advice on keeping fit, healthy and fashionable too. There's also an excellent section on the number one topic – sex plus others on wealth, health, sport and a shop that sells subscriptions and recommends the latest gear.

www.menshealthforum.org.uk   UK

STOP MOANING!
An excellent all-rounder revealing the truth behind the state of men's health and lots of discussion about specific and general health issues facing men today – good for links too.

Other men's health sites:
www.dipex.org – excellent cancer help site.
www.orchid-cancer.org.uk – promotes the awareness of testicular and prostate cancer.
www.sda.uk.net – the Sexual Dysfunction Association.
www.vasectomy-clinic.co.uk – no-scalpel vasectomy – honest!

Shopping

www.firebox.com   UK

WHERE MEN BUY STUFF
An online shop aimed totally at boy's toys, with its own bachelor pad containing all you need for the lifestyle. There are masses of games, videos, toys and, of course, the latest gadgets. Delivery costs vary. See also **www.big-boys-toys.net** and **www.boysstuff.co.uk** which are both worth a visit if you can't find what you want at Firebox.

www.mankindonline.co.uk   UK

MALE GROOMING
An above-average shop devoted to male grooming products and gifts, it also offers advice on things like skincare and has a

M

newsletter you can subscribe to. Delivery is free on orders over £60 but otherwise it's £3.50 for the UK.

www.condomsdirect.co.uk UK
CONDOMS UK
Many different types of condoms are available to buy, and you get free delivery if you spend more than £10 – there's even a price promise and the assurance of a fast and discreet service. It's also worth checking out **www.condomania.com**

Motorcycles

www.bmf.co.uk UK
BRITISH MOTORCYCLISTS FEDERATION
At this site you can join the BMF, get involved with their activities or just use the site for information. You can also get club information and e-mail them on any issues. For the international governing body go to **www.fim.ch/en**

www.motorcycle.co.uk UK
THE UK'S MOTORCYCLE DIRECTORY
Essentially a list of links by brand, dealer, importer, classics, gear, books and auctions.

www.moto-directory.com US
THE WORLD'S MOTORCYCLE DIRECTORY
US oriented, but links to hundreds of sites in 24 categories to ensure that you'll know what's going on in motorcycling and find the information you need.

www.motorworld.com US
ALL YOU NEED TO KNOW ABOUT MOTORCYCLES
Good coverage of both machines and events with multimedia features. Although the site is American there's good British coverage.

www.fowlers.co.uk UK
WHERE TO GET YOUR GEAR
A smart new look to this site which houses a good shop and information site dedicated to motorcycles, clothing and accessories, they seem intent on providing good customer service too. Also worth a visit is **www.customlids.co.uk** who offer a wide range of clothing.

See also:

www.autotrader.co.uk/bikes – Bike Trader from *Auto Trader* magazine has a huge number of bikes for sale and a good place to put your bike up for sale too.

www.classic-motorbikes.com – great if you want to purchase a classic bike.

www.hondahornet.co.uk – a good-looking specialist site.

www.mag-uk.org – home of the Motorcycle Action Group dedicated to campaigning on behalf of motorcyclists in the UK.

www.motorcycleshow.co.uk – details of the motorcycle show.

www.scootermania.co.uk – if you love scooters, here's where to go.

www.umgweb.com – owned by the auctioneer e-Bay, here you can find used motorcycles for sale.

Funny, Adult and Entertaining

M

The Good Web Site Guide's Top 10s of the Internet

1. **www.snopes2.com** – urban legends, all true of course.
2. **www.comedy-zone.net** – the place to start, loadsalinks.
3. **www.b3ta.com** – great for the gross.
4. **www.joecartoon.com** – freaky entertainment.
5. **www.emotioneric.com** – pick an emotion and Eric will act it for you.
6. **www.theonion.com** – irony from the US.
7. **www.craptowns.com** – is your town crap?
8. **www.funny-dowloads.com** – excellent for those video clips.
9. **www.funnymail.com** – more jokes than you can shake a stick at.
10. **www.boreme.com** – viral entertainment.

Movies

All you need to know about films and film stars including where to go to get the best deals on DVDs and videos. For information on the stars also check out the celebrities section on page 75.

News and Information

http://uk.imdb.com   US

INTERNET MOVIE DATABASE
The best and most organised movie database on the Internet. It's very easy to use and every film buff's dream with lots of features and recommendations, plus games, quizzes, chat and movie news. Another good database site is **www.allmovie.com** which has a really good search engine.

www.aintitcoolnews.com   US

AIN'T IT JUST COOL
A renowned review site that can make or break a movie in the US. It's very entertaining and likeable, albeit a bit messy. Harry Knowles's movie reviews are by far the best bit of the site, although they can go on a bit. You can search the archive for a particular review or contribute a bit of juicy gossip by e-mailing Harry direct.

See also:
www.metacritic.com – a site that compiles reviews from around the world, and gives the reviewed movies a score based on them. Also covers games, music and books.
www.mrqe.com – the Movie Review Query Engine, just enter the film title and reviews from magazines from all round the world pop up.
www.mymovies.net – a portal, shop, news and e-zine all wrapped up in a fairly poorly designed site. Having said that there's a lot here so patience is rewarded, but you have to subscribe to get the best out of it.
www.rottentomatoes.com – a comprehensive review site and store.

Film Magazine Sites

www.empireonline.co.uk   UK

THE UK'S NUMBER ONE
An epic of a site with masses of information and background on the latest movies and the stars. There are two main review

sections, one dedicated to the cinema and one entitled, 'At home' for DVD and soundtrack and book reviews. You can also see trailers of new films, see pictures of the stars and production stills in the gallery and subscribe to the magazine.

www.insidefilm.com   US
FILM FESTIVAL DIRECTORY
Comprehensive news on the film festival with a calendar and features on awards.

www.eonline.com   US
E IS FOR ENTERTAINMENT
This is one of the most visited entertainment news sites and it has a reputation for being first with the latest gossip and movie news. It's vibrant, well designed and has a tongue-in-cheek style which is endearing; sadly some of the reporters prattle on though.

www.variety.com   US
VARIETY MAGAZINE
The online version of the show business stalwart magazine has an excellent and entertaining site with all the hot topics, news and background information you'd expect plus biographies and international film news. You have to subscribe to get access to many of the sections.

M

www.brightlightsfilm.com   US
FILM JOURNAL
A diverse and well written e-zine devoted to film that covers a wide variety of topics and film styles. It can be quite eccentric, which adds to the appeal, and some of the content is pretty odd, but it's essential reading for film buffs.

For more gossip see:
www.boxofficemojo.com – excellent US film news and box office information site.
www.ew.com – *Entertainments Weekly* has a really attractive site with lots of features.
www.hollywood.com – over 1 million pages of gossip, news, trailers and multi-media library.
www.hollywoodreporter.com – all the latest gossip and you can subscribe to the magazine.
www.teenhollywood.com – aimed at teenagers, following the top teens in Hollywood.

Bollywood

www.bollywoodworld.com   INDIA

> THE BOLLYWOOD PORTAL
> If it's Bollywood, then it's covered on this site. There are the
> movie reviews you'd expect plus lots of news, what's hot and
> what's not, pictures of the stars and much more. There is a
> music channel, radio and chat, but the Bollywoodshop only
> ships within India.
>
> *See also:*
> **www.bollywhat.com** – here you can find a good beginner's guide.
> **www.planetbollywood.com** – odd design but loads of
> information, gossip and awards.

Awards and Industry

www.oscars.com   US

> THE ACADEMY AWARDS
> Stylish and as tastelessly glitzy as you'd imagine it should be,
> this is the official tie-in site for the Oscars. There's an archive
> and even some games to play. For the Golden Globes go to
> **www.thegoldenglobes.com** and for a celebration of the worst
> Hollywood has to offer, the Razzies, go to **www.razzies.com**

www.bafta.org   UK

> BRITISH ACADEMY OF FILM & TELEVISION ARTS
> A site giving all the information you need on the BAFTAs,
> their history and how it all works.

www.bfi.org.uk   UK

> BRITISH FILM INSTITUTE
> A top site from the BFI packed with information on how the
> film industry works with archive material, links and how to
> make movies. Refreshing that there's not much mention of
> Hollywood! For the American Film Institute go to **www.afi.com**
> where you'll find an excellent site.

British Movie Industry

www.britmovie.co.uk   UK

DEDICATED TO BRITISH CINEMA
A site devoted to the history of British cinema and its wider
contribution to film-making in general. There's a great deal of
information, links and background and it's all well cross-
referenced, although it could do with a search facility and being
updated more regularly.

See also:
www.britishfilm.org.uk – excellent set of articles on the history
of British cinema.
www.britishhorrorfilms.co.uk – a very entertaining romp
through the history of British Horror films, with lots of detail!
www.britshorts.com – short British and European films.
www.cinerhama.com/britpage.html – this site has a good
database of movies and actors although it's not that up to date.

Independent Film-making

www.indiewire.com   UK

INDEPENDENT CINEMA
An enthralling site covering independent cinema, the films, people
and gossip. It stands out as a site that genuinely feels like it's
contributing positively to an industry. See also **www.exposure.co.uk**
who cover the low budget end of film-making.

www.kamera.co.uk   UK

ART HOUSE & INDEPENDENT REVIEWS
A well-written review site covering the world of art house and
independent cinema. It also has a good book review section
and interviews with important actors and directors. There's also
a directory and forums where you can put your views.

See also:
http://shootingpeople.org – a community site aimed at the
independent film maker, with lots of advice and help.
www.bifa.org.uk – British Independent Film awards.
www.raindance.co.uk – a high profile sponsor of independent
films, with a useful site and e-zine.

M

Specialist Film Sites

www.bmonster.com   US
COOLEST CULT MOVIES
A highly entertaining site devoted to B movies, oddities and
actors that aren't quite top drawer. It's well categorised and
obviously a labour of love for its contributors. See also
www.badmovieplanet.com

www.moderntimes.com   US

HOLLYWOOD CLASSICS
A great site devoted to classic Hollywood movies, when it really
was the silver screen. It offers up lots of background, interviews
and clips too.

See also:
www.americanwest.com/films/films.htm – good for links to all
things Western.
www.classichorrorfilms.com – not a great site but it's got all
you need on the subject.
www.classicmoviemusicals.com – a well-categorised but
slightly dull site covering musicals.
www.earlycinema.com – excellent site on the first decade of
cinema with timeline, biographical details and information on
the technology they used.
www.horror.net – a database of some 2,300 horror-related sites.
www.ianfleming.org – the place to go for all Bond fans.
www.movie-locations.com – a guide to the world's movie locations.
www.movie-trailers.com – masses of movie trailers going back
many years, it's quite nostalgic.
www.mysterynet.com/movies – the top movies reviewed with
links to other related genres.
www.scifispace.com – excellent fan site with lots of detail
and links.
www.sciflicks.com – a comprehensive site covering the Sci Fi genre.
www.scriptfly.com – buy movie scripts, hundreds to choose from.
www.silentsaregolden.com – a great place to start if you want
to find out about silent movies.
www.silentsmajority.com – an e-zine devoted to silent movies.
www.surfnetinc.com/chuck/trio.htm - The Old Corral, a directory
devoted mainly to westerns.

Cinemas

Listed below are the major cinema companies and their sites:
www.cinemas-online.co.uk – a portal site with links to all the country's cinemas.
www.cineworld.co.uk – straightforward and easy-to-use guide.
www.odeon.co.uk – book online at this attractive site.
www.showcasecinemas.co.uk – lots here to see and do.
www.uci-cinemas.co.uk – good-looking site with all the usual information and previews.
www.ugccinemas.co.uk – standard features including online booking.
www.myvue.com – Vue, the company formed from the amalgamation of Warner Village Cinemas and SBC International Cinemas, has a cleanly designed site with hidden extras.

Movie Humour

www.moderntimes.com   US

LISTEN TO YOUR FAVOURITE MOVIES
Download extracts from over 50 movies, it's a little confusing at first but once you've got the technology sorted out it's good fun.

http://rinkworks.com/movieaminute   US

DON'T HAVE TIME TO WATCH IT ALL?
Summaries of the top movies for those who either can't be bothered to watch them or just want to pretend they did, either way it's really funny.

www.moviecliches.com   US

THE MOVIE CLICHÉ LIST
Clichés listed by topic from aeroplanes to wood, there's something for everyone here…

See also:
www.badmovieplanet.com – a collection of the worst films ever made.
www.continuitycorner.com – the place to go if you're a born nitpicker, it has hundreds of movie mistakes and believe it not one person has submitted over 100 of them.
www.nitpickers.com – more pettiness.
www.razzies.com – awards for the worst movies.
www.thestinkers.com – more awards for bad films.

Film Companies

*Some of the best web sites are those that promote a particular film.
Here is a list of the major film producers and their web sites, all of
which are good and have links to the latest releases. Most have clips,
downloads, screensavers and lots of advertising.*

> **http://spielbergfilms.com**
> **www.disney.com**
> **www.foxmovies.com**
> **www.miramax.com**
> **www.paramount.com**
> **www.spe.sony.com**
> **www.uip.com**
> **www.universalpictures.com**
> **www.warnerbros.com**

Downloading Movies

*There's no doubt that downloading films and TV shows is likely to be
the next big thing in digital. As technology moves on, the facility to
carry large movie files such as MP4 will get ever easier – just check
out Tivo's Tivo to Go concept (**www.tivo.com**) to see the potential.
Once downloaded you can burn your own DVDs too. You'll need a
broadband connection but here are a few sites that are leading the
way (be warned that some carry adult-oriented content).*

> **www.downloadshield.com** – associated with Yahoo, lots of content.
> **www.ezmovies.net** – a good subscription service specialising
> in movies.
> **www.freemovienow.com** – not much free but one of the
> better designs.
> **www.sharedmovies.com** – possibly the one with the most content.
> **www.ultimatemoviedownload.com** – a popular file-sharing program
> with lots of content; costs vary according to what you buy.
> **www.xvidmovies.com** – a well-used service using the
> MP4 format.

Buying and Renting Movies

*It's probably best to start with visiting a price checker site first such
as **www.kelkoo.com** (see page 364) but these are the best of the
movie online stores.*

www.sendit.com formerly www.blackstar.co.uk UK

THE UK'S BIGGEST VIDEO STORE

The biggest online video and DVD retailer, it is very good value,
boasts free delivery and has a reputation for excellent customer
service. If you want to shop around try www.blockbuster.com who
have a less packed site and offers on a wide variety of films.

www.dvdstreet.infront.co.uk UK

FOR DVD ONLY

Part of the Streets Online group, this is a great-value and easy-
to-use site that only sells DVDs. There are lots of other movie-
related features too, such as the latest news and gossip or
reviews. Delivery is free on orders over £19 for the UK.

www.movietrak.com UK

RENT A DVD MOVIE

Rent as many DVDs as you want with packages from £9.95
per month. Pick the title of your choice and it's dispatched the
same day, you then return it seven days later in the pre-paid
envelope and they immediately dispatch the next DVD on your
list. The range offered is excellent covering eleven major
categories plus the latest releases, coming soon and a good
search facility too. See also www.screenselect.co.uk who offer
a similar service.

See also:
www.discshop.com – a wide-ranging DVD shop that sells
hardware too.
www.dvdoptions.com – rent your favourite DVDs from £3.25
for seven nights.
www.dvdpopcorn.com – a good-looking UK-based DVD shop
with some good offers, and prices include postage and packing.
www.dvdreview.com – great for news and reviews.
www.mymovies.net – a good review and film store with a
movie club.
www.play.com – a very strong selection of DVDs and CDs too
with some good offers.
www.zoovies.com – a good rental store with lots of choice,
you can either pay by movie or subscribe.

www.xiddi.com UK

DVD SHARE AND SWAP

A good alternative to DVD rental, here you build up credits

(Xids) that enable you to select from a good range of films
and popular titles, you only really pay for the postage.

Memorabilia

www.vinmag.com   UK
POSTERS, CARDS AND T-SHIRTS
Vintage magazines, stand-up cut-outs, posters, T-shirts and
magazine covers complete the picture from this established
dealer. Shipping to the UK starts at around £1.95, but it
depends on how much you spend.

www.asseenonscreen.com   UK

AS SEEN ON SCREEN
At this site you can buy what you see on the screen, your
favourite star's shirt or dress can be replicated just for you.
You can also search by star, film and TV show.

www.propstore.co.uk   UK
PROPS FOR SALE
An extensive selection of props and replicas await you here with
everything from snow globes to clothing. Each piece is unique
and has been bought from the relevant film company and the
provenance is provided.

See also:
www.efilmposters.com – who sell posters from a good British site.
www.memomine.com – for Hollywood memorabilia.
www.moviemarket.co.uk – posters, framed prints and
memorabilia delivered to your door.
www.ricksmovie.com – some 11,000 posters and related items.
www.vinylandfilmposters.co.uk – film and music related posters.

Music

I've had to completely rewrite this section for every edition of the
Good Web Site Guide, there are more changes in the area of music
downloading than any other bit of the Internet: sites change more
and technology improves very fast. It also takes me a long time to
write as I keep getting distracted by the music and, of course,

I can't resist downloading old favourites and new stuff. So yes, it works out as the most expensive section too!

Most people with a computer know about downloading music and much has been written about the effect that downloading free music has had on the music industry, mainly at the expense of musicians losing income. Some suggest that it's damaging to the industry by taking away their livelihoods, while others say it stimulates sales by enabling potential customers to sample music they wouldn't have heard otherwise. Whatever the stance, some of the sites listed are basically different file-sharing programs that allow users to exchange files easily whether it is music or not. It's best to read up on the subject before downloading any of the programs, but once you're up to speed it couldn't be easier.

Some of these sites are also prone to change, as regulations are introduced to block their activities, it's also quite difficult to establish their origin in some cases. The legal constraints that surround music file sharing are unclear but it's fair to say that in many cases copyright laws are broken. If you're not sure about using them, then I suggest you go to the pay sites. Personally, I think it's only fair that musicians should earn something if we enjoy their creativity and talent. Recently in America, some of the big music companies have prosecuted people who have downloaded music without paying, so be cautious. Having said all that, there are high-quality sites that allow you to sample music, offer legitimate free tracks and charge reasonable prices for the music – it's often still cheaper than buying a CD.

M

Please be aware that some may contain adult material including pornography (music files aren't the only things traded) and many carry some sort of spyware so that they can adapt to your tastes and advertise accordingly. See our security section on page 397 if you want to get rid of spywares. There are compatibility issues too, for example a track downloaded from Napster won't work on an iPod, as they use different software. There are two reasons for this, the first is about securing the track so that the artist gets paid and copyright is maintained, the second is about keeping you loyal to the product. Again it's best to read up on the subject before you buy.

Given the improvements in technology and the ongoing digital rights controversy, no doubt I'll be rewriting this section again next year.

iPod, Audio Players and Download Sites

These are the most popular digital audio players, all offer a basic free version with a full featured version to buy and download. With these you can download music, rip and burn CDs and get access to radio stations. Some offer movies and video playback too.

We'll start with the gadget that has dominated music downloading over the past few years, the iPod.If you own a digital player that is not an iPod, then it probably comes with its own software or is affiliated with one of these programs.

www.apple.com/uk/itunes   US/UK
UK IPOD

If you have an iPod here's where to start, the iTunes program can be used with a PC or Mac and it's very easy to select, buy and download your music choice. They offer possibly the largest quality selection of music and audio products.

See also:
www.dailytunes.com – linked to iTunes, it gives recommendations and rediscovers long-lost songs.
www.ipodhacks.com – all the iPod tips and tricks.
www.ipodlounge.com – excellent site devoted to all things iPod.

*Podcasting is one of the latest crazes, you can download or create your own personal radio shows using technology called RSS. Here are some sites to help you on your way. If you don't own an iPod, then check out **www.feedster.com** and see the news and radio sections on pages 333 and 368.*

www.ipodder.org   US
PODCAST

Home of the ipodder program that allows you to get podcasting, it's also a directory of 'podcasts' and there's lots to choose from. See also **www.podcastalley.com** for a great collection of podcasts.

http://sonique.lycos.com   US
THE SONIQUE PLAYER

A good-looking and versatile audio player with lots of options, it plays all the major formats and with its link to the Lycos search engine it's easy to find music.

www.musicmatch.com   US
MUSIC MATCH PLAYER
A good-looking and popular audio player with lots of functions and
access to a catalogue of some 800,000 songs, competitively priced.

www.real.com   US
REAL PLAYER
A popular and versatile audio and video player; the free version
is probably good enough for most users, the radio features are
great too.

www.winamp.com   US
WINAMP PLAYER
The Winamp player is better looking than most and easy to use,
but the free version isn't as good as some of the other free
players. Having said that, the Pro version costs less than £10 and
is excellent. There's also plenty of stuff to download on the site.

*Here's a list of sites that enable you to download a wide variety
of music and audio files, although I suggest you start your
search at* **www.100topmp3sites.com** *Some of these sites
come with their own downloading formats and players, which
may mean they can't play some formats except their own.*

M

http://magnatune.com – from record label Magnatune, you can
get a decent sample of their artists' tracks before you buy.
www.artistdirect.com – great design, with the latest music
news and tunes from over 500,000 artists.
www.bleep.com – good selection of artists from Warp records.
www.dmusic.com – independent digital music site, but the
good stuff is hard to find.
www.eclassical.com – many free classical greats (seem to be
mainly Polish recordings) and many more to buy.
www.emusic.com – offers exclusive DJ mixes, live
performances and prides itself on quality alternative music,
500,000 MP3s to choose from.
www.launch.com – high-quality offering from Yahoo with lots of
features, the emphasis is on popular music and the latest releases.
www.listen.com – a subscription service, where for $9.95
a month you get the Rhapsody player and access to some
50,000 albums.
www.mp3-mac.com – MP3 directory for Mac users, some
don't have iPods after all.

www.mperia.com – downloads using the BitPass system, which means you don't need to be at your own computer to buy them. A wide range of music styles covered, but mainly it's for independent labels and musicians to sell their work.

www.mycokemusic.com – sponsored by Coke, it's aimed at the popular end of the market and there are lots of features to go with it.

www.napster.co.uk – another re-launch of Napster, it's attractive and easy to use, it also claims to have 1 million tracks available. Prices start at 99p per track or £7.95 per album.

www.peoplesound.com – an attempt to sell the work of unsigned artists by promoting them alongside established artists, some surprisingly good stuff here and much of it is free.

www.onlineclassics.net – streaming classical concerts to your PC.

www.pro-music.org – a useful information site on the music industry and legitimate music downloading.

www.weblisten.com – subscription-based service with over 300,000 songs to choose from, great that there are lots of subscription options.

www.wippit.com – good looking, wide range of downloads and pretty good value with prices starting at only £4.99 a month.

File-sharing Programs and Free Downloading

www.zeropaid.com   US

FILE-SHARING PORTAL

A site that lists all the many file-sharing sites, it seems very comprehensive but is not that easy to navigate as the text is quite dense.

http://opennap.sourceforge.net   US

CONNECTING PEOPLE

A variant of the original Napster program, this is freeware and you can select some of the many specialist and general servers which hold music, then use the program to search them for the music you like.

www.gnutella.com   US

THE GNUTELLA NETWORK

Sounds like something you spread on toast, but is basically a mini search engine and file-sharing system on one site. It consists of a network of thousands of computer users, all of whom use Gnutella software 'clones' which link them directly to other users to find music, movies and other files. Also check out **http://gnucleus.sourceforge.net**

www.imesh.com   ISRAEL
SHARE THE PASSION
No central servers here, you join the network and as a member
you can use the search facility to find music or files available
from other members. Supposed to be spyware free.

www.kazaa.com   US
NUMBER 1
Kazaa rapidly became probably the most popular music
download site in 2003. It has lots of features, it's easy to use
and, unlike some of its competitors, attractive to look at. It
comes with virus protection too, although some files we
downloaded came with spyware attached. It works in a similar
way to iMesh.

www.madster.com   US
IT'S MAD...
This used to be Aimster, although not affiliated to AOL, it
combines their Instant Message service with the ability to
search for files and trade them with other users of the network,
of Gnutella or even of Napster. It includes encryption software,
so nobody can monitor your files while they're in transit and
will even tell you which other AOL messenger buddies use it.
Again it claims to have no spyware attached.

M

www.xolox.nl   HOLLAND
SHARE AND DISCOVER
An excellent program which allows you to search for files and
music across many of the established networks featured above.
It's very easy to use and there's a parental control option.

See also:
www.emule-project.net – an unexceptional peer to peer network,
but one that guarantees that it's free of adware and spyware.
www.musiccity.com – uses the FastTrack file sharing system,
their version is called Morpheus. It's quite secure, but has lots
of ads. Good design, lots of unsigned bands and legal.
www.winmx.com – a very flexible file-sharing program that
does not contain spyware.

www.riaa.org   US
RECORDING INDUSTRY ASSOCIATION OF AMERICA
Get the latest information on their attempts to stop music

piracy, the legal issues plus their awards and industry statistics.
See also the site for Electronic Frontier Foundation **www.eff.org**
who campaign on legal issues surrounding digital media.

www.goaudio.co.uk   UK
DIGITAL PLAYERS
A specialist retailer devoted to digital players with some
competitive prices on iPod's and other makes such as Creative
and Rio.

Buying CDs and Other Audio Products

*It's as well to start by checking prices of CDs through price comparison
sites such as those listed on page 364. These will take you to the store
offering the best combination of price and postage. All the stores listed
below offer good value plus a bit extra.*

www.hmv.co.uk   UK
HIS MASTER'S VOICE ONLINE
Excellent features and offers on the latest CDs and videos.
There are sections on most aspects of music as well as video,
DVD and games with a good search facility. You can listen to
selections from albums before buying if you have RealPlayer.
Sign up for £4.99 per month and download up to 50 tracks per
month. Spoken word or books on tape are available as well.

www.cd-wow.com   UK
OUTSTANDING VALUE
A very easy site to use with some great offers on CDs and there's free
delivery too. Probably the best site for value at the time of writing.

www.cduniverse.com   US
WIDE RANGE AND GREAT OFFERS
There is a massive range to choose from and some good
discounts; delivery normally takes only five days. You can also
buy games, DVDs and videos. Excellent, but can be quite slow,
and delivery is very expensive.

www.minidisco.com   US
HOME OF THE MINIDISC
The minidisc is alive and well here with some good offers on
the players and information on the latest developments.
Delivery to Europe takes about a week, costs vary. See also

www.minidisc.org which is a messy site but contains everything you need to know about minidiscs.

For more great offers on music try these sites:
www.101cd.com – renowned for offering good value.
www.amazon.co.uk – as good as you'd expect from Amazon.
www.andante.com – excellent e-zine and online store.
www.audiostreet.co.uk – some good prices, free delivery in UK when you spend over £19.
www.cdnow.com – one of the originals but now part of Amazon.
www.recordstore.co.uk – choose from thousands of vinyl records, CDs, T-shirts, record bags and assorted DJ gear.
www.timelesstracks.com – devoted to the music of the 50s, 60s, 70s and 80s with some excellent prices on CDs.
www.towerrecords.co.uk – wide variety and some good offers – better service than you get from the real store.
www.virgin.net/music – average music store with reviews, digital downloads from 80p per track.

www.secondsounds.com   UK
THE USED CD STORE
With a huge range to choose from and prices from as low as £1.99 and free delivery so you can't really go wrong, they guarantee mint condition or your money back. You can browse by artist or through the bargain bins, and of course they are interested in buying from you too.

www.htfr.co.uk   UK

HARD TO FIND RECORDS
Although they specialise in new and deleted house, garage, techno, electro, disco, funk, soul and hip-hop vinyl, they will try and find any record previously released. They also offer a complete service to all budding and serious DJs.

See also:
www.eil.com – who specialise in rare and collectible CDs and vinyl.
www.popetc.com – who offer a wide range of memorabilia, sheet music, vinyl and rare CD singles.
www.raregrooves.co.uk – lots of choice and lots of offers too, strong in funk, soul, jazz as well as Brazilian and Japanese music.
www.recordfinders.com – a US-based vinyl specialist.

Bands, Groups and Stars

http://ubl.artistdirect.com US

THE ULTIMATE BAND LIST
It is the place for mountains of information on groups or
singers. It has a totally brilliant search facility, and you can buy
and download from the site as well, although the prices are not
as good as elsewhere. For a similar, but better organised site try
www.allmusic.com where you can also get excellent
information and videos.

www.onehitwondercentral.com US

A CATALOGUE OF ONE HIT WONDERS
US oriented information site on those who only triumphed
once, never to be seen again. It's arranged by decade and you
get some interesting titbits in the artist profiles.

www.musicbrigade.com US

WATCH YOUR FAVOURITE ARTIST
An excellent site where you can download your favourite music
videos; when we visited they had nearly 5,000. In the UK
subscription starts at £4.99 a month or £39.99 per annum.

For Aspiring Bands

www.taxi.com US

FOR UNSIGNED BANDS
Looking to get a music contract for your band? You should start
here, there's loads of information, contacts and links that will
help you on the rocky road to success and stardom – well that's
the theory anyway!

For more places to find something new and get help if you're
in a band, see also:
www.audiogalaxy.com – for sampling new and some
existing bands.
www.bpi.co.uk – the British Phonographic Industry and what
they do.
www.burbs.co.uk – British Underground Rock Bands, home of
the UK's real music scene.
www.iuma.com – massive selection of unsigned groups all well
categorised, and if you sign up you can even get your own web site.

www.joescafe.com/bands   UK

BAND NAMES

So you can't think of a name for your band? Here is the 'Band-o-matic' which will offer all sorts of never before used band names in seconds. This time we got 'Hot Pepper Suppositories'. They've branched into song titles too, but can't imagine 'Dracula Fish Man' making the top 20!

Music TV, Awards and Magazine Sites

www.bbc.co.uk/totp   UK

TOP OF THE POPS

The Top of the Pops sites are different, but the principle site is a great magazine featuring the current charts with loads of good features and articles as well as competitions, trivia and lots of information. For those with longer memories try **www.bbc.co.uk/totp2** for golden oldies, 23,000 artists' biographies, and 1 million sound clips and loads of general interest content.

M

Sport

The Good Web Site Guide's Top 10s of the Internet

1.   **www.sporting-life.com** – a great overview of the major sports.
2.   **www.sportzine.co.uk** – excellent for links to loads of sports.
3.   **www.cricinfo.com** – outstanding site on cricket.
4.   **www.fishing.co.uk** – whether you consider angling a sport or not this is excellent.
5.   **www.football365.co.uk** – the best football e-zine, probably.
6.   **www.racingpost.co.uk** – excellent and informative.
7.   **www.itv–f1.com** – ITV have done a brilliant job here.
8.   **www.scrum.com** – a great rugby union site.
9.   **www.mountainzone.com** – if it's outdoors it's covered here.
10. **www.1ski.com** – the best for snow sports.

www.cdukweb.com
UK

UK'S NUMBER ONE MUSIC SHOW
Considering their boast, the web site is a bit of a disappointment
with not much in the way of information or interaction. There are
some quizzes and competitions, and you can download a few
things but it has none of the buzz of the show.

http://uk.fmagazine.com
UK

F MAGAZINE
This one is for broadband users only. The look is stunning and it's
a pleasure to use. The site is presented as an on-screen
magazine and you turn the pages by clicking on the corner of the
page almost like you would a real magazine. The content is pretty
good too; it's aimed at the UK market and covers the new bands
and artists with interviews and videos as well as articles.

www.grammy.com
US

THE GRAMMY AWARDS
An overview of the awards, who won what and when, and
then where to buy their music. For the Brit awards go to
www.brits.co.uk where you'll find a similar site. The MOBO
awards are celebrated at **www.mobo.net**

www.mtv.co.uk
UK

MUSIC TELEVISION
MTV offers loads of info on events, shows and the artists as
well as background on the presenters and creative bits like
movie and music video clips. Great design.

www.nme.com
UK

NEW MUSICAL EXPRESS
If you're a rock fan then this is where it's at. There's all the
usual information, it's well laid out and easy to access. The
archived articles are its greatest asset, featuring 150,000 artists
and every article, feature and review they've ever published
plus full UK discographies, pictures, e-cards, ring tones and
links to the best web sites.

www.q4music.com
UK

Q MAGAZINE
A music magazine site that reflects its parent magazine
extremely well, with many of the features and all the authority
that goes with it.

M

www.popworld.com   UK

WHERE POP COMES FIRST

Brilliant site that concentrates on pop, it's fun and has great graphics. You have to register to join but once you're in you get access to their new shop, competitions, features on your favourite bands, clips from Popworld TV, fashion tips and much more. You need the latest Flash download from Macromedia to get the best out of it.

www.rollingstone.com   UK

ROLLING STONE MAGAZINE

The archetypal music magazine has an excellent site with all the features you'd expect to see including reviews, photos, articles on the bands, downloads, links and games.

www.thebox.co.uk   UK

SMASH HITS YOU CONTROL

Similar to Q but with added features such as the ability for you to select a tune to be played on their TV channel and you can influence their overall selection by voting for your favourite songs. You need to be a member to get the most out of it.

www.vh1.com   UK

MUSIC CHANNEL

VH1 is a music channel and here's the associated web site which is packed with information, interactive features, preview videos and downloads.

Sites for Specific Types of Music

Blues

www.bluesworld.com   US

HOMAGE TO THE BLUES

If you're into the blues then this is your kind of site. There are interviews, memorabilia, 78 auctions, bibliographies, discographies and lists of links to other blues sites. You can order CDs via affiliated retailers and if the mood takes you, order a guitar too.

Classical and Opera

www.gramophone.co.uk   UK

GRAMOPHONE MAGAZINE
An outstanding site with features, reviews, competitions, shop
and concert listings; there's also an awards section plus the
editor's choice with the top recommendations.

www.classicalmusic.co.uk   UK

CLASSICAL MUSIC REVEALED
Excellent for lovers of classical music, with articles, guides,
reviews and concert listings, you can create your fantasy
concert or just browse the excellent links section.

www.operabase.com/en   US

OPERA BASE
This site offers opera listings, information on festivals and provides
background to the history of opera. For the *Opera* magazine site go
to **www.opera.co.uk** which offers articles and links.

Other key classical music sites:
www.aria-database.com – information on over 1,000 arias.
www.choralnet.org – excellent site devoted to choral music.
www.classical.net – great for information and links.
www.classicallink.com – a very good portal site.
www.eclassical.com – download MP3s, many are free.
www.eno.org – the English National Opera.
www.mdcmusic.co.uk – good offers on CDs.
www.orchestranet.co.uk – excellent selection of links.
www.royaloperahouse.org – book online, see where your seat
is and get the latest news.
www.wno.org.uk – Welsh National Opera.

Country

www.thatscountry.com   CANADA

COUNTRY MUSIC SCENE
A good overview of country music with offers and links as well
as information on the artists and bands.

See also:
www.cmdn.net – country music dance.
www.countrymusic.org.uk – still a very naff site that covers
the UK scene.

www.countrystars.com – good all-rounder with a messy design but the shop does supply the UK.

www.roughstock.com – all-round magazine site, live radio and recommended for its excellent history of country.

Dance and Beat

www.thatscountry.com   UK

DANCE, HOUSE AND GARAGE

Great design combined with brilliant content, there's everything here for dance fans – news, information and samples of the latest mixes or, if you're feeling rich, you can buy them too, although you'll probably find cheaper elsewhere.

See also:

www.artofthemix.org – playlists, create your own or use someone else's.

www.beatport.com – digital download dance and beat specialist, great design.

www.garagemusic.co.uk – reviews and samples plus the latest on the UK scene, annoying adverts though.

www.juno.co.uk – good dance music store with a wide range.

Disco

www.disco-disco.com   US

DISCO FEVER

A great site devoted to all things Disco. It's quite comprehensive but it's also worth checking out **www.discomusic.com** which has lots of downloads and also **www.radiowdrc.com** for the World Disco Community.

Folk

www.folkmusic.net   UK

FOLK ON THE WEB

A straightforward site from *Living Traditions* magazine, a collection of articles, features, reviews and news.

See also:

www.folking.com – a good all-round site with news, downloads and shopping.

www.thetraditionbearers.com – a project aimed at keeping alive our traditional songs.

Hip Hop and Rap

www.sohh.com   US
SITE OF HIP HOP
Voted the best of its kind by *Rolling Stone*, this site offers all
you'd expect in terms of news, reviews, forums, interviews and
samples. It also has links to shops and other related sites.

See also:
www.britishhiphop.co.uk – the story of British hip hop and
artist listing and discography.
www.contrabandit.com – apparently hip hop's last hope…
www.hiphopville.com – where to go for all the gear.
www.rapdict.org – the Rap Dictionary helping you through
hip hop slang.
www.rapsheet.com – wide ranging and well-put-together site
offering much of what SOHH does.
www.rapstation.com – a temperamental site but one that really
delivers in terms of information and news.

Indie

www.playlouder.com   UK
INDIE MUSIC
Great graphics and excellent design make Playlouder stand out
from the crowd, it covers the indie music scene in depth with
all the usual features, but with a bit more style. Another really
well designed web site covering indie music in great depth is
Channel Fly **www.channelfly.com** – take your pick! See also
www.drownedinsound.com which is a very good e-zine
devoted to the scene.

Jazz

www.jazzonln.com   US
JAZZ ONLINE
Reviews, links, artist interviews and a guide to the different
types of jazz are all features here. You can download videos too,
although you need 'Quicktime' to view them.

See also:
www.allaboutjazz.com – well organised, slightly dull but very
comprehensive.

www.jazzcorner.com – a beautifully designed jazz magazine
site and directory.
www.jazzimprov.com – an e-zine about jazz improvisation.
www.jazzreview.com – lots of reviews and discussion plus
a photography section and downloads.

Karaoke

www.streamkaraoke.com   US

SING ALONG
Over 20,000 tunes to download but you have to subscribe,
which costs from $9.95 a month depending on which package
you take. See also the British **www.singtotheworld.com**

Reggae

www.reggaetrain.com   US

REGGAE TRAIN A COME
An excellent and comprehensive portal site devoted to all
things reggae, with several hundred links.

See also:
www.niceup.com – comprehensive reggae archive site with
a massive database and links.
www.reggaefusion.com – a huge site devoted to Jamaican music.
www.reggaereview.com – a monthly web magazine from
California.
www.reggaetimes.com – a good site connected with *Reggae
Times*, lots of reviews and links.

Rock and Heavy Metal

www.rocksite.com   US

INFORMATION THAT ROCKS
Devoted to rock music, there are band listings, tour news,
reviews plus links and a musicians directory. All this wrapped
up in an appropriately designed site.

For more try:
www.heavy-metalinks.com – horrible-looking site but it does
have all the links you'll need.
www.history-of-rock.com – a good overview of the roots of rock
and roll.
www.metal-sludge.tv – essential viewing for heavy metal fans.

www.rockhall.com – the Rock and Roll Hall of Fame has an
outstanding site dedicated to celebrating only the best.
www.rockhaven.co.uk – a UK oriented rock portal site.
www.rocklist.net – a compilation of lists from the major music
magazines categorised by year, from the 50s to date, with links
to the relevant sites.
www.rocknrollzone.com – a good, colourful portal and news site.

World Music

www.fly.co.uk   UK

GLOBAL MUSIC CULTURE
An excellent e-zine devoted to world music, with sections by
continent including features and links and a search facilty.

See also:
www.africanmusic.org – the African Music Encyclopedia.
www.frootsmag.com – a highly rated e-zine.

Music Information

www.clickmusic.co.uk   UK

EVERYTHING YOU NEED TO KNOW ABOUT MUSIC
This is great for all music fans. It has quick access to details on
any particular band, with tickets, downloads, gigs and gossip.
Shopping is straightforward: just click on the store or use the
search engine to find something specific. See also
www.musites.com where you can find a rather variable but
improving music search engine.

www.musicsearch.com   US

THE INTERNET'S MUSIC SEARCH ENGINE
Musicsearch is a directory site with over 20,000 links to
reviewed music sites, the search facility has improved and you
can offer up sites to be included.

www.bl.uk/collections/sound-archive/cat.html   US

BRITISH LIBRARY SOUND ARCHIVE
This catalogue contains over 2.5 million entries, there are only
a few sounds you can listen to online, but more are being put
on the site. You can find out how to get a listening appointment
and order copies of the sounds, music or oral recordings. For more
sound effects check out **www.sounddogs.com**

M

www.musicplasma.com   US

IF YOU LIKE MUSIC, YOU'LL LOVE...
At this site you type in the name of the band or artist you like,
and up pops a graphic depiction of all related performers in the
same genre. It's a great way to extend your music tastes and
the site design is really innovative.

See also:
www.eartothesound.com – a very good music information portal.
www.gracenote.com – what looks like a corporate site also
holds the CD database. Click on the CDDC tab and you get
access to an excellent search facility which also offers relevant
links to bands and labels.
www.hitsquad.com – a well-categorised portal site aimed
primarily at musicians.
www.thisdayinmusic.com – what happened on a particular day
plus quizzes and information on music history, although you
have to join to make the most of it.
www.useyourears.co.uk – extensive music portal, everything
from instrumental help to recording studios.
www.vitaminic.co.uk – a music club, excellent portal and host
to many specialist music sites. You have to join to get the best
out of it, including downloads.

Learning Music

M

Long-winded though the site URL is, it's worth paying a visit to
www.si.umich.edu/chico/mhn/enclpdia.html *where you can find a music*
encyclopedia in which you can sample the sound of many instruments.

www.musicsearch.com   US

LEARN MUSIC WITH A GAME
You download the game, which helps you learn the basics –
the more you learn and the better you get the higher the score.

See also:
www.abachamusic.com.au – who offer a fun approach
to music theory.
www.songplayer.com – online music tuition, download the
player, load a CD and it shows you how to play the notes on
keyboard and guitar.

Sites for Specific Instruments

General

www.backstreet.co.uk – equipment hire and shop from this London-based studio.

www.electricbluesclub.co.uk – hours of fun digging around on this site, with links and online lessons for a range of instruments plus masses of info on a variety of styles not just blues.

www.harmony-central.com – all sorts of instruments reviewed and rated.

www.music4worship.co.uk – a music store covering a wide range of musical instruments.

www.musicianshop.com – another musical instrument store, especially good for guitarists.

www.starland.co.uk – musical instruments by mail order, some good offers too.

www.yamaha-europe.com – information on their full range of instruments, including digital pianos and a range of music technology gear plus info on their music schools and teaching system.

Strings

www.violin-world.com – complete resource for all string instruments.

Wind and Brass

www.saxophone.org – great for info and links.
www.wfg.sneezy.org – woodwind.

Percussion

www.drummersweb.com – drummer's delight.
www.giggear.co.uk – a well-stocked shop for all the band's needs.
www.rhythmweb.com – the place to go for all things percussive.

Guitar

www.accessrock.com – free interactive web site for aspiring rock guitarists, great range of lessons.
www.guitar.com – good all-rounder, all you need to know.
www.guitarsite.com – masses of information.
www.guitarstrings.co.uk – a guitar specialist shop.

Electronic

http://nmc.uoregon.edu/emi – great introduction to electronic music and instruments.
www.etcetera.co.uk – download all the latest sampling and music creation software here.
www.kvr-vst.com – technical site with downloads and reviews of the latest hardware and software.
www.synthzone.com – excellent source for articles, links and reviews for all things to do with electronic music making.

Keyboard

www.pianonanny.com – complete piano course.
www.pianoshop.co.uk – masses of links, pianos for sale and information on learning.

M

Sheet Music

www.sunhawk.com   US
DOWNLOAD SHEET MUSIC
Well-designed site where you can download music from a wide variety of styles including pop, Christian, country, Broadway, jazz and classical; you have to pay but there are some freebies.

See also:
www.musicroom.com – a huge range and free postage in the UK.
www.sheetmusicarchive.net – specialising in classical music.
www.sheetmusicplus.com – US oriented but a wide range and some new stuff.

Lyrics and Songs

www.lyrics.com   US

THE WORDS TO HUNDREDS OF SONGS
There are songs from hundreds of bands and artists including
Oasis, Madonna, Britney Spears and Queen, you'll have to ignore
the directory section that makes up most of the page, there's an
A–Z listing at the bottom. Hopefully they'll redesign soon.

Other good lyric sites:
http://home.iae.nl/users/kdv/en/ring.htm – a web ring for lyrics.
www.azlyrics.com – over 43,000 lyrics.
www.britishacademy.com – support and advice for songwriters.
www.letssingit.com – big archive plus karaoke!
www.songfacts.com – information, background and trivia about
thousands of songs.

www.kissthisguy.com   US

MISHEARD LYRICS
Mr Misheard lists all those lyrics that you thought were being
sung but in reality you were just not quite listening properly.
This time we liked 'Something in the way she boos, attracts
me to her mother's lover' but there are hundreds more.

M

Concerts, Clubs and Tickets

www.bigmouth.co.uk   UK

UK'S MOST COMPREHENSIVE GIG GUIDE
UK based, with lots of links to band sites, news, events listing
and information on what's up and coming. Great search facilities
and the ability to buy tickets make this a really useful site for gig
lovers everywhere. It's geared to rock and pop though.

www.ticketmaster.co.uk   UK

TICKETS FOR EVERYTHING
Book tickets for just about anything and you can run searches
by venue, city or date. The site is split into five key sections:
Theatre – theatre, drama and musical
Performing arts – comedy, classical and opera
Music – gigs, jazz, clubs, rock and pop
Attraction – shows, anything from Disney on Ice to air shows
to museums
Sports – tickets for virtually every sporting occasion.

See also **www.seetickets.com**

www.efestivals.co.uk   UK
> FESTIVALS
> Excellent place to review and preview festivals, there are photo
> galleries and you can buy online too.

www.nightclubbinuk.com   UK
> NIGHT CLUB LISTING
> A pretty comprehensive database of the UK's nightclubs
> and clubs, including a clubbing guide and festival listing.
> See also **www.niteclubbers.net** which is more edgy and
> **www.uk-cl.co.uk** which is great for links.

Nature and the Environment

*The Internet offers charities and organisations a chance to highlight
their work in a way that is much more creative than ever before, it
also offers the chance for us to get in-depth information on those
species and issues that interest us.*

Wildlife and Environmental Organisations

www.panda.org   UK
> WWF
> The official site for WWF with information on projects designed
> to save the world's endangered species by protecting their
> environment. You can find out about how to support their work,
> how to get involved, the latest news, information on the key
> projects and some great photos. There is also some good kids'
> and educational material embedded in the news section. An
> American organisation called the National Wildlife Fund has a
> similar excellent site at **www.nwf.org**

www.foe.co.uk   UK
> FRIENDS OF THE EARTH
> Not as worthy as you might imagine, this site offers a stack of
> information on food, pollution, green power, protecting wildlife
> in your area and the latest campaign news.

N

www.envirolink.org   US

THE ONLINE ENVIRONMENTAL COMMUNITY
A huge site focused on personal involvement in environment issues.
There are several well-categorised sections including: organisations,
educational resources, jobs, governmental resources, actions you
can take to help and environment links. There is also a good search
facility on environment-related topics.

www.environment-agency.gov.uk   UK

WHAT THE GOVERNMENT IS UP TO
The Environment Agency's site offers information on the latest
initiatives and news of the latest research. It also helps with
recycling and gives out information on how to improve the
environment plus contact details regarding any issues you have.

www.planetdiary.com   US

WHAT'S REALLY HAPPENING ON THE PLANET
Every week Planetdiary monitors and records world events in
geological, astronomical, meteorological, biological and
environmental terms and relays them back via this web site. It's
done by showing an icon on a map of the world, which you
then click on to find out more. Although very informative, a visit
can leave you a little depressed.

www.biodiversityhotspots.org   US

CONSERVATION INTERNATIONAL
A pleasure to visit, this site is a great example of how the
Internet can be used to inform us about what is going on in the
world. It highlights 25 places in the world where wildlife and
the environment are in a particularly perilous state. Click on the
interactive map and you get taken to a beautifully produced
micro site with as much information as you need on each
place. It shows how you can help and you can sign up for the
newsletter too.

http://earthobservatory.nasa.gov   US

THE EARTH FROM ABOVE
Really outstanding photography and detailed information on the
environment presented in an interesting and thought-provoking
way. Owned by NASA, the site offers sections on the
atmosphere, land and air as well as the latest news stories.

www.projectearth.com   US

NAVIGATING TOWARDS A BETTER ENVIRONMENT
Outstanding site devoted to recognising the damaging effect
man has on the environment and pointing the way towards a
better future.

*For more or specialised information on ecology, nature and
the environment try these sites:*

http://wcs.org – home of New York's Wildlife Conservation
Society who have a very informative site.

www.ace.mmu.ac.uk/eae – most of your questions answered here
at the excellent Encyclopedia of Atmospheric Environment.

www.airquality.co.uk – a site devoted to monitoring the air
quality around the UK.

www.cat.org.uk – a messy site from the Centre for Alternative
Technology, but contains good information.

www.defra.gov.uk – the Department for Environment, Food and
Rural Affairs has a newsy site that offers lots of information and
does it pretty well when you consider the size of their brief.

www.environmentwebsites.co.uk – a portal for environmental sites.

www.ewg.org – an excellent and detailed site from the
Environmental Working Group, dedicated to the fight against
pollution – warning, contains some scary information.

www.futureforests.com – a charity that helps individuals and
organisations to reduce carbon emissions. You can find out how
much you produce and get an idea of what you can do to reduce it.

www.genewatch.org – an organisation devoted to monitoring
the development and effect of GM plants and other uses of
gene modification and testing.

www.greenpeace.org – find out about their latest activities and
how to get involved.

www.grist.org – an e-zine devoted to nature and the environment.
It's well written and in places pretty funny. You can have your say
in the forums and catch up with the latest news.

www.ifaw.org – home of the excellent International Fund for
Animal Welfare

www.nhpa.co.uk – staggeringly beautiful nature photography
from a commercial site, although you have to pay for images
it at least reminds us what it's all about.

www.scorecard.org – the facts on local pollution from the US
oriented but informative site.

www.traffic.org – a campaigning site working against the illegal
and sometimes appalling trade in animals throughout the world.

N

www.ufaw.org.uk – improving animal welfare using scientific knowledge.

www.wildlive.org – sponsored by a mobile phone company, you can get the latest environment news, sponsor wild animals or give money to charity, all from the site or downloaded to your mobile.

www.wri.org – World Resources Institute promoting effective campaigning for a far better world.

Eco Help

www.coralcay.org   UK

HOW YOU CAN JOIN IN

In Coral Cay's words its aim is 'providing resources to help sustain livelihoods and alleviate poverty through the protection, restoration and management of coral reefs and tropical forests'. Sign up for an expedition or a science project in Malaysia or the Philippines.

See also:

www.ecoclub.com – a network providing a wealth of information about all aspects of ecotourism.

www.eco-portal.com – a messy but huge database and links site.

www.ecotourism.org – American site with useful links.

www.ecovolunteer.com – if you want to give your services to a specific animal benefit project.

www.environmentjob.co.uk – jobs and volunteer work in the environment industry.

Natural Phenomena and Geology

http://library.thinkquest.org/C003603/   US

FORCES OF NATURE

An amazing site that covers all the known natural disasters, giving background information, simulations and multimedia explanations with experiments for you to try at home.

See also:

http://gldss7.cr.usgs.gov – the Earthquake Hazards Program has plenty of information on earthquakes. In fact it's amazing how many there are.

http://volcano.und.nodak.edu – all you need to know about volcanoes, the site is poor but the photos are spectacular.

www.fema.gov/kids – Federal Emergency Management Association site aimed at young kids.

www.geographyiq.com – comprehensive geography site.

www.geology.com – an American site covering the whole subject.

www.geologylink.com – an educational bias to this site from a specialist publisher.

www.naturalhazards.org – interesting site with basic information on natural phenomena and links.

www.rockwatch.org.uk – an ebullient site aimed at bringing geology to life for young people.

For information on the Tsunami of December 2004 investigate:
http://serc.carleton.edu/NAGTWorkshops/visualization/collecti ons/tsunami.html – an amazing site devoted to tsunami of December 2004 with excellent animation.

www.tsunami.org – the Pacific Tsunami Museum with stories photos and links.

www.dec.org.uk – if you want to donate to the Tsunami Appeal.

Dinosaurs

www.jpinstitute.com   US

JURASSIC PARK

Excellent offering from the Jurassic Park Institute, particularly for kids, with loads of games and activities, well organised information on hundreds of dinosaurs, timelines and details about the different geologic era. The 'dinolab' is slow to load and best for broadband users.

See also:
www.bbc.co.uk/dinosaurs – excellent site with lots of features.

www.dinodata.net – easy to use and information packed.

www.dinosauria.com – masses of information and articles for the serious-minded adult and child.

www.prehistoricplanet.com – good but out of date.

www.strangescience.net – an interesting site showing how scientists have developed the latest theories about dinosaurs and made mistakes along the way.

www.ucmp.berkeley.edu/diapsids/dinolinks.html – horrid URL but phenomenal list of dino-related web links.

www.ukfossils.co.uk – excellent and informative site on where to find fossils in the UK, includes information on geology too.

Nature Information and Media

www.nhm.ac.uk   UK

THE NATURAL HISTORY MUSEUM
A superb user-friendly web site that covers everything from ants
to eclipses. You can get the latest news, check out exhibitions,
take a tour, browse the Dinosaur database or explore the
wildlife garden. There are details on the collections, galleries,
educational resources and contacts for answers to specific
questions. See also the Smithsonian National Museum of
Natural History, which also has a great site at **www.mnh.si.edu**

www.bbc.co.uk/nature   UK

WILDLIFE EXPOSED
A brilliant nature offering from the BBC with sections on key
wildlife programmes and animal groups. The information is
good and enhanced by video clips.

Other nature sites worth checking out are:
www.enature.com – an American magazine site with a huge
amount of information and features on all aspects of nature.
www.kalama.com/~mariner/qserwild.htm – basically just a list
of good sites devoted to nature; it has a US bias.
www.naturephotographers.net – a magazine devoted to wildlife
photography with a great selection of shots and advice.
www.virtualparks.org – just stunning photography from the
parks of Canada and the US.

Rain Forest and Plant Conservation

www.rainforest-alliance.org   UK

RAINFOREST INFORMATION
Excellent for information and links to related sites, with lots of
news and background on major rainforest projects. A good
place to start any research.

See also:
http://ths.sps.lane.edu/biomes/rain3/rain3.html – a long URL
but worth a visit for the information it contains. It also offers
possibly the worst combination of background and text colours
we've seen so be prepared!

www.greenpeace.org.uk/forests formerly **www.saveordelete.com** – a campaigning site from Greenpeace aimed at exposing the tragic loss of rain forests throughout the globe.

www.plantlife.org.uk – devoted to saving wild habitats and conserving botanically important sites.

www.rainforest.org – home of the Tropical Rainforest Coalition with up-to-date information on rainforest destruction and how you can help.

www.rainforestconcern.org – home of a charity which aims to protect the world's rainforests. The site gives an overview of the problems faced and details on how you can help.

www.rainforestlive.org.uk – a UK education site, it could do with an update, but there is some good stuff here.

www.rainforestweb.org – a comprehensive portal devoted to all things to do with rain forests.

www.ran.org – Rainforest Action Network, another group devoted to saving the rainforest, this one is American. You can't help asking why these charities don't get together?

www.rbgkew.org.uk/conservation – the conservation schemes from the Royal Botanical Gardens at Kew

British Nature

www.naturenet.net   UK

UK COUNTRYSIDE, NATURE AND CONSERVATION
Ignore the rather twee graphics and you'll find a great deal of information about nature in the UK. Their interests include: countryside law, upkeep of nature reserves, voluntary work, education and environmental news. There is also a useful guide to planning regulations.You can also search the site for specifics and there is a good set of links to related sites.

www.uksafari.com   UK

BRITAIN'S WILDLIFE
A good overview of the UK's wild animals with a section on each and tips on wildlife gardening, a photo gallery and lots of additional stuff like film clips, facts and figures and information on nature sites.

www.phenology.org.uk   UK

NATURE'S CALENDAR
Phenology is the study of nature through recurring natural phenomena; this site aims to catalogue all that's relevant to the

UK. It has several excellent sections, in particular the children's and the one devoted to mapping, where you can create your own records.

See also:
www.british-trees.com – information on native trees with good links.
www.englishnature.org.uk – supply maps, photos and information on all our nature reserves and explains why reserves are so important – all on an excellent site.
www.forestry.gov.uk – Forestry Commission has details of its work and how you can help sustain our woods and forests.
www.snh.org.uk – excellent site on Scotland's nature and heritage.
www.treecouncil.org.uk – inspiring a love of trees, it comes with a section on some of our favourite trees.
www.wildlifetrusts.org – one of our most wide-ranging nature charities, highlighting the work of the 47 Wildlife Trusts and 2,500 nature reserves around the UK.
www.woodland-trust.org.uk – dedicated to protecting our woodland heritage.

General and Endangered-animal Sites

www.arkive.org   UK

RAISING AWARENESS OF ENDANGERED SPECIES
Sponsored by the Wildscreen Trust this site's aim is to catalogue and picture all the world's endangered species and has a separate section for the UK. Each animal and plant has a page devoted to it giving details on how and where it lives, including pictures and movie clips. You can help by donating pictures and film.

See also:
http://digimorph.org – a collection of x-ray and computer generated photos of many animals including dinosaurs, fascinating stuff.
http://netvet.wustl.edu/e-zoo.htm – a fun portal site devoted to the animal kingdom, good for research and homework.
www.animalworlddirectory.com – a massive site with a large collection of articles on many aspects of nature and wildlife, from care to tourism.
www.endangeredspecie.com – American site with lots of good photography and background on the causes of species decline.
www.naturecom.de/eng/index.html – a good nature site, some of which is aimed at children.

www.rarespecies.org – an organisation that works out conservation strategies, very interesting to find out how they do it.

www.redlist.org – the Red List of critically endangered and threatened species.

www.wildlifesearch.com – links to sites on almost every animal.

Zoos and Safari Parks

www.safaripark.co.uk   UK

SAFARI ONLINE
A detailed site on the UK's safari parks including opening times, animal information and facts on endangered species.

www.sandiegozoo.org   US

DAN DIEGO ZOO
Probably the best zoo site. You can get conservation information, check out the latest arrivals and browse their excellent photo gallery. The highlights are definitely the zoo cams featuring pandas, elephants, apes and polar bears (remember the 8-hour time difference).

Other good zoo sites:
www.bristolzoo.co.uk – good looking and fun for kids.
www.dublinzoo.ie – slow but good content.
www.londonzoo.co.uk – excellent and comprehensive zoo site, also covers Whipsnade Wildlife Park.
www.marwell.org.uk – masses to see and do.
www.mbayaq.org – beautiful site from Monterey Bay Aquarium with web cams, online field guide and info on ocean research projects.
www.seaworld.com – information on holidays and the attractions at their three zoos.

www.bornfree.co.uk   UK

ZOO CHECK
Zoo Check is a charity whose mission is to promote Born Free's core belief that wildlife belongs in the wild. They expose the suffering of captive wild animals and investigate neglect and cruelty. They want tighter legislation and the phasing out of all traditional zoos. If you want to know more then this is where to go.

African Wildlife and the Big Cats

www.africam.com SOUTH AFRICA

ALWAYS LIVE, ALWAYS WILD

Web cameras have come a long way and this is one of the best uses of them. There are strategically placed cameras at water holes and parks around Africa and other of the world's wildlife areas, and you can tap in for a look at any time. You have to register to get the best out of it, but even a quick visit is rewarding.

See also:
http://elephant.elehost.com – an excellent elephant-only portal site.
www.5tigers.org – excellent site on tigers and how we can help to save the remaining five species.
www.cheetahspot.com – all you need to know about the cheetah.
www.greatcatsoftheworld.com – an overview of the big cats from a US nature centre.
www.lioncrusher.com – all large carnivores and a good picture archive.
www.wildnetafrica.com – this wildlife portal provides information on African animals and how to see them.

Insects

www.bugbios.com US

N

BUGS AND INSECTS

A beautifully designed site exposing insects as miracles of nature, with amazing macro-photography, information and links. See also **www.virtualinsectary.com** which contains some great photography. Home of the Invertebrate Conservation Trust a visit to **www.buglife.org.uk** is also very informative.

http://butterflywebsite.com US

BUTTERFLYING

Not that great design-wise but an interesting site on butterflies. Although it's biased towards the US, it does have sections that cover Britain and it also has a very good links section. For another excellent site devoted to British butterflies go to **www.butterfly-conservation.org** who hold information on all resident and migrating butterflies and moths found in the UK.

Birds

www.birds.com   US

ALL ABOUT BIRDS
An online directory and guide to birds covering both wild and
pets. It's biased towards America but otherwise excellent,
except that it's a bit too commercial.

See also:
www.birdguides.com – informative site with free videos and
a specialist store.
www.birdlinks.co.uk – some 500 bird-related links.
www.birdsofbritain.co.uk – a strong monthly web magazine
for British bird watchers.
www.bto.org – tracking birds and their behaviour.
www.ornithology.com – a good, if serious, site dedicated to
wild birds.
www.rspb.org.uk – the Royal Society for the Protection of Birds
have a nice site detailing what they do, and how you can help.

For Garden Lovers

The Good Web Site Guide's Top 10s of the Internet

1. **www.rhs.org.uk** – home of the Royal Horticultural Society.
2. **www.gardenworld.co.uk** – for a garden centre near you.
3. **www.crocus.co.uk** – the best gardening shop.
4. **www.gardenweb.co.uk** – excellent for chat and information.
5. **www.hdra.org.uk** – the authority on organic gardening.
6. **www.bbc.co.uk/gardening** – great stuff from the Beeb.
7. **www.ngs.org.uk** – home of the excellent National Garden Scheme.
8. **www.chilternseeds.co.uk** – masses of seeds, order online.
9. **www.nhm.ac.uk/science/projects/fff** – our wild flora and fauna.
10. **www.allotments–uk.com** – all you need to know about
    your allotment.

Apes and Early Humans

www.becominghuman.org   US
> HUMAN ORIGINS
> A superb site detailing the progress of human evolution,
> showing our development in an interactive and enthralling way.
> Beautifully illustrated throughout; however, it can be a little
> slow, so best seen by broadband users.
>
> *For other sites that feature our evolution and our nearest
> relatives try:*
> **www.archaeologyinfo.com/evolution.htm** – good site on
> human evolution, the Hall of Skulls is great for showing our
> development through time.
> **www.chimps-inc.com** – a non-profit organisation devoted
> to chimpanzees.
> **www.gorilla.org** – home of the Gorilla Foundation and Koko.
> **www.greatapeproject.org** – campaigning on rights for apes.
> **www.janegoodall.org** – very well-put-together site featuring the
> work of this pioneer with biographical details and information
> on chimpanzees and how you can help preserve them.
> **www.unep.org/grasp** – the Great Apes Survival Project aims
> to help preserve the species, specifically orangutans, bonobos,
> gorillas and chimpanzees.

Bears

www.bears.org   US
> BEAR BELIEFS
> An overview of the major species of bears with lots of
> background, photos, myths and also detailed information
> on their habits and lifestyles.
>
> *See also:*
> **http://nationalzoo.si.edu/Animals/GiantPandas** – excellent site
> on pandas from the Smithsonian.
> **www.polarbearsalive.org** – the web's largest polar bear site!
> Lots of info and photos too.

Marine

www.wdcs.org   UK

WHALE AND DOLPHIN SOCIETY

All the latest news and developments in the fight to save
whales and dolphins. There's also information on them, how
and where they live, a 'Sightings and Strandings' section and
details of how to book a whale-watching holiday.

See also:
www.cetacea.org – an excellent site where you can get
background info on every species of dolphin, whale and porpoise.
www.flmnh.ufl.edu/fish – the University of Florida's
Department of Ichthyology has a good site where you can find
an overview of all things fishy plus links and a good selection
of photographs.
www.seasky.org – one man's love affair with the sea and
space. In the sea half you'll find some excellent sections on
such things as coral reef and ocean exploration.
www.seawatchfoundation.org.uk – here you can learn more
about cetaceans, and their sightings around the UK.

News and the Media

*The standard of web sites in this sector is usually very high making
it difficult to pick out one or two winners, just find one which appeals
to you and you won't go far wrong. Nowadays it's easy to create your
own news feeds, in this section we show you how.*

N

World News

www.sky.com/skynews   UK

WITNESS THE EVENT

Sky News has fast developed a reputation for excellence and
that is reflected in their web site. It has a well-rounded news
service with good coverage across the world as well as the UK.
You can view news clips, listen to news items or just browse
the site. There are special sections on sport, business,
technology and even a few games.

www.bbc.co.uk/news   UK

FROM THE BBC
As you'd expect the BBC site is excellent – similar to Sky but without
the adverts. You can also get the news in several languages and
tune into the World Service or any of their radio stations.

www.channel4.com/news   UK

AWARD-WINNING NEWS
High quality journalism reflects the independent and serious
nature of their news coverage. There are some interesting links
and a forum – you can even register to receive 'Snowmail' from
John Snow himself.

www.itn.co.uk   UK

INDEPENDENT TELEVISION NEWS
As well as links to independent TV and radio news sites, ITN
houses the world's largest TV-based video archive and is also
home to the ITN stills collection. It's not cheap (video starts at
£100 and stills at £25 for a one-off use) and is aimed at the
professional market, but there is some amazing stuff here.

www.cnn.com   US

THE AMERICAN VIEW
CNN is superb on detail and breaking news with masses of
background information on each story. It has plenty of feature
pieces too. However, it is biased towards the American
audience, for a similar service try **www.abcnews.com**

www.newsnow.co.uk   UK

NEWS NOW!
A superb news gathering and information service that you can
tailor to your needs and interests. The layout is confusing at
first but it allows you to flick between latest headlines from
3,000 leading news sources without visiting each site
separately, you can then read their choice of stories in full on
the publishers' web sites. It's updated every five minutes!

www.ananova.co.uk   UK

NEWS ON THE MOVE
Ananova has been changed a few times and in the latest guise
you get a well-put-together site that is much clearer than some.
They've also teamed up with Orange to produce a mobile text
messaging news service.

www.moreover.com   US

DYNAMIC CONTENT

With real-time news and rumour reporting, Moreover has
become the news site of choice for many business people and
journalists as it enables them to target the type of news and
information they are looking for, saving time and effort all
round. You need to subscribe to gain access.

http://english.aljazeera.net   UAE

AL JAZEERA

The English version of the well-known Arab news agency. It's
very good for world events and as you'd expect outstanding
when it comes to gaining an insight into the Arab world. See
also **www.arabnews.com** the Arab English language daily.

Other news sites worth a visit are:
www.anorak.co.uk – humorous newspaper reviews.
www.copydesk.co.uk – a very good blog site devoted to news
and popular culture, it's great for news links too.
www.economist.co.uk – business, world events and in-depth
reports.
www.findarticles.com – an article search engine from
LookSmart with access to some 900 publications.
www.irishnews.com – a competent site from *Irish News.*
www.newseum.org – an attempt to archive US newspapers.
www.nuzgeeks.com – excellent links.
www.positivenews.org.uk – for a positive spin on the news.
www.private-eye.co.uk – some of the best features from the
mag, but not much news if truth be told.
www.publist.com – a news search engine covering over
100,000 titles world-wide.
www.reuters.co.uk – strong site from this world-renowned
news agency. Those with broadband can benefit from their
excellent TV news feeds.
www.thefridayproject.co.uk – UK news and politics.
www.theregister.co.uk – for technology news.
www.time.com – an excellent site from *Time* magazine.
www.topix.net – a news collation site which is exceptional for
American news.
www.worldflash.com – download a news ticker and get the
latest news as it happens.

N

Events and Future News

www.drudgereport.com   US

NOW FOR THE REAL NEWS

One of the most visited sites on the web. It's a pain to use, but the gossip and tips about upcoming features in the papers make it worthwhile. One of its best features is its superb set of links to other news sources.

www.foreignreport.com   UK

PREDICT THE FUTURE

Owned by Janes, the Foreign Report team attempt to pick out trends and happenings that might lead to bigger international news events. Browsing through their track record shows they're pretty good at it too.

www.wwevents.com   UK

WORLD EVENTS

Details of events that are happening in the world today, tomorrow and this weekend all available at the touch of a button, it really is that simple. You can search by country or even region and county.

Newspapers Online

www.telegraph.co.uk   UK

THE TELEGRAPH

The Telegraph has the best site for news and layout with all its sections mirrored very effectively on the site.

Other major newspapers with sites worth a visit include:
www.dailymail.co.uk – not so much the paper as a portal for Associated Newspapers, which is disappointing, but there are some good articles and features.
www.guardian.co.uk – clean site with lots of added features and guides.
www.independent.co.uk – good online debate as well as news.
www.thesun.co.uk – very good representation of the paper with all you'd expect.
www.timesonline.co.uk – no surprises here.

www.fish4news.co.uk UK

LOCAL NEWS MADE EASY
An outstanding web site, just type in your postcode and back
will come a collated local 'newspaper' with regional news
headlines, sport and links to the source paper sites and small
ads. Also see **www.newspapersoc.org.uk** and go to 'newspaper
links' to find your local paper.

www.whatthepaperssay.co.uk UK

WHEN YOU'VE NOT GOT TIME
Can't be bothered to sift through the papers? At this site you
can quickly take in the key stories and be linked through to the
relevant newspaper site too. You can also sign up to its daily
e-mail bulletin so you need never buy a paper again. See also
www.thepaperboy.com which is a bit more colourful and has
a good search facility.

Creating Your Own Newspaper or News Feed

*RSS or Really Simple Syndication is one of the latest Internet toys and
its use enables you to create your own news feeds, tailoring them to
your tastes. You can even share them with friends and family.*

*First you download your 'aggregator' program (see below for the list)
then look out for sites that offer a feed; they usually have an RSS or
XML sign at the bottom of the page or on an orange button. Most
major sites have them while some programs and sites allow you to set
up your own.*

http://uk.my.yahoo.com UK

MY YAHOO
Probably the simplest way to construct your own news feed, sign up
then follow the well-written instructions. It's pretty easy to maintain;
however, you are limited in terms of look and design.

www.feeddemon.com US

FEED DEMON
Considered to be one of the best RSS newsreader programs,
it's certainly very straightforward and easy to set up. It costs
$29.95, although you can download a trial version. Everything
is explained and for those new to this technology, it's probably
the best on the market.

www.whatthepaperssay.co.uk   UK
FREE NEWS READER
Possibly not quite as user friendly for beginners as Feed Demon
but, as it's free, it's probably worth starting off with this program.
See also **www.pluck.com** which is popular and also free.

See also:
www.completeRSS.com – a useful directory of news feed links.
www.crayon.net – nice design and easy to use but geared
solely to the US market.
www.feedster.com – free and it's relatively easy to set up,
although you'll ideally need to know your news feed URLs first.
www.myrsscreator.com – a wide range of options here, we
especially liked the news maps.
www.syndic8.com – another news feed and directory site.

Organiser and Diary

www.opendiary.com   UK
THE ONLINE DIARY FOR THE WORLD
Your own personal organiser and diary, easy to use, genuinely
helpful and totally anonymous. Simply register and away you go
but follow the rules faithfully or you get deleted. Use it as you
would any diary, go public or just browse other entries.

See also:
http://pim.kde.org – a free suite of programs including an
address book and organiser, good for Linux users in particular.
http://uk.calendar.yahoo.com – Yahoo has an excellent, free
and easy-to-use calendar facility.
www.calendars.net – create your own calendar here, especially
good for web masters.
www.calendarzone.com – information on calendars,
categorised by subject from astrology to the religious.
www.datereminder.co.uk – never forget a birthday or
anniversary again, just load them in here and you'll get
reminded near the time.
www.filofax.co.uk – if you can't live without the real thing.
www.iping.com – wake up calls, reminders and much more…
www.livejournal.com – download your own journal and
customise it to suit.

www.supercalendar.com – good for groups and businesses as
well as individuals but it costs around £10 per annum.
www.yourorganiser.com.au – good-looking site, easy to use
with a personal or group organiser facility.

Over 50s

*If you're over 50 then you're part of the fastest growing group of
Internet users, and some sites have cottoned on to the fact with
specific content just for you.*

Magazines, Fun and Advice

www.saga.co.uk   UK

THE SAGA GROUP
While this is a commercial organisation aimed at the over 50s, it
offers much in the way of advice, help and information in key areas
such as health, travel and money plus the magazine is excellent.

www.idf50.co.uk   UK

I DON'T FEEL FIFTY
Graham Andrews is retired and this is his irreverent and
opinionated magazine site. It's very positive about the power of
being over fifty and it has a great deal of motivational advice on
how to get the best out of life combined with a superb set of
links to useful sites.

See also:
www.theoldie.co.uk – *The Oldie* magazine, which is great fun.
www.togs.org – where devoted fans of Terry Wogan meet.
www.over50s.com – a well-designed magazine-style site,
good information and financial advice.

Links

www.50connect.co.uk   UK

LIVE LIFE TO THE FULL
A very strong portal site with masses of information and links
covering a wide range of topics. It's incredibly useful; however,
there are plenty of annoying adverts to go with it.

See also:
www.age-net.co.uk – another portal site but one that takes a magazine-style approach.
www.laterlife.com – a comprehensive site with lots of links and advice in many categories.
www.lifes4living.co.uk – an upbeat site dedicated to chat and links, some good offers too.
www.seniority.co.uk – a very comprehensive offering covering all you are likely to need with advice and links. Not exactly the most inspiring design though.
www.silversurfers.net – not the easiest site to get to grips with but it has a huge number of links in over 50 categories.

Information and Help

www.over50.gov.uk   UK

ARE YOU OVER 50?
A useful and informative site from the government devoted to helping older people by offering practical help. You'll find many links to government departments and voluntary organisations, plus help guides to download. There's a separate section devoted to Scotland.

www.ageconcern.co.uk   UK
WORKING FOR ALL OLDER PEOPLE
Learn how to get involved with helping older people, get information and practical advice on all aspects of getting old. You can also make a donation. There are also over 100 links to related and special interest sites.

www.helptheaged.org.uk   UK
HELP THE AGED
Find out how you can get involved in their work, what they do plus the latest news. You can also go to 'home shopping' and buy all sorts of useful gadgets to make life easier.

www.grandparents-association.org.uk   UK
THE GRANDPARENTS' ASSOCIATION
Offers a newsletter, factsheets, advice and support for grandparents who are caring for their grandchildren as well as those who have lost touch with theirs.

www.hairnet.org   UK

TECHNOLOGY EXPLAINED

So you've bought the PC and now you need to know how to
work it properly? Hairnet explains all through a series of forums
and specific courses designed to help you get the most from
technology. See also **www.seniornet.org** which is a pretty
boring but comprehensive guide.

www.u3a.org.uk   UK

LIFELONG LEARNING

An organisation working to improve the lives of older people
through the concept of life-long learning and learning for the
pleasure of it. The site offers details of the subjects covered
and how to contact the relevant groups.

www.age-exchange.org.uk   UK

MAKE YOUR MEMORIES MATTER

Share your experiences and pass them on, Age Exchange aims to
'improve the quality of life for older people by emphasising the value
of their memories to old and young, through pioneering artistic,
educational, and welfare activities' they are also active in improving
care for older people. This site gives details of how you can join in.

See also:
www.csv-rsvp.org.uk – home of the Retired and Senior
Volunteer Program.
www.experiencecorps.co.uk – voluntary work and a positive
use of your experience.
www.laterlife.com – lots of information, links and chat.
www.wiseowls.co.uk – dedicated to tackling ageism, and
a good community site.

Travel

www.saga.co.uk/travel   UK

HOLIDAYS FOR THE OVER 50S

A superbly illustrated and rich site from Saga who've been
specialising in holidays for older people for many years. Here
you'll find everything from top-quality cruises to weekend breaks.

See also:
www.classicski.co.uk – a skiing operator specialising in mature
skiers whether they be beginners or experienced.

www.**eldertreks.com** – a good site from a specialist in adventure travel for the over 50s.

www.**responsibletravel.com** – have an excellent range of environmentally sensitive holidays for over 50s in their 'activities' listing.

www.**travel55.co.uk** – a great database of travel sites specialising in travel for older people.

Parenting

As a source of advice, the Internet has proved its worth, and especially so for parents. As well as information, there are useful sites that filter out the worst of the web and give advice on specific problems. Some of the education web sites, page 115, also have useful resources for parents as do the health sites, page 225. For shopping, see the children's section on page 82 and the general shopping section, starting on page 402. In addition, there is loads of useful stuff for parents in the travel section on page 518 about taking children on holiday and activities to do with the children in the UK.

Advice and Information

www.babyworld.co.uk   UK

BE PART OF IT
Babyworld is an online magazine that covers all aspects of parenthood. There's excellent advice on how to choose the right products for your baby and for the pregnancy itself. The layout is much improved and it's easier to find information.

www.babycentre.co.uk   UK

A HANDS-ON GUIDE
A superb site with a massive amount of information and links to all aspects of pregnancy, childbirth and early parenthood. The content is provided by experts and you can tailor-make your profile so that you get the right information for you. There's also a series of buying guides to help you make the right decision on baby shopping.

www.babyzone.com   US

THE NORTH AMERICAN WAY
From the massive American site on parenting, here you get a

week-by-week account of pregnancy, information on birth and
early childhood. The links are very good and there's plenty of
information on offer to parents. See also the similarly well-put-
together **www.parentsoup.com**

www.raisingkids.co.uk
UK

FROM BIRTH TO...
An information-laden site devoted to helping parents get
through the minefield of child raising with sections on every life
stage, it's particularly good on parenting teens. You can also
ask an expert, and, amongst many sections, there's advice on
travel, education and safety.

www.netmums.com
UK

LOCAL INFORMATION
A very useful support site for mums that provides localised
information about what's going on and what help is available.

www.ukparents.co.uk
UK

YOUR PARENTING LIFELINE
Chat, experiences, stories and straightforward advice make this
site worth a visit – there are competitions, links and plenty of
opportunities for interaction.

www.all4kidsuk.com
UK

IF YOU'RE LOOKING FOR SOMETHING TO DO
This aims to be a comprehensive directory covering all your
parental needs from activities to schools. It's got an easy-to-use
search engine, where you can search by county if you need to.

www.miriamstoppard.com
UK

MIRIAM STOPPARD LIFETIME
An excellent web site from the best-selling author with lots of
advice on being a parent, how to cope with pregnancy and
keeping yourself and your family healthy. New information is
continually being added, so it's very up to date and will become
a great resource for parents.

www.parentalk.co.uk
UK

THE SENSIBLE APPROACH
Interesting articles and sensible advice characterise this site.
There is a helpful section for working parents and one for

employers plus a good links section for expert advice on a wide range of topics. If the advice here isn't enough, you can buy their books or take the course. For another good site with the same aims try **www.parentlineplus.org.uk**

www.parentcentre.gov.uk   UK
THE LOW-DOWN ON EDUCATION
The Parent Centre is for all parents and carers who want to help their child or children to learn. It really covers everything from choosing a school or nursery to detailed information on what a child should learn. It also provides information about the rights and responsibilities of parents in a wider sense, advice and links.

www.babydirectory.com   UK
A–Z OF BEING A PARENT
The Baby Directory catalogue is relevant to most parts of the UK. It lists local facilities plus amenities that care for and occupy your child. The quality of information varies by area though.

www.tommys.org   UK
PREMATURITY, MISCARRIAGE AND STILLBIRTH
Information on getting through some of the tragedies that occur in pregnancy plus details on how you can help.

Other useful sites:
www.allkids.co.uk – a well-categorised portal site covering all things for children including good shopping directory.
www.babyandkids.co.uk – an American-style advice site aimed at the UK.
www.babynames.com – over 6,500 names to choose from plus other services and lots of adverts!
www.ncb.org.uk – home of the National Children's Bureau who provide support for children's charities and support organisations.
www.nctpregnancyandbabycare.com – a well-designed and informative site from the NCT covering the first year or so.
www.parenthood.com – lots of advice from this US-oriented site.
www.pinkparents.org.uk – support site for lesbian, gay and bisexual parents and parents-to-be and their children. You need to subscribe to get access to all areas.

Problem Relationships

Sites of particular interest to fathers are found on page 288 and mothers on page 538.

www.ondivorce.co.uk   UK

MANAGING DIVORCE AND SEPARATION
The first place to go when faced with divorce or separation.
There is sound financial, legal, practical and emotional support
and excellent links. See also **www.family-solicitors.co.uk**

www.gingerbread.org.uk   UK

SUPPORT FOR LONE-PARENT FAMILIES
Gingerbread is an established charity run by lone parents with
the aim of providing support to lone parents. The site is fun to
use and well designed, and is one of the few web sites that is
available in several languages. For more advice on being a
single parent see **www.oneparentfamilies.org.uk** who have a
useful 'helpline' information search facility.

www.fathers-4-justice.org   UK

FIGHTING FOR ABSENT FATHERS' RIGHTS
Learn more about their well-publicised campaign for truth, justice
and equality in family law. Here you can join the movement, find
out about forthcoming events and buy the T-shirt. For an
alternative approach try Families Need Fathers at **www.fnf.org.uk**
and also **www.fathersdirect.com** an informative site from the
National Information Centre on Fatherhood.

See also:
http://britishdna.co.uk – paternity testing.
www.blendedfamilybliss.com – offers US-style practical and
sympathetic advice.
www.ncds.org.uk – National Council for the Divorced and
Separated, information on their network of local clubs.
www.relate.org.uk – relationship counselling for couples or
families, face to face, online or by phone.
www.reunite.org – a charity specialising in international child
abduction provides an impressive site with loads of information.
www.stepfamilies.co.uk – chat with other step-parents, read
articles, submit poetry all on an informal, upbeat site.

P

Childcare

www.bestbear.co.uk   UK

MARY POPPINS ONLINE
Select your postcode and they will provide you with a list of
reputable childcare agencies or nurseries in your area. There
are also homepages for parents, childcarers and agencies all
with information and ideas. There is also a parents' forum. See
also **www.sitters.co.uk**

www.childcarelink.gov.uk   UK

SURESTART
Surestart is part of the government's childcare programme and
the web site is designed to provide information about childcare
options in a given locality. Search by postcode or town name.
It also has a good links section.

www.daycaretrust.org.uk   UK

CHILDCARE ADVICE
Daycare Trust is a national childcare charity which works to
promote high-quality, affordable childcare for all. This site is
designed to give you all the information you need on arranging
care for your child; there are sections on finance and news,
and you can become a member.

Dealing With Areas of Parental Concern

General

www.childline.org.uk   UK

A CHILD'S-EYE VIEW
There's a huge amount of advice on a wide range of issues
from bullying, domestic violence, dealing with death, racism
and exam stress. The advice is aimed at youngsters, but it is
worth parents looking at that advice too.

www.nchafc.org.uk   UK

NATIONAL CHILD HELP
A charity aimed at helping children and parents across a wide range
of subjects, issues and problems. A good place to start getting help.

Achohol

See the section on drugs and alcohol on page 349.

Allergies

www.anaphylaxis.org.uk   UK
ALLERGY AND ANAPHYLAXIS
A useful site with information and links on food allergies
and their reactions, it's very much oriented to the US so also
try **www.anaphylaxis.org.uk**, which is also very helpful and
UK based. For info on E-numbers go to **www.foodag.com**

Bereavement

www.childbereavement.org.uk   UK
CHILD BEREAVEMENT TRUST
Support for those who have suffered the loss of a loved one.
There is a section dedicated to families and one for young
people. The Cruse Bereavement Centre also has a site aimed
at young people at **www.rd4u.org.uk**

Homework and Learning

TOP 10

The Good Web Site Guide's Top 10s of the Internet

1. **www.homeworkelephant.co.uk** – masses of help and info,
    top site.
2. **www.homeworkhigh.co.uk** – from Channel 4, great for the
    most popular subjects.
3. **www.kevinsplayroonm.co.uk** – award-winning and popular site.
4. **www.learn.co.uk** – sponsored by the *Guardian*, quality assured.
5. **www.schoolsnet.com** – an impressive one stop shop for education.
6. **www.schoolzone.co.uk** – a superb education search engine.
7. **www.samlearning.com** – tips, past papers, even competitions.
8. **www.gridclub.com** – another great C4 site this one aimed
    at 7- to 11-year olds.
9. **www.underfives.co.uk** – a brilliant education site for pre-school kids
10. **www.nc.uk.net** – the home of the National Curriculum.

P

Bullying

www.bullying.co.uk   UK

> HOW TO COPE WITH BULLYING
> Advice for everyone on how to deal with a bully; there are sections
> on tips for dealing with them, school projects, problem pages and
> links to related sites. See also **www.successunlimited.co.uk.**
> Another good site to try is **www.kidscape.org.uk**

Child Protection

www.teachernet.gov.uk/wholeschool/   UK
andcommunity/childprotection

> KEEP THEM SAFE
> Although primarily aimed at teachers, this site gives the low-
> down on child protection law and policy. The 'Advice and
> Guidance' is particularly useful as it addresses the wider
> community and parents, and provides further links.

Computers and the Internet

www.cyberpatrol.com   US

> INTERNET FILTERING SOFTWARE
> The best for filtering out unwanted web sites, images and
> words. As with all similar programs, it quickly becomes
> outdated but will continue to weed out the worst. You can
> download the very commercial free trial from the site. See also
> **www.netnanny.com** whose site offers more advice and seems
> to be updated more regularly.

www.pin.org.uk   US

> PARENTS' INFORMATION NETWORK
> Provides good advice for parents worried about children using
> computers. It has links to support sites, guidance on how to
> surf the Net, evaluations of software and buyer's guides to PCs.

> *See also:*
> **www.iwf.org.uk** – the Internet Watch Foundation who combat
> child online abuse.
> **www.kidsmart.org.uk** – aimed at schools, this is a good course
> on how to stay safe on the net.
> **www.parentsonline.gov.uk** – a government site used to
> promote the benefits of the Internet as an educational tool to
> parents. Excellent for links.

www.safekids.com – a basic site that is a useful place to go for links and resources if you're worried about your children coming across something unsuitable on the Net.

Disability and Rare Disorders

www.cafamily.org.uk   UK

SUPPORT FOR FAMILIES

A charity that provides support and advice to parents of children with a medical problem or disability. They have information on over 1,000 rare syndromes and can often put families in touch with others facing similar problems. See also the Council for Disabled Children at **www.ncb.org.uk/cdc**

Divorce

www.itsnotyourfault.org   UK

DIVORCE AND SEPARATION

A useful site with sections for parents, teens and children that attempts to take some of the anguish and guilt out of divorce and separation. See also page 345.

Drugs and Alchohol

www.theantidrug.com   US

TRUTH: THE ANTIDRUG

An outstanding site devoted to the fight against drugs with help for parents and children alike. There's plenty of advice, articles and general information and it's all written in an accessible style, and in several languages.

www.talktofrank.com or **www.ndh.org.uk**   UK

TALK TO FRANK

The NHS's drug site has non-judgemental, factual information on all the major recreational drugs with useful information on what to do in an emergency – or call The National Drugs Helpline 0800 776600, and **www.hit.org.uk** or **www.drugscope.org.uk.**

Dyslexia/Dyspraxia

www.bda-dyslexia.org.uk   UK

BRITISH DYSLEXIA ASSOCIATION

A good starting point for anyone who thinks that their child might be dyslexic. There is masses of information on dyslexia, choosing a school, a list of local Dyslexia Associations where you can get assessment and teaching, articles on the latest research and educational materials for sale. There is also information on adult dyslexia. For similar material visit **www.dyslexia-inst.org.uk** who also offer testing and teaching through their centres. If you're thinking of opting out and taking the home education route go to **www.dyslexics.org.uk**

www.dyspraxiafoundation.org.uk   UK
DYSPRAXIA EXPLAINED
Information and practical help aimed at anyone who is coping with a dyspraxic child including how to find your local support group and up-to-date research news.

Eating Disorders

www.edauk.com   UK
EATING DISORDERS ASSOCIATION
If you think you have a problem with eating then at this site you can get advice and information. It doesn't replace going to the doctor but it's a place to start. There are helplines – youth is 01603 765 050, others 01603 621 414.

Health

www.iemily.com   US
GIRL'S HEALTH
A massive A–Z listing of all the issues and problems you might face. It's easy to use and the information is straight to the point and often accompanied by articles relating to the subject.
See also the sections on health advice, page 225, and women's health on page 541.

www.kidshealth.org/teen   UK
IT'S GOT IT COVERED
An excellent American site divided into three sections: parents, kids and teens. It is really comprehensive and a good place to go if you want information about an illness, developmental concern of just some advice. The teen section is particularly good, especially on food and its relation to health.

Law

www.childrenslegalcentre.com   UK

FREE LEGAL HELP
A charity that provides free and confidential legal advice and an
information service, covering all aspects of the law affecting
children and young people. They can help provide advocates in
disputes with the Local Education Authority and campaigns for
children's rights in the UK and overseas. To keep in touch with
policy changes relating to children and young people go to
www.childpolicy.org.uk

Missing Children

www.missingkids.co.uk   UK

UK'S MISSING CHILDREN
This site is dedicated to reuniting children with their families.
The details of those missing are based on police and home
office data. You can search by town or date and there's also
a section on those who've got back together.

Also try:
www.missingpersons.org – the missing persons helpline
0500 700700.
www.salvationarmy.org.uk – for their family tracing service.

Racism

www.britkid.org   UK

DEALING WITH RACISM
A game that shows how different ethnic groups live in the Britain of
today, full of interesting facts and information. There's a serious side,
which has background information on dealing with racism,
information on different races and their religious beliefs.

Safety

www.childalert.co.uk   UK

CHILD SAFETY
This is about bringing up children in a safe environment; there are
tips, product reviews and a shop, stories, links and masses of advice
and information. Except for the shop, the site is well designed and
it's easy to find things. See also **www.yoursafechild.com**

www.childcarseats.org.uk   UK
> CAR SAFETY
> All you need to know about buying, fitting and using child car seats.

Sex

*The following sites provide accessible, factual information. The
sections on health, page 225, men, page 289, teens, page 453,
and women, page 541, may also provide relevant information.*

www.playingsafely.co.uk   UK
> HERE TO ANSWER YOUR QUESTIONS
> Great site that has lots of information on sex as well as games
> and links to related sites. The emphasis is on safe sex and
> AIDS prevention. See also the Terence Higgins Trust at
> **www.tht.org.uk** this is the leading AIDS charity.

www.likeitis.org.uk   UK
> TELLING IT LIKE IT IS
> A really outstanding site from the Marie Stopes Institute giving
> good, straight information on all the major issues around sex
> and puberty that face teenagers today. The 'Cool or Fool' quiz is
> excellent and there's a 'Dear Doctor…' facility too.

www.fpa.org.uk   UK
> FAMILY PLANNING ASSOCIATION
> Straightforward and informative, you can find out where to get
> help and there's a good list of web links too. See also the
> British Pregnancy Advisory service at **www.bpas.org**

Speech

www.speechteach.co.uk   UK
> SPEECH THERAPY
> Information, help and advice on what to do if your child has
> speech problems or communication difficulties. The site aims
> to provide a learning resource for parents and teachers alike.

Stress and Mental Health

www.rethink.org/at-ease   UK
> YOUR MENTAL HEALTH
> At-ease offers loads of good advice on how to deal with stress and
> is aimed specifically at young people. Go to the A–Z section, which
> covers a large range of subjects from dealing with aggression to
> exam stress to how to become a volunteer to help others. See also
> **www.youngminds.org.uk**

www.isma.org.uk/exams.htm   UK
> EXAM STRESS
> Top tips on coping with exams from the International Stress
> Management Association.

Party Organising

In this section you'll find all you need to organise the perfect party.

www.partydomain.co.uk   UK
> PARTY PARTY!!
> Probably the best of the party shop sites with a wide range of
> fancy dress gear, lots of themed party ideas and options plus a
> party calendar. Shopping is secure with lots of delivery options.

> *See also:*
> **www.charliecrow.co.uk** – a wide range of fancy dress costumes
> primarily for kids' parties.
> **www.evite.com** – where you can create your own invitations.
> **www.justforfun.co.uk** – a good selection of party products here.
> **www.kids-party.com** – a great resource, find out all you need
> to hold a kid's party in your area.
> **www.partypieces.co.uk** – very experienced party suppliers with
> a wide range of products and 48-hour delivery.
> **www.partyzone.co.uk** – specialises in supplying gear and
> goods for children's parties.
> **www.printed4u.co.uk** – party invitations printed.

P

Pets

Here's a selection of web sites devoted to pets: shop and information sites, and specialists too.

www.mypetstop.com   UK
MULTINATIONAL PETS
Apparently the only multilingual web site about pets. It's superb for information and health advice as well as links too. It has sections devoted to each type of pet and animal, and each is pretty comprehensive.

For other good online pet information, services and stores visit:
www.allaboutpets.org.uk – excellent advice and care site from the Blue Cross charity.
www.bluepet.co.uk – specialists in organic food for pets.
www.lostpets.co.uk – an informative site on what to do if you lose your pet, includes a lost pet finder service.
www.newpet.com – advice and help for those who are thinking about getting a pet for the first time.
www.petpack.co.uk – an attractive store, advice and care site with a wide range of products.
www.petpals.com – at-home pet-care services.
www.petplanet.co.uk – good for the shop and up-to-the-minute news.
www.petsathome.com – a fairly basic site from this pet retailer.
www.petsmiles.com – a good directory site featuring some 35,000 companies.
www.ukpets.co.uk – a directory of pet shops and suppliers, plus advice and a magazine devoted to pets.

P

Pet Insurance

www.pethealthcare.co.uk   UK
PET INSURANCE
This is a good place to start looking for insurance to cover your vet's bill. It also has lots of good advice on how to look after pets and what to do when you first get a pet.

See also:
www.animalfriends.co.uk – an insurance company that devoted all profits to animal charities.
www.petplan.co.uk – one of the largest pet insurers.

Travel

www.pethealthcare.co.uk   UK

UK HOLIDAYS WITH PETS
This site is devoted to finding holiday accommodation where
your pets are always welcome – simply arranged by region,
easy. There's also a bookshop and a good set of links.

See also:
www.defra.gov.uk/animalh/quarantine/index.htm – animal
quarantine and advice on overseas travel.
www.preferredplaces.co.uk – a holiday specialist with a good
'pets welcome' section.

Animal Charities

www.rspca.org.uk   UK

THE RSPCA
News (some of which can be quite disturbing) and information
on the work of the charity plus animal facts and details on how
you can help. There's also a good kids' section. It's a good site
but a bit tightly packed.

Other charity sites:
www.aht.org.uk – applying clinical and research techniques to
help animals.
www.animalrescue.org.uk – fight animal pain and suffering.
www.animalrescuers.co.uk – a directory of centres and people
who will help distressed animals.
www.animalsanctuaries.co.uk – index of charities and animal
rescue centres.
www.bluecross.org.uk – excellent site with information, help
and advice.
www.pdsa.org.uk – People's Dispensary for Sick Animals has a
good-looking site with details on how to look after pets and how
you can help.

www.giveusahome.co.uk   UK

RE-HOMING A PET
A nice idea, a web site devoted to helping you save animals
that need to be re-homed; it's got a large amount of information
by region on shelters, vets and the animals themselves as well
as entertainment for kids.

TV-related

www.channel4.com/petrescue UK

PET RESCUE
Details of the programme plus information and links on animal charities and sites, there are also stories, games and chat. See also the excellent BBC web pages on pets which can be found at **www.bbc.co.uk/nature/animals/pets**

Sites for Different Species

Birds

www.avianweb.com US

FOR BIRD ENTHUSIASTS
A massive site devoted to birds, it's especially good for information on parrots. There are sections on species, health and equipment as well as advice on looking after birds.

See also:
www.boglinmarsh.fsnet.co.uk – racing pigeons.
www.birdcare.co.uk – lots of articles and advice on avian health.
www.parrot-rescue.co.uk – excellent site devoted to rescuing and looking after birds that have out-grown their owners or need help.
www.rspb.org.uk – mainly wild birds but some good advice.
www.theaviary.com – oddly designed American site but one with lots of information and links.

Cats

www.cats.org.uk UK

HOME OF CAT PROTECTION
A well-designed and informative site, with advice on caring, re-homing, news and general advice, an archive of cat photos and competitions for the best. The online shop offers delivery in the UK but charges vary.

See also:
www.catoutofthebag.com – a wide range of cat-related products from a good-looking site. It also includes things like homewares and gifts.
www.crazyforkitties.com – nice site devoted to all things cat and kitty.

www.fabcats.org – a charity devoted to cat care.
www.freddie-street.com – fantastic and funny: the story of the Freddie Street cats. There's some good information in there too.
www.i-love-cats.com – a directory of cat sites.
www.moggies.co.uk – home of the Online Cat Guide, not an easy site to use, but it has exceptional links to pet sites.

Dogs

www.the-kennel-club.org.uk   UK

DOGS OFFICIAL

The place to go for the official line on dogs and breeding with information on Crufts and links to related web sites, plus shop and tips on looking after you pooch.

www.dogs.co.uk   UK

COMPLETE DOGS

A comprehensive if slightly unattractive site that seems to have all bases covered when it comes to dogs – although it's mainly a good shop. There are also forums and links.

See also:
www.bugsie.co.uk – yes, it's a mobile dog washing service!
www.canismajor.com/dog – an American magazine site.
www.chazhound.com – for information, fun and games.
www.dogmadshop.com – good-looking doggie-oriented shop with lots of interesting products for you and your pooch.
www.dogpatch.org – a directory and search engine devoted to dogs.
www.dogs-and-diets.com – comprehensive nutritional information for dogs and you can buy a bow-lingual bark translator!
www.dogster.com – yes, you can set up a web site devoted to your dog alone...
www.howtoloveyourdog.com – a children's guide to caring for dogs.
www.i-love-dogs.com – a directory of web sites devoted to dogs.
www.woofwoofdirect.com – daft-sounding title but a very good dog-related gift and accessory shop.

P

www.ncdl.org.uk   UK

THE DOG'S TRUST

Excellent web site featuring the charitable works of the Dog's Trust (formerly the National Canine Defence League) the largest charity of its type. Get advice on how to adopt a dog, tips on looking after one and download doggie wallpaper. For Battersea Dogs Home go to **www.dogshome.org** who have a well-designed site.

Fish

www.ornamentalfish.org   UK
ORNAMENTAL AQUATIC TRADE ASSOCIATION
An excellent site beautifully designed and well executed. Although much of it is aimed at the trade and commercial side, there is a great deal of information for the hobbyist about looking after and buying fish.

See also:
www.aquariacentral.com – a huge site with masses of information on every aspect of looking after fish.
www.fishdoc.co.uk – excellent site of fish illnesses and ailments.
www.fishlinkcentral.com – a good directory site for information on fish.

Horses

www.equiworld.net   UK
GLOBAL EQUINE INFORMATION
Not the most helpful design but a directory, magazine and advice centre in one, with incredible detail plus some fun stuff too including video and audio interviews and footage, holidays and the latest news. The shop consists of links to specialist traders.

See also:
www.equine-world.co.uk – lots here too including classified ads, shopping and links.
www.horseadvice.com – a health-oriented site that supplies a huge amount of information.

Rabbits and Rodents

http://www.rabbit.org   US
HOUSE RABBIT SOCIETY
It's all here, from feeding, breeding, behaviour, health advice and even info on house-training your rabbit. Has a nice kids' section and plenty of cute pictures.

See also:
www.rabbitwelfare.co.uk – lots of chat, advice and links from the Rabbit Welfare Association.
www.rabbitworld.com – a personal tribute to rabbits, which also has information on caring for your fluffy friend.
www.caviesgalore.com – information, forums, games and names.
www.cavycapers.com – a guinea pig haven on the web! A nice site too.
www.gerbils.co.uk – home of the National Gerbil Society.
www.rodentfancy.com – good all-round site about the small creatures.

Other Pets

http://exoticpets.about.com – comprehensive information and news stories.
www.ameyzoo.co.uk – a specialist exotic pet shop with fact sheets on how to look after them properly.
www.easyexotics.co.uk – attractive site covering exotic plants as well as pets, it aims to take the mystery out of looking after them, sections on tarantulas and arrow frogs.
www.kingsnake.com – an American community site devoted to snakes.
www.petreptiles.com – comprehensive pet reptile information.
www.ukreptiles.com – an OK directory site for reptile enthusiasts, good for links.

Photography

http://www.rabbit.org   UK
COMMUNITY OF PHOTOGRAPHERS
A good portal site with links to all aspects of photography, there's information on everything from models to lessons. For more links and research try **www.photolinks.net** which is pretty comprehensive.

www.rps.org   UK
THE ROYAL PHOTOGRAPHIC SOCIETY
Slowish site dedicated to the works of the RPS. There are details on the latest exhibitions and the collection, you can become a member and get the latest news about the world of

photography. Good for photographic history and links, while the shop has some related merchandise.

www.nmpft.org.uk   UK
NATIONAL MUSEUM OF PHOTOGRAPHY,
FILM AND TELEVISION
Details of this Bradford museum via a high-tech web site, opening times and directions, what's on, education resources and a very good museum guide.

www.eastman.org   US
THE INTERNATIONAL MUSEUM OF PHOTOGRAPHY
George Eastman founded Kodak and this New York-based museum too. This site is comprehensive and amongst other things, you can learn about the history of photography, visit the photographic and film galleries, or obtain technical information. Become a member and you're entitled to benefits such as free admission and copies of their *Image* magazine.

www.nationalgeographic.com/photography   US

NATIONAL GEOGRAPHIC MAGAZINE
Synonymous with great photography, this excellent site offers much more. There are sections on travel, exhibitions, maps, news, education, and for kids. In the photography section pick up tips and techniques, follow their photographers' various locations, read superb articles and accompanying shots in the 'Visions Galleries'. Good links to other photographic sites.

www.life.com/Life   US
LIFE MAGAZINE
Life magazine, is wonderfully nostalgic and still going strong. There are several sections, features with great photos, excellent articles, and an option to subscribe; however, they could do much more and it's a little frustrating to use.

www.panoramas.dk   DENMARK
PANORAMIC PHOTOGRAPHY
A great use of the Quicktime program, thousands of sites and movies all devoted to or celebrating panoramic photography.

See also:
www.iphotocentral.com – a dealer in old photographs.

www.photographymuseum.com – odd site from the American Museum of Photography.
www.photonet.org.uk – home of London's Photographer's Gallery, find out what's on and buy prints.
www.rleggat.com/photohistory – the history of early photography.

Great Photographers

www.masters-of-photography.com   US

ONLINE GALLERIES
A simple site with a superb array of galleries devoted to the real masters of the art of photography – you can spend hours browsing here.

See also:
www.adamsgallery.com – the excellent Ansel Adams gallery.
www.anseladams.com – a great place to buy Ansel Adams photos.
www.davidbaileyphotography.com – the official site with some great shots to view.
www.npg.org.uk – National Portrait Gallery offer up interviews, biographies and the work of some of the great photographers.

Photo Libraries

www.bapla.org   UK

PICTURE LIBRARIES
Home of the British Association of Picture Libraries and although it's basically an industry site it has lots of information and links to all the major libraries in the UK.

P

See also:
www.corbis.com – one of the biggest libraries much of which is free.
www.freefoto.com – who say they offer the largest free image database.
www.freeimages.co.uk – 2,500 free quality pictures.
www.gettyimages.com – the leading commercial library with lots of royalty-free images to download.
www.webshots.com – which is great for wallpaper and screensavers.

Photographic Advice

www.bjphoto.co.uk   UK

THE *BRITISH JOURNAL OF PHOTOGRAPHY*
An online magazine with loads of material on photography.
Access their archive or visit picture galleries that contain work
from contemporary photographers, find out about careers in
photography and where to buy the best photographic gear.

www.betterphoto.com   UK

TAKE BETTER PICTURES
A very well-laid-out and comprehensive advice site for new and
experienced photographers with a buyer's guide plus introductions
to and overviews of traditional and digital photography.

See also:
www.88.com/exposure – a temperamental site but one that
offers up a great deal of information both for beginners and the
well versed.
www.photo.net – an American site with lots of advice and reviews.
www.photozone.de – a brave attempt at providing a rounded
community site covering most aspects of photography with
reviews and technical help.
www.shortcourses.com – all you need to know about
digital photography.

Photography Stores and Equipment Reviews

www.jessops.com   UK

TAKE ADVICE TAKE GREAT PICTURES
Jessops are the largest photographic retailer in the UK and they
offer advice on most aspects of photography plus courses and
free software for their digital printing service. They do give you
an opportunity to go shopping for your camera and accessories.

See also:
www.bestcameras.co.uk – good range and a clutter-free site.
Recommended but delivery charges vary.
www.cameras2u.com – this store has a wide range, good
prices and you can download their helpful guides too.
www.camerasdirect.co.uk – a well-designed store.
www.dcresource.com – information and reviews on digital cameras.

www.digitaltruth.com – unusual design, but very comprehensive equipment shop and portal site.

www.dpreview.com – digital photography cameras and equipment reviewed.

www.ffordes.com – a good site offering used equipment alongside the new.

www.internetcamerasdirect.co.uk – a good-value, independent store with reviews and a digital dictionary. Delivery starts at £6.

www.ofoto.com – excellent site from Kodak.

www.photoglossy.com – specialists in paper, material and printing accessories.

www.photographicdirect.co.uk – more than just a shop, this site has been redesigned and is now much more interactive with forums chat and galleries.

Photo Storage, Development and Sharing

http://photos.fotango.com   UK

ONLINE DEVELOPERS

Fotango will take your film and digitise it, then place your pictures on a secure site for you to view and select for printing the ones you like. The service is quick and easy to use; costs don't seem much different from the high street although single prints can be expensive. See also **www.photobox.co.uk** – great design, probably the best for digital photo storage.

www.flickr.com   CANADA

PHOTO COMMUNITY

A fast-growing membership and an indication of what will be the way forward for sharing photos with friends, family and colleagues. It's very easy to set up with the best feature being the facility to tag your photos with key words making it easier to search and share your collection. It's also got good security should you only want to share your album with a few people. See also **www.ofoto.com** an excellent site from Kodak.

www.fotopages.com   US

PHOTO BLOG

Here you can set up your own photo blog, which you can share with friends and family. It's pretty easy to get going and it's really effective, you can archive material, add captions, text and even links. See also **www.my-expressions.com**

Miscellaneous Photography Sites

www.getmapping.com   UK

AERIAL PHOTOGRAPHS
Just type in your postcode and get a picture of your home taken
from above on a sunny day last year. There are lots of cost
options and you can also get a map to go with it.

www.playingwithtime.org   US

TIME-LAPSE PHOTOGRAPHY
This site is part of a larger photographic project, here you can see
incredible movies filmed with time-lapse photography. Excellent.

Price Checkers

*Here's a good place to start any online shopping trip – a price
comparison site. There are many price checker sites; however, the sites
listed here allow you to check the prices for online stores across a much
wider range of merchandise than the usual books, music and film.*

www.kelkoo.co.uk   UK

COMPARE PRICES BEFORE YOU BUY
Kelkoo is probably the best price-checking site with 20 categories
in their shop directory including books, wine, white goods, even cars
and utility bills – they have links with eBay. There are plenty of
bargains to be had, in fact they keep popping up on every page.

www.checkaprice.com   UK

CONSTANTLY CHECKING PRICES
Compare prices across a huge range of products, from the usual
books to cars, holidays, mortgages and electrical goods. If it can't
do it for you, it patches you through to a site that can.

Other good sites:
www.buy.co.uk – excellent for the utilities – gas, water and
electrical as well as credit cards and mobile phones.
www.dealtime.co.uk – easy-to-use directory and price checker
covering a wide range of goods.
www.pricechecker.co.uk – a straightforward site which also
covers flights and telephone tariffs.

www.pricerunner.com – a good all-rounder with a news section giving the latest information on deals and technology updates.
www.pricescan.com – all the usual, plus watches, jewellery, sports goods and office equipment – good store finder.
www.price-search.net – mainly computers and gadgets.
www.pricewatch.co.uk – good for computers and personal finance.
www.unravelit.com – unravel your troubles and get the best deal here. Good for utilities and finances.

Property

Every estate agent worth their salt has got a web site, and in theory finding the house of your dreams has never been easier. These sites have been designed to help you through the minefield. For advice on building your own house go to page 260 in the home section.

www.upmystreet.com   UK

FIND OUT ABOUT WHERE YOU WANT TO GO
Type in the postcode and up pops almost every statistic you need to know about the area in question. Spooky, but fascinating, it's a good guide featuring not only house prices, but also schools, the local MP, local authority information, crime and links to local services and trades people. It also has a classified section and puts you in touch with the nearest items to your area. See also **www.hometrack.co.uk** which is a subscription service but offers a huge amount of data about house prices and the area.

www.landreg.gov.uk   UK

LAND REGISTRY
An OK site for information on house prices by region, you can also make inquiries about property and land values. Could be loads better.

www.conveyancing-cms.co.uk   UK

CONVEYANCING MARKETING SERVICE
Conveyancing is a bit of a minefield if you're new to it, but this site aims to help with advice and competitive quotes. See also **www.easier2move.com** which is nicely designed and very informative.

www.reallymoving.com   UK

MAKING MOVING EASIER
A directory of sites and help for home buyers including mortgages,
removal firms, surveyors, solicitors, van hire and home
improvements. You can get online quotes on some services and
there's good regional information. The property search is fast and
has plenty to choose from. For a helpful directory of removal and
storage companies with information and advice try
www.helpiammoving.com and also the British Association of
Removers has an informative site at **www.barmovers.com**

*For more properties try these sites, some are just for buyers,
but many have homes to rent too:*
www.assertahome.com – great all-rounder, excellent site with
lots of advice, information, houses and associated services.
www.beach-huts.co.uk – great site, providing you want to buy
or rent a beach hut.
www.easier.co.uk – free, no-hassle advertising, also has a
finance section.
www.findaproperty.com – over 86,000 properties listed, biased
to the South East.
www.heritage.co.uk – covers listed buildings only for sale plus
information on their upkeep.
www.hol365.com – really good site design and a massive
range of services and properties from 6,000 estate agents.
www.houseweb.co.uk – highly rated with comprehensive
advice and thousands of properties for sale.
www.itlhomesearch.com – independent home search and
advice site that also covers Spain and Ireland – rent or buy.
www.knightfrank.com – world-wide service, easy-to-use site.
www.naea.co.uk – National Association of Estate Agents with
their code of conduct, links and the latest property news.
www.propertyfinder.co.uk – Britain's biggest house database.
www.rightmove.com – very clear information site with a good
property search engine.
www.smartnewhomes.com – search engine dedicated to
new homes.
www.themovechannel.co.uk – an OK portal site. Each agent
or property site gets a review and a link. Better than it looks
at first glance.
www.ukpad.com – details of property auctions in the UK.
www.ukpropertyshop.com – claims to be the most
comprehensive covering 3,000 towns in the UK.

www.vebra.com – above-average property search engine, much faster than most.

www.home-repo.org   UK

HOME REPOSSESSION
A very useful and informative site that blows the lid off the goings on behind what happens when a house is repossessed and what you should do if you find yourself in arrears. It's assertive and entertaining too.

Renting

www.landlordzone.co.uk   UK

RENTAL PROPERTY KNOWLEDGE
Very useful for landlords and tenants alike with the latest news available and lots of advice too. It's great for links and easy to navigate though a bit advert heavy.

See also:
www.arla.co.uk – home of the Association of Residential Letting Agents with lots of useful information.
www.homelet.co.uk – claim to take the risk out of renting by offering sound advice and insurance for both tenants and landlords – good design.

www.flatmate.com   AUSTRALIA

FIND A FLATMATE
With more people unable to afford homes there has been a huge increase in people wanting flats to share or rent. Here you can find a suitable flat or advertise your vacancy.

P

See also:
http://uk.easyroommate.com – thousands available.
www.flatshare.com – great for London.
www.shareflatmates.com – also US, Canada and Australia.

Property Abroad

www.french-property.com   UK

NO.1 FOR FRANCE
If you are fed up with the UK and want to move to France this is the first port of call. They offer properties for rent or for sale in all regions and can link you with other estate agents.

www.overseaspropertyonline.com   UK
MOVING ABROAD
This site was formerly **www.spanish-property-online.com** and remains a good starting point if you want to find property and advice on buying in Spain. However, it has extended its range to cover Europe, the Caribbean, North America, Australia and New Zealand.

See also:
www.adhspain.com – excellent site from this Spanish property specialist.
www.bulgariandreams.com – it's the place to be, apparently.
www.buy-property-dubai.com – Dubai property.
www.fopdac.com – home to the Federation of Overseas Property Developers, a trade association site that has some useful advice and contact information.
www.french-property-news.com – a poorly designed site, but good advice and links.
www.islandsforsale.com – yes, buy yourself a whole island!
www.latitudes.co.uk – French property specialists.
www.prestigeproperty.co.uk – links with estate agents in nine countries.
www.realestateslovakia.net – beautiful chateaux in Eastern Europe.
www.worldclasshomes.co.uk – properties in Spain, Portugal, France and Bahamas…

Radio

You need a decent downloadable player such as RealPlayer or Windows Media Player before you start listening. The downside is that quality is sometimes affected by Net congestion although that's becoming less of a problem these days. See the music section on page 302 for information on Podcasts and RSS.

www.mediauk.com/directory   UK

DIRECTORY OF RADIO STATIONS
Excellent site. You can search by station, presenter or by type, there's also background on the history of radio and articles on topics such as digital radio. The site also offers similar information on television and magazines.

See also:

http://dir.yahoo.com/News_and_Media/Radio – Yahoo's list of nearly 1,300 stations and related sites.

http://windowsmedia.com – home to Microsoft's media listings, which is very comprehensive.

www.comfm.com – a French site with access to over 11,000 stations.

www.icecast.org – download the player and get access to many radio stations and video streams.

www.live365.com – good-looking site with thousands of radio stations to choose from and it's easy to customise to your tastes too. The basic service is free, but for CD-quality sound and to broadcast your own radio station, you have to pay.

www.publicradiofan.com – ugly site with thousands of stations listed but they are listed by time-zone so you should be able to find something you like playing at any one time.

www.radio-locator.com – a huge directory of radio, US-oriented.

www.radio-now.co.uk – radios to buy, plus lots of links.

www.shoutcast.com – another huge selection using the Winamp player. If you fancy yourself as a DJ, it's to free to join in and broadcast here.

www.spinner.com – a virtual radio which comes with over 175 stations.

www.virtualtuner.com – tune in to a vast number of stations at this good-looking site, the top 500 is interesting in itself.

www.radioacademy.org   UK

UK'S GATEWAY TO RADIO

Radio Academy is a charity that covers all things to do with radio including news, events and its advancement in education and information. It has a list of all UK stations including those that offer web casts. You get more from the site if you become a member.

www.bbc.co.uk/radio   UK

THE BEST OF THE BBC

Listen to the news and the latest hits while you work, just select the station you want. There's also information on each major station, as well as a comprehensive listing service. Some features such as football commentary on certain matches will be missing due to rights issues. Most of the stations have some level of interactivity, with Radio 1 being the best and most lively, you can also tap into their local stations and of course the World Service.

www.virginradio.co.uk   UK

VIRGIN ON AIR

Excellent, if slightly messy with lots of ads plus plenty of stuff about the station, its schedule and stars. There's also a good magazine with the latest music news. You can listen if you have Quicktime, Windows Media Player or RealPlayer.

Other independent radio stations online are:
www.capitalfm.com – Capital Radio.
www.classicfm.com – classical music and background information.
www.coolfm.co.uk – Northern Ireland's number one.
www.galaxyfm.co.uk – good range of dance music.
www.heart1062.co.uk – London's heart.
www.jazzfm.com – live broadcasts, cool site too.
www.lbc.co.uk – two stations providing the voice of London.
www.resonancefm.com – London-oriented arts station.
www.studentradio.co.uk – Internet Student Radio.

Railways

These are sites aimed at the railway enthusiast. For information on trains and timetables see page 523.

www.nrm.org.uk   UK

NATIONAL RAILWAY MUSEUM

An excellent museum site packed with information and details on their collection, you can even take a virtual tour. See also Great Western's very informative museum site at
www.steam-museum.org.uk

www.heritagerailways.com   UK

HERITAGE RAILWAY ASSOCIATION

This site offers an online guide to the entire heritage railway scene in the UK, including details of special events and operating days for all heritage railways with lots of links world-wide. Formerly
http://ukhrail.uel.ac.uk

www.narrow-gauge.co.uk   UK

NARROW GAUGE

The new and improved Narrow Gauge Heaven (formerly Narrow Gauge on the Web) steams in with latest news and a better photo gallery plus all the narrow gauge information you'll need. You can also contribute your own articles or just browse.

See also:
www.drcm.org.uk – good site on the Darlington Railway Museum.
www.gensheet.co.uk – keep up to date with timetable changes and diversions.
www.heritagerailway.co.uk – geared to selling the mag but plenty of links and some archive material.
www.mylinkspage.com/rail.html – the brain resource centre.
www.pcrail.co.uk – a rail enthusiast's dream: simulations of railway operations and journeys. The site is well designed and simulations cost around £33.
www.railcentre.co.uk – the Stockton and Darlington railway.
www.railway-technology.com – the latest industry news.
www.rpsi-online.org – Ireland's Railway Preservation Society.
www.steamlocomotive.com – steam trains in the US.
www.trackbed.com – some 2,500 pages on Britain's railway heritage a labour of love.
www.trainorders.com – a US rail community site, it's pretty poorly designed but there's a lot here, if you can be bothered to search for it.
www.trainspotters.de – a good site from a German rail fan.
www.trainweb.org – a directory of train-and railway-related sites.
www.uksteam.info – a well-organised site covering steam train preservation.
www.vintagetrains.co.uk – home of the Birmingham Railway Museum.

Reference and Encyclopedia

If you are stuck with your homework or want an answer to any question, then this is where the Internet really comes into its own. With these sites you are bound to find what you are looking for. For schoolwork, also refer to the education section, page 115.

R

www.refdesk.com   US

THE BEST SINGLE SOURCE FOR FACTS
Singled out for its sheer size and scope, this site offers information and links to just about anything. Its mission is 'only about indexing quality Internet sites and assisting visitors in

navigating these sites'. It has won numerous awards and it never fails to impress, but for users outside the US it is possibly too biased toward that country.

www.knowuk.co.uk   UK

ALL ABOUT BRITAIN

A subscription service that offers a massive amount of data about the UK from the arts to the civil service, education, government, law, travel and sport. Although most of the information can be accessed through separate sites, the advantage here is that you only need the one. Prices aren't listed on the site but you can contact them for a free trial.

www.about.com   US

IT'S ABOUT INFORMATION

A superb resource, easy to navigate and great for beginners learning to search for information. Experts help you to find what you need every step of the way. It offers information on a wide range of topics from the arts and sciences to shopping.

www.ipl.org   US

THE INTERNET PUBLIC LIBRARY

Another excellent resource, there are articles on a vast range of subjects, its particularly good on literary criticism. Almost every country and its literature is covered. If there isn't anything at the library, there is invariably a link to take you to an alternative web site. Check out their children's section 'kidspace' for first-class children's reference materials and 'teenspace' for young people.

See also:

www.archive.org – an excellent resource in the making. The 'Wayback Machine' is fun, though it has a serious side; it catalogues old sites so that they may never be lost.

www.ibiblio.org – holds a huge collection of textual, audio and software resources.

www.libraryspot.com – is similar in scope to IPL, but has a more literary emphasis and an entertaining trivia section for those obsessed by top 10s and useless facts.

www.questia.com – claims to be the biggest online library with over 50,000 books and almost 400,000 articles. Excellent search facility.

www.theanswerbank.co.uk   UK
QUESTIONS ANSWERED
Just go to any one of the listed categories and type in your
question, and you'll get a list of articles and links relating to
your query. Some results returned are quite odd so you have to
be quite specific. It may be better to use a search engine such
as **www.ask.co.uk**

www.homeworkelephant.co.uk   UK
LET THE ELEPHANT HELP WITH HOMEWORK
A resource with some 5,000 links and resources aimed at
helping students achieve great results. There's help with specific
subjects, hints and tips, and help for parents and teachers.
It's constantly being updated, so worth checking regularly.

See also:
www.homeworkhigh.co.uk – Channel 4's excellent homework
help site.
www.kidsclick.org – more than 600 topics and subjects covered.

Aimed at Women

The Good Web Site Guide's Top 10s of the Internet

TOP
10

1. **www.handbag.com** – the most useful place for women on the
    internet, apparently.
2. **www.bbc.co.uk/radio4/womanshour** – excellent magazine spin off.
3. **www.healthywomen.org** – get healthy, get informed.
4. **www.journeywoman.com** – safe travel.
5. **www.womengamers.com** – for a great selection of games.
6. **www.pinknoises.com** – promoting women's music.
7. **www.ivillage.co.uk** – a great magazine site.
8. **www.fashionangel.com** – all the fashion links you'll ever need.
9. **www.womanmotorist.com** – proving that cars aren't just for men
    to enjoy.
10. **http://shinyshiny.tv** – a girl's guide to gadgets.

R

Encyclopedias

www.wikipedia.org   US

THE FREE ENCYCLOPEDIA
In an amazingly short time Wikipedia has become something of
an Internet phenomenon. Basically, it's an encyclopedia created
by anyone who wants to contribute. The English version has
almost 500,000 entries and although the quality varies, it's a
great place to go for researching. Some people have been
incredibly generous with their input.

http://encarta.msn.com   US

THE ENCARTA ENCYCLOPEDIA
Even though the complete thing is only available to buy, there is
access to thousands of articles, maps and reference notes via
the concise version. It's fast and easy to use, though navigating
it is a bit of a pain.

Other useful encyclopedias:
http://encyclozine.com – wide range of topics covered plus
good use of games, quizzes and trivia.
http://i-cias.com/e.o/index.htm – Encyclopedia of the Orient –
for North Africa and the Middle East.
www.babloo.com – interactive encyclopedia aimed at kids.
www.bartleby.com – one of the best. It offers access to a huge
amount of reference work, but also fiction, verse and narrative
non-fiction, largely with an American bias.
www.eb.com – *Encyclopedia Britannica* for $11.95 per month.
www.encyclopedia.com – possibly the most comprehensive
free encyclopedia on the net, nice design too.
www.everything2.com – similar in concept to Wikipedia with
masses of information but they can't be bothered to organise it,
so unless you have plenty of time, try something else.
www.highbeam.com – outstanding site with access to huge
amounts of data, from newswires to books, maps and images. You
have to subscribe though ($14.95 per month) to get full access to
the information although you can preview texts for free.
www.infoplease.com – the biggest collection of almanacs, plus
an encyclopedia and an atlas.
www.seop.leeds.ac.uk – UK mirror site for Stanford
Encyclopedia of Philosophy.
www.si.edu/resource – encyclopedia and links to the massive
resources of the Smithsonian.

www.spartacus.schoolnet.co.uk – Spartacus Encyclopedia
is excellent for history homework.
www.utm.edu/research/iep – the Internet Encyclopedia
of Philosophy.
www.wsu.edu/DrUniverse – ask Dr Universe a question,
any question...

Specialist Reference Sites

Classics and Literature

www.eserver.org   US

  THE ENGLISH SERVER
  A much-improved humanities site, which provides a vast
  amount of resource data about almost every cultural topic.
  There are some 34,000 texts, articles and essays available
  on subjects from the arts and fiction through to web design.

http://classics.mit.edu   US

  THE INTERNET CLASSICS ARCHIVE
  An excellent site for researching into the classics, it's easy to
  use and fast, with more than enough information for homework
  whatever the level. See also the excellent **www.bibliomania.com**
  for a wider range of resource materials.

www.perseus.tufts.edu   US

  PERSEUS DIGITAL LIBRARY
  An excellent source of data for ancient classics and mythology,
  history and early science. It also offers most of Shakespeare
  and Marlowe and, although it concentrates largely on pre-
  1600, it's ever expanding.

  See also:
  www.mythweb.com – an enjoyable and informative site
  devoted to Greek mythology.
  www.pantheon.org – which contains over 6,000 definitions
  covering mythology, legends and folklore.

R

Dictionaries and Words

*For information on grammar, pronunciation, plain English and
learning English see the English usage section on page 129.*
For language and translation go to page 282.

www.askoxford.com   UK

ASK OXFORD UNIVERSITY

A pretty decent effort at making a dry subject interesting. You can ask an expert, get advice on how to improve your writing and, of course, use the famous dictionary and thesaurus. See also **www.oed.com** where you suscribe to the Oxford English Dictionary at a cost of £50 for 3 months.

www.cup.cam.ac.uk/elt/dictionary   UK

CAMBRIDGE UNIVERSITY

This site has seven dictionaries: English, American English, idioms, phrasal verbs, a learner's dictionary, French/English and Spanish/English – all free.

www.onelook.com   US

DICTIONARY HEAVEN

Onelook claim to offer access to 992 dictionaries and over 6 million words, at a fast, user-friendly site. It also offers a price checking service for online shopping.

See also:

www.allwords.com – a well-categorised portal site on everything to do with words, including help with crosswords and translation.

www.collins.co.uk/wordexchange – Collins dictionary with several useful word tools including a Scrabble dictionary.

www.dictionary.com – here you can play word games as an added feature.

www.wordorigins.org – the origins of some 400 words and phrases explained.

www.wordspy.com – the latest on how words are being used and new words.

www.worldwidewords.org – International English from a British point of view, new words and phrases analysed.

www.yourdictionary.com – very comprehensive, the last word in words, apparently.

www.thesaurus.com   US

IF YOU CAN'T FIND THE WORD

Based on Roget's Thesaurus, this site will enable you to find alternative words – useful but not worth turning your PC on for in place of the book. The site is related to **www.dictionary.com** and has several other facilities including translation into 11 languages.

www.visualthesaurus.com   US

THE VISUAL THESAURUS

If you get bored looking up words or looking for alternative meanings for words in the usual way, then check out the Visual Thesaurus. It's fun to use, if a bit weird. Unfortunately, it now requires a subscription after the free trial.

www.peevish.co.uk/slang   UK

DICTIONARY OF SLANG

A comprehensive dictionary of English slang as used in the UK, with good articles and search facility.

www.acronymfinder.com   US

WHAT DO THOSE INITIALS STAND FOR?

If you don't know your MP from your MP3, here's where to go. With over 150,000 acronyms it should help you find what you're looking for.

www.symbols.com   US

WHAT DOES THAT SYMBOL MEAN?

Here you can find the meaning of over 2,500 symbols, with articles on their history.

www.techweb.com   US

THE TECHNOLOGY DICTIONARY

Get the latest business and technology news plus an excellent technology encyclopedia. For a dictionary that specialises in jargon and Internet terms only go to either **www.jargon.net** or **www.netdictionary.com** for enlightenment.

Other word-related sites:

www.ag.wastholm.net – if you need an aphorism, it's probably here.
www.identifont.com – identify any font and find one that you like, also has information on the many different types available.
www.rhymezone.com – type in a word, up pop all those that rhyme with it.
www.word-detective.com – a magazine devoted to words and wordplay.

Maths and Numbers

www.mathsisfun.com   UK
MATHS RESOURCES
A good site devoted to the basics of maths, it covers all the
bases and was started by a British maths teacher. All is well
explained with lots of diagrams. See also the helpful
www.amathsdictionaryforkids.com which provides a useful
visual dictionary of mathematical terms.

http://www.tractorz.com/Zimmer/Other/metriccalc.htm   US
CONVERSION CHART
Simply a very useful conversion device for the metric and
imperial systems, covering length, temperature, weight,
volume, distance and speed.

See also:
http://tcaep.co.uk – if you need details on a particular
equation. It's almost certainly to be here.
www.easymaths.com – Key Stage maths help.
www.google.com/help/features.html#calculator – this link
takes you to Google's very useful calculator function.
www.math.com – a very comprehensive US maths site.
www.mathguide.de – a German maths portal and search engine.
www.math-net.de/links/show?collection=math – maths links.
www.megaconverter.com/mega2 – annoying design but some
useful converters.
www.univie.ac.at/future.media/moe – a useful collection of
advice, tools and information.

Geography and International Statistical Data

See also the section on geology on page 324.

www.nationmaster.com   US
WORLD STATS
A well-designed site, which is excellent for comparative
statistics on countries and people. The great benefit to this one
is that it also includes access to a good encyclopedia.

www.ntu.edu.sg/Library/Collections/Databases   SINGAPORE
STATISTICS AND MORE STATISTICS
Free information and statistics about national economies –
not that easy to use at first, but it's all there.

See also:
www.cia.gov/cia/publications/factbook – the CIA's famous
fact book.
www.citypopulation.de – a really impressive site with a world
population database including maps and flags.
www.geohive.com/index.html – population statistics combined
with information on other key economic factors.
www.geosense.net – a good geography quiz game.
www.population.com – has a huge amount of data
and information.
www.prb.org – the Population Reference Bureau holds masses
of data on the world on as well as on the US.
www.statistics.gov.uk – great for statistics on the UK.

www.internetgeographer.com   UK
GEOGRAPHY WEB RING
A good source of information on geography for all ages with
quizzes and a population clock which enables you to see the
population grow before your eyes. An alternative portal on physical
geography can be found at **www.geog.le.ac.uk/cti/phys.html** which
includes climatology, geomorphology, hydrology, oceanography
and volcanology.

Atlases

www.atlapedia.com   US
THE WORLD IN BOTH PICTURES AND NUMBERS
Contains full colour political and physical maps of the world
with statistics and very detailed information on each country. It
can be very slow, so you need patience, but the end results are
worth it.

www.geographyiq.com   US
THE WORLD LISTED
A great site covering all the information you'd expect. List freaks
will love the rankings pages: they cover everything from largest
to oldest to richest. Great for homework.

R

See also:
http://plasma.nationalgeographic.com/mapmachine – home of
the National Geographic's Map Machine where you can zoom
in to any part of the world.
www.plcmc.org/forkids/mow – where you can find depicted all
the flags of the world.
www.worldatlas.com – a pretty comprehensive world atlas
and gazetteer.

Practical Skills

www.ehow.com   US
HOW TO DO THINGS
A directory and search site that provides information on how to
do a mass of jobs and everyday tasks – categorised by subject.

Religion

*In this section we've attempted to list sites that are of general interest
and try to explain the philosophy of the religions, rather than those
sites that simply reflect the opinions of those who preach.*

www.omsakthi.org/religions.html   US

RELIGION WORLD-WIDE
This site provides a clear description of each world religion
including values and basic beliefs with links to books on each
one. For links see also the World Religion Gateway at
www.academicinfo.net/religindex.html and the extensive
www.adherents.com who offer statistics on some 4,000
religions and religious bodies.

More general information sites about religion:
http://about.com/religion – About has an excellent overview of
the major religions and some minor ones. It also offers a
newsletter and covers areas such as spirituality too. Rutgers
University has made available a library of information on the
world's religions.
http://virtualreligion.net/vri formerly
http://religion.rutgers.edu/vri/index.html – an excellent portal
on religions, ethics, religious philosophy and psychology.
www.bbc.co.uk/religion – the BBC's excellent site on religion
and ethics.

www.beliefnet.com – a wide-ranging and multi-faith approach
to spirituality.
www.divinedigest.com – a good overview of the major religions.
www.infidels.org – a serious starting point for sceptics, check
out the library for links to sites on atheism and humanism.
www.religioustolerance.org – an organisation devoted to
religions co-operating with each other, it has good information
on all major faiths and attempts to explore controversial issues
from various viewpoints.

The Key Religions

Buddhism

http://buddhanet.net – the world-wide Buddhist information
and education network. A huge site with, one would guess,
everything you need to know.
www.ciolek.com/wwwvl-Buddhism.html – the Buddhist
studies virtual library.

Christianity

www.anglicancommunion.org – the world-wide Anglican
Communion.
www.anglicansonline.org – a huge resource site devoted to
Anglicanism with over 10,000 links.
www.catholic.net – a slick site devoted to the Catholic religion,
here you'll find everything on the religion, and it seems very
comprehensive.
www.cofe.anglican.org – home of the Church of England.
www.crossearch.com – a directory of Christian web sites.
www.methodist.org.uk – the official line in Methodism.
www.newadvent.org/cathen – the Catholic encyclopedia.
www.pres-outlook.com – a magazine site covering all forms
of Presbyterianism; US orientated.
www.quaker.org.uk – information on what it is to be a Quaker.
www.russian-orthodox-church.org.ru/en.htm – the home site
with the latest news.
www.salvationarmy.org.uk – excellent site with lots of
background information.
www.ship-of-fools.com – excellent radical Christian magazine.
www.thetablet.co.uk – a well-designed Catholic news site.
www.vatican.va – the official site of the Vatican, slow but
informative.

R

Druidism

www.druidnetwork.org – an overview of Druid beliefs with links and database.

Hinduism

www.hindu.org – a good overview of this complex religion with excellent directory.

Islam

www.al-islam.org – informative site with good information and links.
www.islamicity.com – a newsy site aimed at explaining Islam and creating more awareness of the religion.
www.islamonline.net – very comprehensive and interesting news and Islamic information site.
www.islamworld.net – a good overview of Islam.
www.salaam.co.uk – wide-ranging site covering all aspects of Islamic culture.
www.ummah.net – an excellent Muslim directory site.
www.usc.edu/dept/msa/reference/glossary.html – a glossary of Islamic terms and concepts.

Judaism

http://shamash.org/trb/judaism.html – a good overview of Judaism plus lots of links.
www.chiefrabbi.org – the official site of the Chief Rabbi.
www.jewfaq.org – an encyclopedia devoted to Judaism.
www.ritualwell.org – ceremonies for Jewish living.

Scientology

www.scientology.org.uk – comprehensive site on Scientology and what it is.

Sikhism

www.panthkhalsa.org – information on the Sikh nation.
www.singhsabha.com – understanding the religious and philosophical teachings of Sikhism.

Science

The Internet was originally created by a group of scientists who wanted faster, more efficient communication and today, scientists around the world use the Net to compare data and collaborate. In addition, the layman has access to the wonders of science in a way that's never been possible before, and as for homework – well now it's a doddle.

Pure Science

www.scirus.com   US

> SCIENCE SEARCH
> A straightforward and easy-to-use search engine devoted to scientific information only.

www.royalsoc.ac.uk   UK

> THE ROYAL SOCIETY
> An attractive site where you can learn all about the workings of the society, how to get grants and what events they are running. They've improved the content to include more links and more interactivity.

www.scicentral.com   US

> LATEST SCIENCE NEWS
> Apart from being a very good portal, this site offers the latest news in the major categories of science, plus a searchable database of articles gleaned from papers and magazines around the world.

http://scienceworld.wolfram.com   US

> PURE SCIENCE EXPLAINED
> Eric Weisstein's World of Science contains encyclopedias and detailed information written in accessible language on astronomy, scientific biography, chemistry, maths and physics. The design is easy on the eye and the site is logical to use.

> *See also:*
> **www.firstscience.com** – accessible and colourful, good for older children.
> **www.treasure-troves.com** – an eccentric site on various aspects of science, quite fun in places too.

S

Magazines

www.newscientist.com   UK
NEW SCIENTIST MAGAZINE
Much better than the usual online magazines because of its
creative use of archive material, which is simultaneously fun
and serious. It's easy to search the site or browse through back
features, however, you have to subscribe to get access to
premium content and the online archive of over 60,000
articles. For a more traditional science magazine site go to
Popular Science at **www.popsci.com** – great for information on
the latest gadgets.

www.sciencemag.org   US
SCIENCE MAGAZINE
A serious overview of the current science scene with articles
covering everything from global warming to how owls find their
prey. The tone isn't so heavy that a layman can't follow it and
there are plenty of links too. You need to register to get the best
out of it.

See also:
www.discover.com – articles from *Discover* magazine.
www.scitechdaily.com – the latest science news.

Popular Science

www.sciencemuseum.org.uk   UK
THE SCIENCE MUSEUM
An excellent site detailing the major attractions at the museum
with 3-D graphics and features on exhibitions and forthcoming
attractions. You can also shop and browse the galleries.
You can't help feeling they could do more though. See also
www.exploratorium.edu a similar but more child friendly site
by an American museum.

www.discovery.com   US

THE DISCOVERY CHANNEL
A superb site for science and nature lovers, it's inspiring as well
as educational. Order the weekly newsletter, get information on
the latest discoveries as well as features on pets, space, travel,
lifestyle and school. The 'Discovery Kids' section is very good
with lots going on.

www.howstuffworks.com US

HOW STUFF REALLY WORKS
An outstanding and popular site, it's easy to use and truly
fascinating. There are sections ranging from the obvious, like
engines and technology, through to food and the weather. The
current top 10 section features the latest answers to the
questions of the day. It's written in a very concise, clear style
with lots of cross-referencing.

www.si.edu/science_and_technology US

SMITHSONIAN SCIENCE AND TECHNOLOGY
Another excellent set of pages from the outstanding
Smithsonian site, which cover everything from biology to flight
and there are some really well-written and interesting articles
and sections too.

www.extremescience.com US

ULTIMATE SCIENCE EXPERIENCE
Not sure that it really lives up to it's billing, but it is a really
entertaining site with lots of useful and useless facts to bamboozle
your brain. Features include a time portal where you can learn the
effects of relativity and other sections on weather, maps, technology,
nature and the earth. It uses the word 'cool' a lot.

www.dangerouslaboratories.org US

DON'T DO IT YOURSELF
Science with a smile: here you get details of various
'experiments' in a range of scientific fields. It all looks very
amateur and fun as well as educational too.

www.voltnet.com US

DON'T TRY THIS AT HOME!
This is literally a high-voltage site devoted to electricity and how
it works. While there is a serious side, by far the best bit is
where they 'stress test' all sorts of objects by sending 20,000
volts through them.

www.science-frontiers.com US

SCIENTIFIC ANOMALIES
Science Frontiers is a bimonthly newsletter providing digests of
reports that describe scientific anomalies – 'those observations
and facts that challenge prevailing scientific paradigms'. There's

S

a massive archive of the weird and wonderful; it takes patience but there are some real gems.

www.world-mysteries.com US

WEIRD SCIENCE

All the mysteries and unexplained phenomena are here, explained and illustrated in a fairly unbiased way. It makes for an interesting browse.

www.improbable.com UK

THE IG NOBLE AWARDS

These awards are for those inventors whose project initially makes others laugh, then makes them think about the science behind it. To quote the site, they 'celebrate the unusual and honour the imaginative'. The site also offers much in the way of unusual scientific gems.

http://whyfiles.org US

SCIENCE BEHIND THE NEWS

If you've ever wondered why things happen and what's the real story behind what they tell you in the papers, then a visit here will be rewarding. With in-depth studies and brief overviews Why Files is easy to follow and you'll get the latest news too.

See also:

www.scienceagogo.com – a popular science discussion and news site.

www.unmuseum.org – a site devoted to the unexplained and natural phenomena, there's some good stuff but the poor site design gets in the way.

Scientists

www.nobelprize.org NORWAY

NOBEL PRIZE

Excellent site on the prize with lots of background information and biographies of the winners.

See also:

http://galileo.rice.edu – excellent site on Galileo.

www.aip.org/history/curie – Marie Curie.

www.mos.org/leonardo – the most useful Leonardo Da Vinci site.

www.newton.cam.ac.uk/newton.html#ini – Isaac Newton.
www.rutherford.org.nz – Ernest Rutherford.
www.thomasedison.com – Edison.
www.westegg.com/einstein – Einstein online.

Chemistry

www.webelements.com   US

THE PERIODIC TABLE
So you don't know your halides from your fluorides, with this
interactive depiction you can find out. Just click on the element
and you get basic details plus an audio description, all in all a
great teaching aid.

www.chemsoc.org   UK

CHEMICAL SOCIETY
A really creative site that covers not only industry issues, but
also educational ones too, all in a very entertaining fashion. The
timeline is especially well done and there is a very useful links
page too.

Practical Science and Science for Children

www.doscience.com   US

EXPERIMENTS: FUN AND SERIOUS
A slightly messy but entertaining site that has a number of
experiments to try both at home and outside. It's informative
and most of the experiments seem easy to do.

www.planet-science.com   US

FAST FORWARD TO THE FUTURE
A visually gratifying site with lots to offer by way of helping
children (and adults for that matter) to learn about science in
an interactive and entertaining way.

S

www.madsci.org   US

THE LAB THAT NEVER SLEEPS
A site that successfully combines science with fun. You can ask
a question of a mad scientist, browse the links list or check out
the archives in the library.

See also:

http://insideout.rigb.org – a good, if a little dull, educational e-zine from the Royal Institute.

www.amasci.com – for the science hobbyist, an ugly site.

www.extremescience.com – a messy but fun oriented science education site.

www.funsci.com – a serious site with many experiments to try both hard and easy.

www.spartechsoftware.com/reeko – a quirky site, but a great source of science and chemistry experiments designed to inspire school children, but will appeal to kids of all ages.

www.tryscience.org – bright site aimed at children, with a few experiments.

Innovation, Invention and Technology

www.21stcentury.co.uk   UK

YOUR PORTAL TO THE FUTURE
A stylish site that gives an overview of the latest technology put over in an entertaining style. Whether you're using it for homework or just for a browse, it's useful and interesting. They have 12 categories from cars through to humour, people and technology and they even cover fashion.

www.nesta.org.uk   UK

THE CREATIVE INVENTOR'S HANDBOOK
The National Endowment for Science Technology not only helps inventors get their ideas off the ground with support and guidance, but also encourages creativity and innovation. They'll also inspire you, as a visit to this well-designed site will show. See also the creatively designed **www.inventorlink.co.uk**

www.invent.org   UK

THE INVENTOR HALL OF FAME
This outstanding and beautifully designed site is sponsored by Hewlett Packard. It features advice on how to patent inventions and gives details of those who have been inducted into the Hall of Fame. If for no other reason, just go to appreciate the web site design.

www.innovations.co.uk   UK

GADGETS GALORE
Impress your friends with your knowledge of the newest

gadgets, innovations or what's likely to be the next big thing. Innovations is well established and has one of the best online stores with a wide range. There's a reward scheme with delivery costs being a flat £3.95. See also **www.streettech.com** who specialise in the latest hardware and also **www.firebox.com** who have a good selection.

www.robotstoreuk.com   UK
ROBOSHOP
A store devoted to selling robot parts and designs, including kits and a useful introduction to robotics.

Science Fiction and Fantasy

Science fiction and fantasy deserves its own section given that so many top movies and books are based on science fiction or fantasy. Here are a few of the massive number of sites that are around. A big vote of thanks should go to George Walkley from Ottakar's for his help with this section.

Directories and Reviews

www.thealienonline.net   UK
THE ALIEN ONLINE
Great for Sci Fi news, reviews and information, with opinionated comments on books, films, television, comics and games from some of Sci Fi's biggest names, and links to a host of web sites.

See also:
www.feministsf.org – comprehensive, dour offering on the role of women in Sci Fi.
www.locusmag.com – the online version of US Sci Fi magazine *Locus.* Dull but authoritative.
www.scifisource.com – a directory of all things Sci Fi, not pretty or easy to navigate but it seems comprehensive.
www.sfrt.com – good for reviews, links and forums.
www.sfsite.com – the dated design doesn't detract from the fact that this is one of the most comprehensive review sites you can find; it's quite dense so you need time to digest it.

S

Awards and Organisations

www.sfwa.org   US
SCI FI WRITERS OF AMERICA
A helpful and informative site from the SFWA including details
of their prestigious Nebula awards. If truth were told it's not a
great site but the links and writing advice are good.

See also:
www.appomattox.demon.co.uk/acca – home of the UK's
Arthur C Clarke Awards.
www.asfa-art.org – the Association of Sci Fi and Fantasy Artists
with an index of artists and galleries.
www.bsfa.co.uk – this chatty site represents the British Science
Fiction Association.
www.wsfs.org – an amateur-looking site from the World
Science Fiction Society home of the Hugo awards and with
details of the World Science Fiction Convention.

TV and movies

www.sciflicks.com   US

SCI FI FILM REVIEW
A comprehensive listing of Sci Fi films with reviews, links,
descriptions, cast listing and so on. There's plenty of detail and
there is also information on forthcoming movies.

www.scifi.com   US

THE SCI FI CHANNEL
An excellent site from the Sci Fi Channel with a very strong
emphasis on film and television, although it also includes
books, games and other products. It's beautifully designed, easy
to navigate, and there is a wealth of extra features, including
weekly newsletters.

www.sfon.tv   UK
SCI FI ON TV
A very good site featuring everything Sci Fi on television from
the famous and obscure. Dr Sci Fi will even attempt to answer
your Sci Fi questions. There's also a good movie review section.

See also:

www.bbc.co.uk/cult – the BBC's cult television page includes all the favourites.

www.greatlink.org – a UK-oriented site devoted to all things Trek.

www.sadgeezer.com – great for fans of Sci Fi cult TV, though pretty difficult to navigate, it has plenty of other Sci Fi resources too; you should be aware that it is possible to access some adult-oriented content.

www.startrek.com – everything you need to know about Star Trek and its spin off series.

www.starwars.com – outstanding official Star Wars site.

www.superherohype.com – lots of stuff on super heroes plus interviews from those involved in the films and downloads too.

www.timelord.co.uk – Dr Who and much more.

The writing

http://isfdb.tamu.edu/sfdbase.html   US

INTERNET SPECULATIVE FICTION DATABASE
This excellent resource is an encyclopedic guide to authors of 'speculative fiction', which includes every Sci Fi, fantasy and horror writer you could think of. The trouble is that it looks more like a library catalogue than a modern web site.

See also:

www.fantasticmetropolis.com – this good-looking and acclaimed site is dedicated to 'new wave' alternative authors, it includes fiction, essays, interviews, reviews and more. It also has an excellent links section.

www.infinityplus.co.uk – original fiction and non-fiction by many top names.

www.sff.net – somewhere amongst the commercial bits there's a really good website, you just have to be patient and sign up.

www.sfnovelist.com – a writing group who believe in Sci Fi based on hard science, some good short stories, but you need to be a member really.

www.technovelgy.com – a fun site devoted to the inventions of Sci Fi writers and whether they would really work and what they would look like.

S

The writers

www.lordoftherings.net   US

LORD OF THE RINGS
Slick on the movie trilogy, including information on the films,
interviews, picture galleries, trailers and other downloads. Best
accessed on broadband. See also **www.tolkien.co.uk** which is
home to the official UK web site from Tolkien's publishers,
including a biography, his books, artwork, downloads and other
information. Ordering facility through Amazon.

www.discworldmonthly.co.uk   UK

TERRY PRATCHETT
Probably the best of the many sites devoted to this massively
popular author and his Discworld creation with lots of links and
regular articles and updates.

Other key authors:
Clive Barker – **www.clivebarker.com**
Terry Brooks – **www.terrybrooks.net**
Katherine Kerr – **www.deverry.com**
Stephen King – **www.stephenking.com**
George RR Martin – **www.georgerrmartin.com**
Philip Pullman – **www.philip-pullman.com**
Tad Williams – **www.tadwilliams.com**

Below is a list of key Sci Fi and fantasy publishers:
www.2000adonline.com – home to the venerable British
comic, featuring Judge Dredd.
www.marvel.com – great interactive site from *Marvel* Comics
with all their major characters suitably involved.
www.orbitbooks.co.uk – home of authors such as Robert
Jordan and Iain Banks, it's an attractive, frequently updated site
with author pages, new releases, sample chapters, a monthly
e-mail newsletter and exclusive offers.
www.titanbooks.com – the UK's largest publisher of graphic novels
– also features information on their range of film and TV tie-ins.
www.voyager-books.co.uk – home of HarperCollins's Fantasy
and Sci Fi publishing. It's a classy-looking site, with author
profiles, news, new titles, sample chapters, interactive features
and extras such as downloadable screensavers.

Search Engines

The best way to find what you want from the Internet is to use a search engine. Even the best don't cover anywhere near the of available web sites, so if you can't find what you want from one, try another. These are the best and most user friendly. For children's search engines see page 93.

www.searchenginewatch.com   US

A GUIDE TO SEARCHING
This site rates and assesses all the search engines and it's a useful starting point if you're looking for a good or specific search facility. There's a newsletter and statistical analysis plus strategies on how to make the perfect search. See also **www.searchengineshowdown.com** who do much the same thing but it's less comprehensive.

Money, money, money...

The Good Web Site Guide's Top 10s of the Internet

1. **www.fsa.gov.uk** – the place to start, the Financial Services Authority.
2. **www.find.co.uk** – the biggest and best financial portal site.
3. **www.fool.co.uk** – for those who want some fun with their finance.
4. **www.bankfacts.org.uk** – all the information on internet banking and more.
5. **www.uswitch.co.uk** – switch services here and save money.
6. **www.inlandrevenue.gov.uk** – home of the tax man.
7. **www.unbiased.co.uk** – go here to find a financial adviser.
8. **www.pensionguide.gov.uk** – excellent advice on pensions.
9. **www.moneysavingexpert.com** – expert Martin Lewis dispenses financial joy.
10. **www.paypal.com** – the secure way to pay for stuff online.

S

General Searching

www.google.co.uk   UK

BRINGING ORDER TO THE WEB
Google is a massive success story and is one of the most useful
sites around. Apart from the simple search facility it also has a
host of other features including a directory, image search,
calculator, translation tools and many specialist research facilities;
you can even access it via a mobile. If you want to get the best
out of Google then pay a visit to the non-affiliated but very helpful
www.googleguide.com, you may also want to try one of our
favourites **www.teoma.co.uk** for general and advanced searches
it's more focused and you can refine more easily.

http://search.msn.co.uk   US

MSN SEARCH
New at the time of writing, this search engine is supposed to be
Microsoft's answer to Google. It's very fast and it seems to be the
business. You also get access to the Encarta Encyclopedia too.

www.ask.co.uk   UK

ASK JEEVES
Just type in your question and the famous old butler will come
back with the answer. It may be a bit gimmicky but works very
well; it's great for beginners and reliable for old hands too. See
also **www.ajkids.com** which is the child-oriented version.

www.lii.org   US

THE LIBRARIANS INDEX TO THE INTERNET
This is a search engine with a difference in that all the source
material has been selected and evaluated by librarians
specifically for their use in public libraries. This doesn't stop you
using it though, and it is very good for obscure searches and
research – like putting together a web site guide, for example.

S

www.dmoz.org   WORLD-WIDE

THE OPEN DIRECTORY PROJECT
The goal is to produce the most comprehensive directory of the
web and relies on an army (some 65,000) of volunteer editors
to do so; if you want to get involved it's easy to sign yourself
up. If it can't help with your query, it puts you through to one
of the mainstream search engines.

Finding the search engine that suits you is a matter of personal requirements and taste. Here are some other very good, tried and trusted ones:

http://uk.altavista.com – limited but very efficient, offers up a list of related options on every search.

www.accoona.com – a good alternative to Google, it allows you to prioritise your searching easily.

www.alltheweb.com – no frills, similar to Google.

www.bbc.co.uk – BBC's search engine is simple to use.

www.blabble.com – a specialist search engine covering blogs.

www.copernic.com – download a free search program.

www.dogpile.com – straightforward and no mess…US oriented.

www.infoplease.com – good for homework, one of the best for research.

www.looksmart.com – good, all sites handpicked.

www.pluck.com – a useful little free program that can be used as a search tool, it's also got a useful news feed facility.

www.spurl.net – a search program enhanced with the ability to manage links and bookmarks in a proactive way.

www.yahoo.com – one of the most comprehensive and popular. It's much more than a search facility, which can sometimes get in the way of finding what you want.

Clustering Search Engines

www.vivisimo.com   US

CLUSTERING TECHNOLOGY
With Vivisimo instead of the usual list, you get your search results back categorised by subject, or clustered. It makes for easy researching and is one of the three search engines I most use.

www.mamma.com   US

THE MOTHER OF ALL SEARCH ENGINES
Mamma have technology enabling them to search the major search engines thoroughly and get the most pertinent results to your query – it's fast too, your query comes back with the answer and the search engine it came from.

www.A9.com   US

THE WEB AND BEYOND
One to watch this, it uses Google to search the web but enhances that search with information from the Internet Movie

Database, Amazon's Search inside the book service and other reference sources. It's a little slow but you get quality results.

See also:
http://turbo10.com – claims to search the bits of the Internet where the major search engines don't go, this is one of the most impressive results-wise.
www.37.com – a bit of a mess but can search 37 other search engines in one go.
www.clusteredhits.com – clutter free, good for technical, scholarly and corporate data although US oriented.
www.metacrawler.com – uses similar technology to Mamma and is a popular choice.
www.profusion.com – an advanced search tool, takes results from several major search engines.
www.search.com – a solid performer from CNet.
www.ungoogle.com – searches many of the major search engines and is good for when 'Google lets you down'.

http://eurekster.com   US

SEARCHING WITH FRIENDS
Here you get the usual search facility with clustered results but you can also sign up with a group of friends, then when one of them does the same search your preferred result will appear higher up their list of results. It's excellent if you share a particular hobby or interest.

UK-oriented Searching

http://uk.yahoo.com   US

FOR THE UK AND IRELAND
The UK arm of Yahoo! is the biggest and one of the most established search engines. It's now much more than just a search facility as it offers a huge array of other services: from news to finance to shopping to sport to travel to games. You can restrict your search to just UK or Irish sites. It's the place to start, but it can be a little overwhelming at first.

www.mirago.co.uk   UK

THE UK SEARCH ENGINE
Mirago searches the whole web but prioritises the search for UK families and businesses. It's very quick, easy to use and offers many of the services you get from Yahoo! You can tailor your search very easily to exclude stuff you won't need.

For other UK-oriented search sites try:

http://UK20.co.uk – a good-looking site, it's OK as a search engine too.

www.4ni.co.uk – scroll down beyond the info and there's a good search engine serving Northern Ireland.

www.britishinformation.com – well designed and comprehensive.

www.clickclick2.net – odd design and more of a directory.

www.lifestyle.co.uk – a massive directory of specially selected sites for the UK.

www.lycos.co.uk – easy to use and popular, good for highlighting offers.

www.scotland.org – small Scotland-oriented site.

www.searchinwales.com – does what it says in the title (i.e. searches relevant to Wales).

www.searchsaint.com – good looking and easy to use.

www.wotbox.co.uk – excellent for UK-oriented searches, each site is denoted with its flag of origin.

www.watchthatpage.com   US

CHANGES ON THE WEB
Not strictly a search engine but if you have specific interests you can download the program, input the URLs and it will let you know when the site or page has been updated. You can also use it to search and hunt out specific articles.

Security

Keeping your computer, its contents and those who use it safe is one of the biggest priorities for any user; albeit unlikely you'll have any problems. Here's a list of sites that will help you keep secure and some protection software that's available for nothing.

www.watchthatpage.com   US

INTERNET SECURITY REVIEW
An exhaustive overview of Internet security with explanations and sections on all the major aspects of the subject.

www.grc.com US

SHIELDS UP!
Click on the 'Shields Up' logo and follow the instructions. You can then leave the program to run a security revue of your PC – it probably won't make happy reading, it depends on how anxious you are about security. For their check up Mac users can go to **www.symantec.com/mac/security**

www.firewallguide.com US
HOME PC FIREWALL GUIDE
According to my DK Internet Dictionary, a firewall is a piece of filtering software that protects your PC and prevents unknown users from sending material to it. But which is the best one? Find out here. For a good and well regarded firewall program that has a free version available go to **www.zonelabs.com**

www.software-antivirus.com US
THE INDEPENDENT ANTI-VIRUS RESOURCE
All the anti-virus programs reviewed and rated. This site sets out to blow the myth that once you have virus technology installed you're safe, or that the best-selling products are actually the best at the job. An authoritative site written by several experienced computer experts.

See also:
http://housecall.antivirus.com – a free virus scanner.
www.avast.com – one of the most reliable free anti-virus programs.
www.grisoft.com – for the free AVG anti-virus scanner.
www.kaspersky.com – home of the top-rated anti-virus program.
www.macafee.com – security specialists.
www.norton.com – where to go for Norton products.
www.pandasecurity.com – another top-rated program.
www.viruslist.com – if you're really interested in viruses, then go here where you'll find a virus encyclopedia.

www.anti-trojan-software-reviews.com US
THE ANTI-TROJAN RESOURCE
OK so you thought you were protected, but not entirely. Trojans are programs that pretend to be other programs and usually hitch a ride into your PC on the back of e-mail attachments. Go here to find the best anti-Trojan programs or just ensure that your anti-virus software does the job on Trojans too.

www.spyware.co.uk   UK
> WHO'S WATCHING YOU?
> As if viruses and Trojans weren't enough, the chances are that
> you've got some spyware on your PC sending information on
> your surfing activities to one of many companies who provide
> marketing data to retailers for example. Here you can get an
> overview of the problem plus advice on what to do about it.
>
> *See also:*
> **www.lavasoftusa.com** – home of the excellent AdAware program.
> **www.pctools.com** – advice and free downloads.
> **www.safer-networking.org** – home of SpyBot, a useful
> spyware destroyer.
> **www.spywarewarrior.com** – more information, background
> and downloads.

www.cookiecentral.com   US
> COOKIES EXPLAINED
> An excellent site dedicated to explaining the workings of that
> mysterious animal the 'cookie' and how you can deal with them.

http://nclnet.org/essentials   UK
> PRIVACY
> An informative site giving an overview of security and privacy
> issues on the Internet, it has plenty of helpful advice and links
> to related sites.

www.windowsstartup.com   UK
> START UP PROBLEMS
> A useful little program that helps with cleaning up your PC's
> start up.

Ships and Boats

S

*For shipping and boating enthusiasts here are a few sites that may
interest you. Sailing is listed under Sport, page 443, and water-borne
holidays can be found in the travel section, page 478.*

Boats

www.totallyboaty.co.uk   UK
BOATING DIRECTORY
A very good portal site devoted to all things boating, it's easy to find
what you're looking for and it's developing fast, see also
www.aboard.co.uk which offers a similar service and also
www.boatlinks.com which is well-categorised, US-oriented directory.

http://boatbuilding.com   UK
THE BOAT BUILDING COMMUNITY
If you want to repair or build a boat then here's where to go,
with features and discussion forums to help you on your way.
There's also a very good directory of links to suppliers and
resource sites.

www.boats-for-sale.com or **www.buyaboat.co.uk**   UK
BUY A BOAT MAGAZINE
Primarily a vehicle to get you to subscribe to the magazine, the
site offers information on brokers and the details of over 14,000
boats for sale. See also the well-designed **www.boats.com**

See also:
www.boatingnews.com – news and classifieds.
www.boatingontheweb.com – an American boating directory.
www.boatlaunch.co.uk – a mapping service showing all the
places in the UK where you can launch your boat.
www.uscgboating.org – a good site for advice and information
on safe boating.

Ships and Navy

www.royal-navy.mod.uk   UK

THE ROYAL NAVY
An excellent site from the Royal Navy giving details of the
ships, submarines and aircraft and what it's like to be a part of
it all. There's a video gallery featuring highlights from the fleet
and details of all the Royal Navy ships. Apart from all the
information, you can have a go on the interactive frigate and
take part in a strategic game.

www.hazegray.org   US

NAVAL HISTORY AND PHOTOGRAPHY
A well-categorised and comprehensive site featuring naval
histories, background on the world's ships and navies and also
shipbuilding. It's oriented to the US.

More naval and historical sites:
www.cronab.demon.co.uk – poor site but with some good
articles and links.
www.mightyseas.co.uk – a history site on the boats and ships
from NW England.
www.naval-history.net – a messy site, but good for the 20th
century and links.
www.navsource.org – a thorough unofficial overview of the
US navy.
www.nmm.ac.uk – a good site from the National Maritime
Museum in Greenwich.
www.skipper.co.uk – nautical publishers and booksellers.
www.tallship.co.uk – a magazine-related site with articles and
photo gallery.

www.red-duster.co.uk   UK

RED DUSTER MAGAZINE
Red Duster is a merchant navy enthusiasts' site offering lots in
the way of history covering sail, stream and shipping lines.
There's also a section on the history of customs. To find out
what the current merchant navy are up to go to
www.merchantnavyofficers.com where you can find
information and links.

www.maritimematters.com   UK

OCEAN LINERS AND CRUISE SHIPS
An informative site with data on over 100 ships from the
earliest liners to the most modern, each has its own page with
quality pictures and some virtual tours. It is also good for news
and links to related sites.

Other Watercraft

www.hovercraft.org.uk   UK

HOVERCRAFT
If you're into hovercraft or are just interested, here's the place to

look with three sections – Britain, Europe and the world, which just about covers it all.

www.jetskier.co.uk   UK

JET SKI

Home of *Jetskier* magazine and while it's geared to sell the mag, the site does offer much in the way of links and advice. For more tips, forums and chat go to the US-oriented **www.jetskinews.com**

www.rontini.com   UK

SUBMARINE WORLD NETWORK

A directory site with over 1,000 links all devoted to the world of submarines. It covers everything from navies to models.

See also:

www.lr.org – Lloyd's register.

www.nao.rl.ac.uk – home of the Nautical Almanac Office.

www.paddling.net – for buying canoes and kayaks.

www.tpl.lib.wa.us/v2/nwroom/ships.htm – the Tacoma public library has a searchable database of some 13,000 ships.

Shopping

*To many people shopping is what the Internet is all about, and it does offer an opportunity to get some tremendous bargains. Watch out for hidden costs such as delivery charges, import duties or finance deals that seem attractive until you compare them with what's available elsewhere. For help on finding comparative prices, see the price comparison sites on page 364, in fact, starting your shopping trip at a site like **www.kelkoo.co.uk** may prove to be a wise move. There is also a section on consumer information on page 101 for the low-down on your rights and what to do when things go wrong. For shopping ethically see the new section on page 131.*

www.tradingstandards.gov.uk   UK

TRADING STANDARDS CENTRAL

Find out where you stand and what to do if you think you're being ripped off or someone is not trading fairly – you can even take a quiz about it. There are advice guides to print off or

download and there is help and advice to businesses and
schools as well as consumers.

Two other consumer-oriented sites worth checking out are:
www.consumer.gov.uk – rights advice from the Department
of Trade and Industry.
www.howtocomplain.com – advice on how to go about airing
your grievances and getting a result.

http://froogle.google.co.uk   UK

SHOPPING SEARCH ENGINE
A useful facility from Google: just type in what you want to buy
and up pops a list with prices and links to relevant shops. It's
quick but the search results don't appear in price order.

www.which.net   UK

WHICH? MAGAZINE
A good place to start your shopping experience but you have to
be a member to get the best out of it. There's a good shopping
directory plus their 'product picks' section, which highlights the
'best in class' on a wide variety of products. There are also the
useful sections that you associate with the magazine such as
legal advice and personal finance.

www.dooyoo.co.uk   UK

MAKE YOUR OPINION COUNT
Media darling Doo Yoo is a site where you the consumer can
give your opinion or a review on any product that's available to
buy, this way you get unbiased opinions about them – in
theory. They cover a wide range of 'products' from books to TV
shows and it's easy to contribute. See also **www.ciao.co.uk**
where you can actually get paid a small amount of money for
your opinion.

www.recallannouncements.co.uk   UK

CONSUMER SAFETY
An informative site listing all the latest product recalls covering
the US, UK and Australia, it also offers a consumer guide, an
'ask the experts' facility and statistics on recalls. Some of the
site can only be accessed if you register.

S

The Virtual High Street

www.marks-and-spencer.co.uk   UK

CLOTHES AND GIFTS

A clear, attractive site that has a good selection of products from
clothes to gifts for all, as well as fashion advice and a quick
order facility. There's not much emphasis on offers, more on
quality. Delivery costs start at £3.50.

www.boots.com   UK

BOOTS

All that nice 'well being' stuff has gone and been replaced by an
online shop that reflects what you see when you visit the real store.
There's lots of choice and it's well categorised, functional too,
although slightly jerky, which can be irritating after a while. You can
get points with your purchase and delivery starts at £4.50, although
at the time of writing it is free if you spend £40 or more.

www.whsmith.co.uk   UK

WHSMITH

The Smith's site has a clean, easy-to-navigate format, with the
emphasis on offers and best-sellers. There is a great deal here
though including the usual books, music, mags, games,
stationery and DVDs. Delivery starts at £1.64 for a single CD
and increases according to the size and type of order. It's free if
you collect the goods from your nearest store, which sort of
defeats the object of buying online, but you can also claim
loyalty points with online purchases.

www.woolworths.co.uk   UK

WELL WORTH IT

A bright and breezy site from Woolworths with all you'd expect
in terms of range and prices. They are particularly good on kids'
stuff with strong prices on movies, chart music, clothes and
games; delivery is a bargain at £1.50 per order.

www.argos.co.uk   UK

ARGOS CATALOGUE

Argos offers an excellent range of products (some 13,000) across
thirteen different categories as per their catalogue. There are
some good bargains to be had. You can now reserve an item at
your local store, once you've checked that they have it in stock.

There's a good search facility and you can find a product via its catalogue number, if you've a catalogue handy that is. Delivery is £4.95 unless you spend more than £150 in which case it's free. Returns can be made to your local store. It's no wonder that this is the UK's most popular shopping site.

www.debenhams.com   UK
AWARD-WINNING FAMILY SERVICE
Not a common sight on the high street but Debenhams have a very good site aimed at their retailing strengths: gifts, weddings and fashion. Delivery costs vary.

www.johnlewis.co.uk   UK

NEVER KNOWINGLY UNDERSOLD
A really attractive and usable site with a wide range of products and some good offers too. Delivery costs start at £3.95, free over £150. Especially good if you haven't got one of their excellent stores near by. For more upmarket gear check out **www.liberty.co.uk** and also **www.selfridges.com,** which both have interesting site designs and products to match.

Foodies

The Good Web Site Guide's Top 10s of the Internet

1. **www.epicurious.com** – more recipes than you'll ever need.
2. **www.waitrose.com** – excellent for something special and great articles and feature sections too.
3. **www.food.gov.uk** – food news and advice from the Food Standards Agency.
4. **www.delia.co.uk** – outstanding site from the queen of cookery.
5. **www.tudocs.com** – cookery sites rated and listed in this excellent directory.
6. **www.3fatchicks.com** – no-nonsense healthy eating and diet advice.
7. **www.edible.com** – if it moves, it's edible…
8. **www.savoria.co.uk** – 'i veri sapori d'Italia'.
9. **www.cheese.com** – the ultimate site on cheese!
10. **www.vegweb.com** – attractive and very useful vegetarian site.

www.virgin.net/shopping   UK
LIFESTYLE AND SHOPPING GUIDE
Virgin's shopping guide is comprehensive covering all major
categories while allowing retailers to feature some of their best
offers. It also attempts to be a complete service for
entertainment and leisure needs with excellent sections on
music, travel and cinema in particular

Other High Street names…
www.bhs.co.uk – no online shopping but they do have a
store locator.
www.houseoffraser.co.uk – good store directory but you can
only buy vouchers online.
www.index.co.uk – Index is part of the Littlewoods empire and
has a similar offering to Argos.

General Retailers, Directories and Online Department Stores

www.2020shops.com   UK
THE SHOPPER'S FRIEND
A really likeable site with a great ethic – they don't do cosy
deals with other retailers for exposure so the shops they select
and rate are there on merit. They are one of the few that give
extra information on the shops such as delivery costs, plus
some shopping advice and price comparisons. It's fast too.

www.shoppingunlimited.co.uk   UK
INDEPENDENT RECOMMENDATION
Owned by the *Guardian* newspaper, this site offers hundreds of links
to stores that they've reviewed. It also offers help to inexperienced
shoppers and guidance on using credit cards online. There are also
links to other *Guardian* sites such as news and sport.

www.goldfish.com/guides/guide.html   UK
GOLDFISH GUIDES
Another good place for consumer advice and an easy approach
to selecting the right store. The Goldfish guides cover a range of
(mainly electrical) shopping categories all written by
independent journalists. Essentially the idea is that you read up
on it, compare prices on it then buy it – simple really. The site
is well designed and easy to use.

www.shopperuk.com UK

UK SHOPPING DIRECTORY
An excellent directory of UK shops both specialist and general.
It's well categorised by both type and alphabet; a genuinely
useful site with each store having a write up and a list of
related stores alongside.

www.edirectory.co.uk UK

IF IT'S OUT THERE, BUY IT HERE
A nice-looking directory of some 500 shops, it has a good
reputation for service as well as being topical.

See also:
http://theukhighstreet.com – a good UK directory, with the
shops rated by you the customer.
www.abound.co.uk – an excellent site offering a wide range of
clothes and leisure and electrical products; it's well executed
and has some good offers too.
www.buy4now.ie – an Irish shopping portal with a massive
selection of goods with prices quoted in Euros.
www.eshopone.co.uk – posh products and cheap prices.
www.eshops.co.uk – great design, loads of shops listed in the
directory with some excellent offers and a good search engine.
www.l-stores.com – a very good store search engine and directory.
www.letsbuyit.com – claiming over a million members and the
best prices.
www.mailorderexpress.co.uk – excellent for toys and kids' stuff.
www.shoptour.co.uk – links to over 1,000 secure shops in 14
categories, with a price comparison tool.
www.ukshopsearch.com – above average search engine and
quality design make this stand out from the crowd, you can
also vent your frustrations on the shopping experience in the
shoppers' forum.
www.ukshopsnet.com – well-designed and well-categorised
store directory site and search engine.
www.worthaglance.com – great-looking shop with some
outstanding bargains.

TV Shopping Channels

www.qvcuk.com UK

TV SHOPPING ONLINE
As a shopping channel on satellite or cable, QVC was already

successful; this well-put-together site shows off the breadth of their range and has some good offers. In total they display some 10,000 products.

See also:
www.bestdirect.tv – loads of bargains and celebrity endorsements.
www.idealworld.tv – just details of their channels and presenters, not much to buy.
www.price-drop.tv – the shop with lots of offers, and you can watch it live too.
www.screenshop.co.uk – very limited range on offer.
www.simplyshoppingtv.co.uk – with emphasis on health and home.

Value for Money

www.onlinediscount.com   US
THE VERY BEST DISCOUNTS
Online Discount specialise in monitoring Internet stores and highlighting those giving the best discounts in any one of 16 major categories. You are quickly put through to a list of the key shops and their bargains.

www.thesimplesaver.com   UK
WHERE TO GET THE BEST DEAL
What started off as a simple e-mail conversation about where to go for savings has snowballed into a web site and newsletter that lets the whole world know where the best shopping bargains are to be had.

www.gooddealdirectory.co.uk   UK
THE BARGAIN HUNTER'S BIBLE
Based on the book of the same name, this is basically a searchable directory of discount shops and sales. It's easy to use and the information seems comprehensive.

British Shopping

www.british-shopping.com   UK
UK SHOPPING LINKS AND DIRECTORY
An excellent comprehensive portal site specialising in British

shops; it also has plenty of related links and information.
www.somucheasier.co.uk also offers a comprehensive UK-oriented shop listing.

For more quintessentially British shops check out these sites:
www.brooksandbentley.com – classy British gifts.
www.classicengland.co.uk – the best British products on a fun-looking and easy-to-use site.
www.distinctlybritish.com – a British shop directory with a wide range of food, clothing, gift and children's retailers on offer.
www.harrods.com – a selection of their products available to buy from an attractive-looking site.

www.scotsmart.com   UK
SCOTTISH
A Scottish directory of sites, not just for shopping but covering most areas, you can search by theme or category and the shopping section is split into books, clothing, food, gifts and highland wear. See also **www.scotch-corner.co.uk** which is Scottish through and through.

www.wales-direct.com   UK
WALES DIRECT
A well-categorised shop devoted to all things Welsh, it has a wide range and some offers too, as well as a good links section.

Gifts

The following sites should help you find the perfect gift, but if you're shopping for the women in your life, there are more gift sites recommended in the men's section on page 288.

www.hard2buy4.co.uk   UK
GIFT IDEAS
Excellent gift shop with a wide range of unusual products including celebrity items, activities and gifts for men, women and children in separate sections, some good offers too.

S

See also:
www.apieceofafrica.co.za – for gifts of an African origin.
www.buyagift.co.uk – activities and experiences for those who have everything.
www.find-me-a-gift.co.uk – gifts, both products and special experiences, can be found here, loyalty scheme and wish lists thrown in too.

www.girlstuff.co.uk – gifts and products aimed at women young and old.

www.hawkin.com – odd design but good for range, children and the unusual.

www.iwantoneofthose.com – for more unusual gifts and stuff you don't need but would really like; it has a great gift finder.

www.jun-gifts.com – Japanese gifts and other products, excellent for the unusual.

www.michaelajdavies.co.uk – a great example of a showcase site with some nice gifts from around the world. If you're a retailer, they'll even make a range especially for you.

www.needapresent.com – very good site with some out-of-the ordinary gifts.

www.rebirth.co.za – authentic African art and gifts.

www.thesharperedge.co.uk – some good stuff in amongst the tat.

So You Can't be Bothered to Shop...

www.webswappers.com   UK

SWAP IT!
An interesting angle, at this site you can swap almost anything from the smallest item to a car or house! It's all backed by a confidential e-mail service and it looks quite good fun too.

www.anythingforhire.co.uk   UK

HIRE IT!
A comprehensive directory of goods and services for hire across the UK, well laid out and easy to use.

Skiing and Snowboarding

These sites tend to include information on both skiing and related travel, so we've moved it from Sports to create a combined section devoted to all things snowy.

www.fis-ski.com   UK

INTERNATIONAL SKI FEDERATION
Catch up on the news, the fastest times and the rankings in all forms of skiing at this site. Very good background information and a live online section enabling events to be monitored as they happen.

www.ski.co.uk
UK

THE PLACE TO START – A SKI DIRECTORY

Straightforward site, the information in the directory is useful and the recommended sites are rated. The sections include holidays, travel, weather, resorts, snowboarding, gear, fanatics and specialist services. See also **www.skicentral.com**

www.1ski.com
UK

COMPLETE ONLINE SKIING SERVICE

With a huge number of holidays, live snow reports, tips on technique and equipment, and the ultimate guide featuring over 750 resorts, it's difficult to go wrong. The site is well laid out and easy to use. There's a good events calendar too.

Other good ski and snowboarding sites:

www.descent.co.uk – specialists in luxury alpine holidays.

www.flexiski.co.uk – tailor-made skiing holidays.

www.ifyouski.com – comprehensive skiing site that has a very good holiday booking service with lots of deals.

www.iglu.com – holiday specialists with lots of variety and offers.

www.mountainzone.com – great for features, articles and ski adventurers.

www.natives.co.uk – aimed at ski workers, there's info on conditions, ski resorts, a good job section, where to stay and links to other cool sites all wrapped up on a very nicely designed site.

www.skiclub.co.uk – Ski Club of Great Britain with lots of offers and information too.

www.skidream.com – skiing and snowboarding in America and Canada.

www.skireunited.com – a Friends Reunited but for skiing holidays and workers.

www.skisolutions.com – one of the oldest travel companies specialising in skiing holidays, with a huge range of holidays and expertise.

www.snow-forecast.com – weather forecasts for snow areas.

www.snowlife.org.uk – very good directory come advice centre.

www.snowrental.net – online equipment rental, all seems very easy.

S

www.boardtheworld.com
UK

SNOWBOARDING

Masses of information and links covering the world of snowboarding, the site is well designed and doesn't seem to miss out any aspect of the sport.

See also:
www.boardz.com/snowboard/snowboardcentral.html – the snowboarding e-zine from Boardz.
www.goneboarding.co.uk – the UK boarding community with lots of information and chat.
www.snowboardinguk.co.uk – forums and snowboarding chat.

Social Networking

Here's how to start up a social network with your friends and consequently with their friends. It's a great way to share experiences, data or photos and particularly good for clubs or if you're fed up with the traditional dating sites. Here are some of the best and most useful sites.

www.friendster.com   US
COMMUNITY
A very easy-to-use set up with clear instructions and design; it's oriented towards dating but it's really adaptable.

See also:
www.dudecheckthisout.com – here you can get together online with people who share your interests basically by sharing the contents of your favourites box.
www.furl.net – not really a social networking program but its facilities make it useful for sharing internet information in this context.
www.linkedin.com – popular especially in the business community.
www.meetup.com – one of the easiest to use and well designed.
www.orkut.com – affiliated to Google, it has the air of an exclusive club but it's very popular and the design is excellent.

Software, Upgrades and Debugging

If you need to upgrade your software, then these are the sites to go to. Shareware is where you get a program to use for a short period of time before you have to buy it, freeware is exactly what you'd think – free. Debugging programs fix problems in established programs that weren't previously identified.

www.softwareparadise.co.uk   UK
THE SMART WAY TO SHOP FOR SOFTWARE
With over 42,000 products and excellent offers, this site should
be your first stop. It's a bit messy but easy to use; there's a
good search facility and plenty of products for Mac users.

www.download.com   US
CNET
A superb site covering all types of software and available
downloads. There are masses of reviews as well as buying tips
and price comparison tools; it also covers handheld PCs, Linux
and Macs.

www.softseek.com   US

ZDNET
Another excellent site with a huge amount of resources to
download, it's all a little overwhelming at first but the download
directory is easy to use and there's lots of free software
available.

www.tucows.com   US

TUCOWS
Probably less irritating to use than ZDNet and CNet, the
software reviews are also entertaining in their own right, the
best thing about it though is that it's quick.

If you feel like shopping around a bit more see also:
http://freshmeat.net – lots of shareware, also good for Linux fans.
http://home.netscape.com/plugins – if you're a Netscape fan then
you can improve its performance with 'plug-ins' from this site.
www.annoyances.org - a good site devoted to fixing problems
in Microsoft Windows.
www.completelyfreesoftware.com – hundreds of free programs
for you to download, from games to useful desktop accessories;
if it's available free, then its here. Membership is essential
costing around £10 per year.
www.cooltool.com – some of the best and 'coolest' software
specially selected by this team of toolsters...
www.freewarehome.com – a great selection of free programs
including a specialist site aimed at software for children,
www.handango.com – a good site specialising in downloads for
handheld PCs.
www.kidsfreeware.com – Internet freebies for kids.

S

www.neatnettricks.com – an archive of useful tips and downloads with regular updates, you need to subscribe though, which costs about £8 per year.
www.versiontracker.com – a massive selection, particularly good for Mac software.
www.vnunet.com – UK-orientated review and download site.
www.winplanet.com – specialises in software downloads and reviews for small businesses.
www.wired.com – popular technology magazine with all the latest news and reviews.

www.winzip.com   US

MANAGE FILES
Winzip allows you to save space on your PC by compressing data, making it easier to e-mail files and unlock zipped files that have been sent to you. It takes a few minutes to download. For Macs go to **www.allume.com** where you'll find Stuffit.

Space

E-zines and Reference Sites

www.space.com   US

MAKING SPACE POPULAR
An education-oriented site dedicated to space; there's news, mission reports, technology, history, personalities, a games section and plenty of pictures. The science section explores the planets and earth. See also Think Space at **http://library.thinkquest.org/26220** which is great for photos and links, pity it has not been regularly updated.

www.spacedaily.com   US

YOUR PORTAL TO SPACE
A comprehensive newspaper-style site with a huge amount of information and news about space and related subjects. It also has links to similar sister sites covering subjects like Mars, space war and space travel. See also the eccentric **www.astspace.demon.co.uk** – a good portal, once you find it.

www.astronomynow.com   UK

THE UK'S BEST-SELLING ASTRONOMY MAG
Get the news and views from a British angle, plus reviews on
the latest books. The store has widened out to include patches,
T-shirts and videos as well as the magazine and posters.

www.windows.ucar.edu   US

WINDOWS TO THE UNIVERSE
A well-designed site that provides information about the earth,
solar system and universe at three levels of detail making it
suitable for everyone from children to the most serious-minded.
There are interesting sections exploring the link between the
world's mythology and space, and history and space. There are
also sections on geology, space exploration and art.

www.heavens-above.com   US

IT'S ABOVE YOUR HEAD
Type in your location and they'll give you the exact time and
precise location of the next visible pass of the International
Space Station or space shuttle. They also help you to observe
satellites, flares from Iridium satellites and start charts
customised to your location. You have to register now, but that
means they keep the details of you location for your next visit.

See also:
www.astronautix.com – a comprehensive encyclopedia of
astronomy.
www.astronomy.ac.uk – study astronomy.
www.bbc.co.uk/science/space – superb pages on space from
the BBC with interactive features.
www.deepcold.com – a dark view of the space race, on an
interestingly designed site.
www.skypub.com – a magazine-related site with shop, archive
and the latest news.
www.spacescience.org – an American space education site.
www.universetoday.com – a space news-gathering service.

Space Organisations

www.nasa.gov   US

THE OFFICIAL NASA SITE
This huge site provides comprehensive information on the US

National Aeronautical and Space Administration. There are details on each NASA site, launch timings, sections for news, kids, project updates, and links to their specialist sites such as the Hubble Space Telescope, Mars and Earth observation. The site has become more vocal since we last visited and there are a range of multimedia activities including NASA TV.

www.esa.int   FRANCE
EUROPEAN SPACE AGENCY
Learn about the Agency's activities, the specific missions and what's planned to come.

See also:
www.arianespace.com – attractive site from the makers of the Ariane rocket.
www.bnsc.gov.uk – Britain's place in space, with links and details of missions and the latest news.
www.iki.rssi.ru/eng – Russian space research.
www.isro.org/space_science – the Indian space program.
www.jpl.nasa.gov – the goings on at the Jet Propulsion Lab with excellent photography.
www.russianspaceweb.com – a good overview of the Russian space program with a history and the latest news.
www.sinodefence.com/space/facility/spaceagency.asp
– information on China's national space programme.

The Solar System and Beyond

www.seds.org/billa/tnp   UK
THE NINE PLANETS
A multimedia tour of the nine planets, stunning photography, interesting facts combined with good text.

http://hubblesite.org   US
THE HUBBLE TELESCOPE
An action-packed site covering the photographs and discoveries made by the Hubble Telescope, which has been orbiting the earth for several years now. It contains some amazing and staggeringly beautiful pictures, some of which you can download.

www.redcolony.com   US

MARS
A superb site all about the red planet. There is a synopsis of its

history, plus details on past and future space missions with a focus on the colonisation of Mars. There's a great deal of information on things like terra forming and biogenesis, it's all taken very seriously too. See also the equally imaginative **www.exploremarsnow.org** where you can find a plausible manifestation of what a Mars mission could look like, backed up with outstanding graphics. At **http://marsrovers.jpl.nasa.gov** you can learn about the latest Mars missions.

For more planetary resources try:
http://chandra.harvard.edu – learn all about space exploration with x-rays here.
http://exoplanets.org – an interesting site on those planets found outside our solar system.
http://planetary.org – home of the Planetary Society.
http://seds.lpl.arizona.edu/billa/twn – a site about Nebulae with some beautiful pictures.
www.asi.org – an organisation campaigning for the colonisation of the moon.
www.fourmilab.ch/earthview – views of the earth and the moon from space.
www.solarviews.com – excellent encyclopedic site on the planets.
www.spaceweather.com – a detailed site on solar activity with excellent links pages.
www.the-solar-system.net – great for pictures and links, you can also test yourself by taking the quiz.

Is There Life Out There?

www.setiathome.ssl.berkeley.edu   US

GET IN TOUCH WITH AN ALIEN
To borrow the official site description 'SETI@home is a scientific experiment that uses Internet-connected computers in the Search for Extraterrestrial Intelligence (SETI).' You can participate by running a free program that downloads and analyses radio telescope data. Millions have participated and 5 billion potential signals have been located; they're pointing their scopes at the most promising now. There's still time for you to be the first!

www.ufosightingsuk.co.uk   UK

UFOS IN THE UK
This is a great catalogue of 'eye witness' accounts of encounters with

UFOs in the UK. Whether you believe in it or not, it makes for an interesting read. For another glimpse at mysterious phenomena, crop circles, take a look at **www.cropcircleresearch.com** where there is also fascinating evidence of extraterrestrial contact.

Miscellaneous and Specialist Sites

www.spaceadventures.com   US
SPACE TOURISM
OK so you want to be an astronaut? Well now you have a golden opportunity, so long as you have $2 million! Having said that there are actually some cheaper options including shuttle tours and a trip to the edge of space.

www.badastronomy.com   US
DEBUNKING THE MYTHS
A site devoted to exploring some of the myths and stories that surround astronomy and science fiction. It gives the facts in a straightforward and (because the site owner sometimes gets on his 'high horse') entertaining way.

www.lpl.arizona.edu/impacteffects   US
WHAT HAPPENS WHEN AN ASTEROID HITS...
A cheery little site, you input all the data about the size and related details of your asteroid or meteor, then the site tells you what will happen when it hits and whether you'll survive. Some of it is very technical but it's mostly explained well.

www.telescopeplanet.co.uk   UK
TELESCOPE SHOP
A wide range of telescopes for sale, plus accessories and some good offers too. See also **www.skyviewoptics.co.uk** and **www.rothervalleyoptics.co.uk**

S

Spectacles

Buying glasses and contact lenses online isn't as daft as you'd think there are great savings to be had...

www.glassesdirect.co.uk   UK
FROM £15
A well-designed site with sections on standard, rimless, semi-rimless
and bendable glasses. There's also advice on how to interpret your
prescription and what sort of frame would suit. You can order trial
glasses to see if the frames fit comfortably too.

See also:
www.antiquespectacles.co.uk – maybe you'd rather go for an
antique pair?
www.boots.co.uk – advice-laden section, you can book an
appointment for an eye test.
www.specs2go.co.uk – good range and money back guarantee.
www.specsavers.co.uk – see their whole range of frames and
contact lenses.

Sport

*One of the best uses of the Internet is to keep up-to-date with how
your team is performing, or if you're a member of a team or
association, keep each other updated.*

General Sport Sites

www.sporting-life.com   UK
THE SPORTING LIFE
A very comprehensive sport site, with plenty of advice, tips,
news and latest scores. It's considered to be one of the best,
and is good for stories, in-depth analysis and overall coverage
of the major sports.

www.bbc.co.uk/sport   UK

BBC SPORT COVERAGE
They may have lost the right to broadcast many sporting events
but their coverage at this level is excellent – much broader than
most and it's always up to date.

www.skysports.com   UK
THE BEST OF SKY SPORTS
Excellent for the Premiership and football in general, but also covers
other sports very well particularly cricket and both forms of rugby.
Includes a section featuring video and audio clips, and there are

interviews with stars. You can vote in their polls, e-mail programmes
or try sports trivia quizzes. Lots of adverts spoil it.

www.rivals.net   UK

THE RIVALS NETWORK
Independent of any news organisations, Rivals is basically a
network of specialist sites covering the whole gamut of major
and some minor sports. Each site has its own editor who is
passionate about the sport they cover. In general, its promise is
better than the delivery, but what there is, is excellent with
good quality content and pictures.

www.sportonair.com   UK

HEAR ALL ABOUT IT...
If you can't see it then you can always come here to listen to it,
this site offers up lots of audio content including interviews and
commentary from most of the major sporting events. There's a
good archive and most major sports are covered.

http://sport.telegraph.co.uk   UK

THE DAILY TELEGRAPH
Very comprehensive and well written with lots of archive
material. All the major sports are covered and with contributors
like Mike Atherton, Henry Winter and Sebastian Coe, you know
it has authority.

Other good all-rounders and sites with good links:
http://dmoz.org/sports/ – links galore at the Open Directory project.
http://sport.independent.co.uk – good all-round coverage from
The *Independent* newspaper.
http://sportsillustrated.cnn.com – the latest in American sport
from CNN.
www.EL.com/elinks/sports – list of American-oriented sports links.
www.eurosport.com – the world of European sport.
www.sportsline.com – excellent coverage from CBS.

Miscellaneous

www.sportspubs.co.uk   UK

WHERE TO WATCH SPORT
A building directory of pubs where you can watch sport. You
can search it by sport or by region and there's a good links
section too.

www.culture.gov.uk/sport   UK

> WHAT THE GOVERNMENT IS UP TO
> Here's where to go to find the latest policies, what the minister
> for sport does and how they are helping sport develop in the
> community at large. Lots on the London Olympic bid, fairly dull
> site though.

www.streetplay.com   US

> URBAN SPORT
> An interesting site covering the development of sports that have just
> sprung up in cities and parks all over America.

Sites on Specific Sports

American Football

www.nfl.com   US

> NATIONAL FOOTBALL LEAGUE
> American football's online bible, it's a huge official site with
> details and statistics bursting from every page. It's got
> information on all the teams, players and likely draft picks;
> there's also information on NFL Europe and links to other key
> sites. All it really lacks is gossip!
>
> *See also:*
> **http://football.espn.go.com/nfl/index** – ESPN's site is
> authoritative and offers links to other sports.
> **www.hot-iron.co.uk** – a very good Scottish e-zine.
> **www.nfleurope.com** – thorough coverage of the European league.
> **www.nflplayers.com** – for the latest news and background on
> all the key people in the game plus nostalgia from ex-players.
> **www.ukgridiron.co.uk** – the UK-oriented view of the game.

Archery

www.archery.org   UK

> INTERNATIONAL ARCHERY FEDERATION
> Get the official news, events listings, rankings and records
> information from this fairly mundane site.
>
> *See also:*
> **www.bownet.com** – *Bow International Archery* magazine.
> **www.scottisharchery.org.uk** – the Scottish Archery Association.

www.theglade.co.uk – an entertaining and chatty site, basically an e-zine, devoted to all forms of archery.

Athletics and Running

www.iaaf.org   UK

INTERNATIONAL ASSOCIATION OF ATHLETICS FEDERATIONS
The official site of the IAAF is a results-oriented affair with lots of rankings in addition to the latest news. There's also a multimedia section where you can see pictures, listen to commentary or watch video of the key events. There's a good links page and information on the organisation's activities.

www.ukathletics.net   UK

THE GOVERNING BODY
Many official 'governing body' sites are pretty boring affairs, not so UK Athletics which contains lots of features, is newsy and written with an obvious sense of enthusiasm. There are details on forthcoming events, reports on aspects of the sport, records, biographies of key athletes and advice on keeping fit. Somehow you get the impression the site is sponsored...

www.athletix.org   UK

THE ATHLETICS SITE
A statistics and results-led site with coverage of all the major events and some minor ones. It covers international competitions as well as having a good gallery and biographical details of some of the major athletes, it's also good for links.

www.runnersworld.com   US

RUNNER'S WORLD MAGAZINE
A rather dry site with tips from getting started through to advanced-level running. There's lots of information, news and records plus reviews on shoes and gear. See also the less visually exciting but comprehensive **www.runnersweb.com**

www.realrunner.com   US

A RUNNING COMMUNITY
A very well-put-together site with lots of resources to help runners in terms of both equipment and advice. There's an online health check, details of events, marathons and loads of information on Ron Hill. Good design ensures that the site is a

pleasure to use. For equipment advice try Runnersworld
www.runnersworld.ltd.uk

See also:
www.athletics-online.co.uk – *Athletics Weekly* magazine.
www.bal.org.uk – results from the British Athletics League.
www.boja.org – a great site for young athletes; there's not
much to look at but it contains lots of information.
www.british-athletics.co.uk – a boring site but it has a
directory of clubs and regional events. It's good for links to
newsgroups though.
www.gbrathletics.com – great for statistics and rankings.
www.marathonguide.com – all you need to know about
marathons with news and advice.
www.nuff-respect.co.uk – see what Linford Christie is up to
these days.
www.runnersweb.co.uk – a good site covering all aspects of
running including marathon training.
www.runtrackdir.com – details of all the UK's running tracks
and their facilities.
www.trackandfieldnews.com – all the latest from *Track & Field
News*. US bias.

Booze

The Good Web Site Guide's Top 10s of the Internet

1. **www.realbeer.com** – 150,000 pages on beer!
2. **www.bbr.co.uk** – the best wine shop.
3. **www.wine-lovers-page.com** – to learn about wine.
4. **www.winespectator.com** – the most comprehensive wine site.
5. **www.superplonk.com** – Malcolm Gluck's great site.
6. **www.idrink.com** – recipes for 5,000 cocktails.
7. **www.camra.org.uk** – the Campaign for Real Ale.
8. **www.whiskeyweb.com** – a whisky-lovers dream.
9. **www.sportspubs.co.uk** – pubs where you can watch sport.
10. **www.wine–searcher.com** – the wine lover search engine.

S

Australian Rules Football

www.afl.com.au   AUSTRALIA
AUSTRALIAN FOOTBALL LEAGUE
A top-quality site covering all aspects of the game including
team news, player profiles and statistics as well as the latest
gossip and speculation.

Baseball

www.mlb.com   US
MAJOR LEAGUE BASEBALL
All you need to know about the top teams and the World
Series. It's not the best-designed site but there's good
information, statistics on the game and notes about the key
players as well as related articles and features.

See also:
www.baseball1.com – very detailed.
www.baseball-links.com – easy to use and has over 10,000 links.
www.gbbaseball.co.uk – all about the game in the UK.

Basketball

www.nba.com   UK

NATIONAL BASKETBALL ASSOCIATION
A comprehensive official site with features on the teams,
players and games; there's also an excellent photo gallery and
you can watch some of the most important points if you have
the right software.

See also:
www.basketball.com – really extensive coverage including the
women's game.
www.basketball365.co.uk – comprehensive overview of the
game with news of what's going on both sides of the Atlantic.
www.bbl.org.uk – the official site of the British Basketball League.
www.britball.com – a newsy site taking in the British and
Irish games.

Bowls

www.bowlsengland.com UK
ENGLISH BOWLING ASSOCIATION
A straightforward design making it easy to find out all you need to know about lawn bowls in England, including a good set of links to associated sites.

www.eiba.co.uk UK
ENGLAND INDOOR BOWLING ASSOCIATION
A pretty basic site giving an overview of the game, links and background information on competitions and rules.

See also:
www.bowlsclub.info – a portal site devoted to lawn bowls.
www.bowlsinternational.com – home of a bowls magazine, good for links.
www.esmba.org.uk – informative site from the English Short Mat Bowling Association.
www.short-mat-magazine.com – aimed at selling the mag, but has information on the Irish, English and Welsh games.

Boxing

www.boxinginsider.com US
BOXING INSIDER
An effective site with lots of information on the sport plus chat and stats. There's a bout-by-bout guide, lots of links and the writing is pretty good too.

See also:
www.bbc.co.uk/boxing – great for the latest news and background information.
www.heavyweights.co.uk – who cover the hype around heavyweight boxing.
www.ibhof.com – the International Boxing Hall of Fame has information on the best ever boxers, it's great but could still do with more photos.
www.secondsout.com – excellent magazine and portal site for fight fans everywhere.

S

For the different boxing authorities:

www.aiba.net – the official site from the Amateur International Boxing Association.

www.wbaonline.com – the WBA has an OK-looking and functional site.

www.wbcboxing.com – a straightforward site from the World Boxing Council.

www.wbu.cc – the World Boxing Union covers the sport well from an unusual site.

www.womenboxing.com – a very comprehensive site devoted to women's boxing.

Clay Shooting

www.clayshooting.co.uk   UK

CLAY SHOOTING MAGAZINE

A good introduction to the sport with a beginner's guide to start you off and a good set of links to key suppliers and associated sites. There's also an online shop where you can buy the odd essential item such as global positioning systems and dog food.

Serious shooters can go to the comprehensive **www.hotbarrels.com**

Cricket

www.cricinfo.com   UK

THE HOME OF CRICKET ON THE NET

The best all-round cricket site on the Internet, with in-depth analysis, match reports, player profiles, statistics, links to other more specialised sites and live coverage. There's also a shop with lots of cricket goodies.

www.lords.org   UK

THE OFFICIAL LINE ON CRICKET

A pretty measly site these days with basic information, ticket sales details and fixtures, plus a top line history of the place. See also **www.play-cricket.com** which is home to the English Cricket Board and a fine source of information and statistics on the game.

www.webbsoc.demon.co.uk   UK

WOMEN'S CRICKET ON THE WEB

There are not many sites about women's cricket; this is probably the best, with features, news, fixture lists, match reports and player profiles. Nothing fancy, but it works.

S

www.theprideside.com   UK

CRICKET TO THE ROOTS
A good attempt at encouraging young people to take an interest in cricket with an overview of the game on a really interesting and interactive site.

See also:
http://sport.guardian.co.uk/cricket – good-looking and up-to-the-minute site from the *Guardian* newspaper.
www.334notout.com – a history of the Ashes and the 'bodyline' controversy.
www.cricketonly.com – a comprehensive and news-oriented cricket enthusiasts' site.
www.cricketrecords.com – one for the statistics freaks, lots of pop up adverts too.
www.cricketsupplies.com – a good-looking online store specialising in cricket gear, delivery is £6 per order.
www.cricnet.co.uk – the Professional Cricketers' Association official site.
www.windiescricket.com – keep up to date with the West Indies team here, it also covers the game by island too.

Cycling

These are sites aimed at the more serious sportsman, for more leisurely cycling see page 104 and for holidays turn to page 476.

www.bcf.uk.com   UK

BRITISH CYCLING FEDERATION
The governing body for cycling, their site has become more comprehensive, you can get information on events, rules, clubs and rankings, as well as contact names for coaching and development, plus a news service.

www.bikemagic.com   UK

IT'S BIKETASTIC!
Whether you're a beginner or an old hand, the enthusiastic and engaging tone of this site will convert you or enhance your cycling experience. There's plenty of news and features, as well as reviews on bike parts and gadgets, a classified ads section and a selection of links to other biking web sites, all of which are rated.

www.letour.fr
FRANCE

TOUR DE FRANCE

Written in English and French this site covers the Tour in some depth with details on the teams, riders and general background information.

www.mtbbritain.co.uk
UK

MOUNTAIN BIKING

Routes, tips, advice and gear: it's all here whether you're a real enthusiast or just a weekender.

Darts

www.planetdarts.co.uk
UK

PROFESSIONAL DARTS CORPORATION

A messy site but one that has lots of league information, statistics, news, articles and rules.

See also:

www.bbc.co.uk/darts – basic information only.
www.cyberdarts.com – a darts e-zine, which contains lots of information such as articles, chat, forums and rules too.
www.dartbase.com – rules, techniques and equipment advice.

Dog Racing

For the gambling side of dog racing, see page 193.

www.thedogs.co.uk
UK

BRITISH GREYHOUND RACING BOARD

A well-designed site offering an overview of the sport, the top dogs and track information, also has help for owners and all the results.

See also:

www.retiredgreyhounds.co.uk – how to adopt a retired greyhound.
www.ugo4u.co.uk – the Union of Greyhound Owners.

Equestrian

www.bhs.org.uk
UK

BRITISH HORSE SOCIETY

A charity that looks after the welfare of horses. Here you can get information on insurance, links, riding schools, competitions, events and trials.

For more information try:

http://horses.about.com – About.com's excellent suite of pages devoted to all things equestrian.

www.badminton-horse.co.uk – background and information on the famous horse trials with lots of extra features and links.

www.britishdressage.co.uk – very good site covering this aspect of the sport.

www.britisheventing.com – an attractive text-based site with details on the sport and links.

www.horseandhound.co.uk – excellent magazine site from the leading authority.

www.horseselect.co.uk – buying and selling competition horses.

Extreme Sports

www.extreme.com   US

EXTREME SPORTS CHANNEL

The official site of the Extreme Sports Channel is hi-tech but quite slow; however, once downloaded it's got lots to offer in terms of information, shopping and the latest headlines.

See also:

www.adventuredirectory.com – useful activity-by-sport portal site.

www.awezome.com owned by **www.extremists.com.au** – informative and wide ranging.

www.expn.go.com – excellent extreme sports magazine with a US bias.

www.extremepie.com – good extreme sports gear shop.

www.extreme-sports-world.com – very useful portal site.

Fishing

www.fishing.co.uk   UK

HOME OF UK FISHING ON THE NET

A huge site that offers information on where to fish, how to fish, where's the best place to stay near fish, even fishing holidays. There's also advice on equipment, a records section and links to shops and shop locations. Shop on-site for fishing books and magazines.

See also:

www.anglersnet.co.uk – good magazine site with lots of information and chat.

www.anglers-world.co.uk – great for fishing holidays.

www.bdaa.co.uk – home of the British Disabled Anglers Association and a comprehensive offering it is too.

www.fishandfly.co.uk – another good magazine site, this one devoted to fly fishing.

www.fisheries.co.uk – excellent for coarse fishing and links.

www.nfsa.org.uk – home of the National Federation of Sea Anglers with lots of links and information.

www.nimpopo.com – basic site with over 3,000 tackle bargains.

www.pacgb.com – the Pike Anglers Club, a bit specialist perhaps, but a good site nonetheless.

www.specialist-tackle.co.uk – excellent store for equipment plus much more in the way of chat and information.

www.tackledirectory.com – a store 'run by anglers for anglers'.

www.thefishfinder.com – yes it's a fish search engine and a pretty good one at that.

Football

www.football365.co.uk   UK

FOOTBALL NEWS

Probably the best of the football e-zines in terms of the combination of looks, quality writing and features, although it can be a bit dense at times.

http://www.goal.com   UK

GOAL!!

Excellent portal and news site with lots of articles and coverage of the latest gossip; it also covers many of the European leagues as well.

www.teamtalk.com   UK

CHECK OUT THE TEAMS!

The most respected place to go if you want all the latest gossip and transfer information. It's opinionated but not often wrong. They have many top journalists on their books, so the information is likely to be on the ball.

www.soccerbase.com   UK

SOCCER STATISTICS

The site to end all pub rows, it's described as the most

comprehensive and up-to-date source of British football data on the Internet.

www.footballgroundguide.co.uk   UK

FOOTBALL GROUNDS

Details of all 92 English league football club grounds, locations and facilities, incredibly useful for all away supporters. Excellent for team links too.

It's worth having a look at the sites listed below; just pick the one you like best.

http://pinkfootball.com – a girls guide to football.

http://skysports.planetfootball.com – news, information and OPTA statistics and the world game, now part of the Sky Sports site.

www.4thegame.com – a messy and commercial football news site.

www.conferencefootball.tv – coverage of some of the key conference clubs including replays.

www.e-soccer.com – hundreds of links and the latest news.

www.fansFC.com – gossip and rumours, plus fans' forums for chat and debate.

www.football-rumours.com – the latest transfer gossip and detailed information on the players.

www.footballtransfers.info - very detailed transfer information and likely moves.

www.guardian.co.uk/football – great writing and irreverent articles, uncluttered design.

www.icons.com – site host to many major players, lots of background info plus the latest news.

www.laughfc.co.uk – a humorous look at the game, good for jokes and chants, some adult content.

www.linkupfootball.com – over 3,372 football-related links in 83 categories.

www.pureworldcup.com – a fun and informative look at the World Cup.

www.ratetheref.co.uk – where you can get your revenge on the ref if you feel mistreated.

www.soccerbot.com – great for basic information, with interesting interactive league tables.

www.soccerhighway.com – a strange site but good for links.

www.soccernet.com – well-put-together by ESPN, comprehensive but a bit boring.

www.wsc.co.uk – home of the magazine *When Saturday Comes*.

www.footballaid.com

FOOTBALL CHARITY
Football aid is a charity that helps good causes by running
football events, you can sign on to play for the team of your
choice or just send a cheque.

Football Authorities

www.fifa.com

FIFA
This is FIFA's magazine where you can get information on what
they do, the World Cup and other FIFA competitions. For the
UEFA go to **www.uefa.com** where you can see how everyone is
faring in the Champions League and UEFA cup.

See also:
www.irishfa.com – the Irish Football Association with a pretty
standard site.
www.leaguemanagers.com – home of the League Manager's
Association.
www.premierleague.com – the FA official site, covering the
latest news and information.
www.scotprem.co.uk – a comprehensive offering with links too.
www.welsh-football.net – an independent magazine on the
Welsh soccer scene.

Golf

www.golftoday.co.uk

THE PREMIER ONLINE GOLF MAGAZINE
An excellent site for golf news and tournaments with features,
statistics and rankings also a course directory. It's the best all-
round site covering Europe. There are also links to sister sites
about the amateur game, shops and where to stay.
GolfToday.com also hosts a comprehensive site on the amateur
game; you can find it at **www.amateur-golf.com**

www.golfweb.com

PGA TOUR
The best site for statistics on the PGA, and keeping up with
tournament scores, it also has audio and visual features with
RealPlayer. For the official word on the tour go to **www.pga.com**

while for the European tour go to **www.europeantour.com** and
for a good overview of the Ryder Cup visit **www.rydercup.com**

www.golf.com   US

THE AMERICAN VIEW
Part of NBC's suite of web sites, this offers a massive amount
of information and statistics on the game, the major tours and
players, both men and women.

www.golfingguides.net   UK

UK GOLF COURSES
Detailed information on selected golf courses classed as 'gems',
plus contact information on those lesser courses. A good search
facility rounds it off, plus the fact it's pretty well designed.

www.uk-golfguide.com   UK

GOLF TOURISM
A useful directory of courses and hotels with courses, with
links to travel agents for the UK and abroad, you can also get
information on golf equipment suppliers and insurance. See
also **www.whatgolf.co.uk**

www.onlinegolf.co.uk   UK

GOLF EQUIPMENT
A good-looking and comprehensive golf store with lots of offers
and a good range, it has a ladies section and a good search
facility. Delivery on orders over £50 is free in the UK.

See also:
http://golfbidder.co.uk – store for second-hand clubs
and equipment.
www.golflinks.co.uk – a large, UK-oriented site database.
www.grassrootsgolf.com – for summer camps for junior golfers,
corporate golf and golf tours.

Gymnastics

www.gymmedia.com   GERMANY

GYMNASTIC NEWS
A bilingual site giving all the latest news, it covers all forms of
the sport and offers lots of links to related sites.

See also:
www.british-gymnastics.org – an official site offering lots of information and advice.
www.intlgymnast.com – the latest news from *International Gymnast* magazine.
www.scottishgymnastics.com – comprehensive coverage but tied to the magazine so it's not all it could be.

Hockey

www.hockeyonline.co.uk   UK

THE ENGLISH HOCKEY ASSOCIATION
A slick site covering the English game with information and chat on the players, leagues and teams for both the men's and the women's games. For the Scottish game go to **www.scottish-hockey.org.uk** and for the Welsh **www.welsh-hockey.co.uk** The latter is not great on design but both give all the relevant information.

See also:
www.fieldhockey.com – advert laden with a dull design but has all the latest news.
www.hockeydirect.co.uk – good equipment store.
www.hockeyweb.co.uk – chat, news and links.

Horse Racing

For sites that cover the gambling side of horse racing go to page 193.

www.racingpost.co.uk   UK

THE RACING POST
Superb, informative site from the authority on the sport, every event covered in depth with tips and advice. To get the best out of it you have to register, then you have access to the database and more.

www.bhb.co.uk   UK
BRITISH HORSE RACING BOARD
A very well-put-together site offering up information and background on the sport including interviews, details of the latest meetings and horse ownership advice.

www.racenews.co.uk   UK
RACING, COURSES AND BETTING
A slightly different spin from Racenews, they have three main

sections: their news service, a course guide and a tipsters column.
There's also an excellent links section covering racing world-wide.

www.flatstats.co.uk UK

FLAT RACING STATISTICS
This site contains masses of detailed and unique statistics –
horse, trainer, jockey, sire and race statistics, favourites
analysis, systems analysis and much more. You have to be a
member to get the best out of it; subscription costs £24.95 per
month. See also **www.workrider.com**

www.thejockeyclub.co.uk UK

THE JOCKEY CLUB
A campaigning site aimed at promoting confidence in racing.
It has news, details on the rules and how stewarding works,
as well as links and sporting guidelines. See also
www.jockeysroom.com which has an A–Z of jockeys with
biographies and pictures.

Other sites worth a visit are...
www.attheraces.co.uk – live action, tips and the latest news
plus great design.
www.bbc.co.uk/racing – the BBC's excellent race pages.
www.racecall.co.uk – hear all the action on your phone.
www.teletext.co.uk – the information pages have gone, but
under 'mobile services' you can sign up for racing alerts direct
to your phone.

Ice Hockey

www.nhl.com US

NATIONAL HOCKEY LEAGUE
Catch up on the latest from the NHL including a chance to
listen to and watch key moments from past and recent games.

www.icehockeyuk.co.uk UK

ICE HOCKEY UK
The official site with bags of information and background on the
game. It's well designed and great for beginners and those who
want to find out more about the sport.

See also:
www.azhockey.com – home of the encyclopedia of Ice Hockey.

www.crazykennys.com – ice hockey equipment suppliers.
www.icehockeyhistory.co.uk – a sparse site covering the history of the game in the UK.

Ice Skating

www.frogsonice.com/skateweb   US
LINKS
Not a great design but it offers lots of links to all aspects of skating.

See also:
www.iceskating.org.uk – the official site of the National Ice Skating Association of the UK; good-looking site covering all aspects of ice skating.
www.iceskatingintnl.com – for competitive skating news, US bias.
www.iceskatingworld.com – comprehensive US site with excellent links and the latest news.
www.sisa.org.uk – the Scottish Ice Skating Association.
www.skating-shop.co.uk – for all your skating gear.

Martial Arts

www.martial-arts-network.com   US
PROMOTING MARTIAL ARTS
Possibly qualifies as the loudest introduction sequence, but once you've cut the volume or skipped the intro, the site offers a great deal in terms of resources and information about the martial arts scene, including *Black Belts* magazine. Its layout is a little confusing and the site is quite slow.

www.britishjudo.org.uk   UK
JUDO
Judo has a proud tradition in the UK, and if you want to follow that you can get all the information you need at the British Judo Association site. It gives a brief history of judo, a shop and event information. For a broader view go to **www.judoinfo.com**

www.btkf.homestead.com   UK
BRITISH KARATE FEDERATION
Information on all forms of the discipline as well as events listings, fun pages and an online martial arts club, which is hosted by Yahoo.

See also:

http://physical-arts.com – a site in the making, more a way of life than combat.

http://uk.dir.yahoo.com/recreation/sport/martial_arts – a huge number of links.

www.martialinfo.com – slow but comprehensive site with an online magazine.

www.practical-martial-arts.co.uk – useful advice on techniques and an overview of key combat types, there are also forums where you can have your say.

www.ryoku.co.uk – where to go for your gear.

Motor Sport

www.crash.net
UK

MOTOR SPORT PORTAL
An excellent but very commercial news and directory site covering the major motor sports and most of the minor ones too. There's an online shop selling motor sport merchandise amongst other things and there's a good photo library.

www.ukmotorsport.com
UK

INFORMATION OVERLOAD
This site covers every form of motor racing; it's got lots of links to appropriate sites covering all aspects of motor sport. There are also chat sections and forums plus links to product and service suppliers. They promise a site overhaul soon – not before time.

www.MSport-UK.com
UK

UK MOTOR SPORT
A good site covering all aspects of motor sport in Britain, highlights include the 'must see' section (I wish more sites had one) and the links page. As they've kept out clutter, it's fast to use.

www.autosport.com
UK

AUTOSPORT MAGAZINE
Excellent for news and features on motor sport plus links and an affiliated online shopping experience for related products such as team gear, books or models.

www.linksheaven.com
US

THE MOST COMPREHENSIVE LINKS DIRECTORY

Whatever, whoever, there's an appropriate link. It's biased towards Formula 1, CART and Nascar though.

www.worldmotorsport.com   UK

MOTOR SPORT DEBATE
Many forums covering all aspects of racing. If you want a say or get something off your chest then here's where to go.

Sites Covering Specific Types of Racing

www.itv-f1.com   UK

F1 ON ITV
This web site is excellent, it doesn't miss much and there is plenty of action. There's all the background information you'd expect plus circuit profiles, schedules and a photo gallery.

See also:
www.atlasf1.com – outstanding for information on F1.
www.f1-world.co.uk – more information and background plus links too.

www.fota.co.uk   UK

FORMULA 3
Formula 3 explained plus info on the teams, drivers and circuits. It's the breeding ground for F1 drivers of the future which adds to the excitement reflected in the energy of this site.

www.indycar.com   US

INDY CARS
A comprehensive offering with coverage of all that goes on in the Indy car scene.

www.rallysport.com   UK

COVERING THE WORLD RALLY CHAMPIONSHIP
Good for results and news on rallying in the UK and across the world.

See also:
http://rally.racing-live.com/en – all the latest news, plus follow races stage by stage.
www.rallyzone.co.uk – a comprehensive international e-zine.

www.btccpages.com UK

BRITISH TOURING CAR CHAMPIONSHIP

This site offers a great deal of information and statistics on the championship, driver and team profiles, photos and links to other related sites. There are also a number of forums you can get involved with if you feel like chatting to fellow enthusiasts.

www.karting.co.uk UK

GO KARTING

A well-laid-out portal site to all things karting in the UK, with links and directories covering the tracks, manufacturers, events and a photo gallery plus the latest news. See also **www.gokartingforfun.co.uk**

www.monstertrucks.net US

TRUCKS

All aspects of truck racing, exhibitions and shows, if you like your motor sport large, then go here.

Motorcycling

www.motorcyclenews.com UK

NEWS AND VIEWS

A very good magazine-style site giving all the latest news, gossip and event information, there are also sections on buying a bike, where to get parts and the latest gear, off-road biking and a links directory. There's also a chat room and a good classified section.

www.acu.org.uk UK

AUTO-CYCLE UNION

The ACU is the governing body for motorcycle sports in the UK and this site gives information on its work and the benefits of being a member. There are also links and details of their magazine.

www.motoGP.com UK

TRACK AND OFF-ROAD

A well-laid-out magazine site, covering the world of Moto Grand Prix with results, background and biographical details. Available in eight languages.

www.british-speedway.co.uk   UK

SPEEDWAY
Provides information on the leagues as well as the latest news,
there's also an events calendar and links to related sites.

www.motocross.com   US

MOTOCROSS
An authoritative site covering the sport but it's centred on the
US, although it has got some information on the European
scene. See also **www.motolinks.com**

Mountaineering and Outside Sports

www.mountainzone.com   US

FOR THE UPWARDLY MOBILE
Thoroughly covers all aspects of climbing, hiking, mountain
biking, skiing and snowboarding with a very good photography
section featuring galleries from major mountains and climbers.

www.ukclimbing.com   UK

CLIMBING NEWS
Excellent and very informative site covering all aspects of
climbing, it has plenty of opportunities for chat along with the
latest news. There's also weather information and a very good
database of climbs with comments and essential information
for each one.

www.rockrun.com   UK

ALL THE RIGHT EQUIPMENT
Excellent equipment shop covering climbing and walking gear,
which is also pretty comprehensive on the information front too.
Delivery starts at £3.50 for the UK. See also
www.gearzone.co.uk, who have a similar offering.

Other good climbing sites:
www.blacks.co.uk – good camping and equipment store.
www.bouldering.com – an odd site but one devoted to climbing
big boulders…
www.climb-guide.com – the guides are pretty basic but there a
good links page.
www.cruxed.com – nice-looking site with advice on techniques
and training, good links.

www.onward-outward.co.uk – a good outdoor clothing store with a wide range and the best brands.
www.outdoorgear.co.uk – everything you need for the outdoors.
www.thebmc.co.uk – good all-round climbing and hill-walking magazine-style site from the British Mountaineering Council with good links pages.
www.ukcrags.com – some good guides to popular climbs, but the site was for sale at time of visiting.
www.upandunder.co.uk – a Welsh mountaineering store with a good links section.

Netball

www.netball.org   UK

INTERNATIONAL FEDERATION OF NETBALL ASSOCIATIONS
Get information on the work of the federation and the rules of the game, plus rankings and the events calendar. See also **www.netballcoaching.com** which is good for advice and links.

Olympics

www.olympics.org   UK

BRITISH OLYMPIC ASSOCIATION
An expanded site featuring highlights of the Athens' games and looking forward to Torino in 2006 and Beijing in 2008. You can learn more about 300 Olympic heroes, access an athlete's medal tally and learn more about the sports featured in the games. There's information for collectors and also the doping policy. For a history of the games there's the Olympic museum link and links to sports federations and committees.

www.london2012.org   UK

THE LONDON BID
Find out what's planned and where, download the interactive map, discover who's backing the bid, get the latest news, and you can even sign up to be a volunteer.

See also:
www.olympianartifacts.com – good site featuring an Olympic memorabilia store.
www.olympics.com – the official site of the Olympic movement.

Rowing

www.ara-rowing.org　　　　　　　　　　　　　　　　　　UK

AMATEUR ROWING ASSOCIATION
This site offers information on the history of the sport, plus the latest news, coaching tips and links.

See also:
www.steveredgrave.com – Sir Steve's official site offers biographical information, training instruction and tips, links and background on the sport.
www.total.rowing.org.uk – a good rowing portal site.

Rugby

www.scrum.com　　　　　　　　　　　　　　　　　　　UK

RUGBY UNION
An excellent site about rugby union with impressively up-to-the-minute coverage. For a similar but lighter and more fun site go to **www.planet-rugby.com** which has a comprehensive round-up of world rugby with instant reports, lots of detail and information on both union and league. **www.rugbyheaven.com** is also worth checking out. For the history of rugby union go to the **www.rugbyfootballhistory.com** which is also good for links.

www.rfu.com　　　　　　　　　　　　　　　　　　　　UK

RUGBY FOOTBALL UNION
Masses of features, articles and news from the official RFU site, it's got team news and information, links and a shop where you can buy gear – delivery starts at £3.

www.rleague.com　　　　　　　　　　　　　　　　　　UK

WORLD OF RUGBY LEAGUE
Another very comprehensive site, featuring sections on Australia, New Zealand and the UK, with plenty of chat, articles, player profiles and enough statistics to keep the most ardent fan happy. See also the magazine site **www.totalrugbyleague.com** and also **www.ozleague.com**

www.rugbyrelics.com　　　　　　　　　　　　　　　　UK

RUGBY MEMORABILIA
A good memorabilia store covering most countries and aspects of the game, everything from autographs to ties and programmes.

Sailing

www.madforsailing.com   UK

> THE DAILY SAIL
> An informative and well-laid-out site covering all aspects of
> sailing both as a sport and as a hobby. There are some really
> good and well-written articles, video clips and features such as
> a crew search facility and weather information.

www.yachtmonster.com   US

> FOR ALL THINGS YACHTING
> A combination of search engine and site directory all devoted to
> one subject – yachting.

www.ukdinghyracing.com   UK

> UK DINGHY RACING
> Devoted mainly to this one aspect of sailing, it covers the sport
> comprehensively and gives advice on buying, and hosts links to
> auctions and specialist shops.

www.ellenmacarthur.com   UK

> ELLEN MACARTHUR
> An interesting and well-put-together site where you can find out
> what Ellen is up to as well as biographical details. When she is
> sailing, you can follow her progress, access the charts and
> weather forecasts while listening to her latest transmission. Best
> viewed with broadband.

> *See also:*
> **www.rya.org.uk** – a good advice-laden site from the Royal
> Yachting Association, very informative at all levels.
> **www.sailing-411.com** – excellent American sailing portal.
> **www.uksail.com** – a sailing portal site offering some 1,000 links.

> *Skiing and Snowboarding – see page 410.*

Snooker

www.embassysnooker.com   UK

> WORLD CHAMPIONSHIPS
> As a tobacco sponsored site, you have to declare that you are
> over 18 to enter. If eligible, you'll find an overview of the world

championships from their sponsor. The site is comprehensive and there are good features such as a hall of fame, rankings and a look behind the scenes.

See also:
www.snooker.net – great for the latest news and gossip.
www.snookersports.co.uk – a snooker equipment shop.
www.worldsnooker.com – an informative site, which is run by the games governing body.

Tennis and Racket Sports

Tennis

www.lta.org.uk   UK

LAWN TENNIS ASSOCIATION
An excellent and attractively designed all-year tennis information site run by the Lawn Tennis Association, it has information on the players, rankings and tournament news, as well as details on clubs and coaching courses. There's also an online tennis shop where you can buy merchandise and equipment. Check out their portal **www.totaltennis.net** for chat, news and resources to download. See also **www.atptour.com** which gives a less UK-biased view of the game, with excellent sections on the players, tournaments and rankings.

www.wimbledon.org   UK

THE OFFICIAL WIMBLEDON SITE
Very impressive, there's a great deal here and not just in June, but you need to be patient. Apart from the information you'd expect, you can download screensavers, visit the online museum and eventually see videos of past matches. The shop is expensive.

Other tennis sites worth a look:
www.cliffrichardtennis.org – excellent site aimed at encouraging children to take up the game.
www.pwp.com – a comprehensive tennis- and racket-sport-related store, free delivery on orders over £59.
www.racquet-zone.co.uk – a good racket shop also with free delivery on orders over £59.
www.tennis.com – good magazine, with gear guides, tips and hot news.
www.tennisnews.com – the latest news updated daily and e-mailed to you.

Badminton

www.badders.com   UK

BADMINTON COMMUNITY NETWORK
A very good example of a site that pulls together an interest
group. It's excellent for news and chat as well as links and
information on the sport.

See also:
www.badzone.co.uk – a pretty comprehensive offering,
interesting design!
www.baofe.co.uk – the site of the Badminton Association
of England with all the latest news.
www.intbadfed.org – home of the International
Badminton Federation.

Squash

www.squashplayer.co.uk   UK

WORLD OF SQUASH AT YOUR FINGERTIPS
A really comprehensive round up of the game, with links galore
and a great news section, there's also a section for the UK,
which has club details and the latest news. See also
www.worldsquash.org for a good site on what's going on
world-wide.

Table Tennis

www.ittf.com   UK

INTERNATIONAL TABLE TENNIS FEDERATION
A messy site but one that covers most aspects of the sport around
the world. See also **www.ettu.org** for the European view.

Tenpin Bowling

www.btba.org.uk   UK

BRITISH TENPIN BOWLING ASSOCIATION
The home of the game in the UK with rules, information on
clubs and background on what the governing body does.

See also:
www.bowluk.co.uk – a useful directory of bowling centres, shops, links and events.
www.probowluk.co.uk – a serious site with useful tips and links.

Water Sports and Swimming

Swimming

www.swimnews.com   US
SWIMMING NEWS
It's up to date and offers a wide coverage of news, with other features such as rankings, events calendar, shopping and competition analysis.

www.pullbuoy.co.uk   UK
UK SWIMMING
A good site that covers the UK scene. You can find unusual features such as a job finder and time converter. It's great for links too.

Other good swimming sites:
www.learn-to-swim.co.uk – learn-to-swim holidays.
www.swiminfo.com – US magazine site with articles, information and results.
www.swimmersworld.com – pretty average site with news and links.
www.webswim.com – forums, articles and help.

Surfing

www.coldswell.co.uk   UK

SURFING THE UK COAST
Includes forecasts for weather and surf, satellite images, live surf web cams from around the world and a complete directory of surfing web sites.

S

See also:
www.britsurf.co.uk – home of the British Surfing Association.
www.coastalwatch.com – great, if you're in Australia.
www.surfline.com – check out weather, sea conditions, the latest gear – all you need before you go, essentially.
www.surflink.com – good coverage of surfing world-wide.

www.surfstation.co.uk – for links, shopping and surf speak.
www.thesurfingmuseum.co.uk – the museum itself opens in
Brighton in 2006 but here you can get a bit of a preview.
www.troggs.com – good for surfing gear.

www.2xs.co.uk   UK

WINDSURFING IN THE UK
Where to go windsurfing, plus tips and the latest sports news,
shopping, weather information and advice.

Water-skiing

www.waterski.com   US

WORLD OF WATER SKIING
An American site which features information about the sport,
how to compete, news, tips, equipment and where to ski. See
also **www.bwsf.co.uk** although not an attractive site, it does
have UK-based information on places to ski, clubs,
competitions and a message board. Another good site is
www.planetwaterski.com – an American site with a global
guide to places to ski.

Diving

www.ukdiving.co.uk   UK

DIVING RESOURCE
A very good resource site with the latest news. It seems to
cover all aspects of the sport with some good articles, useful
advice and is good for links too. The wreck of the week is
particularly intriguing.

See also:
www.bsac.com – the British Sub Aqua Club, a basic site with
info on what they do.
www.cmas2000.org – the World Underwater Federation with
an odd but informative site.
www.divegirl.com – a magazine site about women and scuba.
www.padi.com – the place to start when you want to learn
to dive.
www.saa.org.uk – home of the Sub Aqua Association with links
and information.

S

Wrestling

www.wwe.com   US
WORLD WRESTLING ENTERTAINMENT
Whether you think it's sport or soap opera, here you can keep
up with the twists and turns plus all the action at this exciting
site, which has news, clips and of course a merchandise shop.

See also:
www.amateurwrestlingnews.com – amateur wrestling scene
with US bias.
www.prowrestling.com – all the latest news and controversy.
www.wrestlingusa.com – a more serious and credible
magazine site.

Sports Clothes and Merchandise

www.sweatband.com   UK
SHOP BY SPORT
A wide-ranging shop that supplies equipment for many sports,
but it's especially good for tennis, rugby and cricket. Delivery
costs depend on the weight of your parcel. See also
www.newitts.com which is comprehensive.

www.kitbag.com   UK
SPORTS FASHION
Football kits and gear galore from new to retro; it covers cricket
and rugby too. Costs on delivery vary according to order. Also
offers shopping by brand and a news service.

www.sportsbooksdirect.co.uk   UK

TAKING SPORT SERIOUSLY
Sportspages and Sports Books Direct have joined forces to
create an online book store that also stocks video and DVD.
Concentrating on sport, they offer a wide range at OK prices,
even signed copies. Great for that one thing you've been unable
to find. Free delivery to the UK. Formerly **www.sportspages.co.uk**

www.sportsworld.co.uk   UK
SPORT TRAVEL
Specialists in making travel arrangements to sporting events; at
this site you can book tickets and find out about future events.

It's particularly good for corporate hospitality; they seem to feel the need to talk to you on the phone though!

www.sportingheritage.co.uk UK
SPORTING GIFTS
A selection of prints, gifts and collectibles available to buy from this well-laid-out site and they cover all the major sports.

Stationery

www.stationerystore.co.uk UK
STATIONERY STORE
A well-designed and easy-to-use stationery store supplying everything from paperclips to office machinery. There are also sections on green stationery, electronics and lots of offers. Delivery is free for orders over £40.

www.staples.co.uk UK
NOT JUST STAPLES
A good all-rounder with a wide range and some good offers; next day delivery is available and free if you spend more than £30 ex VAT. However, this service is still only intended for business purposes.

For other stationery stores try:
www.cardcorp.co.uk – good place to go for your business cards and other printing needs.
www.office-world.co.uk – Office World have at last introduced an online shopping service. Delivery is next day and free if you spend over £35.
www.paperchase.co.uk – you can't buy online but it looks great.
www.viking-direct.co.uk – excellent range, now serving everyone, not just business customers.
www.whsmith.co.uk/stationery – another good WHSmith site with some offers and multi-buys but a limited range, which does include some of their fashion stationery.

S

www.katespaperie.com US
POSH PAPER
To many people it's just 'paper with bits in' but for those who pay regular homage to the New York stores, Kate's Paperie

represents the best in hand-made stationery and wrapping paper. Here you can buy online, but shipping can be expensive.

http://rps.gn.apc.org   UK

TOTALLY RECYCLED
For all your stationery needs from computer paper to art supplies, all recycled and several ranges to choose from. They will also print your letterheads and customise promotional goods. There's lots of information on paper making and recycling too. Free delivery on orders over £50. See also **www.greenstat.co.uk**

See also:
www.paper-caper.co.uk – nice range of notebooks and gift stationery – all fair trade.
www.remarkable.co.uk – for pencils made from recycled plastic cups.

Student Sites

There's masses of information for students on the Internet. Here are some sites worth checking out. The links are generally very good, so if the topic isn't covered here, it should be easy to track down.

Universities and Colleges

www.ucas.co.uk   UK

THE UNIVERSITY STARTING BLOCK
A comprehensive site listing all the courses at British universities with entry profiles. You can view the directory online and order your UCAS handbook and application form. If you've already applied, you can view your application online. There are links to all the universities plus really good links to related sites. There is good advice too. If you want to study abroad you can try finding a course through **www.edunet.com**

www.nusonline.co.uk   UK

STUDENTS UNITE
Lots of relevant news and views for students on this really
good-looking site. You need to register to get assess to their
discounts directory and special offers. Once in, you can send e-
cards and use their mail and storage facilities too.

See also these other useful sites:
www.braintrack.com – a comprehensive directory of links to
universities world-wide.
www.britishcouncil.org/education – the student section is full
of options for further education and training.
www.careers-portal.co.uk – an excellent portal site that is part
of the National Grid for Learning.
www.findaphd.com – find a PhD, Masters or Post Doc course.
www.hotcourses.com – a very good database of courses for
students at all levels, with careers and money advice thrown in.
www.slc.co.uk – home of the Student Loan Company.
www.unn.ac.uk/~iniw2/bestsite.htm – a useful directory of
sites for students.

PC Essentials

The Good Web Site Guide's Top 10s of the Internet

1. **www.download.com** – all your software needs.
2. **www.itreviews.co.uk** – read the reviews before you buy.
3. **www.kelkoo.co.uk** – for the best prices.
4. **www.isr.net** – all you need to know about internet security.
5. **www.pcmech.com** – how it all works, how to repair it.
6. **www.tucows.com** – software reviews and downloads.
7. **www.compman.co.uk** – good offers on computer manuals.
8. **www.cooltool.com** – for the coolest software.
9. **www.handango.com** – the best for PDA software.
10. **http://grc.com** – get your PC checked for security.

S

Working Abroad and Job Finding

www.gapyear.com   UK

> COMPLETE GUIDE TO TAKING A YEAR OUT
> Whether you fancy helping out in the forests of Brazil or
> teaching in Europe you'll find information and opportunities
> here. There's loads of advice, past experiences to get you
> tempted, chat, a message board, competitions and you can
> subscribe to their magazine (an old-fashioned paper one).

www.payaway.co.uk   UK

> FIND A JOB ABROAD OR A WORKING HOLIDAY
> A great starting place for anyone who wants to work abroad.
> There is an e-zine with reports from travellers, and you can
> register with their online jobs service. They've missed nothing
> out in their links section from embassies to travel health.

www.anyworkanywhere.com   UK

> JOBS IN THE UK AND WORLD-WIDE
> A bright and breezy site with jobs and all the right advice,
> plus links.

> *See also:*
> **www.bunac.co.uk** – combine work and travel with these
> programmes from an experienced specialist.
> **www.yearoutgroup.org** – a mass of information and help for
> both those taking a gap year and their parents too.

Careers

www.prospects.ac.uk   UK

> CAREER OPTIONS
> Home of the official graduates' careers guide offering a huge amount
> of information, which is all packed into a pretty dense site.

Discount Cards

www.prospects.ac.uk   UK

> INTERNATIONAL STUDENT TRAVEL CONFEDERATION
> Get your student and youth discount card as well as info on working
> and studying abroad. Also help with such things as railpasses,

phonecards, ISTC registered travel agents world-wide, plus e-mail,
voice mail and fax messaging. For a European youth card for
discounts within the EU go to the cool **www.euro26.org**

Student Life

www.studentuk.com   UK

STUDENT LIFE
A good-looking, useful and generally well-written student's
e-zine featuring news, music and film reviews, going out, chat,
even articles on science and politics. There's also some
excellent advice on subjects such as gap years, accommodation
and finance.

www.good2bsecure.gov.uk   UK

FIGHT CRIME AGAINST STUDENTS
Students are more likely to be victims of crime than any part of
society, here you can get advice on security and keeping safe.

www.studenthealth.co.uk   UK

CLICK IT BETTER
Written by doctors for students, this site offers printable advice
leaflets on 277 topics along with some funny jokes and good
competitions. They estimate that they provided over 2 million
leaflets in 2004 – that's over 6,000 a day, so I guess everyone
already knows about this site.

Links

www.lazystudent.co.uk   UK

SITE LISTING
The perfect site for those who can't be arsed to look things up
properly. It's well categorised and has listed virtually any site
that a student might need.

Teenagers

*Here's a small selection of the best sites aimed at teenagers. Many of the
most hyped sites are just heavily disguised marketing and sales operations,
treat these with scepticism and enjoy the best, which are done for the love*

*of it. We've also indicated the sort of age group that the magazines are aimed at. We should add our thanks to all those who keep writing in to us suggesting sites for this section. Don't forget your personal safety if you chat online, see page 80 for details or go to **www.thinkuknow.co.uk** for a cartoon-based interactive look at the issues.*

Teenage Magazines

www.globalgang.org.uk   UK

WORLD NEWS, GAMES, GOSSIP AND FUN
See what the rest of the world gets up to at Global Gang. You can find out what kids in other countries like to eat, what toys they play with, chat to them or play games. Lastly you get to find out how you can help those kids less fortunate than yourself. *10 plus*

www.girland.com   UK

GIRL AND...
An excellent, really attractive and well-put-together site aimed at teenage girls. It has chat forums, news and lots of features, but you do have to register. It has won loads of awards and the environment is safe. *11 plus*

www.mykindaplace.com   UK

IT'S MY KINDA PLACE
Excellent site for teens, with the latest news, gossip and celebrity features. Aimed squarely at girls it seems to have everything, including lots of adverts! *11 plus*

www.dubit.co.uk   UK

GAMES, ARTICLES – THE LOT
Dubit combines 3-D graphics with chat, games, video, music and animations in a fun and interactive way. It's a completely different approach to the normal teen magazine. It needs a little patience but it's worth it in the end. Registration is required, which is a pity as it is a pain and very slow. *12 plus*

www.teentoday.co.uk   UK

FOR TEENAGERS BY TEENAGERS
Get your free e-zine mailed to you daily or just visit the site: which has much more games, chat, news, entertainment, free downloads, ringtones and message boards. It's well designed and genuinely good with not too much advertising. *13 plus*

http://www.bbc.co.uk/teens   UK

E-ZINES FOR BOTH SEXES
The BBC's teen magazine site addresses the loves and concerns
of the two sexes. Boys get plenty of games, quizzes, cartoons
and useless facts while the girls get a dose of celebs, beauty,
horoscopes plus some fun and games too. There are excellent
advice and information sections for both sexes and both are
treated to some brilliant competitions, prizes and fun articles
too. *13 plus*

www.alloy.com   US

ALLOY MAGAZINE
On the face of it, this is great; it's got loads of sections on
everything from personal advice to shopping albeit a bit
American. But with too many adverts, it all seems to be geared
to getting your name for marketing purposes and selling stuff.
13 plus

Music

The Good Web Site Guide's Top 10s of the Internet

1. **www.apple.com/itunes** – great design, songs from 79p.
2. **www.kazaa.com** – possibly illegal but for free downloads
    none better.
3. **www.cd-wow.com** – for those who still buy CDs, here's the
    best for value.
4. **www.htfr.co.uk** – Hard-To-Find-Records has been a saviour
    to many.
5. **http://ubl.artistdirect.com** – info on virtually anyone who has
    recorded a song.
6. **www.clickmusic.co.uk** – all you need to know on the subject.
7. **www.lyrics.com** – stop the arguments, the lyrics to hundreds
    of songs.
8. **www.ticketmaster.co.uk** – for your concert tickets.
9. **www.sunhawk.com** – the place to download sheet music.
10. **www.mediauk.com/directory** – more radio stations than
    you'll ever need.

www.cheekfreak.com   US

FOR THE FREAK IN ALL OF US
Best for stories, blogging and reviews. It's got chat sections,
forums and a search engine. Some of the forums are devoted to
serious topics such as suicide, sexual hang-ups and family
break-up, as such they may prove helpful in dealing with
teenage angst. *13 plus*

www.cyberteens.com   UK

CONNECT TO CYBERTEENS
One of the most hyped sites aimed at teenagers, it contains a
very good selection of games, news, links and a creativity
section where you can send your art and poems. Don't bother
with the shop, which was still being re-designed at the time of
writing, but on previous visits it was expensive, as is the credit
card they offer. *13 plus*

www.4degreez.com   US

INTERACTIVE COMMUNITY
A friendly and entertaining site with reviews, poetry, jokes, polls
and links to other related sites. You have to become a member
to get the best out of it though. *15 plus*

Directories

www.teensites.org   US

WEB DIRECTORY FOR TEENS
A huge directory of sites covering loads of subjects of interest to
teenagers. It's biased to the US, but if you don't mind that, then
it should have everything you need.

www.ipl.org/div/teen   US

TEEN SPACE
Part of the Internet Public Library, these pages offer a directory
of links for help and information on everything from careers,
homework, issues, fashion and dating.

See also:

http://directory.google.com/Top/Kids_and_Teens – good directory from Google.

www.kidgrid.com – well laid out and easy to use, with a US bias.

www.kidsclick.org – massive database of sites put together by a group of librarians.

www.surfnetkids.com – a comprehensive directory put together by an American journalist.

Advice

www.worriedneed2talk.org.uk   UK

CRUELTY TO CHILDREN MUST STOP!

A site from the NSPCC aimed at helping teenagers and children cope and deal with violence, family problems and drug advice. Also available in Welsh.

www.mindbodysoul.gov.uk   UK

GET THE LOW-DOWN ON HEALTH

A health site for teenagers. It covers all you'd expect, all wrapped up in good-looking graphics; it's also not too densely written or too patronising. See also the US-based **www.teenwire.com** and also **www.thehormonefactory.com**

www.thesite.org.uk   UK

THE SITE

This site offers advice on a range of subjects: careers, relationships, drugs, sex, money, legal issues and so on. Aimed largely at 15- to 24-year olds, it's well laid out and very informative.

Telecommunications

In this ever-changing section there's information on ADSL and computer-related communications, where to go to buy mobiles, get the best out of them and even have a little fun with them. For phone numbers see the section entitled Finding Someone on page 159. For broadband/ADSL see page 58.

www.ofcom.org.uk   UK

THE REGULATOR

Ofcom is the regulator for the UK communications industries, with responsibilities across television, radio, telecommunications and wireless communications services. Theirs is a useful site with the latest news and consumer information surrounding this complex world. If you have a complaint, here's where to seek redress. See also **www.icstis.org.uk** for the Independent Committee for the Supervision of Standards of Telephone Information Services, and the Telecommunications Ombudsman at **www.otelo.org.uk**

www.gbnet.net/net/uk-telecom   UK
UK TELECOM FAQS
One man's work, an encyclopedic list of FAQs relating to the UK's telecommunications system. All you need to know and more...

www.magsys.co.uk/telecom   UK
COMPARE TARIFFS
A potentially useful site if you want to see how your tariff compares with those of other phone companies; it's not exactly user friendly though.

Mobile Phones

www.carphonewarehouse.com   UK
CHOOSING THE RIGHT MOBILE
You need to take your time to find the best tariff, then take advantage of the numerous offers. Excellent pictures, details of the phones and the information is unbiased. There's a shop that also sells handheld PCs and delivery is free too. You can download a wide range of new phone ring tones, from classical to the latest pop tunes.

www.mobileedge.co.uk   UK
MOBILE INFORMATION
A quirkily designed site with help on buying the right mobile, it also offers information on health and mobiles, links and contact numbers, pre-pay deals, global networks, ring tones, shop and much more.

See also:
www.b3k.net – excellent site with a wide range of phones and accessories, good for the hard to get bits too.
www.dialaphone.co.uk – another phone shop. They'll match anyone else's prices though; let's hope they continue to survive.

www.expansys.com – dense site with masses of information and competitive prices.
www.mobilefun.co.uk – a huge range of phones and accessories.
www.mobileshop.com – nice design and lots of offers.
www.onestopphoneshop.com – nicely designed site with a deal finder. Also promise to match competitors' prices.

Here's where to find the major phone operators:
www.motorola.co.uk
www.o2.co.uk
www.orange.co.uk
www.three.co.uk
www.t-mobile.co.uk
www.virginmobile.com
www.vodafone.co.uk

Recycling

www.oxfam.org.uk/what_you_can_do/recycle/phones   UK

SEND YOUR OLD MOBILES HERE
If you have all your old mobiles hanging around the house then go here to find out how you can put them to good use. See also **www.nru.org.uk/mobilephones.htm**

Ring Tones and Text Messaging

www.yourmobile.com   UK

NEW RING TUNES FOR YOUR PHONE
There are several hundred tunes, icons and logos that you can download on to your mobile using text messaging and most are free.

www.treasuremytext.com   UK

SAVING YOUR TEXTS
Here you can store your text messages online, even create a mobile blog and share your text conversations with your friends.

See also:
www.onmymob.com – offering hundreds of free ring tones and logos.
www.ringtones2go.co.uk – massive selection, all the latest tunes.

T

www.chatlist.com/faces.html   UK

TEXT MESSAGING
Confused about your emoticons? %-) Here's a list of several
thousand for you to choose from.

Accessorising Your Phone

www.coverfrenzy.com   UK

DESIGN YOUR OWN PHONE COVER
You can use one of their images or one of your own to create a
unique phone cover; however, it costs £18.50. It's available for
a wide range of Nokia phones but their range of options is
expanding not only to phones but apparently to hairdryers too.

Services

www.buzzme.com   UK

NEVER MISS A CALL
An online answering machine that gives you the option of
accepting, ignoring or sending voice messages, very useful if
you only have the one line.

www.mediaring.com   SINGAPORE

PC TO PHONE COMMUNICATION
Media Ring offer a PC to phone service through their My Voiz
technology. This enables users to communicate at a much
lower cost than phone to phone, it's especially useful if you use
the phone a lot.

www.mapminder.co.uk   UK

MOBILE PHONE TRACKING
Map Minder' phone tracking service is excellent if, for example,
you're big brother or a parent wanting to keep track of your kids or
you're a business wanting to co-ordinate sales teams. It combines
their mapping which is pretty clear with mobile technology. See also
www.mapaphone.co.uk and also **www.verilocation.com**

www.jiwire.com   US

WIFI
A very useful site if you travel with a laptop and need to know
where the nearest WiFi spots are. There is also a great deal of
advice on how to get the best out of it and keep secure too.

Faxing

www.efax.com   UK

FAX USING E-MAIL

A paid-for service that makes it easy for you to send faxes via
your e-mail service. See also **www.j2.com** who offer a similar
service. For more information go to **www.tpc.int**. It's also worth
checking out **www.download.com** for fax programs.

Lowering the Costs

www.skype.com   US

FREE CALLS

Free from the makers of Kazaa, the popular music sharing
program, this one allows you to make free calls using the
Internet. It's pretty straightforward and easy to use.

See also:

www.18866.co.uk – cheaper international calls.
www.gossiptel.com – free and cheap calls using your
broadband connection.

Technology

www.bluetooth.com   US

OFFICIAL BLUETOOTH

A superb official Microsoft site devoted to Bluetooth technology;
it's amazing how fast it's become so widespread.

www.3g.co.uk   UK

3G

Excellent site devoted to bringing you the latest information and
developments in this technology.

See also:

www.gprshelp.co.uk – helpful site covering GPRS.
www.mobiledevelopers.com – the latest information on what's
happening in the world of mobile telecommunications.

T

Television

*TV channels, listings and your favourite soap operas are all here –
some have great sites, others are pretty naff, especially when you
consider they're in the entertainment business. Television now shares
a regulator with telecommunications in general. See Ofcom above.*

www.ofcom.org.uk   UK
> OFCOM
> Ofcom is the regulator for the UK communications industries
> including television, radio, telecommunications and wireless
> communications services. If you've a complaint, here's the
> place to go – they've made it quite easy.

www.tvlicensing.co.uk   UK
> TELEVISION LICENCE
> All you need to know about your TV licence, how to pay and
> how to deal with problems.

Channels and Digital

www.bbc.co.uk   UK

> THE UK'S MOST POPULAR WEB SITE
> The BBC site deserves a special feature, it is huge with more than 2
> million pages and it can be quite daunting. It has sections covering
> everything from business to the weather and there are also regional
> sections, a web guide, as well as tips on how to use the Internet
> and you can subscribe to a newsletter. There are feature sites on all
> their major programme and most of the minor ones too it's a
> fantastic site and more than a useful resource.

www.itv.co.uk   UK
> ITV NETWORK
> ITV has a pretty straightforward site with links to all the major
> programmes, soaps, topics and categories, their related web
> sites and a 'what's on' guide, plus a few extras such as quizzes.

www.citv.co.uk   UK
> CHILDREN'S ITV
> A bright and breezy site that features competitions, safe surfing,
> features on the programmes including all the favourite characters
> and much more. You need to join to get the best out of it though,
> and because there's so much on the site, it can be a little slow.

T

www.channel4.co.uk   UK
>   CHANNEL 4
>   A cool design with details of programmes and links to specific
>   web pages on the best-known ones. There are also links to
>   other initiatives such as Filmfour and the 4learning programme.

www.channel5.co.uk   UK
>   CHANNEL 5
>   The usual programme information, scheduling details, news
>   and competitions. There are also some useful programme-
>   related factsheets and a bright and breezy children's section
>   featuring the *Milkshake* magazine.

www.sky.com   UK
>   SKY TV
>   Links to the main Sky sites – news, sport etc, plus information
>   on their digital packages.

www.nick.com   US
>   NICKELODEON
>   Bright doesn't do this site justice, you need sunglasses! It's got
>   info on all the top programmes plus games and quizzes.

www.freeview.co.uk   UK
>   FREEVIEW
>   Details of the Freeview service and where it's available in the UK.

www.wwitv.com   US
>   WORLD-WIDE INTERNET TV
>   Watch several international channels, the BBC and listen to
>   radio too. Probably best for broadband users. See also the
>   excellent **www.liketelevision.com** which is very much geared
>   to broadband.

TV Fans and Nostalgia

www.sausagenet.co.uk   UK
>   CULT AND CLASSIC TV
>   An outstanding nostalgia site devoted to popular children's TV
>   programmes from the past 40 years. You can download theme
>   tunes or buy related merchandise via the excellent links
>   directory. See also **www.sadgeezr.com** which is Sci Fi-oriented.

www.televisionheaven.co.uk   UK

PRESERVING TV MEMORIES

An excellent site devoted to archiving reviews and memories of as many TV favourites as they can. A visit is very nostalgic and very time consuming. Good for links too.

www.transdiffusion.org/emc/   UK

MEDIA HISTORY

A selection of articles, sites and links which look back at television history. It's pretty diverse and not easy to navigate but there's some excellent stuff here especially in the Halcyon Days section.

www.uktvadverts.com   UK

TV ADVERTS

A collection of TV adverts and background information now you can find out who did that voiceover. See also **www.adwatch.tv**, who offer a similar collection. And about that piece of music… www.commercialbreaksandbeats.co.uk is the place to go.

See also:

http://epguides.com – a massive database of episode guides covering a wide variety of US and some UK TV shows and series.

www.625.uk.com – a personal celebration and overview of the rights and wrongs of British telly,. with downloads of logos and even public information films.

www.advertsongs.co.uk – find music used in adverts, pretty out of date though.

www.beonscreen.com/uk/index.asp – the chance to appear on your favourite show.

www.bigglethwaite.com – great for TV-related links.

www.clappers-tickets.co.uk – be part of the TV show audience, free tickets for selected shows.

www.petford.net/kaleidoscope – the site of a voluntary organisation devoted to the appreciation of classic TV, lots of links and information to be found here.

www.sitcomsonline.com – a huge amount of information on US sitcoms.

www.whirligig-tv.co.uk – a great site for 50s TV nostalgia.

TV Review and Listings Sites

www.digiguide.co.uk   UK

THE DOWNLOADABLE GUIDE
If you have Sky digital, you'll be familiar with this guide. It follows a
similar format, although you can customise it. Simply download the
program and you get 14 days, forward programming for up to 200
channels, masses of links and background information. It costs
£8.99 per annum.

www.radiotimes.com   UK

THE *RADIO TIMES*
Excellent listings e-zine with a good search facility for looking
up programme details, plus competitions, links and a cinema
guide. There are also sections on the best-loved TV genres
– children's, sci-fi, soaps and so on.

See also:
www.onthebox.com – a simple and effective daily TV guide.
Lots of pop-up ads.
www.thecustard.tv – a personal, fun and well-put-together
TV and listings guide, which deserves to succeed.

Theatre

Here's a great selection of sites that will appeal to theatre goers
everywhere. Be aware that some online ticket services charge large
processing fees for the privilege plus postage as well. Check the
invoice carefully before you commit yourself.

www.whatsonstage.com   UK

HOME OF BRITISH THEATRE
A really strong site with masses of news and reviews to browse
through plus a very good search facility and booking service
(through a third party), a real theatre buff's delight.

www.aloud.com   UK

ONLINE TICKET SEARCH
You can search by venue, location or by artist, it's fast and
pretty comprehensive and there's a hot events section –

it mainly covers music and festivals nowadays though it's good for comedy. The review section is good and you can buy tickets.

www.theatrenet.com   UK

THE ENTERTAINMENT CENTRE

Get the latest news, catch the new shows and, if you join the club, there are discounts on tickets for theatre, concerts, sporting events and holidays. You can also search their archives for information on past productions and learn how to become a theatre angel.

www.uktheatre.net   UK

PASSIONATE ABOUT THEATRE

Whether you're a fan or an actor this site has much to offer both as a useful source of information and as a good site directory.

www.uktw.co.uk   UK

UK THEATRE WEB

A cheerful site offering all the usual information on theatre plus amateur dramatics, jobs, chat, competitions and just gossip.

www.rsc.org.uk   UK

THE ROYAL SHAKESPEARE COMPANY

Get all the news as well as information on performances and tours. You can book tickets online although it's via a third party site. There is also loads of information about the life and times of the Bard and synopses of his plays.

www.reallyuseful.com   UK

ANDREW LLOYD WEBBER

At this attractive, hi-tech site you can watch video clips and listen to top audio clips, download screen savers and wallpaper, take part in competitions and chat. There's also a good kids' section plus details on the shows.

www.nt-online.org   UK

THE NATIONAL

Excellent for details of their shows and forthcoming plays with tour information added. You can't buy tickets online, but you can e-mail or fax for them.

www.officiallondontheatre.co.uk   UK

SOCIETY OF LONDON THEATRES

The latest news, a show finder service and hot tickets are just a

few of the services available at this great site. You can also get
a Theatreland map, half price tickets and they'll even fax you
a seating plan. See also **www.thisislondon.co.uk** who have a
good theatre section.

www.dresscircle.co.uk   UK
THEATRE SHOP
A long-established supplier of music, books and products
related to the theatre, with links and the latest news.

www.uktheatrebreak.co.uk   UK
THEATRE BREAKS
A useful site and booking service that allows you to combine
your trip to the theatre with a short holiday or overnight stay.

To book online also try the following sites:
www.lastminute.com
www.londontheatretickets.com
www.ticketmaster.co.uk
www.uktickets.co.uk

Travel and Holidays

*Travel is one of the biggest growth areas on the Internet, from
holidays to insurance to local guides. If you're buying, then it
definitely pays to shop around and try several sites, but be careful,
it's amazing how fast the best deals are being snapped up. You may
find that you still spend time on the phone, but the sites are
constantly improving. The amount of information available is
staggering and it's no wonder this is the biggest section in the book.*

*When checking out travel sites, you should be aware that the same
company may own many sites, for example Lastminute.com has interests
in sites covering everything from skiing holidays to general travel and even
ferry bookings. To complicate matters, they've now been bought by
Expedia. These sites will be listed under their specialist area.*

*If you don't want to deal with a particular company and want to
check, nearly all sites have company information hidden away,
usually at the bottom of the page, or you can quickly check at
Companies House* **www.companies-house.gov.uk**

Information for disabled travellers can be found on page 114.

Starting Out

www.ukpa.gov.uk   UK
UK PASSPORTS
Pre-apply for your passport online and get tips on how to get
the best passport photo amongst other very useful information.

www.visaservice.co.uk   UK
QUICK VISA
This service will get you your visa in double quick time, for a price.

www.hmce.gov.uk   UK
HM CUSTOMS AND EXCISE
All you need to know about visiting the UK, exporting and
importing and the regulations surrounding what you can bring
back with you from your holidays.

www.abtanet.com   UK
ABTA
Make sure that the travel agent you choose is a member of the
Association of British Travel Agents as then you're covered if
they go bust halfway through your holiday. All members are
listed and there's a great search facility with links for you to
start the ball rolling. See also the Air Travellers Licensing home
page **www.atol.org.uk** which is part of the Civil Aviation site.

www.brochurebank.co.uk   UK
BROCHURES DELIVERED TO YOUR HOME
Holiday brochures from the major and specialist travel
companies can be selected then delivered to your home, free of
charge. The selection process is easy and the site is fast.
Delivery is by second class post.

Health, Safety and Tips

www.fco.gov.uk/travel   UK

ADVICE FROM THE FOREIGN OFFICE
Before you go, get general advice or safety or visa information.
Just select a country and you get a run-down of all the issues
that are likely to affect you when you go there, from terrorism
to health.

www.travelhealth.co.uk   UK

STAY HEALTHY

An authoritative site with sections on general health advice and
disease prevention, a shop and links.

For more health and safety travel information and tips...
www.1000traveltips.org – tips from the very well-travelled
Koen De Boeck and friends.
www.bloodcare.org.uk – the Blood Care Foundation offers a
wide range of advice and tips for many illnesses and situations.
www.cdc.gov/travel – official American site giving sensible
health information world-wide.
www.first48.com/guide/features/muslimcode.php – clothing
advice for women travelling to Muslim countries.
www.flyana.com – good advice from an experienced traveller.
www.masta.org – authoritative health advice and an online
shop to get your medicines.
www.medicalert.org.uk – buy a bracelet that contains all your
essential medical details.
www.nealsyardagency.com – healthy holidays.
www.travelhealthresources.com – data on over 250 countries
though US oriented.
www.tripprep.com – country-by-country risk assessment
covering health, safety and politics; it can be a little out of date
so check with the foreign office as well.
www.who.int/en – statistics and health information country by
country.

Family Travel

www.family-travel.co.uk   UK

PRACTICAL INFORMATION

A wide-ranging site covering every aspect of travelling with
children, covering health, hotels, culture, products and just
getting to your destination.

See also:
www.familytravelforum.com – an American site offering lots of
information and advice.
www.flyingwithkids.com – sensible air travel advice for those
travelling with babies and small children.
www.kidstravel.co.uk – bright and breezy design but it could

T

have more content, still some good ideas and travelling tips for
parents though biased to England.
www.opfh.org.uk – good information for single-parent families,
turn the sound off…
www.smallfamilies.co.uk – a wide range of holiday options for
single-parent families.
www.thefamilytravelfiles.com – a US-oriented e-zine with lots
of advice and links.
www.tinytravelers.net – a well-designed and attractive site
offering tips, product reviews and travel advice.
www.travellingwithchildren.co.uk – good for ideas and advice,
if you can put up with the adverts.

Travel Services

www.whatsonwhen.com   UK

WORLD-WIDE EVENTS GUIDE
An easy-to-use site with information on every type of event you
can think of from major festivals to village fêtes.

www.worldtimezone.com   US

TIME ZONE MAP
Useful time zone mapping, although it's heavily advert laden.
See also **www.timeanddate.com**

www.kropla.com   US

PHONE HELP
Here you can find out about where to plug in your modem, if your
mobile will work, international dialling codes, even TV standards.

Also worth checking out for more information:
http://cybercaptive.com – a directory of world cyber cafés.
http://mytravelrights.com – an American site devoted to
travellers rights abroad.
www.cybercafes.com – over 4,000 cyber cafés listed
throughout the world.
www.tipping.org – good advice on how much to tip around
the world.

Luggage and Travel Gear

www.family-travel.co.uk   UK
BUYING LUGGAGE
A wide range and with some good offers, this store is worth
a visit if you have to replace that tatty old case.

www.excessluggage.co.uk   UK
EXCESS LUGGAGE
For problems concerning excess baggage, here's the place to
go. There are lots of options and it's best to discuss your
requirements with them.

www.holidayadditions.co.uk   UK
ESSENTIAL ITEMS
A bright and breezy shop that offers a small range of 'essential'
travel-oriented products from padlocks to mosquito repellents.

Travel Money and Insurance

www.xe.net/ucc   UK

ONLINE CURRENCY CONVERTER
The Universal Currency Converter could not be easier to use,
just select the currency you have, then the one you want to
convert it to, press the button and you have your answer
in seconds. See also **www.oanda.com** and **www.x-
rates.com/calculator.html**

www.taxfree.se   US
GLOBAL REFUND
Find out how to make the most out of tax-free shopping at this
very useful web site.

www.onlinefx.co.uk   UK
FOREIGN CURRENCY DELIVERED
A pretty straightforward and potentially hassle-free way of
getting your currency, just order with you card and it gets
delivered the next working day. There are also other financial
services available such as international transfers.

T

www.travelinsuranceclub.co.uk   UK

> AWARD-WINNING TRAVEL INSURANCE CLUB
> Unfortunately there isn't one site for collating travel insurance
> yet, it's a question of shopping around. These sites make a
> good starting point offering a range of policies for backpackers,
> family and business travel.
>
> *All these companies offer flexibility and good value:*
> **www.costout.co.uk** – well-rated insurance and good value.
> **www.direct-travel.co.uk** – nice design and some good offers
> too, online quotes.
> **www.underthesun.co.uk** – good for annual and six-monthly
> policies.
> **www.worldwideinsure.com** – good selection of policies, instant
> online cover.

Travel Shops and Agents

www.travel-lists.co.uk   UK

> TRAVEL OPERATORS DIRECTORY
> A largely subscription-based service but with free access to their
> database of travel specialists and agents. Each entry has a link,
> contact number and a short overview of what they do.

www.expedia.co.uk   US/UK

> THE COMPLETE SERVICE
> This is the UK arm of Microsoft's very successful online travel
> agency. It offers a huge array of holidays, flights and associated
> services, for personal or business use, nearly all bookable online. Its
> easy and quicker than most, and there are some excellent offers too.
> Not the trendiest, but it's a good first stop. As with all the big
> operators, you have to register. They've also got sections on travel
> insurance, mapping, guides, ferries and hotels.

www.lastminute.com   UK

> DO SOMETHING LAST MINUTE
> Last Minute has an excellent reputation not just as a travel
> agent, but as a good shopping site too. For travellers there are
> comprehensive sections on hotels, holidays and flights, all with
> really good prices. There is also a superb London restaurant
> guide and a general entertainment section. Mostly, you can
> book online, but a hotline is available.

www.thomascook.com   UK
THE WIDEST RANGE OF PACKAGE HOLIDAYS
This site is easy to use and well laid out and, with over 2 million package holidays to chose from, you should be able to find something to your liking. You can also browse the online guide for ideas or search for cheap flights or holiday deals. Again you have to call the hotline to book.

www.e-bookers.com   UK
FLIGHT BOOKERS
Acclaimed travel agents specialising in getting good flight deals, but also good for holidays, special offers and insurance.

www.travel.world.co.uk   UK
FOR ALL YOUR TRAVEL REQUIREMENTS
A massive, comprehensive site, it basically includes most available travel brochures with links to the relevant travel agent. It concentrates on Europe, so there are very few American sites, but provides links to hotels, specialist holidays, cruises, self-catering and airlines.

www.uk.mytravel.com   UK
SEARCH FOR THE RIGHT DEAL
This site has got an excellent search engine that enables you to find a bargain or just the right holiday. There are also good offers and the late escapes holiday auction site.

www.priceline.co.uk   UK
LET SOMEONE ELSE DO THE WORK
You could leave it to someone else to do the travel searching for you, here you provide details of the trip you want and how much you're willing to pay, then they try to find a deal that will match your requirements. If you're flexible about timing then there are some great offers. They cover flights, hotels and car hire. Another site to try is **www.myownprice.com** but both this site and Priceline want your credit card details before you agree to any transaction so you may feel more comfortable using a more traditional route.

www.budgettravel.com   UK
BUDGET TRAVEL
Rubbish design but masses of links and information for the budget traveller plus advice on how to travel on the cheap. It can be difficult to navigate but the information is very good.

See also:

www.aito.co.uk – offers and information from the Association of Independent Tour Operators, excellent for the unusual.

www.bargainholidays.com – probably the best for quick breaks, excellent for late availability offers.

www.dreamticket.com – the usual holiday offers, but the site also offers much in the way of information too.

www.firstchoice.co.uk – bargains from First Choice holidays.

www.firstresort.com – a good general site with some good deals and a price promise, owned by Thomsons.

www.holiday.co.uk – good deals on package holidays from a very well-designed site.

www.opodo.co.uk – slick newcomer from some of the major airlines, worth checking out for flight offers and discounts on hotels.

www.packageholidays.co.uk – late bargain holidays and flights from a wide range of tour operators including Airtours, Cosmos, and Thomson.

www.teletext.co.uk/holidays – much better than browsing the TV, you can now get all those offers on one easy-to-use site. There is also lots of useful travel information to help you on your way.

www.thisistravel.co.uk – in association with the newspaper group that publishes the *Daily Mail*, this is a comprehensive offering with some good offers. Lots of pop-up ads too.

www.thomson.co.uk – for a wide range of package holidays as well as low-cost flights on their airline.

www.travelagents.co.uk – another all-rounder, nothing special but competent.

www.travelbag.co.uk – straightforward and easy-to-use flight and holiday finder. Now part of ebookers.

www.travelcareonline.com – loads of deals and honest information from the UK's largest independent. Winner of the British Travel Awards 2004 'Best Online Travel Agent'.

www.travelfinder.co.uk – lots of options and great bargains at this simple-to-use site.

www.travelmood.com – follows the standard site design for an all-rounder, has some good offers though.

www.travelocity.com – one of the oldest online travel agents; it's similar to Expedia, comprehensive with plenty of advice and background information.

www.tripsworld-wide.co.uk – despite the name it specialises in Latin America and the Caribbean. Some beautiful photography enhances the site.

T

Short and City Breaks

www.eurobreak.com – click on the map for your destination and you get presented with lots of options including hotel details and online booking.

www.shortbreaks.com – hotel breaks in the UK, Europe and US; arranges theatre breaks too.

www.shortbreaksbyair.com – a good selection of city breaks from this specialist operator.

www.webweekends.co.uk – specialists in weekend breaks both in the UK and abroad.

Luxury and Tailor-made Holidays

Here's a list of the best known luxury holiday specialists and a few we've had recommended to us:

www.abercrombiekent.com – one of the most experienced luxury travel operators with a very competent site.

www.amanresorts.com – exclusive hotels and villas in gorgeous locations.

www.audleytravel.com – tailor-made itineraries for escorted groups.

www.balesworldwide.com – for something special, tailor-made holidays to the exotic parts of the world. This hi-tech site is excellent especially now you can book online.

www.bridgetheworld.com – a good site from this multi-award winning company.

www.carrier.co.uk – luxury holiday specialists, nice looking site too.

www.caz-loyd.com – specialists in the more exotic destinations.

www.coxandkings.co.uk – a slightly disappointing site from one of the oldest travel companies.

www.essentialescapes.com – exclusive luxury spa holidays.

www.exsus.com – tailor-made luxury adventures.

www.hayesandjarvis.co.uk – long-haul holiday specialists, lots to choose from.

www.itcclassics.co.uk – luxury everything basically.

www.jeffersons.com – taking a holiday with your own private jet…

www.jewelholidays.com – India, Turkey, Red Sea and Asia.

www.journeysbydesign.co.uk – tailor made, African specialists:

www.luxurylink.com – luxury holiday auctions.

www.originaltravel.co.uk – holidays for activity and well-being, outstanding site design too.

www.pura-aventura.com – active holidays in comfort, mainly Latin America and Spain.

T

www.rbrww.com – opulence and fishing.
www.seasonsinstyle.co.uk – world-wide luxury in the world's finest hotels.
www.tailor-made.co.uk – basic site but the holiday options look good.
www.vjv.co.uk – Voyages Jules Verne with an excellent selection of luxury activity holidays.
www.world-widejourneys.co.uk – tailor-made packages, especially experienced in wildlife holidays.

Cruises

www.cruiseinformationservice.co.uk   UK
CRUISE INFO
A trade site put together to encourage people to take cruise holidays. There's an introduction to cruising, information on the cruise lines, a magazine and links to useful sites. There's also information on how to book and what sort of cruise is right for you.

See also:
www.cruisedeals.co.uk – easy to use, a little sparse on info but some good offers.
www.cruise-direct.com – information, advice and good prices.
www.cruiseline.co.uk – a great site from one of the UK's leading specialist cruise companies.
www.cruisesandvoyages.com – a cruise specialist with a basic site and some good deals.
www.psa-psara.org – useful information from the Passenger Shipping Association.

Activity and Sporting Holidays

Cycling Holidays

The following are mostly UK specialists, but some cover further afield too.

www.ctc.org.uk   UK
WORKING FOR CYCLING
The CTC have a great travel section with routes, tours, offers, links and directories. It's a great place to start your search for the perfect cycling holiday.

Also check out:

www.backroads.com – a US-based specialist with a wide range of options.

www.bicycle-beano.co.uk – Bicycle Beano have a good site covering cycling holidays in Wales and the borders.

www.bikemagic.com – go to the travel pages for an excellent section on where Bike Magic have got partners who'll supply flight deals for cyclists or rail travel and holidays.

www.byways-breaks.co.uk – a nice-looking site, Byways Breaks arrange cycling and walking holidays in the Peaks, Shropshire and Cheshire countryside.

www.cycleactive.co.uk – excellent for action-packed cycle holidays.

www.cyclebreaks.co.uk – cycling holidays in Suffolk.

www.cycle-rides.co.uk – a very good selection of biking tours through Europe and further afield.

www.discoveradventure.com – a great selection of biking holidays for the more adventurous.

www.rough-tracks.co.uk – a wide range of active adventure holidays for beginners and experts.

www.scotcycle.co.uk – Scottish Cycling Holidays are specialists in cycling holidays in Scotland obviously. Nice site too.

www.skedaddle.co.uk – one of the best for variety, everything for the beginner or expert. It covers most of the world too.

www.sustrans.co.uk – the National Cycle Network is featured as part of this campaigning charity site.

Diving Holidays

www.aquatours.com – the site isn't up to much but they offer a world-wide service.

www.divechannel.co.uk – excellent site specialising in diving holidays and travel.

www.divequest.co.uk – lots of detail, prices and choice make this a good site to visit.

www.ifyoudive.com – this portal is a good place to start.

www.regaldive.co.uk – learn to dive in the best diving locations.

Golfing Holidays

T

www.golfbreaks.com – a travel agent specialising in holidays for golfing nuts.

www.grassrootsgolf.co.uk – a naff site but the holidays look great, includes Africa too.

www.prosolgolf.com – holidays on the Costa del Sol, poor spelling lets the site down.

Hobby and Cultural Holidays

www.shawguides.com   UK
LOOKING FOR SOMETHING TO DO?
A massive database of cultural, hobby and learning holidays, mostly American but you can find UK-based ones if you search hard enough.

www.arblasterandclarke.com – wine tours world-wide.
www.epiculinary.com – culinary holidays, online booking.
www.flavours-foodiehols.co.uk – Italian cookery holidays.
www.martinrandall.com – cultural travel with expert lecturers.

Language Learning

See the languages section on page 282.

Riding Holidays

www.equineadventures.co.uk – a good agent for riding holidays.
www.equitour.co.uk – a wide range of riding holidays available for all levels of rider.
www.inthesaddle.com – a good-looking site covering a variety of holiday options.
www.ranchweb.com – excellent site on all forms of ranch holidays mainly in the US.

Sailing

www.sunsail.com   US
SAILING AND WATERSPORT HOLIDAYS
A wide-ranging and informative site with lots to offer whether you're an enthusiast or a beginner, plenty of special offers too.

See also:
www.allafloat.com – lots of choice and online booking.
www.bootoo.co.uk – the luxury yacht Bootoo takes you around the Caribbean.
www.compass24.com – a good shop for sailing enthusiasts, over 8,000 products.

www.elitesailing.co.uk – learn to sail.

www.neilson.com – an odd site, but they run a sailing training school and also do yachting holidays too.

www.sailingholidays.com – specialists in Greece and Croatia.

www.sea-trek.co.uk – specialist in Greece, learn-to-sail holidays too.

www.tenrag.com – charter your own yacht.

Backpacking and Adventure

www.adventuredirectory.com   UK

THE ADVENTURE DIRECTORY
A huge directory of sites devoted to adventure, just click on the world map or search and away you go…

See also:
http://expeditionquest.com – a portal and information site about expeditions.

www.backpackeurope.com – aimed at Americans but useful for Europeans too.

www.changingworlds.co.uk – outstanding site design and presentation from a company that helps people find worthwhile working holidays.

www.footprint-adventures.co.uk – birding, trekking and wildlife all over the world.

www.gvillage.co.uk – specialising in independent travellers and students with some great deals and adventure holidays to the world's most interesting places, excellent round-the-world trip planner.

www.highplaces.co.uk – treks in high places in some 20 countries.

www.iexplore.com – a high-quality offering with a huge amount of information for the adventure traveller.

www.igougo.com – more of an information exchange for global travellers, but you can book trips through them. There are plenty of features and the IgoUgo awards too.

www.madadventurer.com – excellent site design with loads of mad adventures to choose from while helping community development in 23 countries.

www.spicemcr.com – vibrant activity and social club with holidays to match.

www.theleap.co.uk – similar approach to Mad Adventurer but based in Africa.

T

www.trailsource.com – excellent resource covering the world's great trails, categorised by mode of transport.
www.transitionsabroad.com – excellent for long-term travelling and working holidays.

www.bananabuzz.com   UK

GET BACK IN TOUCH
OK so you've had your holiday and lost touch with all those friends you've made, here's where to go. It's a sort of Friends Reunited for backpackers basically. There are also chat and messaging services.

Eco-tourism and Nature

We've introduced this new section to reflect the growing interest in the wider issues surrounding the tourist industry.

www.responsibletravel.com   UK

GIVE THE WORLD A BREAK
Endorsed by Anita Roddick, this site provides a huge range of travel experiences all selected for their sensitivity to the local environment and its people. You can search by destination, activity or accommodation type. If you become a member, you can receive their monthly magazine. There are a several campaigns to join too ranging from protecting wildlife to outlawing child sex tourism.

www.tourismconcern.org.uk   UK

ETHICAL TOURISM
If you're concerned about the impact of your trip, then come here for advice or help with one of their campaigns. It all goes to ensuring that the poorest holiday workers are not exploited.

See also:
www.btcv.org – conservation holidays.
www.changingworlds.co.uk – worthwhile working holidays.
www.checkmytravel.info – check your travel behaviour.
www.coralcay.org – 'providing resources to help sustain livelihoods and alleviate poverty through the protection, restoration and management of coral reefs and tropical forests'.
www.csv.org.uk – information for volunteers.
www.discoveryinitiatives.co.uk – responsible wildlife holidays.
www.ecoclub.com – a network providing a wealth of

information about all aspects of ecotourism.

www.eco-res.com – make a reservation at an eco-friendly lodge, camp or reserve.

www.eco-tour.org – Eco Tourism directory.

www.ecotourism.org – the International Ecotourism Society.

www.ecotravel.com – a US-based site with a magazine and an excellent search facility

www.ecovolunteer.com – if you want to give your services to a specific animal benefit project.

www.exodus.co.uk – specialist agents and winners of the 'Best Tour Operator' in the Responsible Travel Awards 2004.

www.inntravel.co.uk – specialists in walking and cycling holidays, excellent, informative site.

www.naturetrek.co.uk – excellent nature holiday specialists.

www.northsouthtravel.co.uk – a small travel agent which channels much of the profit into aid projects in Africa.

www.sacredearth.com – ethnobiology and eco-travel to South America, for those seriously interested in nature.

www.thetravelfoundation.org.uk – information on the effect of tourism and how you can help.

www.traveltree.co.uk – for eco-sensitive volunteer work overseas.

www.wildshots.co.uk – wildlife photography holidays.

Healthy Holidays

If you want to lie back and relax then try one of these...

www.bodyandsoulholidays.com   UK

SPA BREAKS AND HOTELS

A cool site where you can pick out your treatments or activities and they will select the resort or holiday to suit your needs. There's quite a bit of choice and some of the locations are stunning.

See also:

http://spas.about.com – a useful directory with tips and information on taking a spa holiday.

www.inspa-retreats.com – a combination of luxury and health.

www.thermalia.co.uk – one of the leading specialists in spa holidays.

T

Airline and Flight Sites

www.cheapflights.co.uk   UK
NOTHING BUT CHEAP FLIGHTS
You don't need to register here to explore the great offers
available from this site; you still need to phone some of the
travel agents or airlines listed to get your deal although an
increasing number have web links. If you're after a last-minute
deal, they have a handy calendar that will search for deals from
your local airport.

www.netflights.com   UK
THE AIRLINE NETWORK
Discount deals on over 100 airlines world-wide make The
Airline Network worth checking out for their flight offers page
alone. It's good for flights from regional airports. They also do
all the traditional travel agent things and there are some good
holiday bargains too.

www.openjet.com   UK

NO FRILLS MADE EASY
This site searches the low-cost carriers to find you the best
prices to European destinations and gives you the results for
adjacent days to enable you to fly at the lowest possible price.
See also **www.whichbudget.com**

www.traveljungle.co.uk   UK
FARE COMPARISONS
Travel Jungle have become very popular and it's easy to see
why: here you can compare offers from 24 airlines and 7 travel
agents so you should be able to get a great deal.

For more cheap flight deals try these sites:
www.attitudetravel.com/lowcostairlines – now covering the
world's low cost airlines and where they fly to.
www.bargainflights.com – good search facility and plenty of
offers, but you need to be patient.
www.bmibaby.com – the low-cost arm of British Midland.
www.deckchair.com – a strong site where you can get some
good flight bargains as well as plan the rest of your holiday.
Now part of the Lastminute.com empire.
www.easyjet.co.uk – great for an ever increasing number of
destinations, particularly good for UK flights.

www.flightcentre.com – they guarantee to beat any genuine current quoted airfare!

www.ryanair.com – very good for Ireland, northern Europe, Italy and France. Clear and easy-to-use web site, massive discounts.

www.skyscanner.net – excellent for Europe and comparing the budget airline offers.

www.travelselect.com – good flight selection and lots of different options available at this very flexible site.

www.whichbudget.com – click on the place where you want to go from or to and it lists all the airlines with links that serve that airport. Useful if you want to know what's available from your local airport.

Airport and Airline Information

www.worldairportguide.com   GERMANY

WHAT ARE THE WORLD'S AIRPORTS REALLY LIKE?
It seems that no matter how out of the way, this guide has details on every airport – how to get there, where to park, facilities, key phone numbers and a map. There are also guides on cities, resorts and even world weather. See also **www.airportcitycodes.com**

www.baa.co.uk   UK

BRITISH AIRPORT AUTHORITY
Details on all the major UK airports that are run by the BAA, you get all the essential information plus flight data, weather and shopping information.

www.a2bairports.com   UK

UK AND IRISH AIRPORTS
These pages from A2B Travel offer all the relevant information on all the major airports and lots of the smaller ones too. Another site with information on UK airports is **www.airport-maps.co.uk** which also has flight route information along with maps, facility details and related links.

www.airlinequality.com   UK

RANKING THE AIRLINES
An independent ranking of all the world's airlines and their services, see who's the best and the worst and why. Each airline is rated using a number of stars (up to five) on criteria such as seat quality, catering and staff.

www.sleepinginairports.net
UK

GUIDE TO SLEEPING IN AIRPORTS
Rated 'Good' 'Tolerable' or just 'Hell' here is a sleeper's guide for budget travellers on many of the world's airports. It's actually pretty funny too.

www.airfraid.com
US

CONQUER YOUR FEAR OF FLYING
A good place to go if you're of the opinion that getting on a plane is the last thing you'll ever do. There's advice gleaned from various reputable sources and details on how you can go on courses to help you overcome your fears.

THE KEY AIRLINES
www.aa.com – American Airlines, standard airline site.
www.aerlingus.ie – good, easy-to-use site.
www.airfrance.co.uk – plenty of offers.
www.airindia.com – good offers and travel information and destination guide.
www.alitalia.it – a no-nonsense site.
www.ba.com or **www.britishairways.co.uk**– easy-to-use, efficient site.
www.cathaypacific.com – comprehensive flight service and guide.
www.emirates.com – no-frills design and flight booking facilities.
www.flybmi.com – British Midland, good offers for European destinations.
www.klm.com – good design with lots of offers.
www.lufthansa.co.uk – masses of information and express booking.
www.quantas.com – straightforward booking facility.
www.singaporeair.com – follows the formula but with the added extra of a multi-city flight planner.
www.united.com – United Airlines offers a good all-round service at this site.
www.virgin-atlantic.com – good online booking facility with some offers.

UK Regional Airlines

It's worth trying out regional airlines, not only because they may be cheaper, but also they might fly to your destination from a more convenient local airport. Here are the best of them.

www.air-scotland.com – billed as Scotland's low-cost airline, this lot fly out of Glasgow and Edinburgh to Spanish and Greek resorts. The site follows the usual design and at the time of writing, there were lots of offers.

www.airsouthwest.com – small airline offering great-value flights from the South West of England to London.

www.airwales.co.uk – Awyr Cymru offer a wide variety of flights throughout the UK and Ireland from Swansea and Cardiff, again it looks good value. Better than average site too.

www.excelairways.com – an ambitious and service-oriented charter airline, they offer luxuries, such as leather seating, and fly to a wide range of European and Middle Eastern destinations.

www.flyglobespan.com – a Scottish low-cost airline flying to European holiday destinations on a no frills site.

www.jet2.com – flying from Leeds-Bradford, Manchester and Belfast to a select number of European destinations, Jet2 is offering seats at very low prices

Airport Parking

www.uk-airport-car-parking.co.uk   UK
BOOK YOUR SPACE
Probably the best of the sites dedicated to helping you find somewhere to park your car while you're away. It offers more options and information than the others listed but it's always worth shopping around, so you should try these alternatives.

See also:
www.bcponline.co.uk – easy to use and with some good savings on airport car park rates.

www.holidayextras.co.uk – who are also good for parking, airport hotels, airport lounges and also have information on getting to airports by public transport.

www.parking4less.co.uk – high-quality secured parking assured.

www.securedcarparks.com – as the title suggests, a useful guide to car parks with decent security.

Rail and Coach Travel Abroad

www.seat61.com   UK
THE MAN IN SEAT 61
You can get timetables and book on many routes whether by train, ship or coach. You can compare costs and there's plenty of information and links too.

See also:
www.eurail.com – details of the Eurail ticket, information and prices, and you can now buy online.
www.eurostar.com – through the Channel Tunnel…online booking plus timetables and offers.
www.eurotunnel.com – online passenger bookings.
www.greyhound.com – the famous American coach company.
www.raileurope.co.uk – booking European rail travel.
www.trainseurope.co.uk – European and North American trains with online booking.

Hotels and Places to Stay

www.hotelguide.com   UK

COMPREHENSIVE
With services available in nine languages and specialist sections such as golfing breaks, this site ranks amongst the best for finding the right hotel. It lists around 100,000 at time of writing.

www.hiphotels.net   UK

FOR THE HIPPEST HOTELS
Excellent for the unusual, it's a directory of the unique and off-beat with good illustrations of each hotel, not much in the way of deals, but then they are very special.

www.from-a-z.com   UK

A–Z OF HOTELS
A well-designed British site with over 20,000 hotels to choose from in the UK, Eire and France and a further 40,000 world-wide, it's quick and easy to use and there's online booking available plus plenty of special discounts.

Other good hotel directory and booking sites:
www.all-hotels.com – 90,000 hotels listed with lots of options, American bias.
www.ase.net – some 150,000 listed properties here with many reviews.
www.best-inn.co.uk – another hotel/motel directory containing thousands of entries, very good for London and links to specialist accommodation.
www.discount25.com – great for hotel discounts, primarily in Spain but also the major European cities.

www.octopustravel.com – a huge number of rooms and deals available, one of the most used sites for hotel booking.
www.openworld.co.uk – a collection of links to hotel sites, just use the interactive world map.
www.placestostay.com – simple to use and provides a list of hotels, descriptions, prices, maps and an online reservation service.

Hostels

www.hostels.com   US

INTERNATIONAL HOSTELLING
An excellent resource for anyone looking for budget accommodation. Many of the hostels are reviewed and it's easy to find one using the click-through maps.

See also:
www.hihostels.com – a hostelling booking service with lots of information too.
www.hostellingworld.com – a hostelling club with online booking.
www.yha.org.uk – very good site from the Youth Hostels Association.

Villas

www.cvtravel.net – passionate about villas, mainly in Europe.
www.jamesvillas.co.uk – over 500 villas in the Med.
www.ownerssyndicate.com – a wide choice with some good offers.
www.villa-rentals.com – from Abercrombie & Kent, villas world-wide, some look outstanding.

Travel Guides and Information

www.johnnyjet.com   US

TRAVEL PORTAL
A very detailed and comprehensive portal site devoted to all things travel. It's well categorised but has an American bias.

www.lonelyplanet.com   UK

LONELY PLANET GUIDES
A superb travel site, aimed at the independent traveller, but with great information for everyone. Get a review on most world destinations or pick a theme and go with that; leave a message

on the Thorn Tree; find out the latest news by country; get health reports; read about the travel experiences of others – what's the real story?

www.bugbog.com UK

TRAVEL INFORMATION

An outstanding and well-organised site offering information and advice on all aspects of travel, with guides and a good directory too.

www.tripadvisor.com US

UNBIASED REVIEWS

An excellent site offering guidance on almost any destination with reviews and links. It includes magazine articles as well as guide book reviews and opinions from members.

http://travel.roughguides.com UK

ROUGH GUIDES

Lively reviews on a huge number of places – over 14,000. In addition, there's general travel information, a place to share your travel thoughts with other travellers, or you can buy a guide. Excellent for links and you can get some good deals via the site. You can now order interactive city maps for your PDA or listen to world music on rough guides radio.

www.fodors.com US

FODOR'S GUIDES

These guides give an American perspective, but there is a huge amount of information on each destination. The site is well laid out and easy to use. See also the comprehensive **www.mytravelguide.com**

http://kasbah.com UK

THE WORLD'S LARGEST TRAVEL GUIDE

Clear information, stacks of links and a good search engine should mean that you will find the low-down on most destinations. The highlights on each destination are useful and the 'Global Travel Toolbox' provides info, telecommunications, maps, currency and more.

www.packback.com UK

PACKBACK TRAVEL GUIDE

A good-looking and useful site with an independent travel guide, a growing membership and a reputation for quality reviews. It includes a discussion forum, travel tools and flight booking.

www.guardian.co.uk/travel

UK

FROM THE *GUARDIAN* NEWSPAPER

A good reflection of the excellent *Guardian* weekly travel section with guides, information and inspiration throughout. There's also the latest news and links to sites with offers plus extra features such as audio guides and articles on parts of the UK.

www.gorp.com

US

FOR THE GREAT OUTDOORS

A great title, Gorp is dedicated to adventure, whether it be hiking, mountaineering, fishing, snow sports or riding the rapids. It has an American bias, but is full of relevant good advice, links and information.

www.timeout.com

UK

TIME OUT GUIDE

A slick site with destination guides covering many European cities and an increasing number further afield such as New York and Sydney. Not surprisingly, it's outstanding for London. You can also book tickets and buy books via other retailers.

www.bradmans.com

UK

BRADMAN'S FOR BUSINESS TRAVELLERS

A really excellent city guide with none of your fancy graphics, just a straightforward listing of countries and sensible information on each one, includes restaurant reviews and tips on orienting yourself in the city.

www.vtourist.com

UK

THE VIRTUAL TOURIST

Explore destinations in a unique and fun way. Travellers describe their experiences, share photos, make recommendations and give tips so others benefit from their experience.

Other guides and sites worth checking out are:

http://away.com – lots of links and information hidden away amongst the offers.

http://picturesofplaces.com – here you can find a huge number of photos from around the world.

www.about.com/travel – a comprehensive travel directory from About.com.

T

www.bootsnall.com – aimed at the independent traveller, it has several guides and is packed with information, looks good too.

www.citypopulation.de – lots of information about cities and regions throughout the world.

www.citysearch.com – a listing for mainly US cities with entertainment and orientation guides.

www.citysearch.com – US-oriented site with some excellent city guides.

www.nytimes.com/pages/travel/index.html – travel news and information from the *New York Times*.

www.officialtravelinfo.com – a directory covering the world's official tourism sites.

www.roadnews.com – help and information for those of us who travel with a laptop computer.

www.thetravelportal.com – hotel reviews and an excellent set of links from a bigger web directory.

www.travelintelligence.net – the opinions of more than 100 travel writers.

www.travel-library.com – less entertaining than some but combines recommendation with hard facts very well.

www.world-heritage-tour.org – a list and tour of World Heritage sites around the globe with panoramic views.

www.worldinformation.com – not specifically a travel guide but there is a mountain of information on the world's countries, their culture and advice about how to deal with issues like corruption.

Maps and Route Finders

/.multimap.com   UK

GREAT BRITAIN

Outstanding design, easy to use, excellent for the UK, you can search using postcodes, London street names, place names or Ordnance Survey grid references. Once you've found what you're looking for, you can also see an aerial view of the area.

www.mappy.co.uk   UK

START HERE

Mappy has a great-looking site which is easy to use and has lots of added features such as a personal mapping service where you can store the maps you use most. The route finder is OK, and business users can fill in their mileage allowance and Mappy will calculate how much they should claim.

See also:

http://maps.expedia.co.uk – limited to the US, France, Germany and the UK for detailed maps – modest route finder.

http://maps.msn.com – excellent mapping and route-finding service from MSN.

www.mapquest.com – find out the best way to get from A to B in Europe or America, not always as detailed as you'd like, but easy to use and you can customise your map or route plan.

www.mapsonus.com – it's notoriously difficult to find your way around America, but using the route planner you should minimise your risk of getting lost.

www.memory-map.co.uk – a useful range of downloadable maps based on Ordnance Survey mapping.

www.ordsvy.gov.uk – a good site with mapping for sale but the interactive mapping was suspended at the time of writing.

www.stanfords.co.uk – travel book and map specialists.

www.uk.map24.com – excellent interactive and static mapping but the directions are a little difficult to follow at times.

www.viamichelin.com – a good all-round travel site with an improved route-finder service, which is OK.

www.theaa.co.uk   UK
AUTOMOBILE ASSOCIATION
A superb site that offers route-planning and traffic information, a hotel and restaurant guide with a booking; service, and help with buying a car or even a GPS. There is also information on insurance and other financial help.

www.rac.co.uk   UK
GET AHEAD WITH THE RAC
Great for UK traffic reports, this site has a very reliable route planner, which seems to be very busy and slow at peak times. There's also a good section on finding the right place to stay, and lots of help if you want to buy a car.

Destinations

www.antor.com   UK
ASSOCIATION OF NATIONAL TOURIST OFFICES
A useful starting point for information about the 90 or so countries that are members of the association. It also has very good links to key tourism sites. See also **www.towd.com** who list every official government tourist office and some unofficial ones too.

www.embassyworld.com   US

EMBASSIES AROUND THE GLOBE
Pick two countries, one for 'whose embassy' and one for 'in
what location', press go and up pops the details on the
embassy with contact and essential information.

*Here's an alphabetical list of countries and regions to help you
research your chosen destination and plan your holiday.*

A

www.africaonline.com   SOUTH AFRICA

AFRICA
Exhaustive site covering news, information and travel in Africa,
with very good features and articles.

www.africatravelresource.com   UK

EAST AFRICA
An exceptional site that specifically covers Burundi, Kenya,
Rwanda, Uganda and Tanzania plus the resorts of Lamu and
Zanzibar. The level of detail is great but because the site is
packaged so well, it doesn't overwhelm. A lesson in how a
travel site should be set up.

See also:
http://i-cias.com – an excellent information site covering North
Africa and the Middle East.
www.africaguide.com – detailed country-by-country guides,
discussion forums, shopping, culture and a travelogue feature
make this site a good first stop.
www.africanodyssey.co.uk – African and Arabian specialist agents.
www.africansafariclub.com – cruises and safaris a speciality.
www.backpackafrica.com – excellent site for backpackers with
over 400 links and advice on where to go and what to see.
www.ecoafrica.com – tailor-made safaris with the emphasis on
eco-tourism.
www.onsafari.com – good advice on what sort of safari is right
for you.
www.phakawe.demon.co.uk – safaris in Botswana.
www.sahara-overland.com – the trans-Sahara experience with
information and travellers' reports.
www.travelinafrica.co.za – budget travel in Southern Africa.
www.vintageafrica.com – awesome safaris and destinations
from this specialist travel agent, who will tailor-make holidays
if requested.

www.wilderness-safaris.com – specialises in providing safaris that go to pristine wilderness.
www.wildnetafrica.net – an excellent travel and information portal for safaris to south and south-east Africa.

www.turisme.ad   ANDORRA
ANDORRA
A nice little site extolling the many virtues of this tiny country.

www.polartravel.co.uk   UK
ARCTIC AND ANTARTICA
How to get to the Poles in safety and even enjoy yourself when you get there!

See also:
www.arctic-experience.co.uk – spectacular holidays in the Arctic.
www.iaato.org – International Association of Antarctic Travel Operators, has links to all the major agents.
www.inuitadventures.co.uk – learn about survival in the cold with the Inuit.

www.argentour.com   ARGENTINA
ARGENTINA
Outstanding (but very slow-loading) travel site with video clips, regional information, history and slide shows of the major cities. There's even a section on how to tango. See also
www.argentinatravelnet.com/indexE.htm

www.asiatravel.com   SINGAPORE
ASIA
A horribly designed site packed with travel information about all the Asian countries and beyond. Fortunately, the quality of the information is much better than the site design would suggest and covers accommodation, travel and background facts on the countries and what to buy while you're there.

www.austria-tourism.at   AUSTRIA
AUSTRIA
An excellent site covering all you need to know about the country, with information on skiing and summer holidays too. See also **www.tiscover.at**

www.australia.com   AUSTRALIA
DISCOVER AUSTRALIA
The Australian Tourist Commission offer a good and informative
site that gives lots of facts about the country, the people, the
lifestyle and what you can expect when you visit.

See also:
www.acn.net.au – a directory of Australian cultural and
recreational resources.
www.australianexplorer.com – excellent and well-illustrated site
with some 9,000 pages of information.
www.travelaustralia.com.au – informative site, good for
regional information.
www.travelmate.com.au – a comprehensive site with masses
of information, which is especially good if you're driving.
www.voyages.com.au – stay in luxury at Ayers Rock, or Uluru
as it's officially known now.
www.wilmap.com.au – excellent for Australian maps and links.

B
www.indo.com   INDONESIA
BALI ONLINE
This site covers Bali and its top hotels, but there's also plenty
of information on the rest of Indonesia and links to other
Asian sites.

www.virtualbangladesh.com   US
BANGLADESH
A colourful and atmospheric travel site that contains all the
practical information you need to start planning a trip written in
an informal, welcoming style. You can find out about the
people, customs, flora and fauna, and there is an interesting
section on the politics. For another general tourist site go to
www.discoverybangladesh.com

www.trabel.com   BELGUIM
BELGIUM
The Belgium Travel Network offers a site packed with information
about the country and its key towns and cities. You can get
information on hotels, travelling, an airport guide, flight information
and there's also a good links page. See also the well-designed
www.belgium-tourism.net and **www.visitflanders.co.uk**

www.belize.com   US
BELIZE
A good general site covering the country. It's not just aimed at tourists but its incredibly useful for the visitor.

www.boliviaweb.com   US
BOLIVIA
A useful and well-put-together portal site.

www.botswana.com   SOUTH AFRICA
BOTSWANA
A well-illustrated site covering Botswana's exciting collection of game lodges. It also offers links to hotel and services directories too. See also **www.okavango.com**

www.brazil.com   BRAZIL
BRAZIL
A straightforward, no-nonsense guide, travelogue and listing site for Brazil that also contains information on hotels and resorts.

See also:
www.brazil.org.uk – very informative site from the Brazilian Embassy.
www.carnaval.com – you have to hunt for the information but there's a very helpful site in there.
www.helisight.com.br – book your helicopter tour over Rio.
www.ipanema.com – outstanding site by people who really know Rio, with masses of links and detailed cross referencing.
www.varig.co.uk – the national airline, good site with online booking.

www.travel-bulgaria.com   BULGARIA
EXPLORE BULGARIA
A well-put-together portal site with all the information you should need, Bulgaria is the hottest place for cheap property at the moment. See also the slow **www.bulgaria.com** and the UK-based specialist **www.balkanholidays.com**

T

C

www.cambodia-travel.com
CAMBODIA

HOME OF THE KHMER
A wide-ranging site with some interesting spelling! There are sections on Angkor Wat, the Khmer and the usual accommodation details. See also **www.eyeoncambodia.com**

www.travelcanada.ca
CANADA

EXPLORE CANADA
Did you know that the glass floor at the top of the world's tallest free-standing structure could support the weight of 14 large hippos? Find out much more at this wide-ranging and attractive site, from touring to city guides. See also **www.canadian-affair.com** who offer some excellent low-cost flights and tours, and for an outdoor experience of the country go to **www.out-there.com**

www.turq.com
US

CARIBBEAN
All you need to organise a great holiday in the Caribbean. There's information on flights, hotels, cruises, a travel guide and trip reports to the islands, all on a well-presented and easy-to-use site.

See also:
www.antigua-barbuda.com – competent site from the Antiguan High Commission.
www.barbados.org – great overview of the island with excellent links.
www.caribbeandreams.co.uk – UK travel agent specialising in the Caribbean.
www.caribbeansupersite.com – good information, over 4,000 links.
www.doitcaribbean.com – information, booking and an interactive map.
www.jamaicatravel.com – a pretty comprehensive site devoted to the island with regional guides and help in planning your trip.
www.visittnt.com – basic information site on Trinidad and Tobago.

www.gochile.cl
CHILE

CHILE
A great overview of the country with all the holiday information you'll need including details on Easter Island. See also **www.chile-hotels.com**

www.chinatour.com   CHINA
INFORMATION CHINA
A comprehensive site stuffed with data on China: where to go
and stay, how to get there and what to see, maps and visa
application information. See also the China Travel System at
www.chinats.com who have a good-looking and very polite site
where you can book hotels and tours, get travel information and
chat to others who've experienced China.

See also:
www.chinapage.com/china.html – information on everything
from calligraphy to language to tatoos. Some historical
background information on major sites.
www.discoverhongkong.com – for Hong Kong.
www.haiweitrails.com – organised treks in SW China and Tibet.

www.croatia.hr   CROATIA
CROATIA
An excellent site covering the country and its virtues with
sections on events, attractions, background, accommodation
and an all-round travel guide. For villas and general info check
out **www.croatianaffair.com**

www.cubanculture.com   US
CUBA
A fast, easy-to-use site with the basic information about Cuba
and its heritage. There are lots of useful links too.

www.cyprustourism.org   CYPRUS
CYPRUS
A pretty basic site about the country, well the Greek-run bit anyway.

www.czech-tourism.com   CZECH REPUBLIC
CZECH REPUBLIC
A good directory site providing information and links in 15 categories
from business to the weather including tour operators and a country
guide. See also Czech It Out at **www.goaway.co.uk**

D
www.visitdenmark.com   DENMARK
DENMARK
The official Danish tourist board site where you can get links to

book a holiday and all the advice and information you'd expect
from a well-run and efficient-looking site. See also
www.woco.dk for an excellent site on Copenhagen.

E

www.ecuadorexplorer.com   US

ECUADOR
A very well-put-together directory site covering all you need
for a visit to one of the most beautiful countries on the planet.
For specific sites on the Galapagos go to the thorough
www.galapagos-travel.com and also the Galapagos
Conservation Trust at **www.gct.org** which is full of information
and good for links.

http://touregypt.net   EGYPT

EGYPT
A pretty ugly but very comprehensive site covering the country
and in particular its history. It's really a very good portal site as
well as a travel guide.

See also:
www.ancient.co.uk – archaeological tours with this
specialist operator.
www.discoveregypt.co.uk – a well-illustrated site from a UK-
based specialist.
www.peltours.com – great site from an agent specialising in Egypt.

www.croatia.hr   ESTONIA

ESTONIA
Gushing with enthusiasm for the charms of this small Baltic
state, this site gives you information on travel, accommodation,
history, climate and money. For another view try the no-
nonsense **www.estoniantravel.com**

www.eurotrip.com   UK

BACKPACKING EUROPE
Student and independent European travel with in-depth
information, facts, reviews, articles, discussion, live reports,
links and travel advice on a good-looking and well-designed
site. Also connects to a no-frills airline booking service and
a section with information on finding low-cost air fares.

www.eurocamp.co.uk   UK
SELF-CATERING EUROPE
The leading self-catering company with over 160 holiday parks in 12 countries. Here you can find details of the accommodation and book a holiday; there are some bargains too. See also **www.eurocampindependent.co.uk,** who offer a European campsite reservation service.

www.visiteurope.com   US

EUROPEAN TRAVEL COMMISSION
A site aimed at Americans to encourage them to visit Europe. It's informative and there's a section for each country.

F

www.visitfinland.com   FINLAND
FINLAND
Look under the 'Individual holiday planner' for good-quality information on travelling around, accommodation and outdoor activities. There are also organised tours available for the British traveller. Don't miss out on Santa's homepage and arrange a Christmas visit.

See also:
www.finland-tourism.com – a rather jerky but informative site with holiday planner and links to specialist tour operators.
www.wildnorth.net – a visual treat with fishing and hunting tours.

www.franceway.com   FRANCE

VOILA LA FRANCE!
Excellent site giving an overview of French culture, history, facts and figures, and of course, how to book a holiday. You can also sign up for the newsletter.

See also:
www.brittanytourism.com – a good site on all that Brittany has to offer.
www.cdt-nord.fr – useful site on northern France, but only in French.
www.corsica.co.uk – good site from a Corsican specialist.
www.franceguide.com – official French Government Tourist Office portal site or **www.francetourism.com** the sister site aimed at US tourists.
www.francemag.com – really informative and useful e-zine devoted to France.

T

www.gites-de-france.fr/eng – a wide variety of gite accommodation with online booking.

www.justparis.co.uk – details on how to get there and hotels for when you've arrived.

www.le-guide.com – a messy but informative guide to the South of France.

www.logis-de-france.fr – reliable guide to 3,000 hotels and restaurants throughout France.

www.magicparis.com – good Paris guide with some offers.

www.manchetourisme.com – what to do in La Manche, Normandy.

www.normandy-tourism.org – excellent and informative site on Normandy.

www.northernfrance-tourism.com – a scrappy site on northern France.

www.parishotels.com – a fast booking service for Paris hotels.

www.rhonealpes-tourism.co.uk – information and holidays.

www.vive-la-france.org – very comprehensive and good fun.

G

www.visitthegambia.gm   GAMBIA

GAMBIA

A good tourist site which promotes Gambia's wildlife and ecological sites with particular emphasis on the bird-life and waterways. See also **www.gambia.co.uk**

www.germany-tourism.de   GERMANY

GERMANY – WUNDERBAR

As much information as you can handle with good features on the key destinations, excellent interactive mapping and links to related sites. For further information try **www.germany-info.org**

www.gibraltar.gi/tourism   GIBRALTAR

GIBRALTAR – THE ROCK

A good site devoted to the area with sections on the sights plus travel information.

www.gnto.gr   GREECE

GREEK NATIONAL TOURIST ORGANISATION

An attractive site with the official word on travelling in Greece, also a good travel guide and information for business travellers plus accommodation, advice and details on what you can get up to.

See also:

www.culture.gr – excellent site covering Greek culture and its legends.

www.filoxenia.co.uk – a specialist, good for unusual accommodation in Greece.

www.gogreece.com – a search engine devoted to all things Greek.

www.greekisland.co.uk – an entertaining and personal view of the Greek islands with over 200 links.

www.gtpnet.com – the Greek Travel Pages with the latest ferry schedules for island hoppers.

www.islands-of-greece.com – another specialist operator with a good site and features on the better islands.

www.travelalacarte.co.uk – specialists in holidays in the best of the Greek islands.

H
www.holland.com   HOLLAND

HOLLAND IS FULL OF SURPRISES

A very professional site offering a mass of tourist information and advice on how to have a great time when you visit. There are sections on how to get there, what type of holiday will suit you and city guides.

www.gotohungary.com   HUNGARY

HUNGARY

All the information is here to enable you to plan your trip to Hungary including information on the wide range of cultural events taking place in Budapest. If it's restoration you're after, there's an interesting section on Hungary's curative spas. See also **www.budapest.com** and **www.hungarytourism.hu**

I
www.iceland.is   ICELAND

ICELAND

The official site of the Icelandic Ministry of Foreign Affairs with a wealth of information about the country, the people and its history. It's easy to navigate and there are good links to related sites. See also **www.iceland.com** which is more tourism oriented and also **www.icelandexpress.com** which is good for low-cost fares.

www.incredibleindia.org   UK
INDIAN TOURIST OFFICE UK
Essential tourist information and advice as well as cultural and
historical background on the country and its diverse regions. It
has a massive hotel database as well.

www.indiamart.com   UK
INDIA TRAVEL PROMOTION NETWORK
Basically a shopping site with diverse information including
travel, hotels, timetables, wildlife, worship, trekking, heritage
and general tourism. It's well organised and easy to use.

See also:
www.greavesindia.com – luxury holidays in India and Nepal.
www.hindustantimes.com – full of useful information, news
and gossip.
www.indianrail.gov.in – passenger information and timetables
for the largest rail network in the world.
www.india-travel.com – a really strong travel site with lots of
information and guidance as well as essential links.
www.indiatraveltimes.com – great for links and the latest news.
www.mapsofindia.com – an excellent site with maps of the
country and a rail timetable and route planner.
www.partnershiptravel.co.uk – specialist Indian travel agent.
www.rrindia.com – another good information site offering tour
itineraries and hotel booking.
www.taj-mahal.net – explore the Taj Mahal.

www.tourismindonesia.com   INDONESIA
INDONESIA
A very good overview of the country and its people, with lots of
useful information about travelling there and a good links
section. See also **www.indo.com** and for trips to see the
Komodo Dragon go to **www.komodotours.com**

www.shamrock.org   IRELAND
IRELAND
A wide-ranging site giving you the best of Ireland. Aimed at the
American market, it really sells the country well with good links
to other related sites.

See also:
www.12travel.co.uk – Irish holiday specialists with lots of holiday options.
www.camping-ireland.ie – over 100 parks listed for caravanning and camping.
www.heritageireland.ie – exploring the history of Ireland.
www.iol.ie/~discover – a good travel guide plus lots of links.
www.ireland.travel.ie – the very good official Irish Tourist Board site.
www.irelandhotels.com – a good accommodation directory.
www.timeoutireland.com – specialist in activity tours.
www.visitdublin.com – very comprehensive official guide to Dublin.

www.goisrael.com   ISRAEL
ISRAEL
Excellent site with information on the country, its sights and sites, how to get there and how to organise a tour. See also **www.infotour.co.il** and **www.e-israel.com**

www.italytour.com   ITALY
VIRTUAL TOUR OF ITALY
Good looking, stylish and cool, this site is essentially a search engine and directory but a very good one.

See also:
www.doge.it – a basic but informative site on Venice.
www.emmeti.it – slightly eccentric site with bags of good information, although it takes a while to find it. Very good for hotels, regional info and museums.
www.enit.it – from the Italian State Tourist board, another wacky site but useful nonetheless.
www.initaly.com – another 'Italian' site but generally well organised, informative and useful.
www.itwg.com – Italian hotel reservations with online booking.
www.travel.it – a messy information site but you can book online.
www.tuscanynow.com – villas for rent in Tuscany.

J
www.jnto.go.jp   JAPAN

JAPAN
This excellent site is the work of the Japanese Tourist Association. There's a guide to each region, the food, shopping and travel info with advice on how to get the best out of your visit.

See also:
www.uk.emb-japan.go.jp – a new site for the Japanese
Embassy with details on how to study or work in Japan, plus
visa, tourist and background information.
www.jaltour.co.uk – travel agents specialising in Japan.
www.japan-guide.com – comprehensive information site about
Japan with links, culture notes, shopping and a hotel finder.

www.see-jordan.com   JORDAN
JORDAN
An attractive and interesting site from the Jordanian tourist
board. It is very cultural and informative with good links and a
photo gallery. See also **www.jtehome.com** where you'll find the
attractive site of the Jordan Travel Exchange.

K
www.visit-kenya.com   KENYA
KENYA
A slightly amateurish site with links and information on
travelling in Kenya. There are sections on Nairobi and the coast
as well as the expected safari information.

See also:
www.kenya.com – good-looking site with a safari deal finder
and information on the country too.
www.kenyaweb.com – a good portal site on all things Kenyan.

L
www.lata.org   UK
LATIN AMERICA
The Latin American Trade Association's text-based site has a
good country-by-country guide to the region plus links and
general information.

www.southamericanexperience.co.uk   UK
SOUTH AMERICA
Specialists on South America are hard to come by, but at this site
you can get tailor-made tours to suit you plus some scant
information on the countries and special offers. See also
www.adventure-life.com and **www.gosouthamerica.about.com**
both are very informative and are good for links.

See the sites below, most of which also cover South America:
www.journeylatinamerica.co.uk – lots of tour and country options from this specialist agent.
www.lastfrontiers.com – tailor-made itineraries for holidays across the continent.
www.latinamericatraveler.com – great for links and information.
www.steppeslatinamerica.co.uk – from the Steppes group offering tailor-made packages.

www.nexteurope.com/tourism   LATVIA
LATVIA

A valiant effort with information on what to do when you get there and a good selection of links. They will also arrange for a translator/guide to show you around. For a second opinion go to **www.latviatravel.info**

www.destinationlebanon.com   LEBANON
THE LEBANON

The Lebanon is going through a resurgence and is successfully rebuilding itself. Written with the help of US-aid money to encourage tourism, this site successfully provides all the resources you need to organise a visit and see its many attractions.

www.tourism.lt   LITHUANIA
LITHUANIA

A straightforward offering from the State Department with basic tourist information.

www.luxembourg.co.uk   LUXEMBOURG
LUXEMBOURG

Comprehensive information on the Grand Duchy with good links to other sites. It could do with a few pictures to whet the appetite though.

www.malaysianet.net   MALAYSIA
MALAYSIA

Great for hotels in particular but you'll also find flight information and hidden away is a pretty good travel guide to the country. For air travel info see also **www.malaysiaair.com**

www.visitmaldives.com   MALDIVES
MALDIVES

A good overview of the islands and all the options available to tourists with links and a section on the capital Male.

www.visitmalta.com   UK

MALTA

A text-heavy but informative site about this beautiful island,
with good details on accommodation and interactive mapping.

www.tourbymexico.com   UK

MEXICO

A basic site, but there is a travel guide to Mexico plus
information on tours, hotels, health, tips, links and sights.
See also the bright and breezy European gateway into
Mexico **www.mexicanwave.com/travel**

http://i-cias.com   NORWAY

THE MIDDLE EAST

Probably the best site for information on the Middle East, just
click on the interactive map. There's really extensive information
on selected countries including maps, statistics, history, plus
the religious, economic and political state of each nation. See
also **www.ancient.co.uk**

www.arab.net   SAUDIA ARABIA

RESOURCE FOR THE ARAB WORLD

A wide-ranging site covering North Africa and the Middle East
with excellent country guides. See also
www.arabianodyssey.co.uk

www.tourism-in-morocco.com   MOROCCO

MOROCCO

Take the guided tour and visit the major tourist sites in
Morocco. There are also sections covering museums, tourist
events, Moroccan culture and you can try out a recipe at home.
The site provides links, but for more see **www.morocco.com**
and **www.morocco-travel.com**

N

www.namibweb.com   NAMIBIA

NAMIBIA

Comprehensive as a description doesn't quite do this site
justice, it seems to have covered everything. The result is a little
messy but it's easy to find what you need, and it is a stunning
country to visit.

www.nepal.com   US

NEPAL AND THE HIMALAYAS

A beautifully presented site showing Nepal in its best light.
Business, sport, culture and travel all have sections and it's a
good browse too. The travel section is not that comprehensive,
it has a basic guide, lots about Everest and access to the useful
Sherpa magazine. Also check out entries under China and India
in this section.

See also the specialist tour companies and information sites:
www.himalayankingdoms.com
www.nepaltravelinfo.com
www.rrindia.com/nepal.html
www.trans-himalaya.com

www.purenz.com   NEW ZEALAND

NEW ZEALAND

A good-looking and informative site about the country with a
section devoted to recollections and recommendations from
people who've visited. See also the comprehensive but
www.nz.com and **www.newzealand.com**

www.nicaragua.com   US

NICARAGUA

On the face of it a comprehensive portal devoted to all things
Nicaraguan, it's not what it seems, however, and only the guide
book information seems useful.

www.visitnorway.com   NORWAY

NORWAY

The official site of the Norwegian Tourist Board offers a good
overview of what you can get up-to-when you're there, from
adventure holidays to lounging around in the midnight sun to
cruising the coast. You need an up-to-date browser to get the
best out of the site. See also **www.norway.org** which is the
Norwegian Embassy's site and also **www.norwayshop.com**
great for dodgy patterned jumpers.

T

P

www.tourism.gov.pk   PAKISTAN

PAKISTAN

A pretty lightweight site but it has all the basic information and a good set of links with a travel guide built in. See also **www.pak.org** which is a very comprehensive portal site.

www.enjoyperu.com   US

PERU

It's amazing how much there is to see in Peru and this site does a good job of reflecting the country's assets. It has plenty of tourist information and deals. See also the basic but useful site of the Peruvian embassy **www.peruembassy-uk.com**

www.polandtour.org   US

POLAND

A basic overview of the country, tourist facilities and travel information. For a portal site go to **http://poland.pl**

www.portugal-web.com   PORTUGAL

PORTUGAL

A complete overview of the country including business as well as tourism with good regional information, news and links to other related sites.

See also:

www.madeiratourism.org – all about Madeira although you have to hunt for the English site, we found the link in the top right of the Portuguese page.

www.portugal.com – a news and shopping site with a good travel section.

www.portugal.org – well-designed information site with a good travel section.

www.portugalregional.pt – a shop devoted to Portuguese wine and arts.

www.thealgarve.net – all you need to know about the Algarve.

R

www.rotravel.com   ROMANIA

ROMANIA

Good historical information, maps and regional guides backed up with tourist services for both the independent traveller and those wanting a ready-made tour, make this site a good starting point for the exploration of this central European gem. The Romanian National Tourist Office has a good web site at **www.romaniatourism.com**

www.russia-travel.com   RUSSIA
RUSSIA

The official guide to travel in Russia with good information on excursions, accommodation, flights and trains, there's even a slide show, plus historical facts and travel tips. See also **www.themoscowtimes.com/travel** which offers a more traditional approach. For links go to **www.russia.com**

www.rwandatourism.com   RWANDA
RWANDA

It's good to see Rwanda back on the tourist map and here at the Tourist Board site you can find out what the country has to offer including interactive mapping on the gorilla treks.

S

www.sey.net   US
SEYCHELLES, PARADISE – PERIOD

A good all-round overview of the Seychelles with background information on the major islands and activities. There are also links to travel agents.

See also:
www.seychelles.uk.com – informative and geared to a British audience.
www.seychelleselite.co.uk – specialists in the Seychelles.
www.seychelles-travel.co.uk – excellent site from another specialist agent.

www.sg   SINGAPORE
SINGAPORE

The shortest URL in the book brings up one of the most detailed and comprehensive sites – all you need to know about the country and its people. See also **www.satours.com**

www.slovenia-tourism.si   SLOVENIA
SLOVENIA

A good introduction to the country, which is trying to establish a tourist industry. They boast that a visit here will regenerate 'lost psychophysical strength'.

www.sacr.sk   SLOVAKIA

SLOVAKIA
The official word of the Slovak Republic on their tourist
attractions. For similar but more wordy information go to
www.slovakia.org/tourism who also have an audio guide to
common phrases in Slovak.

www.southafrica.net   SOUTH AFRICA

SOUTH AFRICA
Official tourist site with masses of information about the country
and how you can set yourself up for the perfect visit with
suggested itineraries.

See also:
www.gardenroute.org.za – excellent site covering the Garden
Route and south coast.
www.southafrica.com/travel – very good portal site with a
comprehensive travel section.
www.southafricanaffair.com – tailor-made itineraries, basic
site though.

South America see Latin America on page 504.

www.tourspain.es   SPAIN

TOURIST OFFICE OF SPAIN
A colourful and award-winning web site that really makes you
want to visit Spain. Very good for an overview.

You could also try any of these listed below:
www.costaguide.com – your Costa del Sol companion, lots
of information.
www.iberia.com – the Iberian airlines site, with helpful advice
and offers.
www.majorca.com – great site about the island.
www.munimadrid.es – comprehensive site on Madrid.
www.okspain.org – nice all-round information and travel site.
www.red2000.com – a colourful travel guide, with a good
search instrument!

www.lanka.net SRI LANKA

SRI LANKA

An exhaustive site, which isn't easy to navigate, but it has loads of information and news on the country. See also **www.slmts.slt.lk** for the Ministry of Tourism.

www.sverigeturism.se/smorgasbord SWEDEN

SWEDEN

The largest source of information in English on Sweden. It's essentially a directory site but there are sections on culture, history and a tourist guide. For more details of Sweden's cities see the very good **http://cityguide.se** and **www.visit-sweden.com** and also **www.sweden.com**

www.switzerlandtourism.ch SWITZERLAND

SWITZERLAND

An excellent overview of the country with the latest news, travel information, snow reports and links. See also **www.myswitzerland.com**

T

www.tanzania-web.com TANZANIA

TANZANIA

Find your way around Tanzania with its wonderful scenery, Mount Kilimanjaro, safaris and resorts with this very good and comprehensive online guide from the official tourist board.

www.allaboutzanzibar.com TANZANIA

ZANZIBAR

An outstanding tourist site with concise (then very detailed if your need it) descriptions covering all the information you need, including accommodation and cultural stuff. Other tourism sites could learn a lot from this. See also **www.zanzibar.net**

www.thailand.com/travel THAILAND

THAILAND

Another excellent portal site, which acts as a gateway to a mass of travel and tourism resources. It covers some of South East Asia too and it has a good search facility. The helpful **www.tourismthailand.org** is the official tourist board site and is very informative, as is **www.nectec.or.th/thailand** and also **www.thaismile.co.uk**

T

www.tourismtunisia.com

TUNISIA

TUNISIA

A welcoming and easy-to-use site with lots of interactive links that gives you a good introduction to the country, its tourist sites and its people. There's information on hotels and restaurants – plus what to eat when you get there and links to travel agencies.

www.allaboutturkey.com

TURKEY

TURKEY

The best-looking and most informative site on the country and its people, though some sections are pretty odd. It's the work of one professional tour guide.

See also:
www.exploreturkey.com – pretty boring but comprehensive.
www.tourismturkey.org – great for links and basic information from the Ministry of Culture and Tourism.
www.turkey.org – informative site from the Turkish Embassy in Washington DC.
www.turkeycentral.com – a huge number of Turkish links.

U

www.uae.org.ae

UAE

UNITED ARAB EMIRATES

A useful guide to the seven states that make up the UAE, it carries historical and social information as well as the usual travel guide stuff. See also **www.godubai.com**

www.visituganda.com

UGANDA

UGANDA

A great site and directory from the Ugandan Tourist Board with excellent-quality pictures.

www.usatourism.com

US

US

A state-by-state guide to the US, just click on the interactive map and you get put through to the relevant state site. See also **www.areaguides.net** which is very detailed.

www.usembassy.org.uk

US

VISA INFO

This site gives a dull look at the latest tourist entry requirements plus information on gripping topics such as driving. It also provides some limited but useful links. For tourist information they send you to **www.visitusa.org.uk**

See also:
www.americanadventures.com – great site devoted to budget adventure tours. Now merged with **www.treckamerica.com** to offer an even broader range of holidays.
www.amtrak.com – rail schedules and fares across America.
www.cruiseamerica.com – rent an RV for your fly-drive holiday.
www.disneyworld.com – all you need to know about the world's number-one theme park.
www.gocitykids.com – a family-friendly guide to some of the major cities in the US.
www.gohawaii.com – great site for checking out Hawaii and its many attractions.
www.greyhound.com – coach and bus schedules; for selected cities you can now buy tickets online using the 'will call' option and pick them up before boarding the bus.
www.hawaii-tourism.co.uk – the official site of Hawaii's tourist board, excellent information on all the islands.
www.kidscamps.com – a massive directory of kids' camps, mainly in the US.
www.seeamerica.org – an excellent portal to American travel sites.
www.usa-by-rail.com – the definitive guide book for touring the US by rail, apparently.
www.usahotelguide.com – reserve your room in any one of 55,000 hotels across the US.

V
www.vietnamtourism.com   US
VIETNAM
Vietnam is the hot destination, apparently. Here's the official tourism site, which is informative and good for links.

Z
www.zambiatourism.com   ZAMBIA
ZAMBIA
Comprehensive tourist site with loads of information about places to visit, where to stay and what to do when you get there. There are sections on the animals and birds you might see, plus maps and a good travel directory.

Travel in Britain

www.visitbritain.com   UK

HOME OF THE BRITISH TOURIST AUTHORITY
Selling Britain using a holiday-ideas-led site with lots of help for
the visitor, maps, background stories, images, entertainment,
culture, activities and a planner. There's also a very helpful set
of links.

www.informationbritain.co.uk   UK

HOLIDAY INFORMATION
Where to stay and where to go with an overview of all the UK's
main tourist attractions, counties and regions; it has good cross-
referencing and links to the major destinations.

www.ukholidaybreaks.co.uk   UK

FIND YOUR PERFECT HOTEL
A directory of hotels in the UK, you find the one you want by
drilling down through a series of maps or selecting by category.
It's easy, although results are a bit hit and miss, but it claims to
use the latest technology to find just the right break for you.

See also:
www.aboutbritain.com – attractive, well-laid-out and
comprehensive UK guide.
www.anothertravel.com – a good-looking site, a bit light on
information though.
www.atuk.co.uk – billed as the UK travel search engine,
unattractive design.
www.enjoybritain.com – useful links directory.
www.i-uk.com – useful information on the UK, mainly aimed
at visitors.
www.ukguide.org – well-organised directory with a UK and a
London guide plus mapping.
www.ukvillages.co.uk – not a great design but has good
information on over 30,000 places.

www.knowhere.co.uk   UK

THE USER'S GUIDE TO BRITAIN
An unconventional 'tourist guide', which gives a warts-and-all
account of over 1,000 places in Britain; it's very irreverent and
if you are squeamish or a bit sensitive, then they have a good
list of links to proper tourist sites.

For the separate countries and regions:

England

http://london.flavourpill.net – an excellent and entertaining London city guide which is updated weekly.
http://themeparksofengland.com – reviews and information on all of England's major theme parks.
www.londonhotelreservations.com – some good deals on London hotels.
www.londontown.com – very comprehensive survival and holiday guide rolled into one, with sections on restaurants, hotels, attractions and offers. It is quite slow.
www.timeout.com/london – *Time Out* mag's excellent guide to the capital.
www.travelengland.org.uk – nice online guide to everything English, places to visit and accommodation.

Northern Ireland

www.discovernorthernireland.com – Northern Ireland Tourist Board has an attractive site showing the best that the region has to offer. It has a virtual-tour holiday planner.
www.guide-to-nireland.com – a good directory site and guide.

Scotland

www.aboutscotland.com – excellent site with information on a broad range of accommodation and sights to see, it's fast too.
www.scotac.com – accommodation by region.
www.scotland.com – nicely illustrated site with a good overview of the country.
www.scotland-info.co.uk – very good online guidebook covering Scotland by area; it's quite slow but the information is very good.
www.visithebrides.com – a light and airy site with links and information relating to the islands. See also **www.hebrides.com** which offers beautiful photography.
www.visitorkney.com – from the Orkney Tourist Board a very informative and appealing site. See also **www.orknet.com**
www.visitshetland.com – a definite green theme to this site devoted to Shetland, highlighting its outdoor life and spirit of adventure.

Wales

www.cadw.wales.gov.uk – historic monuments in Wales.
www.data-wales.co.uk – not so much a tourist site, but
excellent for history and culture and quite funny too.
www.stayinwales.co.uk – for hotels, cottages, B&Bs,
campsites, even bunkhouses.
www.valleyconnection.co.uk – a useful directory devoted to all
things Welsh.

The UK's Islands

www.alderney.net – a good-looking site devoted to the third
largest Channel Island.
www.guernseytouristboard.com – all the information you need
on Guernsey.
www.jerseyhols.com – good-looking site with lots of
information on where to stay and what to do. See also
www.jersey.com, who have a very slick site.
www.islandbreaks.co.uk – official site on the Isle of Wight.
www.isle-of-man.com – learn all about this unique island with
help on where to stay and, of course, background on the
famous TT races.
www.sark.info – a lively site with all the information you need
plus online booking for ferries.
www.simplyscilly.co.uk – specialists in travel to the Isles of
Scilly with info on how to get there and what to do.
www.wightlink.co.uk – Isle of Wight ferries and holiday
information.

Things to do in Britain and Ireland

www.sightseeing.co.uk   UK
SIGHT-SEEING MADE EASY
A good-looking and very useful site if you're looking for
something to do. Just type in what you want to see and where
you are, then up pops a list giving basic information on each
attraction, how far away it is, the entrance fee and a map.
However, it would be better if there was more background
information on each attraction or at least a link.

www.daysoutuk.com
UK

TAKE A DAY OFF

An excellent directory of venues and events with lots of search options. It's easy to use and you can get discounts to many attractions too. For a similar but more colourful site go to **www.daysout.co.uk** which includes a useful section for the disabled too.

www.gardenvisit.com
UK

GO TO A GARDEN

A basic text-based site, which lists some 1,000 of the UK's gardens open to the public, giving details of each, how to get there and how they rate. It also covers the US and Europe and there's also an excellent overview of garden history. See also the section on Gardening page 216.

www.nationaltrust.org.uk
UK

PLACES OF HISTORIC INTEREST AND BEAUTY

The National Trust's site has an excellent overview of their activities and the properties they own. There is a very good search facility and up-to-date information to help with your visit. See also **www.nts.org.uk** for the National Trust for Scotland.

See also:

www.castles-of-britain.com – informative and lively site on Britain's castles.

www.english-heritage.org.uk – excellent, high-quality site with information on their properties and an events calendar.

www.hrp.org.uk – pretty boring site devoted to five historic royal palaces – the Tower, Hampton Court, Kensington, Kew and the Banqueting House.

www.statelyhomes.com – comprehensive site devoted to our stately homes, with links and an e-zine to keep you updated.

www.goodbeachguide.co.uk
UK

THE BEST BEACHES

From the Marine Conservation Society you can find out which are Britain's worst and best beaches. It's set out regionally and the site is updated regularly.

T

What to do With the Kids

www.babygoes2.com   UK
ESSENTIAL TRAVEL GUIDE FOR PARENTS
An excellent resource for parents who have children under five,
it covers a wide range of holiday options, plus plenty of advice,
guides and information.

For more ideas try:
www.barracudas.co.uk – activity camp holidays.
www.butlins.co.uk – bright and breezy site from this popular
family-oriented company.
www.campbeaumont.com – a summer camp covering south-
east England.
www.centerparcs.com – attractive site from this holiday village
specialist, covering the UK and parts of Europe.
www.kidscamps.com – a massive directory of kids' camps,
mainly in the US.
www.kidstravel.co.uk – up-beat design but it could have more
content, still some good ideas and travelling tips for parents
though biased to England.
www.pgl.co.uk/holidays – activity holidays for children with lots
of options.
www.xkeys.co.uk – specialist in residential camps for children of all
ages, excellent web site with lots of information and references.

Holiday Cottages and B&B

www.hidays.co.uk   UK
UK COTTAGES
Hidays claims over 26,000 cottages in the UK, Ireland and France.
The site is user friendly and you can search using numerous options
from those that take pets to cottages with pools.

www.bedandbreakfast-directory.co.uk   UK
B&B
A regional directory of B&Bs with a good search facility. Each
entry has contact details, a description and information such as
whether online booking is available.

See also:
www.cottagesdirect.com – click on the interactive map and
away you go, plenty of cottages to choose from.

www.nationaltrust.org.uk/cottages – holiday cottages with a difference.
www.oas.co.uk/ukcottages – over 1,000 cottages available throughout the UK.
www.preferredplaces.co.uk – good site with a wide range of options.
www.seasidecottages.co.uk – all within 10 miles of the sea.
www.selfcatering-directory.co.uk – a very useful directory site listing hundreds of cottages with information and contact details.

Camping and Caravanning

Many of the sites listed specialise in Britain but some have information on camp sites abroad too.

www.camp-sites.co.uk   UK
FIND A SITE
Excellent regional listing of the UK's campsites with comprehensive details on each site and links to other related directories.

See also:
www.eurocampindependent.co.uk – excellent site if you want to go camping in Europe, some special offers and you can chat about your experiences too.
www.keycamp.co.uk – European specialist with sites in seven countries.
www.ukparks.com – directory site covering caravan and camping sites.

www.caravan.co.uk   UK
THE CARAVAN CLUB
This site offers help and advice, and has a huge listing of over 200 sites and some 2,600 other certified locations where you can park up. There's also a European service. You can join the club online and request any of the 50 or so leaflets they publish.

See also:
http://camping.uk-directory.com – a good regional sites directory, with retailing links, caravans for sale and forums. Camping in New Zealand is covered too.
www.campingandcaravanningclub.co.uk – an OK offering with information on sites and technical help and advice too.

T

www.campinguk.com – a basic regional campsite directory for campers and caravanners.
www.caravannersreunited.co.uk – forums, chat, information and meeting up with old friends.
www.caravan-sitefinder.co.uk – listing of over 3,500 caravan sites, with background information on a wide range of topics.
www.clicreports.co.uk – the Chat Line for Internet Campers offers loads of advice in a fun and informative way.
www.cruiseamerica.com – rent an RV for your fly-drive holiday.

Waterways

www.britishwaterways.co.uk   UK

BRITISH WATERWAYS
This organisation is responsible for maintaining a large part of Britain's waterways and this excellent site details their work. On two sites (also **www.waterscape.com**) it features interactive mapping of the routes with a great deal of background information, events, holidays, listings and history.

See also:
www.blakes.co.uk – a boating holiday specialist.
www.broads-authority.gov.uk – excellent overview of the Norfolk Broads.
www.canalholidays.com – an easy way to book your narrow-boat holiday.
www.gobarging.com – luxury barging in Europe.
www.hoseasons.co.uk – great site from the specialists in boating holidays, you can book online too.
www.waterways.org.uk – Inland Waterways Association site, dedicated to keeping canals open and you can find out about their organised activities too.

Adventure and Activity

Listed below are UK-oriented sites, see also page 479 for international adventure specialists.

www.activitiesonline.co.uk   UK

ULTIMATE RESOURCE FOR LEISURE PURSUITS
A directory of adventure and activity holiday specialists covering everything from extreme sports to gardening. You get a

description of the activity, then a list of relevant sites. See also
www.adventuredirectory.com for an excellent portal site.

www.sportbreak.co.uk   UK

THE SPORTS BREAK DIRECTORY
A good directory, apart from sports it covers all activity holidays
including leisure breaks, health clubs, even stag and hen
parties. They specialise in corporate entertaining too. It's easy
to use and the information is well put over.

Other adventure holiday sites:
www.activityholsni.co.uk – Activity Holidays in Northern
Ireland have a great site and lots to do.
www.adventureholiday.com – ProAdventure specialise in
activity holidays in North Wales.
www.hightrek.co.uk – strenuous activities in the mountains of
North Wales.
www.mountainandwater.co.uk – wide range of activities for
adults and children in Wales.
www.sportstoursinternational.co.uk – sports holidays (mainly
running, cycling and swimming) in the UK and abroad, but
many to international events.
www.trailplus.com – the ultimate adventure, offering lifestyle
experiences, adventure camps and much more.
www.uksurvivalschool.co.uk – learn new skills; learn how to
survive in many different situations on the courses.

Walking and Rambling

www.ramblers.org.uk   UK

THE RAMBLERS' ASSOCIATION
News, strong views and plenty of advice on offer here, where
you can find out about the Association's activities and even join
a campaign. There are features on events and details of *The
Rambler* magazine, shopping and holidays.

www.walkingbritain.co.uk   UK

BRITISH WALKS
Some 3,300 pages of information about walking in Britain, it
mainly covers the National Parks but it is expanding to include
less well-known areas. They provide decent route maps and
photos to guide you. There's also a list of handy links and a
good photo gallery.

www.onedayhikes.com   US

WHERE DO YOU WANT TO HIKE TODAY?
A great site, which is basically a directory of hikes that you can
complete in a day, it's not just for the UK either, it covers the
whole world. There's excellent information on each hike plus
pictures and you get the chance to win a digital camera if you
send in a report of a hike you've done and it gets accepted.

www.walkingworld.com   UK

OVER 2,000 WALKS
Each walk has a detailed description and map, and it's easy to
find a good one. In addition, there's advice on difficulty and
what you can expect to see. The walks cost £1.50 or you can
become a member for £17.45 per annum, then they're free.

For more sites for hikers try:
www.gelert.com – equipment for sale, a good-looking site, well
worth a visit.
www.georgefisher.co.uk – another excellent equipment store.
www.hfholidays.co.uk – excellent specialist travel agent with
walking holidays for all levels and all around the world.
www.ramblersholidays.co.uk – Ramblers Holidays specialise
in escorted rambling holidays.
www.trailsource.com – the hiking section of this big site has
some great walks and detailed mapping.

Train, Coach and Ferry Journeys

www.pti.org.uk   UK

PUBLIC TRANSPORT INFORMATION
An incredibly useful site if you're a frequent user of public
transport or if you're using it to go somewhere you're not
familiar with. It categorises all the major forms of public
transport and lists for each area useful numbers, timetables,
web sites and has interactive mapping to help you. It also
includes routes to Europe and Ireland. See also
www.internet.xephos.com which is a subscription service
which offers a high degree of accuracy on train and bus
timetables, and the UK pages at **www.seat61.com** while
http://journeyplanner.tfl.gov.uk is very useful for travelling
around London.

T

www.kizoom.co.uk   UK

TRAVEL SERVICE TO YOUR PHONE
Good-quality travel information to your mobile phone sounds
great and this is a very well-set-up and easy-to-use site.
Unfortunately, it only works with a limited number of WAP
phones, so if you've one of those, you're in luck.

Railway Travel

www.rail.co.uk   UK

RAILWAY LINKS
A directory of useful links including timetables, operators and
associated businesses.

www.nationalrail.co.uk   UK

NATIONAL RAIL
National Rail's site has all the latest information, timetables and
links you need to plan a rail journey. It's very comprehensive
with up-to-the-minute information on what's going on.

www.thetrainline.com   UK

BUY TRAIN TICKETS
You have to log in first but you can book a ticket for train travel,
whether business or leisure (except sleeper, Motorail, and ferry
services). They have an up-to-date timetable and the tickets will
be sent or you can collect. You can now buy European rail
tickets and other travel services from the site. See also the fast-
working **www.qjump.co.uk** which is similar. At both these sites
there are a bewildering number of options and prices, a little
help with what each ticket type and their relative costs wouldn't
go amiss.

See also:
www.gensheet.co.uk – information on unusual rail journeys
in the UK.
www.greatrail.com – escorted railway holidays world-wide.
Well-illustrated site.
www.networkrail.co.uk – what was Railtrack, some useful
information.
www.orient-express.com – details of their holidays and routes.
www.traintaxi.co.uk – useful site if you need a taxi once you're
off the train, with taxi company contact details and advice on
whether there are usually taxis waiting.

T

www.trainweb.com – a huge train portal site, particularly good for Amtrak in the US and Via Rail in Canada.

www.thetube.com   UK

LONDON UNDERGROUND

An excellent and informative site from London Underground with lots of features, articles on visiting London and links to related sites. There's a good journey planner and tube maps too. See also the Tube Planner at **www.tubeplanner.com**, which is a straightforward journey planner and a tube guide and history at **http://owen.massey.net/tubemaps.html**

Coaches and Buses

www.nationalexpress.com   UK

BOOK COACH TICKETS

Organise your journey with this easy-to-use web site from National Express, and then book the tickets. Also offers an airport service, transport to events and tours. See also **www.stagecoachbus.com** where you can find information about Stagecoach services and buy tickets, and **www.citylink.co.uk** for their Scottish Services.

www.megabus.com   UK

NO FRILLS

The coach equivalent of low-cost planes, Megabus is expanding rapidly, currently they serve over 30 towns and cities. Tickets can only be purchased online and all you need is your booking reference to present to the driver on the bus. Tickets start from £1 if you book soon enough, with only a 50p booking charge. Rumour has it they arrive on time too!

See also:
www.busabout.com – for independent travellers, mainly covers Europe and North Africa.
www.eurolines.com – Europe's largest coach network, although online booking is a bit complicated.
www.wallacearnold.co.uk – coaching holiday specialist with online booking.

Ferries

www.ferrysavers.com   UK
BOOK YOUR CROSSING
Low-cost ferry crossings and plenty of special offers on a
number of routes, you can book online but the price promise
seems to have disappeared.

See also:
www.boozecruise.com – for ferry tickets, guides to the French ports
and maps for locating the hypermarkets and shopping areas.
www.brittany-ferries.co.uk – crossings to France and Spain with
online booking and special offers, also cruises and holidays.
www.dfdsseaways.co.uk – details and offers on
Scandinavian routes.
www.directferries.co.uk – claims to offer the widest choice of
routes and crossings.
www.drive-alive.com – motoring holiday specialists who get
good rates on channel crossings as part of their package.
www.ferry.co.uk – great offers on selected crossings.
www.ferrycrossings-uk.co.uk – a helpful site with offers and
links, a shopping guide too.
www.hoverspeed.com – online booking and all the information
you need to make the fastest channel and Irish Sea crossings.
www.irishferries.ie – excellent magazine-style site where amongst
all the features you can find timetables and book tickets.
www.poferries.com – P&O Stena Line with online booking,
details of sailings and offers.
www.seafrance.com – bookings and information on their
Calais–Dover service plus some special offers.
www.seat61.com – has a useful listing of ferry companies
and booking.
www.speedferries.com – a low-cost operator offering crossings
from £25 one-way per car on the Dover–Boulogne fast-ferry
service. Book online to save admin fee.
www.steam-packet.com – get Sea Cat to destinations on the
Irish sea.
www.stenaline.co.uk – details of their routes and offers.
www.transmancheferries.com – the new boys on the south
coast offering Newport to Dieppe at competitive prices.

T

Car Hire

*It's probably best to go to a price-comparison site before going to one of the car hire companies, that way you should get the best prices. One of the best is to be found at **www.priceline.co.uk***

www.holidaycars.co.uk   UK

WORLD-WIDE CAR HIRE
Over 4,000 car hire locations throughout the world means that this site is well worth a visit on your quest, you can get an instant online quote and you can book too. Very good for the US.

See also:
www.easycar.com – low-cost, online car hire specialist, part of the Easyjet group.
www.holidayautos.co.uk – excellent prices and a wide choice too.
www.pelicancarhire.co.uk – competitive rates from this specialist in Europe.
www.insurance4carhire.com – who have a number of options to suit.

Travel Writing

Here are some sites covering the work of our favourite travel writers:
www.palinstravels.co.uk – an outstanding site from Michael Palin with his recommendations, excerpts from the books and video clips as well as competitions and links.
www.randomhouse.com/features/billbryson – an official site from Bill Bryson's publisher, it has a short biography, his book lists and a forum. Given the breadth of material available it could be so much better.
www.timseverin.net – details about his life and his remarkable voyages.
www.paultheroux.com – a biography and details on all his books.

T

Utilities

Get the best prices on your gas, electricity and water and find out what the big suppliers are up to as well.

www.ofgem.gov.uk   UK

GAS AND ELECTRICITY SUPPLIER WATCHDOG
Data on the suppliers and companies. The comparison
information makes for interesting reading. There's also
background on how bills are made up, complaints, government
policy and how energy reaches your home. See also the
independent watchdog Energywatch at **www.energywatch.org.uk**.
They offer impartial advice on many energy-related issues.

www.uswitch.com   UK

CUT YOUR BILLS – COMPARE PRICES
Take a few minutes to check the prices of the key utilities and
see whether you can save on your current bills, its easy and
quick. It also gives you the option to change to a green energy
tariff. In addition you can check out phones, broadband access,
digital TV and loans.

See also:
www.energylinx.co.uk – one of the best switch sites with a
wide range of options, particularly good on renewable energy.
www.greenelectricity.org – switch to green energy.
www.switchandgive.com – switch energy suppliers and give
to charity at the same time.
www.theenergyshop.com – very easy to use and fast results.
www.unravelit.com – savings on gas and electricity plus
numerous other services.
www.utilitydeal.com – helps business users as well as
home owners.

Saving Energy

www.natenergy.org.uk   UK

NATIONAL ENERGY FOUNDATION
Devoted to saving energy in order to benefit the environment.
There's lots of advice and information to help save money too.

U

See also:
www.clear-skies.org – information about grants for those installing renewable energy systems such as solar panels.
www.energysaving.me.uk – energy-saving lighting.
www.est.org.uk – a government trust set up to help fight global warming.
www.ukace.org – Association for the Conservation of Energy.

Electricity and Gas

Here are the main energy sites, who owns them at the time of writing and the highlights of the site.

www.british-energy.com – one of the largest electricity providers with a good-looking but not very useful site.
www.centrica.co.uk – owners of British Gas, this site aims to give information about the group, could be a lot more helpful.
www.esb.ie – messy site from an Irish supplier with online sign-up available.
www.house.co.uk – a comprehensive service from British gas with account viewing and offers.
www.hydro.co.uk – Scottish Hydro Electric has one of the sites most oriented to its customers.
www.edfenergy.com – a stylish site for London Energy, SWEB Energy, Seeboard Energy and Virgin Home.
www.nationalgrid.com/uk – the National Grid, the Railtrack of power.
www.nie.co.uk – Northern Ireland Electricity with customer information on their service, the rest is fairly corporate.
www.npower.com – nicely designed site with online application and the usual incentives to switch to their service.
www.powergen.co.uk – Powergen has a neat site with calculators and a switching service.
www.scottish-southern.co.uk – owner of Swalec, their site is aimed at shareholders and provides company information.
www.swalec.co.uk – Swalec, useful information, special site for kids and renewable energy.

www.transco.uk.com   UK

FOR GAS LEAKS
Transco doesn't sell gas, but maintains the 24-hour emergency service for stopping gas leaks – call 0800 111 999 to report one.

www.corgi-gas-safety.com   UK

COUNCIL OF REGISTERED GAS INSTALLERS
CORGI is the gas industry watchdog; the site has advice on gas installation and where to find a fitter or repairman.

www.calorgas.co.uk   UK

CALOR GAS
Information on your nearest stockists, how best to use Calor Gas and Autogas, there's also corporate background and customer services too. You can also order it online with payment collected on delivery.

Solid Fuel

www.solidfuel.co.uk   UK

SOLID FUEL ASSOCIATION
Information about solid fuels, about which is right for you and what appliances to buy; also covers suppliers and has a wealth of information and links. See also **www.coal.gov.uk**

Travel Sites That Make You Want to Go There

The Good Web Site Guide's Top 10s of the Internet

1. **www.africatravelresource.com** – on East Africa, excellent design.
2. **www.travelCanada.ca** – attractive and informative.
3. **www.franceway.com** – culture, history and travel.
4. **www.jnto.go.jp** – great site from the Japanese Tourist Association.
5. **www.nepal.com** – making the most of what nature has given them.
6. **www.tourspain.es** – colourful and a great overview.
7. **www.allaboutzanzibar.com** – a lesson to other tourism site designers.
8. **www.visitbritain.com** – comprehensive or what!
9. **www.seeamerica.org** – great for links and information.
10. **www.sg** – at least you'll remember the URL, a great portal on Singapore.

U

www.cpldistribution.co.uk   UK

COAL TO YOUR DOOR
Type in your postcode and, if accepted, you have several
delivery and ordering options depending on what type of solid
fuel you want.

Water

www.ofwat.gov.uk   UK

OFFICE OF WATER SERVICES
A relatively poor effort, especially when compared with the
OFGEM counterpart's site; however, you can find out about
what they do and you can contact them for advice. There's a
search facility to help you navigate the site.

The following are the main water company sites:
www.nwl.co.uk – Northumbrian Water with information and
bill-paying info.
www.stwater.co.uk – the consumer site of Severn Trent Water,
it's good looking, useful and easy to use.
www.swwater.co.uk – lots of information and good advice, bill
paying online.
www.thameswater.co.uk – good information and advice.
www.unitedutilities.co.uk – United Utilities, once North West
Water, has a well-designed site with help, information and good
advice for consumers, with online access to your account.
www.wessexwater.co.uk – good site with bill-paying facilities
and information, even which reservoirs you can fish in.

www.wateraid.org   US

WATER FOR LIFE
A charity devoted to helping people for whom getting water is
very difficult or almost impossible, you can find out about their
work and how to help. See also **www.actionaid.org**

The Weather

www.met-office.gov.uk   UK

EXCELLING IN WEATHER SERVICES
Comprehensive information on Britain's favourite topic of
conversation: easy to use with interactive maps. Includes details
on world weather and world weather news, UK weather

headlines and flash-weather warnings, weather for aviators and sailors and you can see what the weather is like on their webcams. There's also a good selection of links and a mobile phone service.

www.bbc.co.uk/weather   UK

ANOTHER WINNER FROM THE BBC
Another page from the BBC site, it gives up-to-the-minute forecasts, and is very clear and concise. It features: 5-day forecasts by town, city or postcode; specialist reports such as ski resorts, pollution, sun index; world weather and the shipping forecast. There are also audio and video forecasts and links.

See also:
www.intellicast.com – a general weather guide from the US.
www.weather.com – geared to the US but has some really good articles and features.
www.weather.org.uk – informative UK weather information site.
www.weatherunderground.com – an entertaining site with colourful, interactive mapping.

www.weatherimages.org   US

SEE THE WORLD'S WEATHER – LIVE
Weatherimages is compiled by a true weather fan. Split into twenty or so areas of interest, there is plenty of information and there's loads to see. The best feature is the network of weather cams from which you can see the best and worst of the world's weather. See also the excellent **www.weather-photography.com**

Other interesting and useful weather sites worth checking out:
www.chasingstorms.com – home of the Storm Chasers and Spotters Association.
www.climateark.org – all the links you'll ever need on climate change.
www.everythingweather.com – information and links.
www.hurricaneadvisories.com – American hurricane information.
www.hurricanes.net – information on tropical storms and their effects.
www.risingslowly.com – an entertaining blog devoted to weather in the UK, with lots of links and other related blogs.
www.spaceweather.com – for daily updates on solar winds and flares plus information on solar weather patterns in general.
www.stormstock.com – the world's premier storm footage library with some stunning clips.

W

www.stormtrack.org – another US storm-tracking site, very comprehensive though.
www.torro.org.uk – the Tornado and Storm Research Organisation, an interesting UK-oriented site.
www.weatherbase.com – statistics on world weather, data on over 16,000 cities.
www.wildweather.com – find out where the wildest weather is, also statistics and links.
www.worldclimate.com – weather data, averages and statistics.

Web Cameras

One of the most fascinating aspects of the Internet is the ability to tap into some CCTV or specially set up web cameras from all around the world. Some sites will contain adult material though.

www.camcentral.com   US
WEB CAM CENTRAL

An excellent selection of cameras, chosen for quality rather than quantity; the wildlife ones are very good in particular but there's a good search facility too.

See also:
www.camvista.com – web cam shots of the UK and the US from a web cam manufacturer, annoying pop-ups
www.webcam-index.com – lists some 500 sites from around the world.
www.webcamworld.com – a big directory of web cams.

Web Site Design

As it's pretty expensive to get a site designed and built professionally, there's been an explosion in the number of books, software and sites dedicated to helping people put their own sites together. These web sites will help enormously and take you through the world of Hypertext Markup Language, Java and Flash.

http://hotwired.lycos.com/webmonkey   US
THE WEB MONKEY

A superb resource for web designers of all skill levels providing everything from basic tutorials to articles from professional designers. The 'How to' library is brilliant and, as you'd expect, the site design is excellent too. See also **www.htmlgoodies.com** who also offer tutorials and lots of tips for those times when things don't go quite the way you want them to.

www.codebeach.com   US
CODE BEACH
Code Beach describe their site as 'your complete guide to free and open source code and tutorials for ASP, C++, ColdFusion, Java, JavaScript, Palm, Perl, PHP, and Visual Basic' and it is. Each language has a section with tutorials, downloads and links for you to get your head around it all.

Other essential sites:
http://cool.infi.net – vote for the coolest sites and find out which are considered the best. This has got very commercial now, so lots of deals and adverts get in the way.
http://webdeveloper.earthweb.com/webjs – a great source of those helpful little Java programs you find on most sites. Why write your own when you can download one for free.
www.allwebco.com – good-value web hosting.
www.blogger.com – a free web-publishing tool and diary facility. See also the section on page 46.
www.cutandpastescripts.com – a great time-saving tool where you can literally cut and paste bits of essential computer graphics.
www.desktoppublishing.com – free web templates and original clip art – excellent.
www.dreamweaver.com – home of one of the leading pieces of web-creation software, here you can download a trial version, get lots of information and more downloads to improve your site.
www.flashkit.com – animate your site, give it life here.
www.fontfreak.com – over 300 different and unusual fonts.
www.freewebs.com – free web site hosting.
www.homepagetools.com – a really strong resource of tools and services you can add to your site once you're up and running.
www.identifont.com – identify fonts, get new ones for your site.
www.internet.com – top tips, news and downloads – a comprehensive offering.
www.learnthenet.com – web site construction made easy, sensible thorough and well designed.
www.netforbeginners.about.com – the beginners pages from About.com.
www.port41.com – manage and update your web site the simple way.

W

www.rnib.org.uk – from the Royal National Institute for the Blind, here you can find information on how to make your web site more accessible for partially sighted and disabled people.

www.spinwave.com – free software to ensure that the pictures you choose fit the site, and load quickly and efficiently too.

www.thecounter.com – find out who visits your site and how often.

www.typepad.com – excellent blog program.

www.ultimateresources.co.uk – advice and information on how to make money from your site.

www.useit.com – great place to go for advice from a bone-fide web-design guru.

www.webaward.org – the so-called top awards for web design, annoying announcer to go with it.

www.webbyawards.com – an attractive and prominent site devoted to rewarding the best of what's on the Internet, learn from those who got it right.

www.webdesignforums.net – your questions answered at this useful forum site.

www.webpagesthatsuck.com – examples of how not to do it, a chastening and humorous experience for some.

Web Site Guides and Directories

If you can't find the site you're looking for in this book, then rather than use a search engine, check out one of these web site directories.

www.just35.com   UK

FIND IT THE EASY WAY
A very good directory site which is well categorised (maximum 35 sites in each category) and easy to use with each site reviewed and rated. You can also get the latest news and personalise the site.

www.uk250.co.uk   UK

1000'S OF QUALITY SITES IN 250 CATEGORIES
Heavily advertised and hyped though this site has been, many people seem to think that it consists of just the top 250 sites, but it's actually a very comprehensive database of Britain's most important and useful .co.uks and .coms. The sites listed are not reviewed but a one-liner gives a brief description of what they are about.

www.thegoodwebguide.co.uk UK
GOOD WEB GUIDE
The best web sites in several key categories are comprehensively
reviewed but you have to subscribe (£10–50 per annum) or buy the
related book (subscription then free to that subject area) to get the
best out of it, although some information is free. It's a good site and
the books are good (if a little expensive), but the problem for the
Good Web Guide team is that you can get all the information at
reduced or no cost elsewhere.

www.ukdirectory.co.uk UK
DEFINITIVE GUIDES TO BRITISH SITES
A massive database of web sites conveniently categorised into
fifteen sections, they don't review, but there are brief
explanations provided by the site owners. See also
www.local.co.uk

www.bored.com US
IF YOU'RE BORED
Basically a directory of unusual and humorous sites to occupy you
when you've nothing better to do; it's quite entertaining really.

Weddings

www.confetti.co.uk UK

YOUR INTERACTIVE WEDDING GUIDE
A good-looking and busy site designed to help you through every
stage of your wedding with information for all participants. There are
gift guides, planning tools, advice, a supplier directory and a shop.
They don't miss much.

www.theknot.com UK
PREPARATION
All (well nearly all) your wedding needs catered for, excellent
and attractive design too. You even get your own web pages
and a useful count down to the day.

www.wedding-service.co.uk UK
UK'S LARGEST WEDDING AND BRIDE DIRECTORY
A huge list of suppliers, service providers and information by
region, everything from balloons to speechwriters are listed. The
site is not that easy on the eye and it takes a little while to find
what you want.

W

www.all-about-weddings.co.uk UK
GETTING MARRIED IN THE UK
Excellent for basic information about planning weddings from
the ceremony to the reception; it also has a good set of links to
related and specialist supplier sites, a travel section and a shop.
It's all wrapped up in suitably matrimonial design with love
hearts flowing across the screen as you browse.

Other good sites for weddings:
http://bridesandgrooms.com – a comprehensive guide and
community site.
www.bridesuk.net – excellent site from *Brides* magazine; get all the
latest in bridal fashion and a guide to where to go on honeymoon.
www.hitched.co.uk – another good all-rounder with the added
feature of a discussion forum where you can swap wedding stories.
www.lastnightoffreedom.co.uk – everything you need to
organise your stag or hen night.
www.limoshop.co.uk – reserve your stretch limo.
www.partydomain.co.uk – if you want to organise your own
party, then this is the site for you with some fairly naff offerings
for hen and stag nights.
www.printed4u.co.uk – invitation printing.
www.pronuptia.co.uk – illustrated details of the range and
stores, not much else.
www.trading-direct.co.uk – your wedding presents taken care
of with an online wedding list service.
www.webwedding.co.uk – lots of expert advice and inspiration,
you need to join up to get the best out of it.
www.weddingguide.co.uk – clean-looking site with shop,
directory, forums and advice plus a good search facility.

Women

The following are a few sites of particular interest to women.

Equality Issues and Politics

www.womenandequalityunit.gov.uk UK
THE WOMEN AND EQUALITY UNIT
Dedicated to promoting a 'vision of equality and opportunity for all'.
Politics aside, the site provides useful information on how

W

government policies impact on women's lives, covering hot topics
such as encouraging women to become more involved
in public life, balancing work and family, domestic violence, money,
health and equal opportunities. Worth visiting for the useful links.
For information on what the UN is doing to promote gender
equality go to **www.un.org/womenwatch** where there is
information on all their initiatives and international treaties.
A dry but informative read.

www.eoc.org.uk   UK
EQUAL OPPORTUNITIES COMMISSION
Know your rights by checking here about sex discrimination in
the workplace, sexual stereotyping in education or work, the
legalities of part-time work, maternity leave etc. A useful
resource although not very user-friendly.

www.aviva.org   UK
INTERNATIONAL FEMINIST WEBZINE
If you want information on the political and social issues facing
women all over the world, this site has plenty of factual articles,
details of meetings and loads of links. There is a nice section
on international women's art too.

www.savingwomenslives.org   US
A GLOBAL PERSPECTIVE
An excellent site to visit for a glimpse into the lives of women
throughout the world. There are heart-wrenching stories,
shocking facts, essays on issues and a newsroom. The US
foundation, The National Organisation for Women, explore
similar issues at **www.now.org**

See also:
www.poptel.org.uk/women-ww – dedicated to supporting the
rights of women workers world-wide.
www.wen.org.uk – the Women's Environmental Network
campaigns and educates on environmental matters

Working Women

www.everywoman.co.uk   UK
NOT JUST FOR BUSINESS WOMEN
A really useful site aimed at women business owners, but the

W

'home' channel provides sound information on personal finance, family and well-being for all women.

www.womenatwork.co.uk   UK

DIRECTORY OF WOMEN IN BUSINESS

If you want to support local women in business, search the site for self-employed freelancers, consultants, home workers, tradeswomen or women running small businesses in your area. If you're one of those women, join here for networking and support.

See also:

www.busygirl.co.uk – a more serious site than the name suggests, their aim is to advance women by supporting the business and career needs of women.

www.flametree.co.uk – a specialist consultancy 'working with organisations to respond effectively to the work-life challenge'. Unfortunately they have abandoned the personal section to concentrate on the corporate'.

www.ivillage.co.uk/workcareer – useful advice and information on a range of employment issues for women.

www.scottishbusinesswomen.com – a good community site aimed at business women in Scotland.

www.the-bag-lady.co.uk – international women's trading portal with plenty of information and links for those in business.

Women and Their Families

Information on divorce, separation and family relationships is found in Parenting on page 345.

www.fulltimemothers.org   UK

FOR FULL-TIME MUMS

This organisation aims to promote the status of stay-at-home mums and campaign for changes in taxation, the benefit system and employment policy to give women more choice. There is also information on how to join a local group, or set one up. See also **www.netmums.com**

For the working mother's perspective see **www.workingmother.com** a campaigning e-zine for working mothers from the US and **www.motheratwork.co.uk** a very useful e-zine for British mothers.

W

See also:

www.matchmothers.org – self-help support site for mothers separated from their children for whatever reason. There is useful information for all, but you need to join to get the most out of it.

www.mothers35plus.co.uk – support and information for older mothers.

www.mumsnet.com – a rather advert-laden site devoted to product reviews with advice and tips thrown in. You have to subscribe to get the best of it.

www.thebritishsecondwivesclub.co.uk – a new site promising support for second wives and the problems they face.

www.womensaid.org.uk – national charity working to end domestic violence against women and children.

Women Students

www.womanstudent.co.uk   UK

FOR WOMEN IN HIGHER EDUCATION
Loads of information for UK and international students with sections on money and careers, travel, health, leisure and universities. There is a helpful section for overseas women planning to come to British Universities.

Magazines

www.handbag.com   UK

THE ISP FOR WOMEN
Described as the most useful place on the Internet for British women, Handbag lives up to that with a mass of information written in an informal style and aimed at helping you get through life. There's shopping and competitions too. For some it's a little too commercial though.

www.ivillage.co.uk   UK

WHERE WOMEN FIND ANSWERS
All the sections you'd expect in a women's magazine, the difference here is that they are trying, and succeeding, to create a community with a range of message boards, advice, a good section on work, even a dating service. Alternatively, visit MSN's Women's Channel at **www.msn.co.uk/womens**

W

www.bintmagazine.com   UK

ALWAYS A PLEASURE
An irreverent weekly that strives to turn the word bint into
something better than its regular usage. It's fun, controversial
and no prisoners are taken.

www.blackwomen.co.uk   UK

THE VOICE OF BLACK WOMEN
A serious magazine-style site which in addition provides a list of
services targeted at Black women living in the UK. See also
www.blackliving.net a good American magazine site with a
British interest; it has a co.uk version under construction.

www.bbc.co.uk/radio4/womanshour   UK

WOMAN'S HOUR
An excellent magazine spin-off from the popular Radio 4
programme, you can listen to programmes, have your say and
go to sections such as those on food, health and history (which
includes a timeline).

www.e-women.com   UK

THE MULTICULTURAL WOMEN'S PORTAL
E-women aims to provide women world-wide with features and links
which are relevant to their lives. There are lots of women's
magazine-type features, a good range of forums, a shopping
directory but less serious comment than when previously visited.

Other general women's e-zines and portals:
http://www.wwwomen.com – US directory site for women,
with extensive coverage.
http://womensissues.about.com – features on a comprehensive
range of women's issues.
www.allthatwomenwant.com – a portal site which offers
links to sites covering a vast range of topics. It needs a search
engine though.
www.femina.com – a useful search engine for women-friendly sites.
www.newwomanonline.co.uk – good representation of
the magazine.

W

Women's Health

Below are a few excellent sources of information on women's health issues. For more general health sites see page 225 and don't rely on web sites; see a doctor if you are unwell.

www.healthywomen.org   US

EDUCATING WOMEN ABOUT THEMSELVES
The layout doesn't do justice to the quality of information on this site provided by the American-based National Women's Health Resource Center. Go to the 'health center' and use the pull-down menu to select a topic such as breast cancer, acupuncture or menopause. The aim is to provide women with good information to help them make informed decisions about their health.

www.womens-health.co.uk   UK

OBS AND GYNAE EXPLAINED
A good starting point for information on obstetrics and gynaecology including pregnancy, infertility, complications and investigations. Has a good search facility and useful links.

www.fpa.org.uk   UK

FAMILY PLANNING
A really comprehensive web site from the Family Planning Association with information on all aspects of birth control written in a clear and helpful style. There is a useful page entitled 'I need help now' plus good links. For a more campaigning approach, try **www.mariestopes.org.uk** for a rundown on contraception choices and information on related topics such as health screening. You can even arrange for him to have a vasectomy online.

See also:
www.ein.org – Infertility Network with information and advice.
www.menopausematters.co.uk – excellent site giving the latest information on the menopause and how to live with it.
www.miscarriageassociation.org.uk – for miscarriage support and information.
www.pms.org.uk – National Association for Premenstrual Syndrome.
www.pni.org.uk – support for those suffering post-natal depression.

W

Travel

www.journeywoman.com   US
>
> PREMIER TRAVEL RESOURCE FOR WOMEN
> Dedicated to ensuring safe travel for women. Registering gets
> you access to the free newsletter plus lots of advice, guidance
> and tips from women who've travelled, traveller's tales and
> health warnings. See also **www.poshnosh.com** which is aimed
> at the 50+ traveller.

www.hermail.net   US
>
> CONNECTING WOMEN TRAVELLERS
> Great idea, once joined up you can be put in e-mail contact with
> women who have knowledge of the destination you're about to visit.
> You can exchange e-mail messages about the weather, restaurants
> or what to pack.

www.womenwelcomewomen.org.uk   UK
>
> CIRCLE OF FRIENDSHIP
> With 2,800 members in 72 countries, the aim is to foster
> international friendship and understanding by enabling women
> from different countries to visit one another. Members range in
> age from teens to over eighties and visit each other's homes as
> individuals or as part of organised gatherings.
>
> *See also:*
> **www.christinecolumbus.com** – travel tips for women plus the
> opportunity to share the experiences of other women.
> **www.goodadventure.com** – opportunities for adventurous travel
> with other active women.
> **www.wildroseholidays.co.uk** – holidays for single women in
> the UK and overseas.

Leisure and the Arts

www.wsf.org.uk   UK
>
> WOMEN'S SPORT FOUNDATION
> The voice of women's sport is committed to improving and
> promoting opportunities for women and girls in sport at every
> level. It does this by lobbying and raising the awareness of the
> importance of women in sport to the organisers and governing
> bodies. Here you can find out how to get involved or get help.

W

www.womengamers.com   US
> BECAUSE WOMEN DO PLAY
> The aim is to provide a selection of reviews and games geared
> specifically to a female audience (although it doesn't stop this being
> an enjoyable site for men to visit). It has up-to-the-minute reviews,
> really well-written articles, lots of content and high-quality design.

www.womeninmusic.org.uk   US
> WOMEN IN MUSIC
> If you're a musician be it classical, jazz, folk or hip hop, then
> you'll find support and encouragement here. It seems
> particularly good for women composers. There's a very good
> 'what's on' section, links and a forum.

www.pinknoises.com   UK
> PROMOTING WOMEN'S MUSIC
> Giving women a voice in the male-dominated international
> electronic music scene by providing music, profiles of artists,
> review, essays, a message board and comprehensive links.
> Truly international in the artists it features and an invaluable
> resource for women DJs and electronic music freaks.

www.nmwa.org   US
> NATIONAL MUSEUM FOR WOMEN IN THE ARTS
> Take a tour of this New York-based museum dedicated to
> women artists. They have paintings and artefacts dating from
> the 16th century up to the present day with a reasonable
> collection available to view online. The shop is tempting, but
> remember delivery from the US is expensive.

http://digital.library.upenn.edu/women   US
> A CELEBRATION OF WOMEN WRITERS
> A site with a passion for the work of women writers; the quality
> and quantity of information on this site is tremendous with links
> to biographical and bibliographical information about women
> writers as well as providing complete books written by women.
>
> *For other sites on women's arts see:*
> **http://web.ukonline.co.uk/n.paradoxa** – feminist art journal
> with good links to artists and women's art associations.
> **http://womenwriters.net/links.htm** – a guide to Internet
> resources as well as book reviews and features.
> **www.blackwomenart.org.uk** – dedicated to black women in

W

fashion, design, crafts and the performing arts.

www.distinguishedwomen.com – biographies and information on women's impact on history.

www.society-women-artists.org.uk – join the Society of Women Artists, learn about their annual exhibition and see some of the exhibits.

www.thewomenslibrary.ac.uk – unfortunately, this extensive collection of archives on women's history is not available online, but you can see the catalogue and book a visit to the reading room.

www.the-womens-press.com – for incisive feminist writing.

Miscellaneous

http://shinyshiny.tv   UK

A GIRL'S GUIDE TO GADGETS

A fun blog which catalogues gadgets and gifts that have particular appeal to women. The authors have great taste and the stuff featured is mostly gorgeous and desirable whoever you are.

www.hintsandthings.co.uk   UK

PEARLS OF WISDOM

Not strictly for women, but it features serious hints and tips on such things as not losing your children, bank statements and computer viruses, but also some tongue-in-cheek information on the rules of cricket and what to do with unwanted CDs. It's a good place to visit for a coffee break.

www.girlsstuff.co.uk   UK

GIFTS GALORE

Loads of silly gifts that you didn't know you wanted and certainly don't need. Delivery starts at £3.95.

W

Stop Press...

Art

www.commissionaportrait.com – if you fancy yourself portrayed on a painting or as a sculpture, then here's the place to go. There are some 100 artists to choose from.

www.storyabout.net/typedrawing – create your own art with this excellent drawing program.

Books

http://amaztype.tha.jp – a book search engine with a difference: type in the title and the results appear in the form of book covers, which you click on to get more results. It's linked to Amazon and its great fun.

Cars

www.liftshare.org – find someone who's going your way, informative and easy to use too.

www.biodieselfillingstations.co.uk
All you need to know about bio-diesel and where to buy it.

Crime

www.cifas.org.uk – the UK's fraud prevention service with lots of advice and help on issues such as identity theft.

www.identity-theft.org.uk – a helpful site designed to help you avoid someone stealing your identity.

www.crimereduction.gov.uk – a useful site with information and statistics on crime in the UK.

Fashion

www.ganesha.co.uk – an excellent store featuring Indian products sold and produced on an ethical basis.

www.closetspy.com – a very good blog site devoted to bringing you the latest in what's fashionable.

Food

www.feedmebetter.co.uk – Jamie Oliver's campaign for better food in schools.

Genealogy

www.1837online.com – home of the 1861 census and other useful resources from this commercial outfit. Charges vary.

Health

www.freedieting.com – an excellent site on dieting with the major diets reviewed, it comes with useful advice and tools to help you lose weight.

www.streetdrugs.org – an American site that gives information on drugs and how to deal with abuse.

History

www.whoyoushouldknow.com – a blog which features a new world leader every weekday, in an attempt to educate Americans about the world. It's turned out to be an educationally useful and informative site.

www.ourdocuments.gov – excellent and advanced site showing the 100 most important documents in US history.

www.iwm.org.uk – home of the Imperial War Museum with an impressive site.

http://afe.easia.columbia.edu/mongols – a comprehensive site covering the Mongol empire and its history.

Home

www.green-bottle.co.uk – recycling glass into usable products such as tiles.

www.aecb.net – the Association for Environmentally Conscious Building has a helpful site with the relevant information.

Humour

www.freakingnews.com – playing with Photoshop to make new pictures is the hobby of many, but here you can enter your masterpiece of deception in competitions.

Music

www.tunetribe.com – this site provides bands and musicians a showcase for their work and they get paid for it too.

www.totalband.com – an excellent web resource for bands and musicians who want to set up their own web site.

Nature

www.discoveringfossils.co.uk – excellent guide to the UK's geology and where to go fossil hunting.

Parenting

www.childhoodinteriors.co.uk – a modern approach to decorating and accessorising your child's room.

www.annegeddesbaby.com – for fans of the world-renowned baby photographer, here's her baby clothes shop. Delivery is expensive.

Science

www.futuristsnetwork.org.uk
Find out what the future could hold for us. Here you'll find essays and discussions on potential events.

Space

www.spaceislandgroup.com – space tourism is on its way!

Travel

www.holiday.co.uk – a portal offering a massive number of package holidays and a wide range of other options from all the major operators.

www.bouncebacksrilanka.org – a great site on how Sri Lanka is getting back on its feet since the tsunami.

www.bwsafaris.com – a stunning site from this Kenyan safari specialist.

www.visithighlands.com – all you need to know about the Scottish Highlands and more.

www.londontown.com – a comprehensive and vibrant site on London.

http://worldhum.com – a descriptive site derived from the rush people get from travelling. Some excellent writing.

www.gridskipper.com – described as an 'urban travel guide' here you'll find a wide variety of personal views on the major cities of the world.

Index

HALLIWELL'S FILM, VIDEO AND DVD GUIDE 2006

26TH EDITION

Edited by John Walker

The biggest and the best film guide available, packed with over one hundred years of entertainment and cinema information. The undisputed bible for film enthusiasts and trivia buffs everywhere – a must-have for every moviegoer.

The longest running guide to the film industry is fully revised and updated to include:

- hundreds of new films
- cast and credit information
- pithy comment on the classics of the silver screen, the latest blockbusters, and everything in between
- critics reviews from as far afield as Iran and Korea
- plot synopses and evaluation
- video cassette, laser disc and DVD availability

Halliwell's delivers all the cast and crew credits, fun trivia and behind-the-scenes information you need on over 23,000 movies, including hundreds of new ones.

This perennially entertaining, comprehensive and indispensable guide also includes reader-friendly icons to denote films suitable for family viewing, Academy Award winners and nominees, soundtrack availability and video format compatibility, plus lists of four-star and three-star films by title and year.

Available October 2005
ISBN 0 00 720550 3
£22.50

HALLIWELL'S TOP 1000

Edited by John Walker

"At the end of the day, Halliwell is top of the pile"
Film Review

Halliwell's Top 1000, in the form of a fully illustrated count-down, with additional top ten lists from industry insiders, film stars and directors.

Each movie provides a plot summary and includes key information, such as:

- cast and crew on the film
- any awards the movie won
- key critical comments on the movie's release
- DVD and soundtrack availibility

plus other interesting information such as original film titles, gossip from behind the scenes and quotes from the critics, director and stars.

Finally with this book the Halliwell's Hall of Fame will be established once and for all!

ISBN 0 00 718165 5
£15.99

HALLIWELL'S WHO'S WHO IN THE MOVIES

4ᵀᴴ EDITION

Edited by John Walker

'A filmic fountain of knowledge'
Guardian

The 4th edition of *Halliwell's Who's Who in the Movies* is the comprehensive guide to the Who, Why, What and How of cinema. Everything you ever wanted to know, explained with wit and concision.

The People:
Biographies and filmographies of stars, moguls, directors, writers and other key players. Plus fictional characters from Ali Baba to Zorro.

The Prizes:
Full year-by-year listings of the Oscars. Plus winners of the world's leading festivals and critics' awards.

The History:
The chronology of cinema from its beginnings to today. Plus a country-by-country breakdown of national film industries.

The Background:
Details of the studios, the genres, the technology and trends. Plus listings of the best film books and magazines.

Halliwell's Who's Who in the Movies is the essential companion to *Halliwell's Film, Video and DVD Guide*.

ISBN 0 00 71697 4
£18.99

THE PRACTICAL DOG LISTENER

The 30-Day Path to a Lifelong Understanding of Your Dog

By Jan Fennell

In her best-selling first book, *The Dog Listener*, Jan Fennell changed the way we think about our dogs. Now, she delves deeper into their hidden language and deals with the day-to-day practicalities of putting those principles to work, distilling her ideas into a simple guide that will enable everyone to establish a new and fulfilling relationship with their best friend.

The Practical Dog Listener shows how to incorporate Jan's powerful method into every element of pet ownership, from introducing a dog to its new home and handling it in public, to dealing with behavioural problems. In 30 days, owners can learn a system they will be able to apply for life.

Throughout the book, key elements of Jan's easy-to-follow method are accompanied by instructive photographs. Jan also illustrates her points with more entertaining, inspiring – and sometimes heartbreaking – real-life examples from her own work with damaged and delinquent dogs.

ISBN 0 00 257205 2
£15.99

Also available in paperback, January 2006
ISBN 0 00 714570 5
£12.99

THE UXBRIDGE ENGLISH DICTIONARY

By Tim Brooke-Taylor, Barry Cryer, Graeme Garden, Iain Patterson and Jon Naismith

Say Goodbye to Wrong-Sounding-Word-Misery.

The Uxbridge English Dictionary is the first comprehensive, illustrated and fully annotated list of NEW DEFIINITIONS for all those old and misleading English words that simply don't mean anything like what they sound like they ought to mean.

How much less complicated it would be to live in a world where a 'bordello' was a blasé greeting, or a 'dossier' was a French tramp; a world where 'dilate' meant to live long, and 'poppycock' was a streaker on November the 11th.

Well now, thanks to *The Uxbridge English Dictionary*, everything you say will actually sound like you mean what you sound like you're actually saying. And doesn't that make sense?

The Uxbridge English Dictionary has been collected from the popular 'New Definitions' round in the award-winning Radio 4 panel game *I'm Sorry I Haven't a Clue*.

INVALUABLE
(Worth nothing)

IMPECCABLE
(Bird-proof)

SPECTACULAR
(Short-sighted vampire)

ISBN 0 00 720337 3
£7.99